Master Drawings from Stockholm

ALBRECHT DÜRER, German, 1471-1528, *Portrait of a Girl*, 1515, black chalk

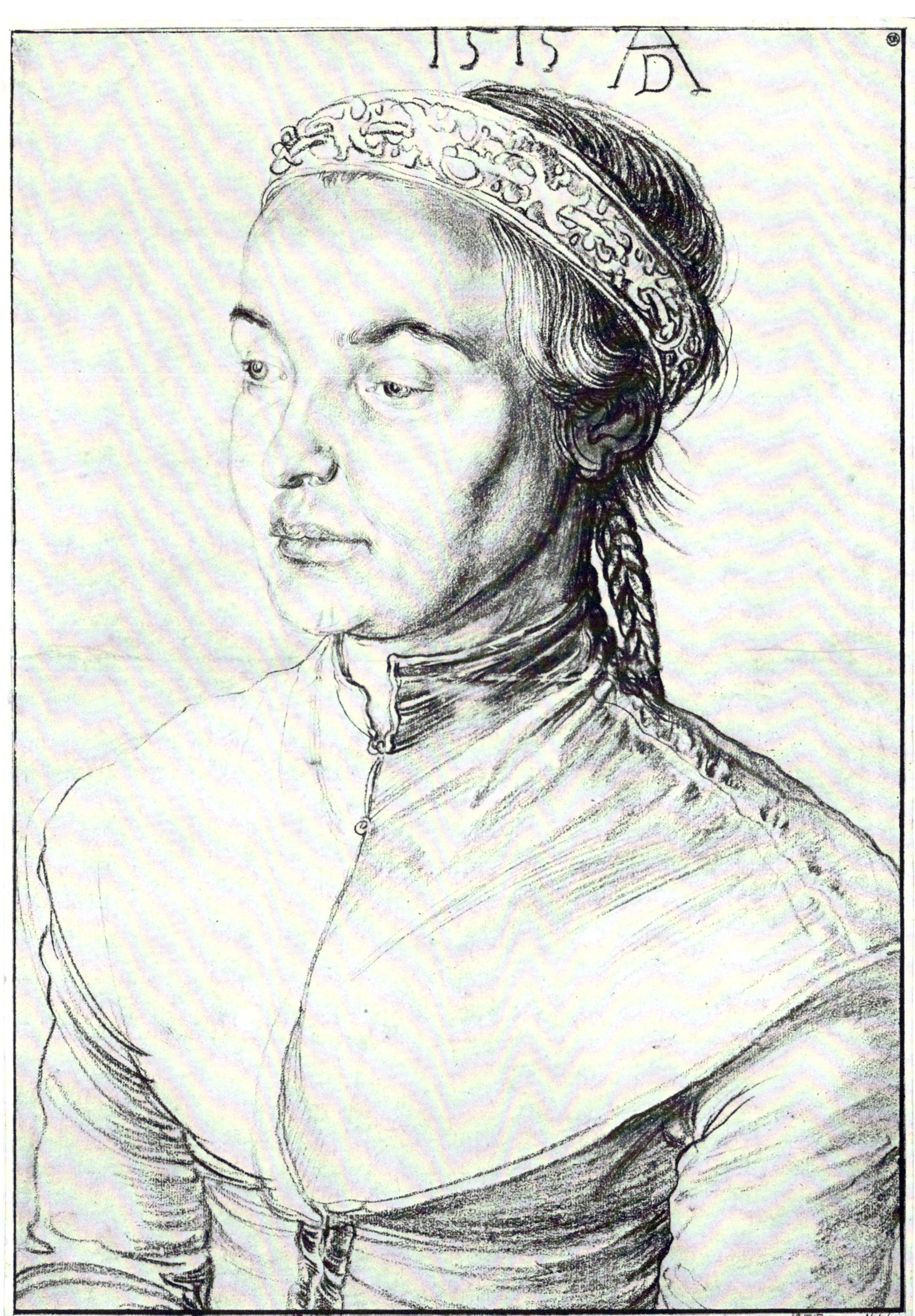

This publication accompanies an exhibition of master drawings from the Nationalmuseum of Sweden, Stockholm.

National Gallery of Art, Washington October 27, 1985-January 5, 1986
Kimbell Art Museum, Fort Worth February 1-April 13, 1986
The Fine Arts Museums of San Francisco May 10-July 20, 1986

DÜRER TO DELACROIX

Great Master Drawings from Stockholm

by

Per Bjurström

with

Ulf Cederlöf and
Börje Magnusson

Kimbell Art Museum
Fort Worth

Dürer to Delacroix: Great Master Drawings from Stockholm is an exhibition organized by the National Gallery of Art, Kimbell Art Museum, and The Fine Arts Museums of San Francisco in association with the Nationalmuseum of Sweden. It is supported by a federal indemnity from the Federal Council on the Arts and Humanities.

Responsibility for individual catalogue entries are as follows:

Per Bjurström	1, 2, 4-11, 13, 19-24, 27-71, 94-102
Ulf Cederlöf	12, 15-18, 103-118
Börje Magnusson	3, 14, 25, 26, 72-93

Library of Congress Catalogue Card Number: 85-80676

Library of Congress Cataloging-in-Publication Data

Bjurström, Per.
Dürer to Delacroix.

"This catalogue is published on the occasion of an exhibition of master drawings from the Nationalmuseum, Stockholm, shown at the National Gallery of Art, Washington, 27 October 1985-5 January 1986, Kimbell Art Museum, Fort Worth, 1 February-13 April 1986, and the Fine Arts Museums of San Francisco, 10 May-20 July 1986"—T.p. verso.
Bibliography: p.
Includes index.
1. Drawing—Exhibitions. 2. Sweden. National museum—Exhibitions. I. Cederlöf, Ulf. II. Magnusson, Börje, 1943-0000. III. Sweden. Nationalmuseum. IV. National Gallery of Art (U.S.) V. Kimbell Art Museum. VI. Fine Arts Museums of San Francisco. VII. Title.

NC15.W37N369 1985 741.94'074'013 85-80676
ISBN 0-912804-21-1 (pbk.)

Catalogue produced by Kimbell Art Museum
Editor: June Taboroff
Manuscript preparation by Karen King
Design by Tom Dawson / Graphic Design
Production art by Tom Dawson
Typeset in Goudy Old Style, Goudy Old Style Italic, Goudy Bold, and Goudy Bold Italic by Fort Worth Linotyping Company, Inc.
Printed by Hurst Printing Company, Dallas

Cover illustration:
REMBRANDT VAN RIJN, 1606-1669
Portrait of Titia Van Uylenburch, 1639
Nationalmuseum, Stockholm
Catalogue No. 89

The exhibition in Washington has been generously supported by Volvo North America Corporation.

TABLE OF CONTENTS

FOREWORD

Dürer to Delacroix: Great Master Drawings from Stockholm is one of the most important drawing exhibitions ever to come to the United States. The introduction of modern drawing techniques by the artists of the Renaissance made a fundamental contribution to the development of Western civilization. Although very few drawings survive from the fourteenth and early fifteenth centuries, the works that have come down to us from subsequent times are one of the richest resources for the understanding of the Western creative achievement.

All of the drawings in the exhibition are on loan from the Nationalmuseum, Stockholm, and only a fraction (less than ten percent) has ever been seen in the United States; the Nationalmuseum ranks with the British Museum, the Louvre, the Berlin State Museums, and the Albertina as one of the ten greatest repositories of graphic arts in the world. The drawings constitute a historical and cultural survey of stylistic changes in the pictorial arts up to the mid-nineteenth century. The exhibition serves as an opportunity to re-examine accepted notions about the creative process and the importance of individual masters. For many it will provide the first chance to view the works outside Sweden and to appreciate their aesthetic and historical significance.

The exhibition consists almost entirely of works by the greatest European artists. Outstanding individual sheets by Dürer, Grünewald, Ghirlandaio, Raphael, Chardin, and Goya, as well as groups of drawings of exceptional merit by Rembrandt, Watteau, Rubens, Van Dyck, Titian, Poussin, Primaticcio, Fragonard, Fuseli, David, and Delacroix are included. The selection demonstrates the high points of European draftsmanship and a full range of artistic expression in various media and types of drawings (sketches, studies, modelli). The exhibition also traces the development of the collecting of drawings beginning with Carl Gustaf Tessin — one of the finest connoisseurs of his time — and other eighteenth-century art patrons. The achievement of a select group of great Swedish artists, for example Johan Tobias Sergel, in the late eighteenth century is presented in the context of their European precursors and contemporaries. Unlike an earlier exhibition of a different group of drawings from the Nationalmuseum seen in New York, Boston, and Chicago in 1969, the present selection includes German as well as Italian, French, and Netherlandish masters and extends into the nineteenth century with important works by David, Géricault, and Delacroix.

It is an honor to share with the American people these precious works by the greatest European masters. The involvement of Dr. Per Bjurström, Director of the Nationalmuseum and one of the world's foremost drawing connoisseurs, has been essential in obtaining the loan of so many treasures. Dr. Bjurström worked closely with representatives of our three institutions—Diane DeGrazia, Robert Johnson, and Edmund Pillsbury—to select the works for the exhibition. He also contributed a valuable essay on the history of the collection as well as numerous individual entries in addition to overseeing the preparation of the catalogue text by Mr. Börje Magnusson and Mr. Ulf Cederlöf of the Nationalmuseum staff. Our profound gratitude extends to him, Mr. Magnusson, and Mr. Cederlöf, as well as to the trustees and entire staff of the Nationalmuseum, for their gracious support and cooperation that has made possible this beautiful exhibition.

We are particularly grateful to Dr. Pehr G. Gyllenhammar, Chairman and Chief Executive Officer of the worldwide Volvo Group for Volvo's support of the exhibition at the National Gallery of Art in Washington. Our thanks go also to the Federal Council on the Arts and Humanities, who provided an indemnity for the exhibition.

J. Carter Brown
Director
National Gallery of Art

Edmund P. Pillsbury
Director
Kimbell Art Museum

Ian McKibbin White
Director
The Fine Arts Museums of San Francisco

INTRODUCTION
by Per Bjurström

The Nationalmuseum of Sweden has visited the United States once before with a major selection of Old Master drawings from its collections. In 1969, a loan exhibition was sent to the J. Pierpont Morgan Library, New York, the Museum of Fine Arts, Boston, and The Art Institute of Chicago. The works in the 1969 exhibition were drawn largely from the Museum's oldest collection, the works on paper assembled by Carl Gustaf Tessin (1695-1770), Sweden's most important collector of art during the first half of the eighteenth century. Five of the non-Swedish drawings shown in 1969 are also included in the present exhibition; otherwise there is no repetition of objects.

Dürer to Delacroix: Great Master Drawings from Stockholm intends to juxtapose time-honored works of art and acquisitions made in recent decades. In the 1960s and 1970s, a series of fortunate circumstances enabled the Print Room of the Nationalmuseum to add a considerable number of important works to its holdings and to carry out scholarship which strengthened the understanding of the existing collections. The acquisitions were made, despite the fact that the Nationalmuseum's resources from government grants and funds are modest by international standards and that Sweden's fiscal system does not encourage private donations. There is no instance among the works exhibited of a personal gift, although some purchases have been funded wholly or in part by the Friends of the Nationalmuseum. Moreover, the systematic appraisal of the collections undertaken during these decades has given rise to a series of critical catalogues[1] which have made it easier to assess the structure of the Museum's collections and to determine which areas need development.

QUEEN CHRISTINA

The first collection of drawings of any consequence in Sweden belonged to Queen Christina (1626-89), who in 1651 through Pieter Spiering Silfverkrona, her minister at The Hague, acquired five or six volumes of drawings. Some, if not all, of these drawings came from the collection that Joachim von Sandrart had assembled in Italy. It included individual volumes of drawings by Raphael and Michelangelo, renderings of "antiques" by Hendrik Goltzius, a volume that contained drawings by Parmigianino, and two volumes with sheets by a variety of Italian masters. It seems that this collection left Sweden with Christina, who resided in Rome from 1655 onwards. In an account of a visit in 1688, the architect and collector Nicodemus Tessin the Younger states that he studied "all seven of the volumes" containing her drawings, which suggests that the collection was largely intact in the Queen's lifetime.

The subsequent fate of these drawings owned by Christina has been researched at length but is still uncertain in many respects. It is known that some Botticelli drawings accompanied Christina's library to the Vatican and that at least part of the collection was bought in Rome in 1692 by Prince Livio Odescalchi, Duke of Bracciano, from the nephew of Cardinal Azzolino, who executed the Queen's will.[2] The latter items were then incorporated in a very extensive collection of drawings, parts of which are still owned by the Odescalchi family. In 1790, some drawings that reportedly belonged to Christina and most recently had been held by the Odescalchi princes, were acquired in Rome by Wilhelm Anne Lestevenon on behalf of the Teylers Stichting, Haarlem.[3]

Apart from these volumes, the largest group of drawings associated with Christina (some 2,500 sheets in 56 volumes) were acquired by the city of Leipzig and kept in its city library until the Museum der Bildenden Künste was founded. This collection came to Leipzig in 1712-14 from Francesco Antonio Rensi, a Roman prior, who is not otherwise known as an art collector. The theory that Christina owned at least part of these works is based upon a note written by Rensi on a loose piece of paper found inserted in one of the volumes. Another indication of a connection to Christina is a seal in two of the volumes that might possibly be Christina's.[4]

One can assume that no drawings from Christina's collection remained in Sweden. However, a provenance from the Queen's collection is theoretically possible in the case of acquisitions made in 1958 and 1975, drawings by Claude Lorrain and Salvator Rosa, respectively, which belonged to volumes identified in the Odescalchi inventory in 1713.[5]

Even more probably part of Christina's collection is a drawing by Pier Francesco Mola, who served in Rome as court painter to Christina after her abdication. It exactly corresponds to the description in the Odescalchi inventory of 1713, where a sheet is listed as: *un chimico prigione* (**sic**) *originale per caricatura del Mola.*[6] This item was acquired by the Museum from a Swedish private collection in 1970.

THE TESSIN

There is no way of knowing whether or not it was Nicodemus Tessin the Younger's visit to Queen Christina that spurred him to start collecting master drawings in addition to architectural drawings. As an architect and director of dramatic performances and *festivitas* at the court, he collected chiefly to obtain material for his professional activities. The drawings of a nonarchitectural character which he obtained reveal a preference for seventeenth-century artists, primarily Roman artists working in the great tradition of ceiling and interior decoration.[7]

In contrast to the predominantly practical approach of Nicodemus Tessin, his son Carl Gustaf applied purely aesthetic criteria to his collection. While visiting Paris in 1715 as a young man, he looked of course for things to complete his father's collection but used his own limited means to acquire counterproofs, probably directly from Watteau, with whom he became closely acquainted. This is the only moment, before the enormous purchases in Paris in 1741, when we can prove that Tessin actually acquired drawings for himself.

Besides shouldering his father's mantle, Carl Gustaf Tessin wished to serve in the government of Sweden and make his voice heard in politics. As a noble he had access to the Estates of the Realm and entered this arena in earnest in 1723. His talents were used above all for embassies abroad; in the three decades from 1714 to 1744, between his nineteenth and forty-ninth years, Tessin was out of the country for almost half of the time.

His next opportunity to purchase art objects occurred in 1728, when he was on an official commission to Paris to study the latest developments in the decorative arts, possibly also to engage artists for the embellishment of the Royal Palace in Stockholm.[8] Already in 1721 painters and sculptors were brought from Paris to the Stockholm Palace where they also instructed young Swedish craftsmen and formed the kernel of a Swedish Academy of Art. The death of Carl Gustaf's father in 1728 and his marriage with a rich heiress the year before had made him a man of means. It was now that he laid the foundation of his collection of French paintings. The drawings he acquired at this time are uncertain.

Between 1735-36, Tessin carried out a diplomatic mission to Vienna. He also paid a brief visit to Venice, in order to contact a Venetian painter to undertake the decoration of several ceilings in the Royal Palace in Stockholm. While in Vienna Tessin added to his library and his collection of engravings; in Venice he acquired several paintings. A letter home from Venice[9] mentions six portrait heads in chalk by Piazzetta, but at this point the list in the letter breaks off and it is not known whether he acquired any other drawings there. In Vienna, Tessin was introduced to Anton Maria Zanetti the Elder (1680-1766), one of the most vibrant personalities in that city's artistic life during the eighteenth century. It was Zanetti who acted as Tessin's guide in Venice and it seems likely, though there is no definite proof, that Zanetti provided Tessin with some of the Venetian drawings which were added to the latter's collection after 1750.[10]

Tessin's most important diplomatic commission was unquestionably the embassy to Paris in 1734-42, aimed at gaining French support for an aggressive policy against Russia. During these years he collected avidly, bringing himself to the verge of financial ruin. After some small purchases in the first two years, the opportunity to establish a really outstanding collection of drawings presented itself in April 1741 at the auction of the fabulous collection of Pierre Crozat. Tessin did not hesitate. Of the more than 19,000 drawings, catalogued for the sale by Pierre-Jean Mariette, he obtained no less than 2,057 for the sum of 5,072 livres 10 sous, making him one of the principal buyers. All the great dealers and connoisseurs of the age were represented at the auction. Among the dealers were Mariette himself, Huguet, Huquier, Hagard, Joulain, and Gersaint; the connoisseurs included the Comte de Caylus, Marquis de Gouverney, d'Argenville, Nourri, Jullienne, Lempereur, and Marquis de Caill-eres. Tessin supplemented his lots with purchases from the dealers Hagard, on six occasions for a total of 949 livres and Huquier, on five occasions for 813 livres. Most of these items probably came from large lots in the Crozat sale which the dealers then broke up to dispose of piece by piece. In March 1741, Tessin had already bought twenty-two drawings from Huquier for the relatively high price of 200 livres, and in 1742 he paid 500 livres for a collection of theatrical designs at an auction after the death of the Prince de Carignan. He again purchased for 220 livres a series of drawings by Gilles-Marie Oppenordt from Huquier. On the other hand, the cashbooks give no indication of any direct purchases of drawings from artists such as François Boucher, Jérome François Chantereau or Jean-Baptiste Chardin, suggesting that Tessin's numerous sheets by these artists were either gifts connected with the purchase of paintings or acquisitions from dealers.

Comparing the total costs of Tessin's purchases of drawings in 1741, some 7,800 livres, with those of his wife's wardrobe, 2,930 livres in the autumn of 1739 alone, and his own gambling debts in that season, 2,130 livres, these can hardly have represented the life-long ambition of an ardent collector. It is also characteristic that after Tessin had supplemented his Crozat lots the same year there is no evidence of further purchases in this field.

Tessin had a scant decade in which to enjoy his collection; financial pressures forced him to sell the greater part of the drawings to the Swedish king in 1755. In 1777, the next monarch, Gustavus III, redeemed the collection from his father's debt-encumbered estate and deposited it in the Royal Library.

At this point the care of Tessin's collection was entrusted to his nephew Fredrik Sparre (who had a function at the Royal Chancellery), who rearranged it exclusively by schools and artists and had the sheets mounted in a single size (51.7 x 36.4 cm.), with gilt-edging all around. Older mountings (for example, those by Vasari) were retained and the other sheets were given borders of different kinds; a golden strip distinguished the more esteemed sheets, a colored border (often bright yellow, pink, or green) marked intermediate pieces, and a simple ink border sufficed for the rest. The collection was also numbered in sequence from 1 to 3,025, the number usually being written on both the drawing itself (in the bottom right-hand corner) and its mount. Thirteen new portfolios were produced for the collection, with the three crowns of Sweden repeated six times on their calfskin spines.

It was in this state that the collection was taken over in 1794 by the newly founded Royal Museum, and practically no additions were made during the first half of the nineteenth century. In 1866, when the Museum was given its present name, Nationalmuseum, its collections were transferred from the Royal Palace to the building in which they are still housed. Acquisitions of new drawings became more frequent, and the collection was recatalogued and renumbered according to a system that is still in use. This work started in 1863 which is why all the Tessin sheets have this date included in their number. The new museum was charged with the important task of building up a collection of Swedish graphic art. By acquiring the various collections left by the Swedish sculptor Johan Tobias Sergel (1740-1814), the Museum became the owner of a small collection of master drawings, as well as sheets by Sergel and his contemporaries and friends in Rome.

In 1896, a substantial addition was made of drawings by foreign masters, collected by a former director of the Museum, Michael Gustaf Anckarsvärd (1792-1878). Although the quality of the 700 or so sheets is uneven, there are a number of important works. In 1918, Christian Langaard, a Norwegian collector, donated a *Klebeband* of mainly German Renaissance drawings (including works by Hans Baldung, Hans Burgkmair, and Wolfgang Huber shown in this exhibition). This donation was all the more welcome since German graphic art is poorly represented in Tessin's collection.

In 1973, the Museum took over the last significant private collection of old master drawings in Sweden. Created around 1800 by Count Jacob Gustaf De la Gardie (1768-1842), this collection had two main sources. While De la Gardie was Swedish ambassador in Vienna from 1799-1801 he received a large gift from Duke Albert of Sachsen-Teschen of drawings, part of which came from the collection of Prince Charles de Ligne. The drawings from de Ligne's collection are very uneven in quality, with just a few important sheets and a great many anonymous works whose identity is only now being established.[11] Several hundred drawings had been in the possession of De la Gardie's father-in-law, Count Gustaf Adolf Sparre (1746-94).[12] The Sparre collection was built up in 1768-72 during his grand tour through England, Holland, Germany, and France. The most notable items are Netherlandish works, but it seems probable that whole sections were purchased en bloc at auctions in Paris.

COLLECTING

It can be argued that every notable collection of drawings, including those in public ownership, carries the imprint of a particular collector's personality. One can hardly overlook the importance of Pierre-Jean Mariette (1699-1774) for the Louvre's collection, Fairfax Murray's for the J. Pierpont Morgan Library, Frans Koenigs' for Museum Boymans-van Beuningen, or Frits Lugt's for the collection in the Institut Néerlandais, Paris.

In the case of Stockholm it is just as natural to recognize the mark of Carl Gustaf Tessin. To what extent Tessin's collection reflects his personal taste as opposed to a social wish to conform to prevailing fashion cannot of course be established with certainty. The paintings he assembled may be judged to represent the fashion of the age: canvases by Chardin, Boucher, Lancret, Pater, and Tiepolo exemplify his acquisitions of contemporary art, while paintings by Rembrandt, Ruysdael, Wouwermans, van Dyck, and Snyders stand for older items of appeal even to official taste. The circumstances behind the creation of Tessin's art collection should be borne in mind. As Sweden's ambassador, Tessin clearly cultivated attention in Paris, striving to make his residence a center for good taste, connoisseurship, and the intellectual élite. He established personal contact with artists, art dealers, and collectors. Many fields of art attracted Tessin as a collector: books, graphic art, coins, medals, porcelain, silver, paintings, and drawings. He did what he could to promote the interests of his country and invested his fortune in this ambition.

Tessin's attitude toward drawings, however, is very different. His purchases at the Crozat auction make it quite clear that he spread his money so as to acquire at least one lot of works by each of the artists or group of artists represented. This makes it all the more interesting to note what he did not buy: nothing by Pietro da Cortona, Ciro Ferri, Giovanni Battista Gaulli, or Carlo Maratta, little Venetian art (nothing by Tintoretto or Jacopo Bassano and only an insignificant lot by Titian), nor did he take anything by Salvator Rosa, but this may have been because Tessin's inheritance from his father included several sheets by or attributed to these Roman artists and Salvator Rosa.

Despite these gaps Tessin's selection shows great foresight. An eminent example of this historical approach is his acquisition of works by early Florentine artists, thirty drawings from lot 1 and the whole of lot 2, which made him the biggest buyer of this group. Tessin himself comments: "Ces desseins interessent l'histoire du progrés des Arts. Ils on été ramassés par Vasari, qui en faisoit grand cas." ("These drawings are interesting for the history of the progress of the arts. They were collected by Vasari, who was making a big fuss about them.")[13] It was probably the same striving for historical completeness that subsequently led Tessin to supplement his purchases at the auction.

At the Crozat auction the early Florentine drawings went extremely cheaply — the 85 sheets cost Tessin 15 livres 10. Otherwise, Tessin's most interesting purchase of surprisingly cheap sheets were 106 drawings by Rembrandt and his school, for which he paid 55 livres. Tessin was the biggest buyer in this group too, taking four of the twelve lots available.

Whatever the grounds for his acquisitions, Tessin left a collection of drawings that, considering its sudden conception, is remarkably multifaceted. The absence of sheets by Michelangelo, for instance, and the paucity of work by Annibale Carracci are most probably a result of deference to Mariette in recognition of his efforts to research and catalogue the Crozat material.

Tessin's selection of contemporary artists seems to have aimed for the variety that characterized the parent collection. François Boucher dominates it with some thirty sheets. François Desportes, Carle Van Loo, Charles Parrocel, and Chantereau are also well represented. The three drawings by Chardin are still the only sheets that can be attributed with certainty to this master. There is something by practically every other artist of note, leading to the impression that even if Tessin was not particularly attracted by an artist, he chose to include him in his portfolio for completeness.

The rich set of Boucher drawings is indicative of Tessin's friendship with this artist as well as his appreciation of Boucher's art. The sheets are numerous but still seem to have been selected with careful consideration of their quality and variety. This is less true of the group by Van Loo, while the drawings by Desportes make a rather one-sided impression. The small lots by François Lemoine and Charles Joseph Natoire indicate a greater ambition to cover the various aspects of their art.

Taken as a whole, however, this part of Tessin's collection illustrates a great many aspects of this important epoch in the art of drawing. What had previously been an object of study for a privileged few was being developed into an ornament for display to an educated public; the distinctive character of drawings as preparatory studies was used to create a new category of intimate pictures, with spontaneity and the proximity of artistic inspiration as important ingredients. It was mainly in the subsequent decades around the middle of the eighteenth century that this tendency evolved into a genre.

The aim of providing a full and many-sided picture of artistic development also meant that Tessin wanted his collection to illustrate different aspects and phases in the work of individual masters. In this he was aided, of course, by the arrangement of the Crozat auction since the drawings were sold as homogeneous lots rather than individually. The work by Rembrandt is a case in point: in the Stockholm collection certain themes occur in a number of variants that enable one to follow the artist step by step.

For those responsible for a collection with this strong tradition there is reason to adapt to and even adopt the valuations and attitudes of the original creator and share his inspiration. Such an approach is more tenable for a public collection of drawings than of paintings where so much allowance has to be made for prevailing demands and values.

Tessin's lead continues to provide a guiding principle today, with the Museum concentrating its purchases on certain artists and even on specific projects. This applies both when filling out the stock of earlier drawings and in the documentation of modern Swedish art, where this principle is obviously easier to follow.

In the 1960s and 1970s, a number of changes paved the way for increased acquisitions. Carl Nordenfalk and Bengt Dahlbäck were both directors who favored the purchase of notable master drawings. Happily a few donations improved the chances of buying French art. As French drawings are an outstanding feature of the Museum's collection, this was an area where new acquisitions would make a most satisfactory whole.

The chief deficiencies in the collections were found in the sixteenth century holdings and in the lack of consistent efforts to emulate Tessin's policy for the period after 1740, when his collection was assembled. The sixteenth century was represented only by sheets by Francesco Primaticcio and Nicolò dell'Abate, though they at least are plentiful and varied. Examination of the theatrical material, also having a Tessin provenance, revealed works by Antoine Caron, while the architectural drawings included a magnificent tomb project by Germain Pilon.

But sixteenth-century portrait art was conspicuously absent, which is hardly surprising when one considers that the French royal family collected these drawings; Catherine de' Medici was able to present her niece, Christine of Lotharingia, with "five hundred and fifty portraits of princes and princesses, noblemen and ladies." Broken up in 1736, this group of drawings is today largely in the hands of the British Museum, the Musée Chantilly, and the Bibliothèque Nationale. When a portrait of just this Christine of Lotharingia, done by François Quesnel, a late but important portraitist, became available in 1974, the Museum managed to acquire it as an example of this remarkable portrait art.

Another very notable acquisition for the French sixteenth century collection is Etienne Delaune's *Dialectic*, which completes what had long been a deficient set of the seven Liberal Arts. The other six drawings in the set were incorporated long ago in public collections in Berlin, Chantilly, and Paris.

The second school of Fontainebleau, artists who worked primarily for Henry IV (1533-1610), is represented by a magnificent drawing by Ambroise Dubois that is probably a full-scale draft for a painting. Influenced by Primaticcio and Nicolò dell'Abate, Dubois exemplifies the waning of mannerism.

The complete absence of work by Claude Lorrain in an otherwise varied and representative collection of French seventeenth century drawings is something of a mystery. One explanation seems to be that when Crozat—and subsequently Tessin—assembled a collection, large parts of Claude's drawing oeuvre were already in England. It is characteristic that the sheets by Claude that the Nationalmuseum acquired in 1958 and 1969 came from old Italian collections—Odescalchi and Camuccini. The earlier purchase consisted of two animal studies and one plant study from the *Animal Album* as well as a landscape of the mid-1640s from the large volume that also stemmed from the Odescalchi and was published later by Röthlisberger as the *Album Wildenstein* (subsequently in the Norton Simon Foundation and ultimately partly dispersed). The landscape was a major acquisition, not least because of the high quality of the drawing. Together with the later acquisition of three renderings of a *Landscape with the Landing of Aeneas in Latium* of 1673, this landscape enables the Museum to provide an indication of Claude's artistic range.

A further addition to the Museum's collection was made in 1982 with the purchase of a recently discovered sketchbook from the period around 1650 and a group of small studies of relatively minor significance, mostly done about twenty years earlier. This was an acquisition made in the spirit of Tessin, whose collection mingles nondescript sketches and finished drawings. Unfortunately an export ban has prevented this acquisition from reaching Stockholm, but the Nationalmuseum is contesting the matter and the sheets are being kept in England pending a renewed assessment. The 1984 acquisition of a monumental tree study from the latter half of the 1630s forms an important complement to the collection of large sheets, which previously had been entirely dominated by compositional studies.

With these recent acquisitions the Claude collection has been rounded out in a way that makes it roughly comparable to the Poussin group, which is part of the old holding. Otherwise the rich collection of seventeenth century drawings has remained largely unaltered. The occasional addition has been made such as two red chalk drawings of a type that is customarily attributed to Jacques Bellange and an important drawing by Laurent de la Hyre (*Hercules Taking Cerberus from the Underworld*), who was previously unrepresented.

In the case of early eighteenth-century drawings it has seemed superfluous to spend scarce resources on supplementing what was already a strong selection. The Museum has had the good fortune to make an "internal acquisition" in the form of two red chalk drawings by Antoine Watteau. These were identified in 1979 in a group of otherwise insignificant sheets that had been hidden away in the Print Room's store for almost a century. There has also been a very costly purchase of the sheet "aux trois crayons" (the mixture of red, black, and white chalks) of *Two studies of a Young Woman*, which belongs to the preparatory work for the Museum's painting *La Leçon d'Amour*. The free composition and fresh observation of this drawing make it a very valuable addition to what was already a handsome collection of Watteau drawings.

Acquisitions on a broad front have been directed, however, to French art after about 1740, when Tessin stopped collecting, and up to the present day, above all to the late eighteenth and early nineteenth centuries. Here it has proved possible to build up a varied group of drawings by Jean-Honoré Fragonard, to create in two stages a Hubert Robert collection dominated by quick studies and sketches, and to supplement these works with some important sheets by Jean-Baptiste Greuze. Gabriel de Saint Aubin's four attractive watercolor sheets that have been in the collection since the nineteenth century, have been augmented in recent years. One of the few landscapes by Mariette has been incorporated in the collection, which is gratifying not least on account of Tessin's personal relationship with this ardent connoisseur and art dealer. Works by less celebrated French artists of the period such as Nicolas Cochin, Hubert François Gravelot, Jacques-André Portail, and Jacques Louis Durameau have also been added.

Another special concern of the Nationalmuseum has been to enrich the collection with works by artists whom Johan Tobias Sergel encountered during his years in Rome from 1767-78 or during his later sojourn there from 1783-84. François-André Vincent, J. B. le Bouteux, Bénigne Gagneraux, and Giuseppe Cades are among these artists. Sergel's own collection, moreover, provided a starting point for late eighteenth-century French drawings. Favorable circumstances enabled the Museum to make a very important purchase in the American art market, one of the few—if not the last—remaining complete albums of drawings from Jean Louis David's time in Rome. The album, containing about a hundred sheets of uneven quality, has interesting examples of figures and landscapes, as well as sketches related to a number of his most famous works. Similarly, the Museum has been able to acquire some sheets by Girodet de Roucy Trioson.

France's outstanding early nineteenth-century master, Jean-Auguste Ingres, has proved more elusive. Just one example of his graphic art has been acquired, a lovely nude study from 1842, but nothing connected with his renowned portraits has been available.

Otherwise the aim of the Museum has been to pursue Tessin's method of following the art of drawing by assembling groups of works by master draftsmen. Since the 1920s and 1930s, the Museum has had a small selection of sheets by Eugène Delacroix, and efforts have therefore been made to build up a similar resource for the other leading Romantic, Théodore Géricault. Today the Museum possesses a collection that illustrates practically every phase of Géricault's development, with links to some of his masterpieces. Victor Hugo is equally well represented, with a range from evocative medieval fantasies to free spot studies. The earlier collection of J. F. Millet has also been systematically enlarged, chiefly with small sketches and studies. Another recent acquisition en bloc comprises study drawings by Thomas Couture. They represent a continuation of the academic tradition and are highly important in Sweden because Couture had a great many Swedish pupils. Since 1936, moreover, the Museum has owned a sketchbook that Paul Gauguin evidently used sporadically from 1876 to 1887. It can be seen as a major document for his drawing prior to the trip to Martinique.

Besides this sort of documentation, the Museum has obtained single works by other great draftsmen to supplement its existing holding or lay a foundation for further acquisitions. Mention can be made of sheets by Pierre-Joseph Prud'hon, two sheets by Honoré Daumier, and a few by Camille Corot, all illustrating different distinct phases in the development of their art.

In time a collection that is built up in this way acquires a structure and can start to perform its pedagogic function of providing an overview of a vital artistic progression. Other acquisitions could, of course, be explained in similar terms. Apart from the French corpus, however, it is really only the Venetian collection that has been improved in this systematic fashion. Other areas have been enriched primarily with single items in an effort to fill particularly obvious gaps. This applies, for instance, to an important sheet by Pietro da Cortona, previously entirely unrepresented in a relatively good collection of Roman artists, and to a drawing by Francisco Goya which is sufficiently powerful to stand on its own.

It is, of course, a privilege to be able to begin with collections of such a high quality and comprehensive range as those at the Nationalmuseum. But the Museum's resources are extremely limited and every acquisition must fill a purpose, while also respecting the existing structure of the collections and articulating this without upsetting the overall balance. Seldom has the Museum been in a position to compete for the great treasures and has then usually gone away empty-handed. Such disappointments are irrelevant here. It is sufficient to note that an institution which has to rely mainly on diminishing government funds must cut its cloth accordingly. The chance of acquiring an important portrait by Ingres has gone forever but there are other happier instances where the price was met.

As previously noted, private donations are by no means encouraged by Swedish law, so in this respect the Nationalmuseum's situation differs radically from that of American museums. The lack of access to massive contributions is offset to some extent, however, by the freedom that the Museum's professional staff enjoys when it comes to making prompt and unconventional acquisitions without regard to headstrong donors, power hungry trustees, or meddlesome politicians. For it is another Swedish tradition that national agencies are completely independent of their ministries as long as they do not exceed their financial allowance.

The Nationalmuseum is a small museum in a small country, but the quality of its collections is very high. It is hardly an exaggeration to say that the collection of drawings ranks among the ten foremost in the world. This also implies a great responsibility and is perhaps the chief reason why the Print Room of the Museum is now pursuing an ambitious acquisition policy.

NOTES

1. See bibliography (works cited in abbreviated form, Bjurström).

2. J. Q. van Regteren Altena, *Les Dessins italiens de la reine Christina de Suède*, Analecta Reginensia, 2 (Stockholm, 1966), p. 26. Van Regteren Altena gives (13-39) the most extensive assessment of Queen Christina as a collector of drawings. The most recent contribution to the study of the Christina collection of drawings is Bert W. Meijer, "Un appunto per la provenienza," *Designi italiani del Teylers Museum Haarlem*, exhibition catalogue, Istituto Olandese di Storia dell'Arte, Florence and Istituto Nazionale per la Grafica, Gabinetto Nazionale delle Stampe, Rome, 1983-84, pp. 11-13.

3. *Les dessins italiens*, p. 34 ff.

4. *Les dessins italiens*, p. 20.

5. *Les dessins italiens*, p. 29 f.

6. *Les dessins italiens*, p. 30.

7. The primary source of information about Nicodemus Tessin's collection is a catalogue (now in the Nationalmuseum's archives) drawn up by Carl Gustaf Tessin some time between 1728, when Nicodemus died, and 1739, when Carl Gustaf left for Paris. It lists architectural drawings from Nicodemus's collection but none of the Crozat items acquired in Paris.

8. C. D. Moselius, *Carl Gustaf Tessins ungdom* (Stockholm 1967), p. 45.

9. For a more detailed consideration of Tessin as a collector of drawings, see P. Bjurström, "Carl Gustaf Tessin as a Collector of Drawings," *Contributions to the History and Theory of Art, Figura Nova Series* 6 Acta Universitatis Upsaliensis (Stockholm, 1967), pp. 99-120 and the references given there.

10. P. Bjurström and G. Cavalli-Björkman, "A newly acquired portrait of Anton Maria Zanetti by Rosalba Carriera," *Nationalmuseum Bulletin*, 1:1 (1977) pp. 31-43.

11. Cf. B. Magnusson, "The De la Gardie (Borrestad) Collection of Drawings," *Nationalmuseum Bulletin*, 6:3 (1982), pp. 113-140, and N. Turner, "Roman Baroque Drawings in the De la Gardie Collection," *Nationalmuseum Bulletin*, 6:3 (1982), pp. 141-159.

12. Another branch of the family inherited the collection of paintings; most of its masterpieces were disposed of and lost for Sweden as recently as the 1980s and are now to be found in American museums.

13. Nationalmuseum, A 88, fol. 19.

COLOR PLATES

1

ANONYMOUS FLORENTINE ARTIST (c. 1460)

Three Figure Studies

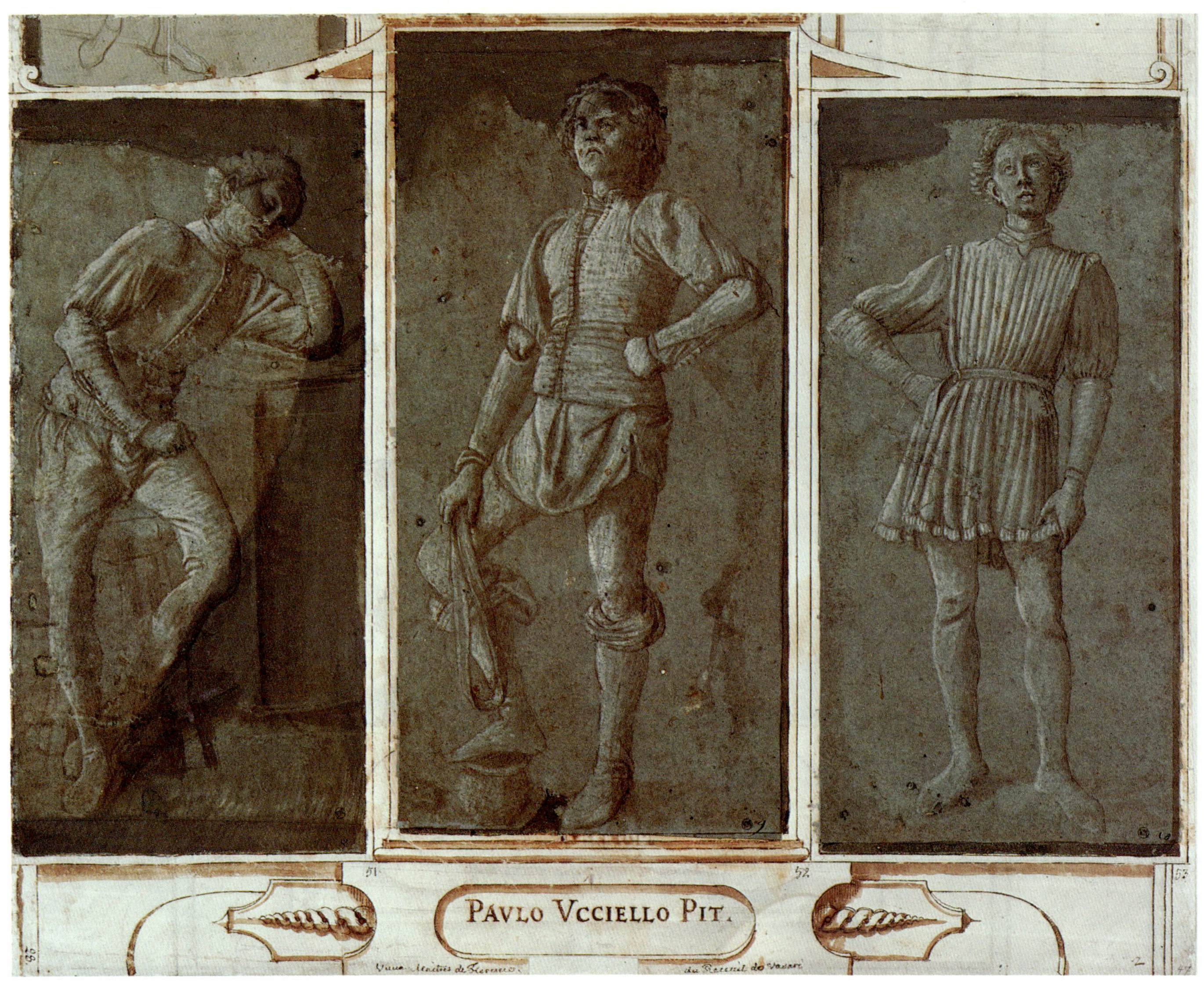

2

DOMENICO GHIRLANDAIO (1449-1494)

Head of an Old Man

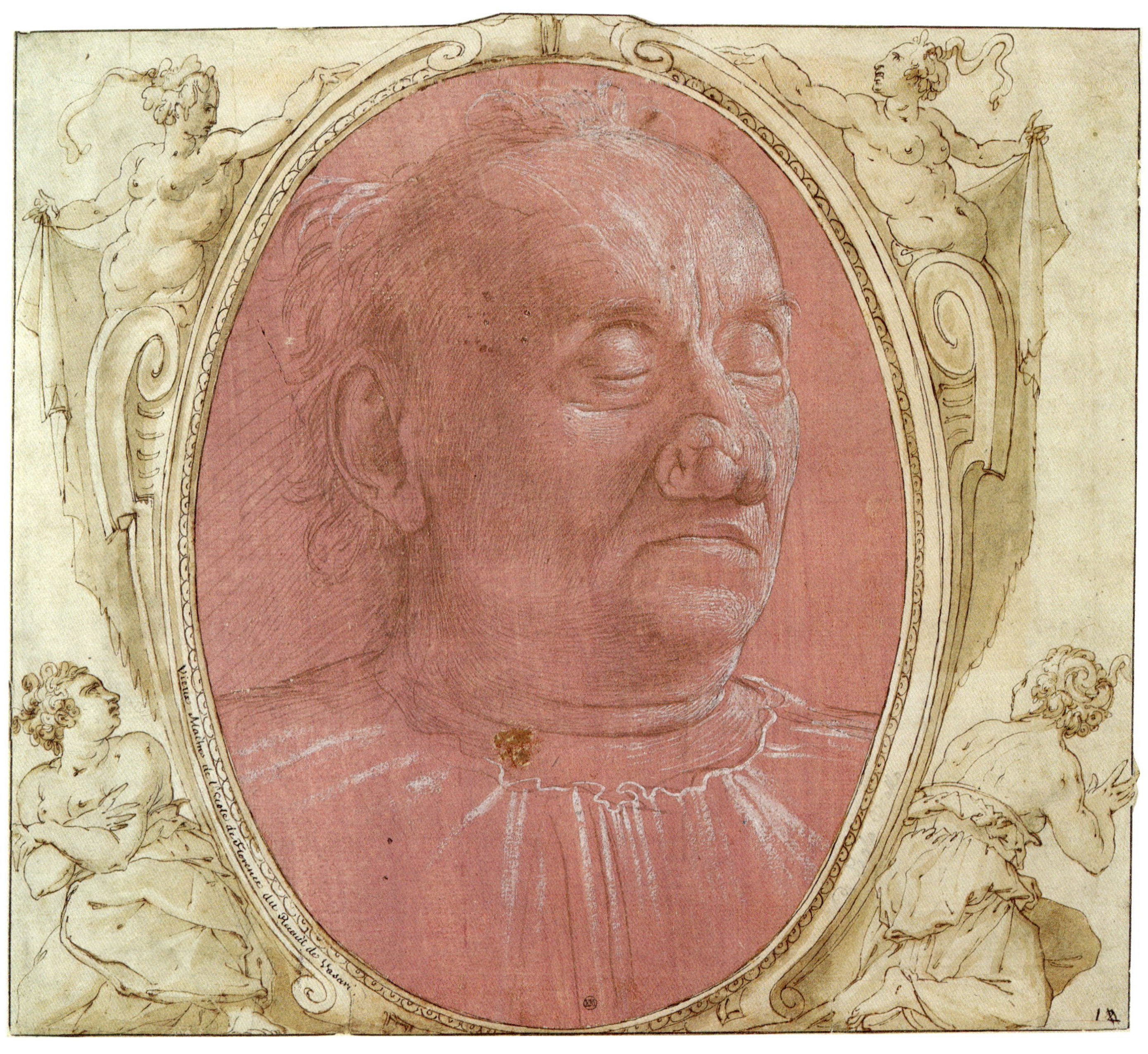

3

SCHOOL OF BERNARDINO PINTURICCHIO

A Boy Standing by a Chair, an Eye, and Three Seated Women

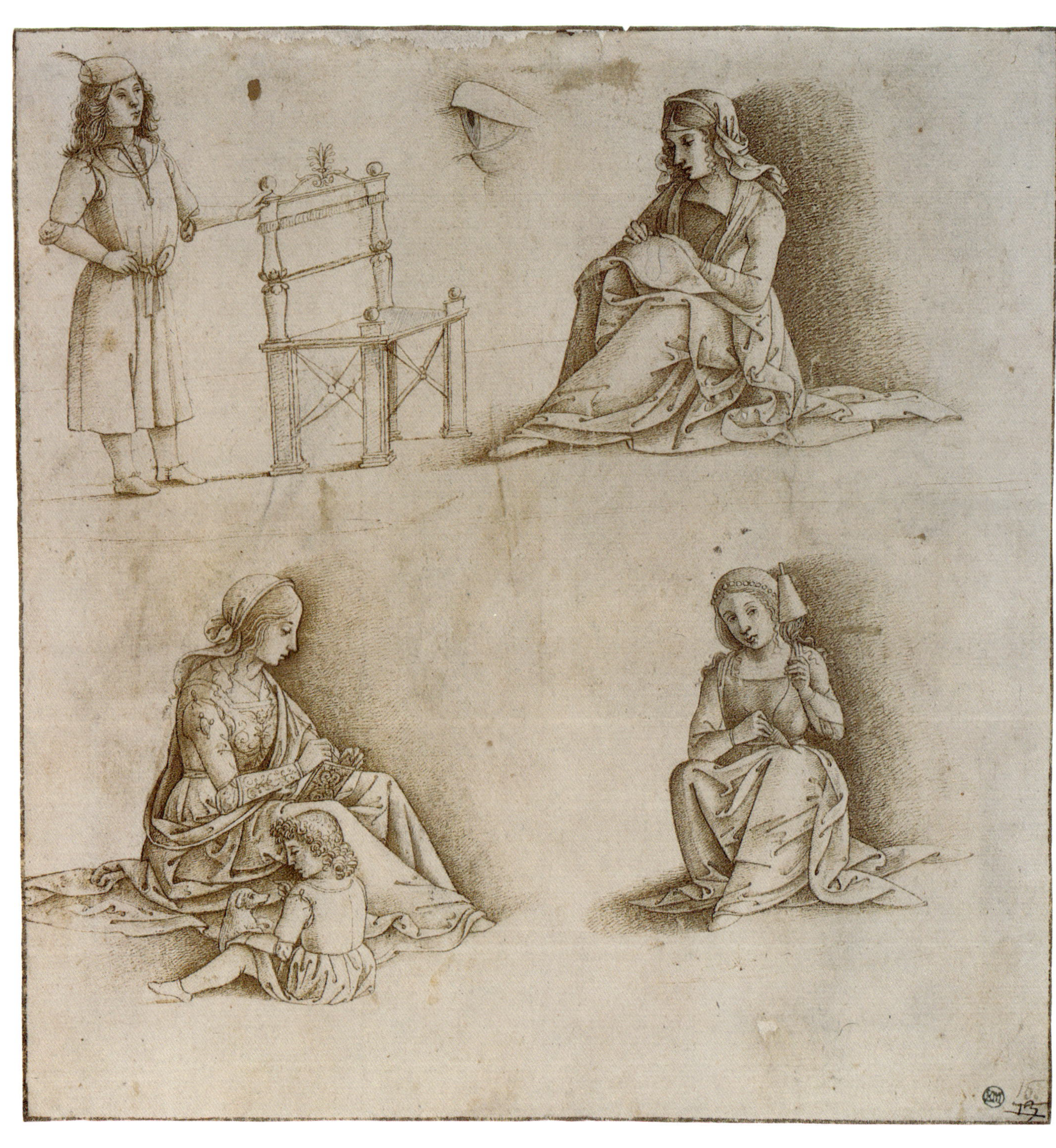

4
RAFFAELE BOTTICINI (1477-c. 1520)
The Virgin Mary Kneeling, Study for a Nativity

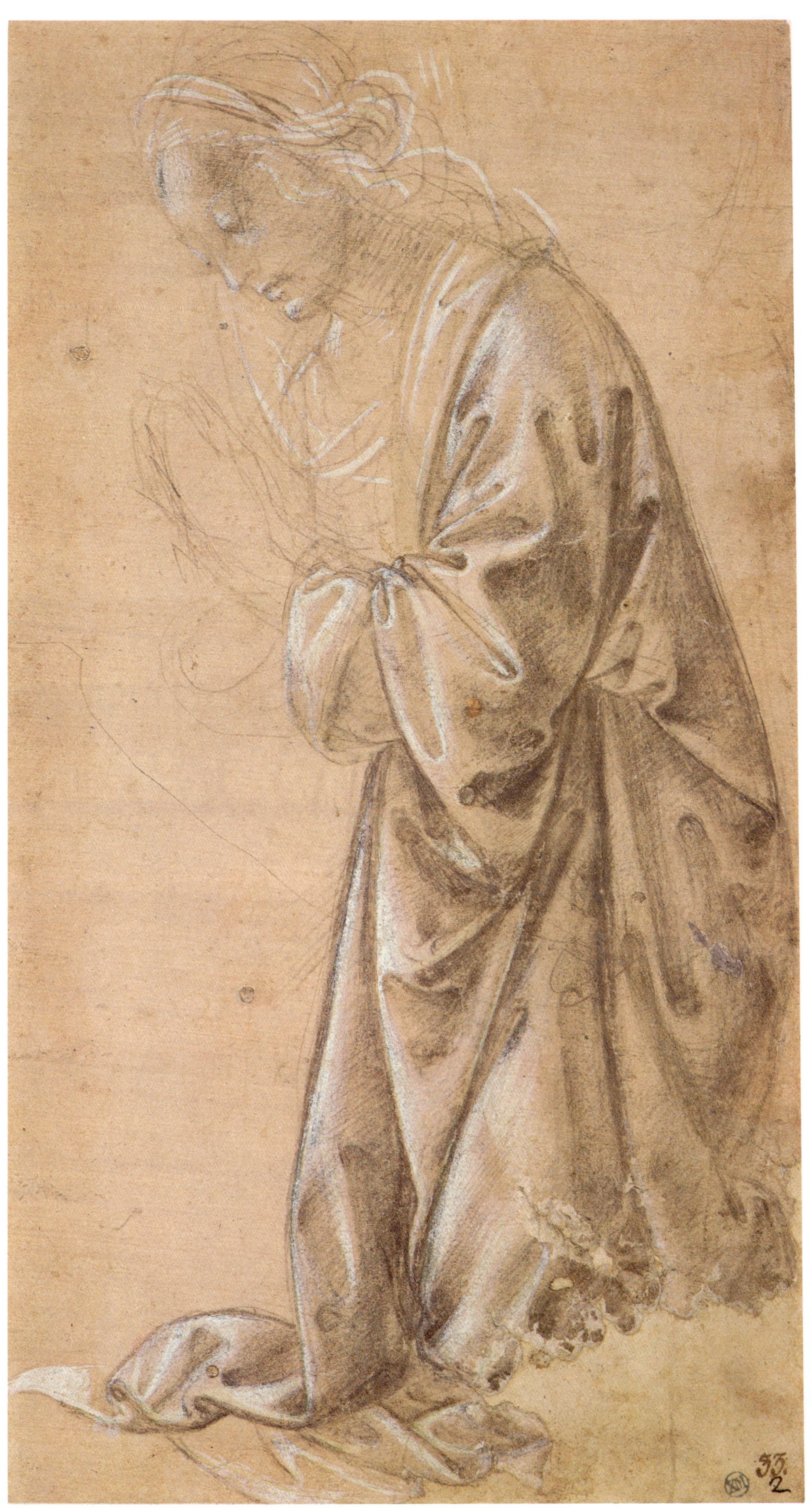

5
LEONARDO DA VINCI ? (1452-1519)

Goddess Standing in a Chariot Drawn by Two Horses, of Which One is Falling

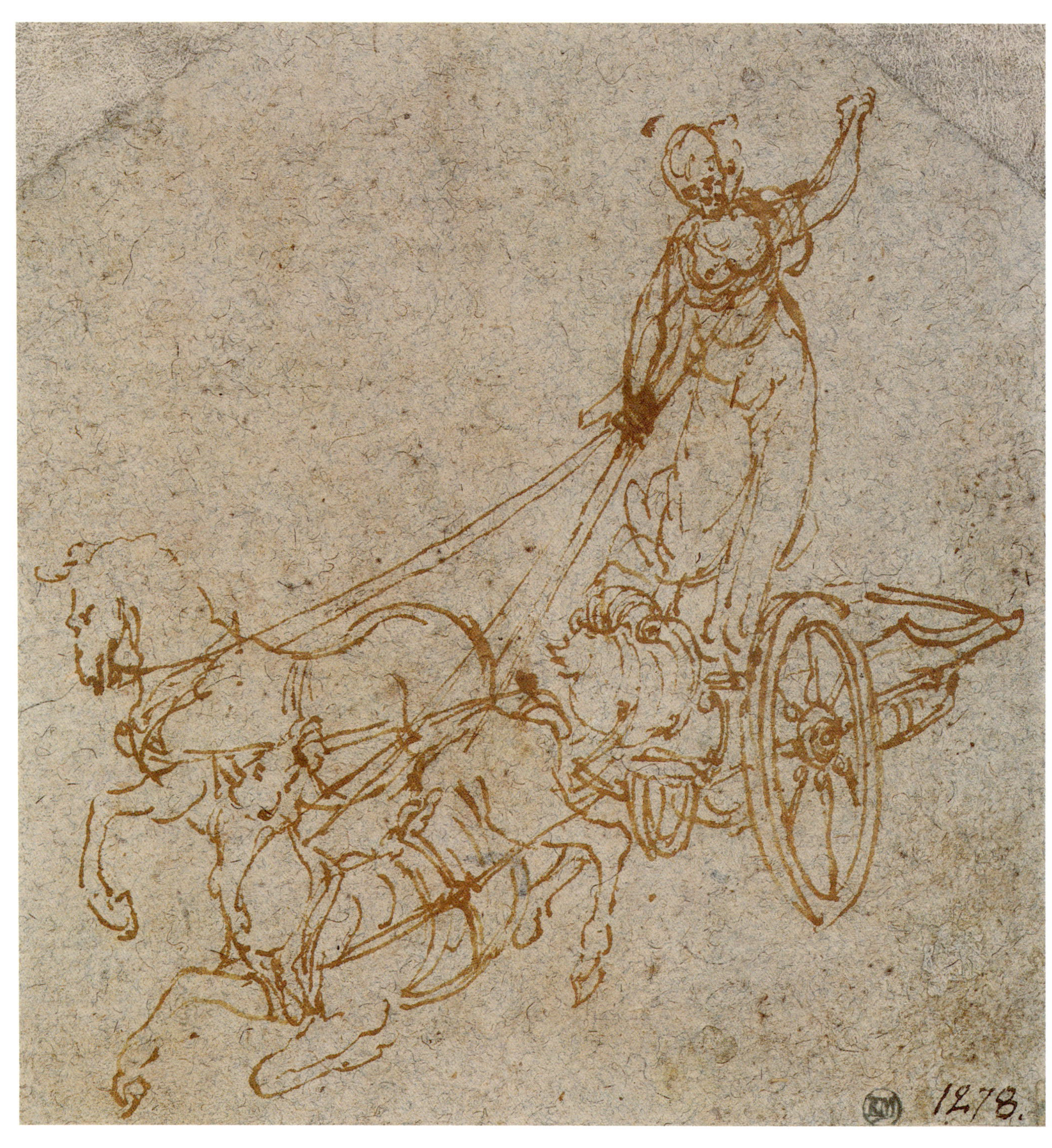

7

GIROLAMO GENGA (1467-1551)

Battle in Front of a Castle

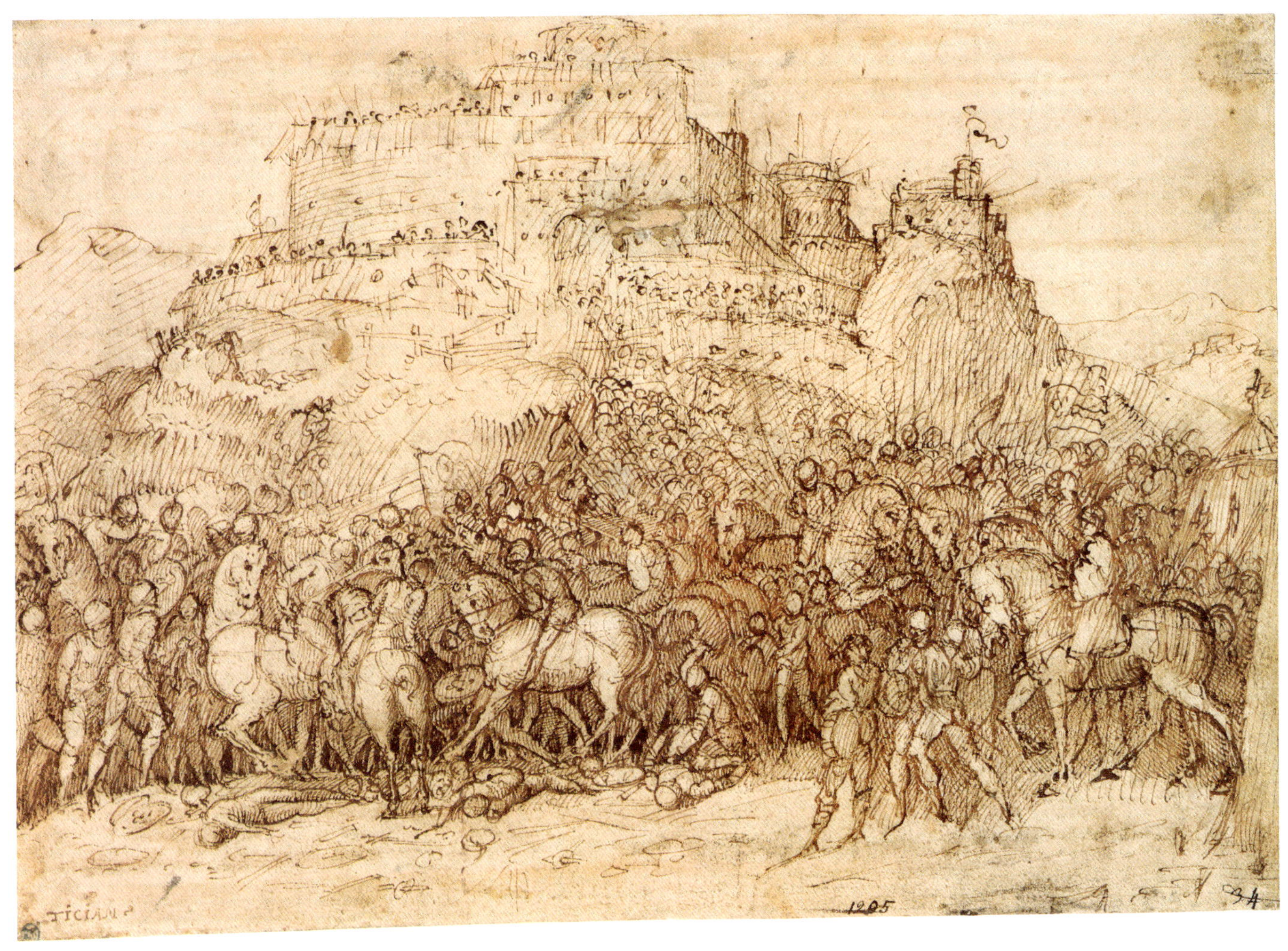

8

TIZIANO VECELLI (1485/88-1576)

Girl Lying on Her Back with One Arm Outstretched

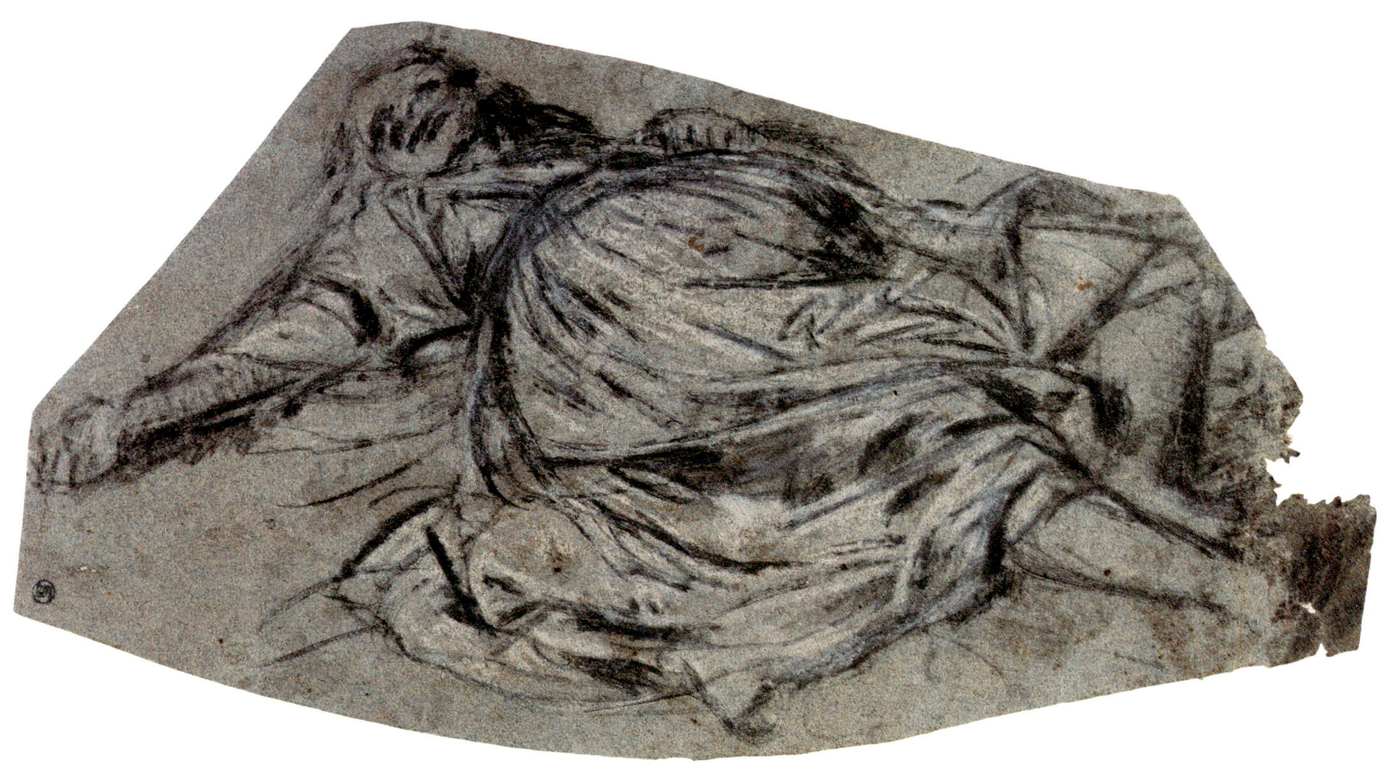

10
GIOVANNI GIROLAMO SAVOLDO (c. 1480-after 1548)

St. John the Evangelist

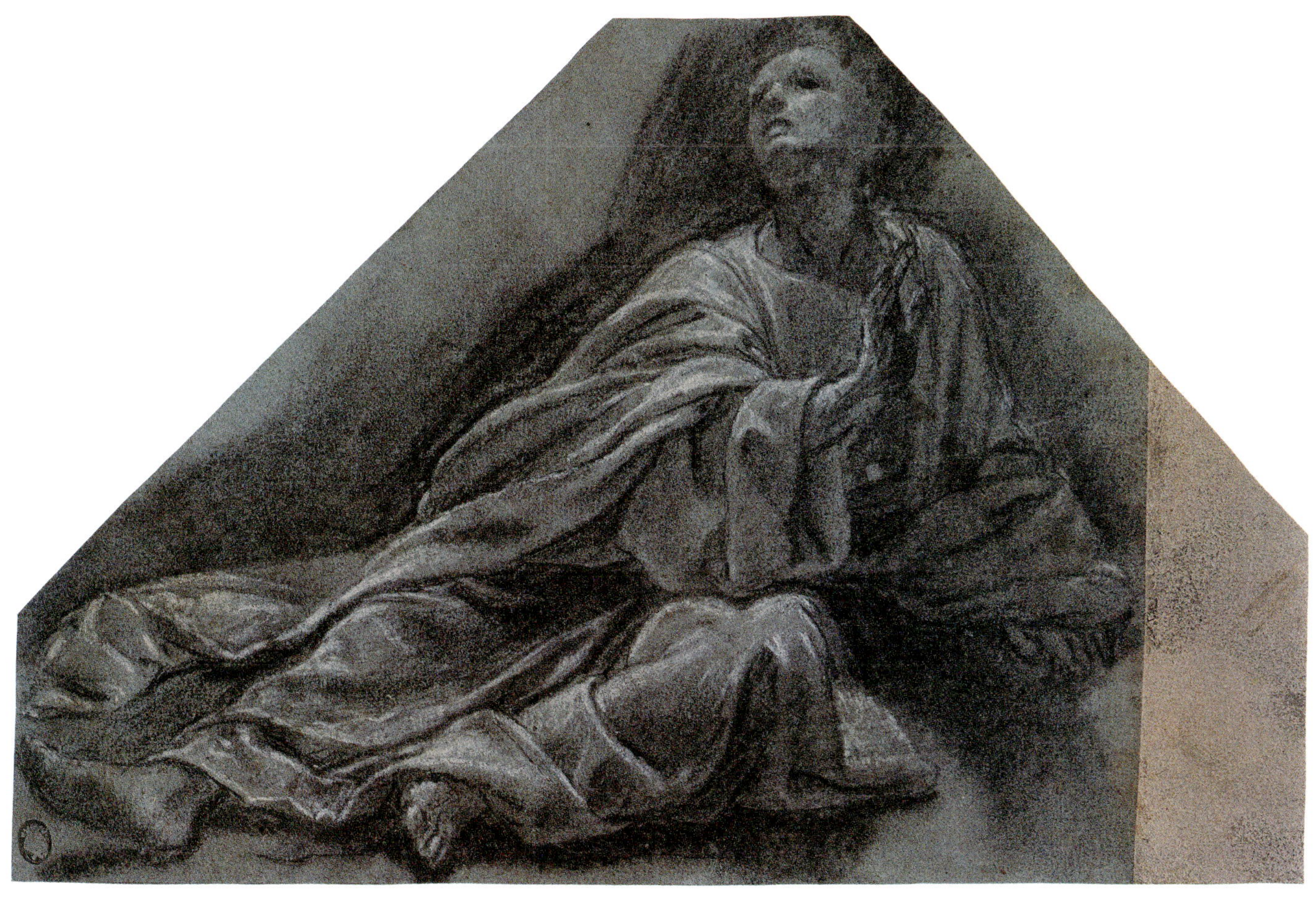

11

PARIS BORDONE (1500-1570)

Walking Male Figure

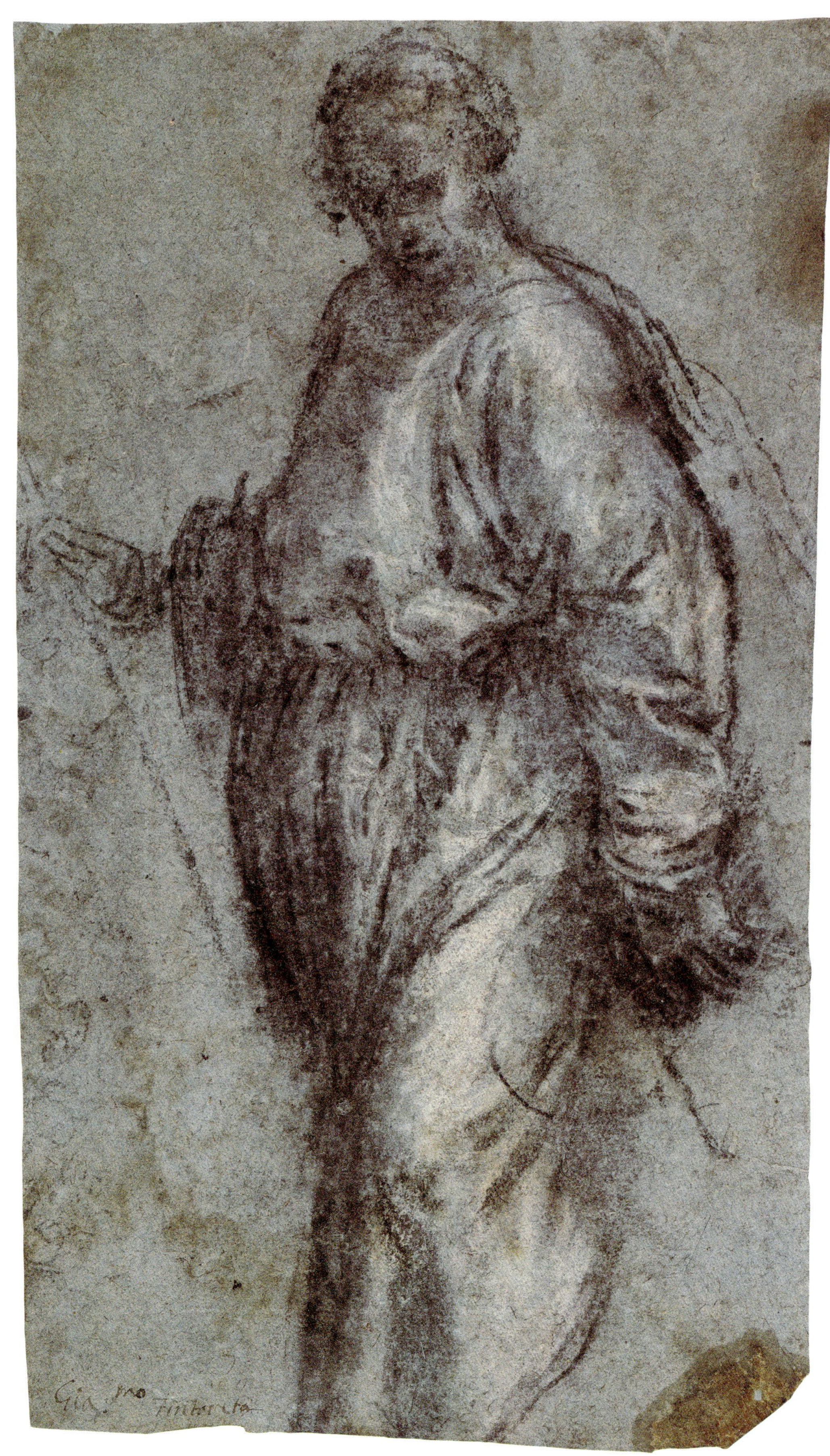

12

RAFFAELLO SANTI, called RAPHAEL (1483-1520)

The Ascension of the Virgin

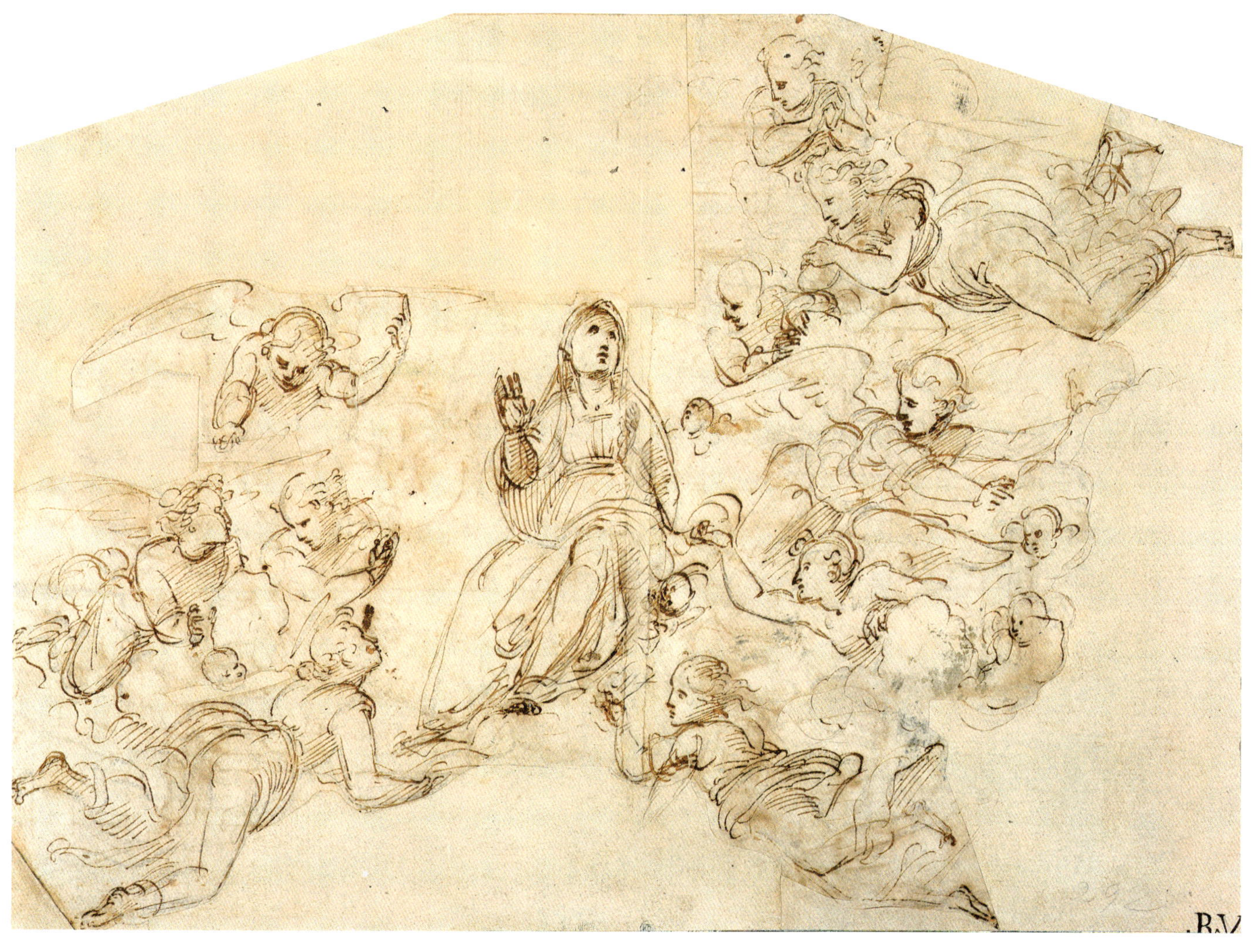

14
POLIDORO DA CARAVAGGIO (1490/1500-1543)

Figure Studies, Possibly for a Triton

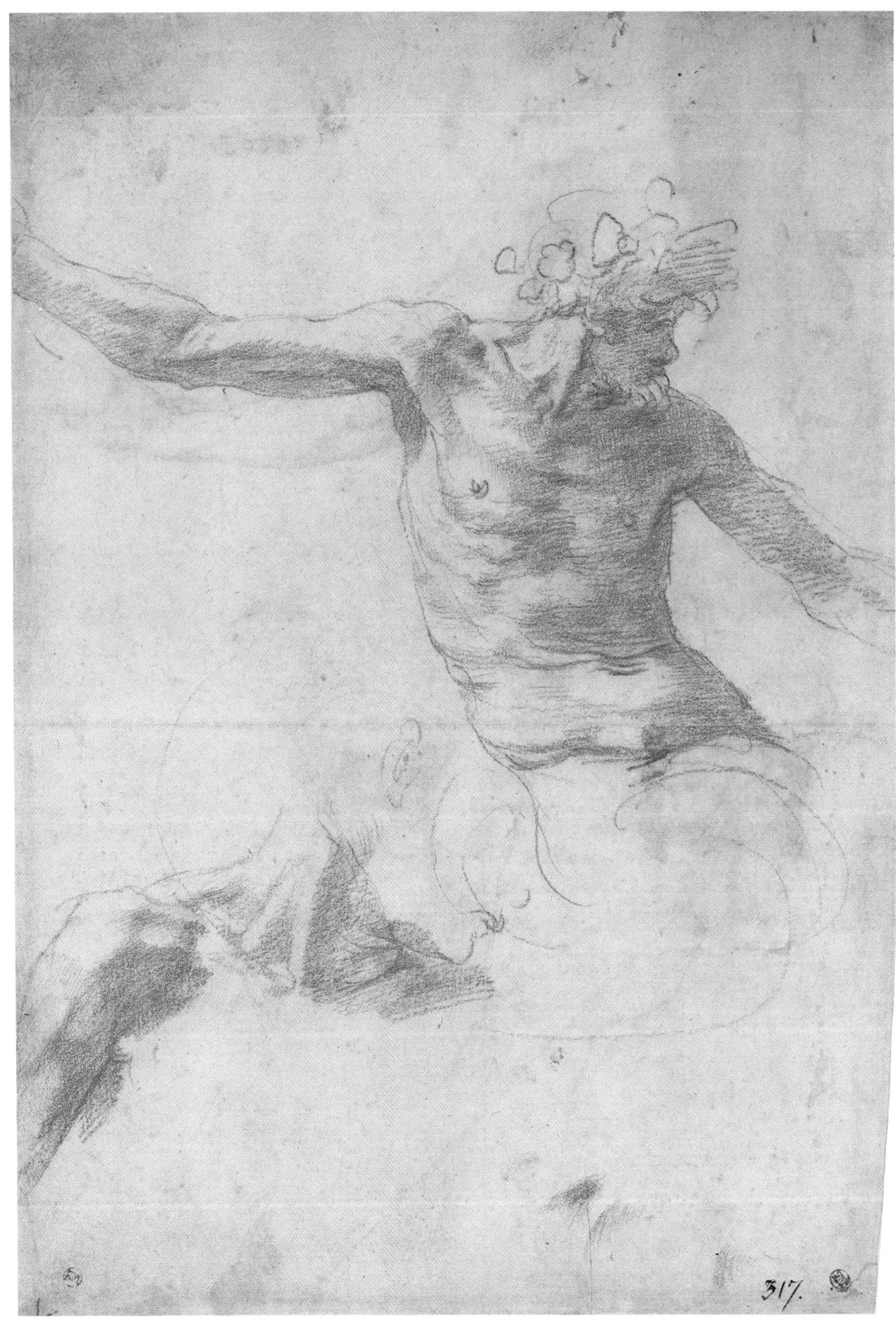

15

GIULIO PIPPI, called GIULIO ROMANO (1493-1546)

Study for Porta della Citadella in Mantua

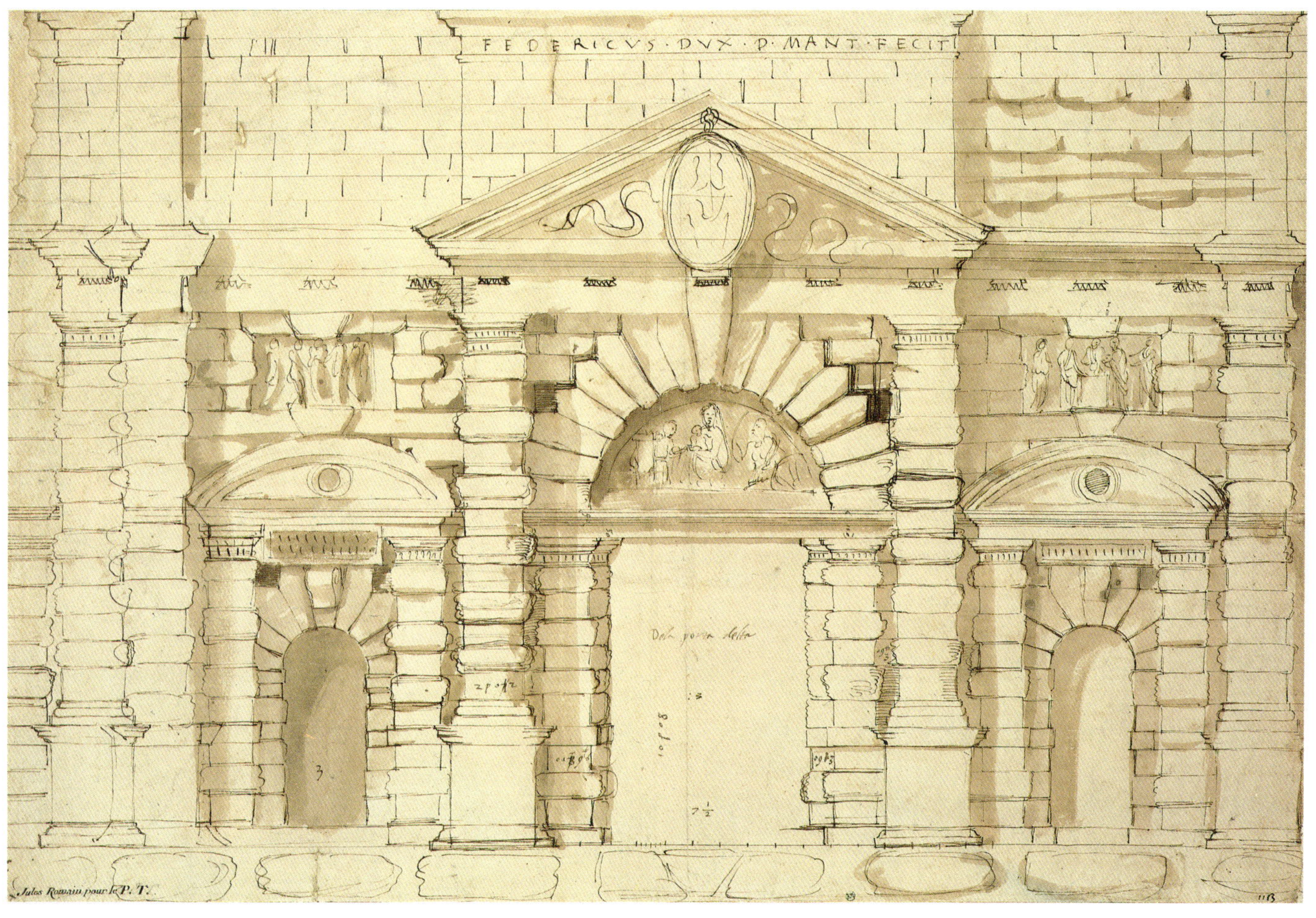

16

TADDEO ZUCCARO (1529-1566)

St. Paul or St. Andrew

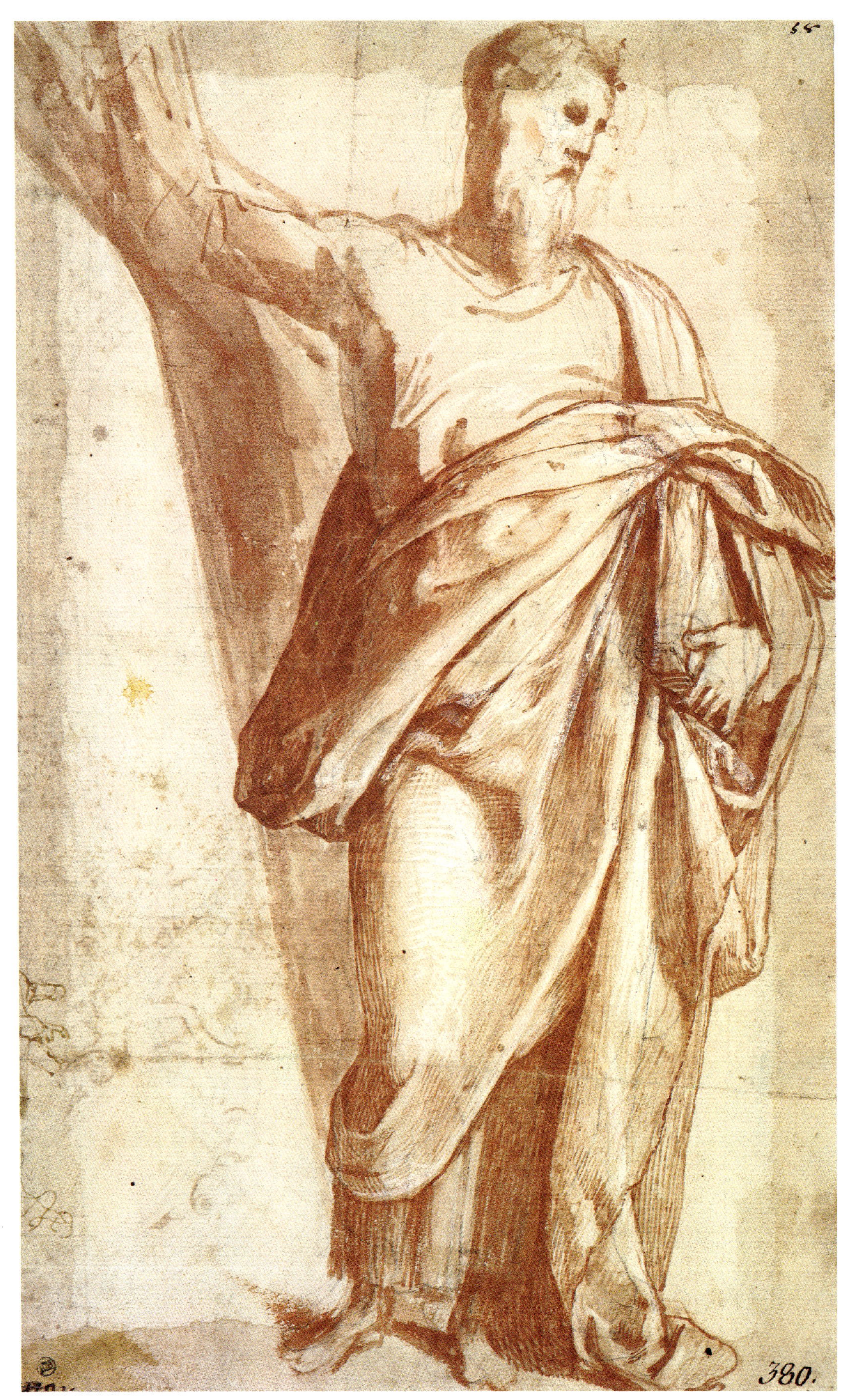

19

FEDERIGO BAROCCI (1526-1612)

Study of a Tree

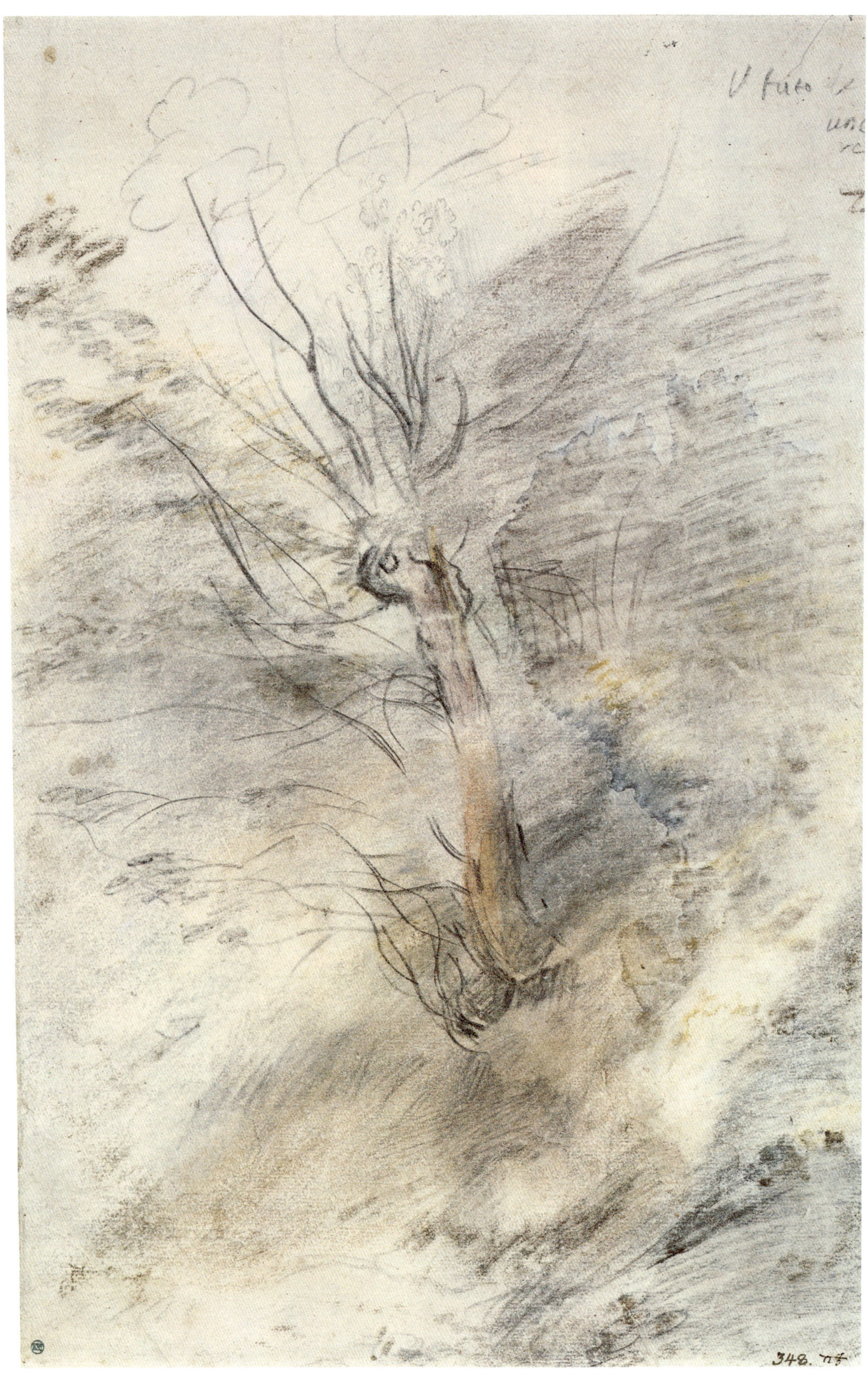

20

FEDERIGO BAROCCI (1526-1612)

Head of a Woman

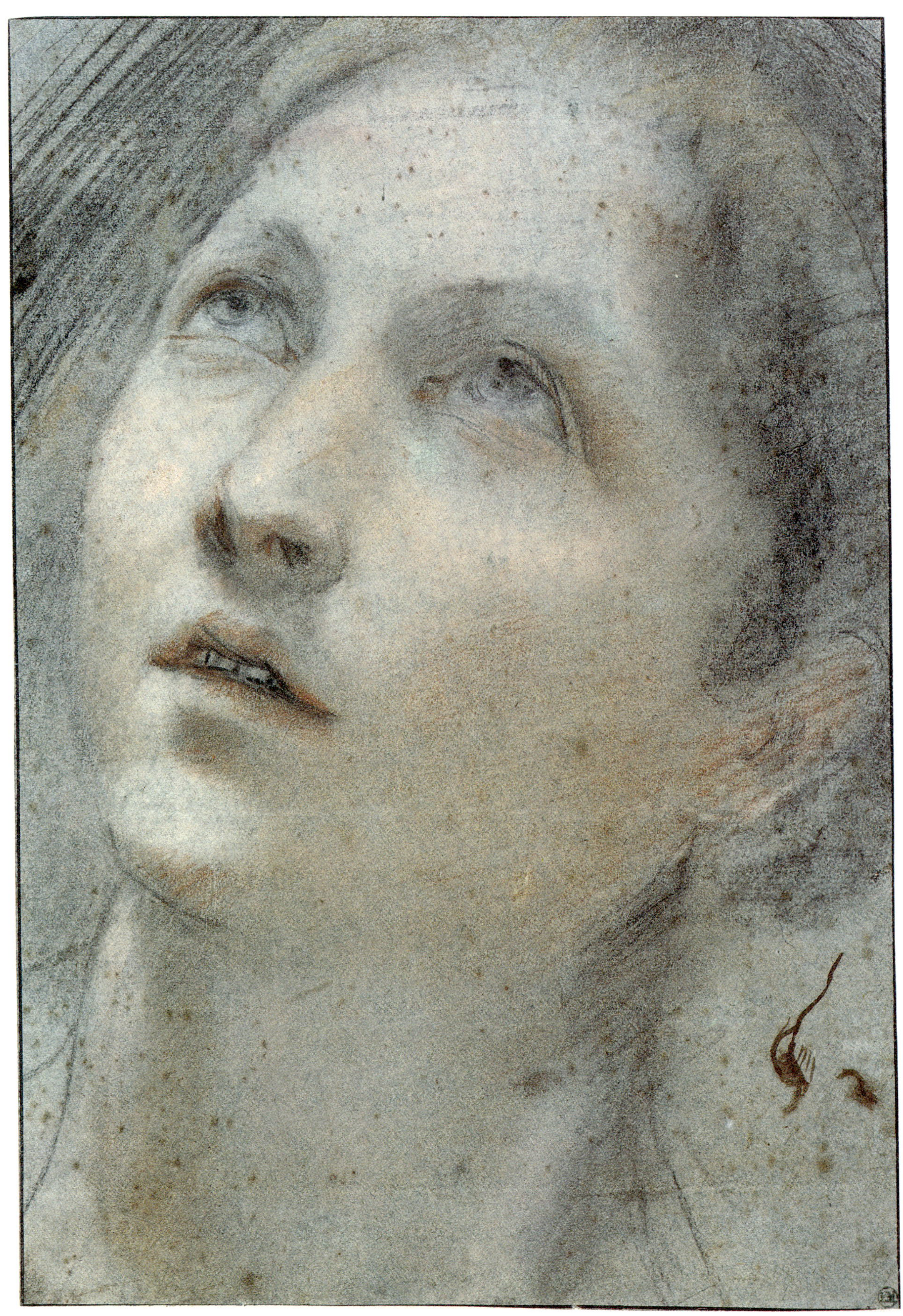

24

SALVATOR ROSA (1615-1673)

Study for The Philosophers' Grove

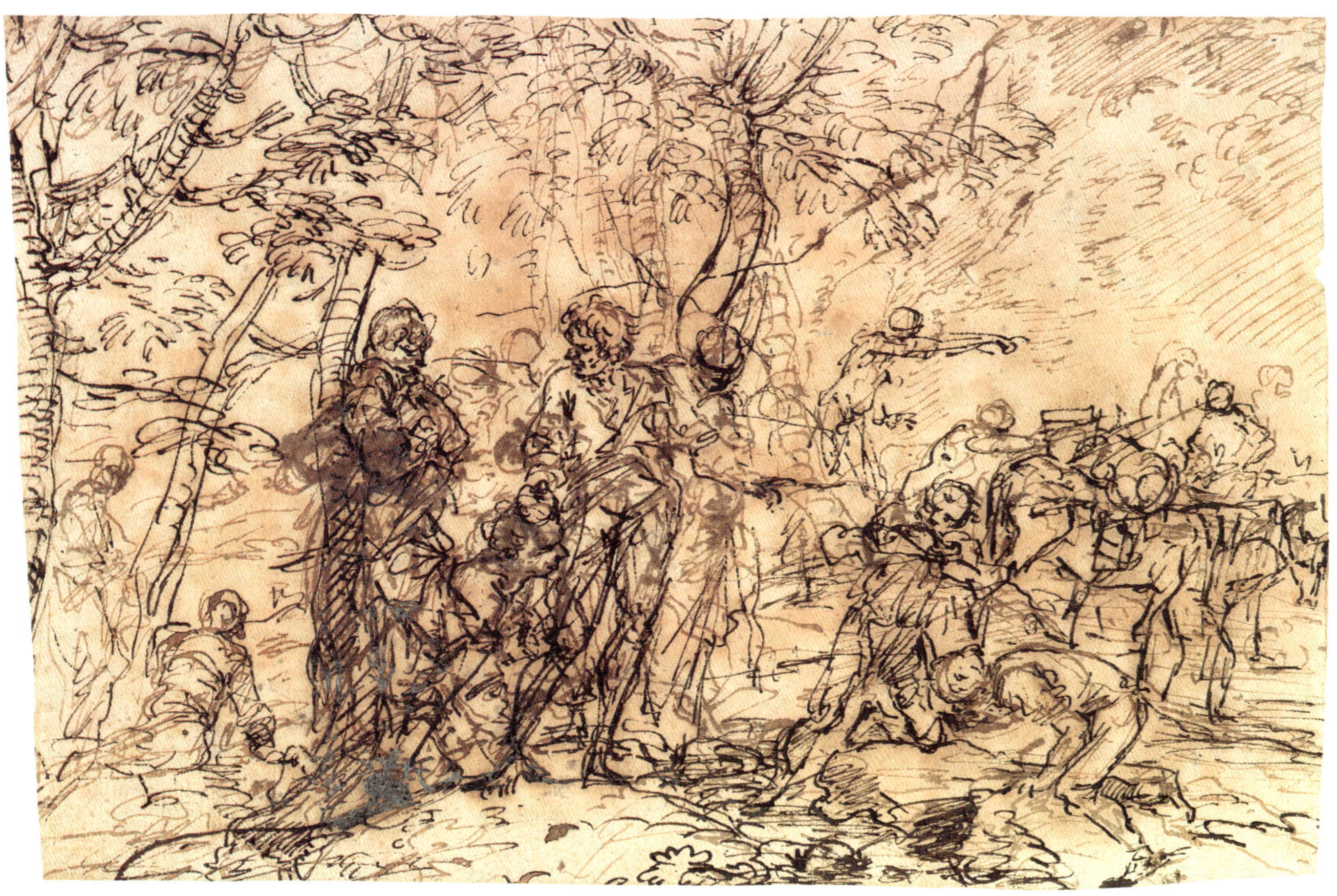

26

GIOVANNI FRANCESCO BARBIERI, called IL GUERCINO (1591-1666)

Virgin and Child on a Pedestal

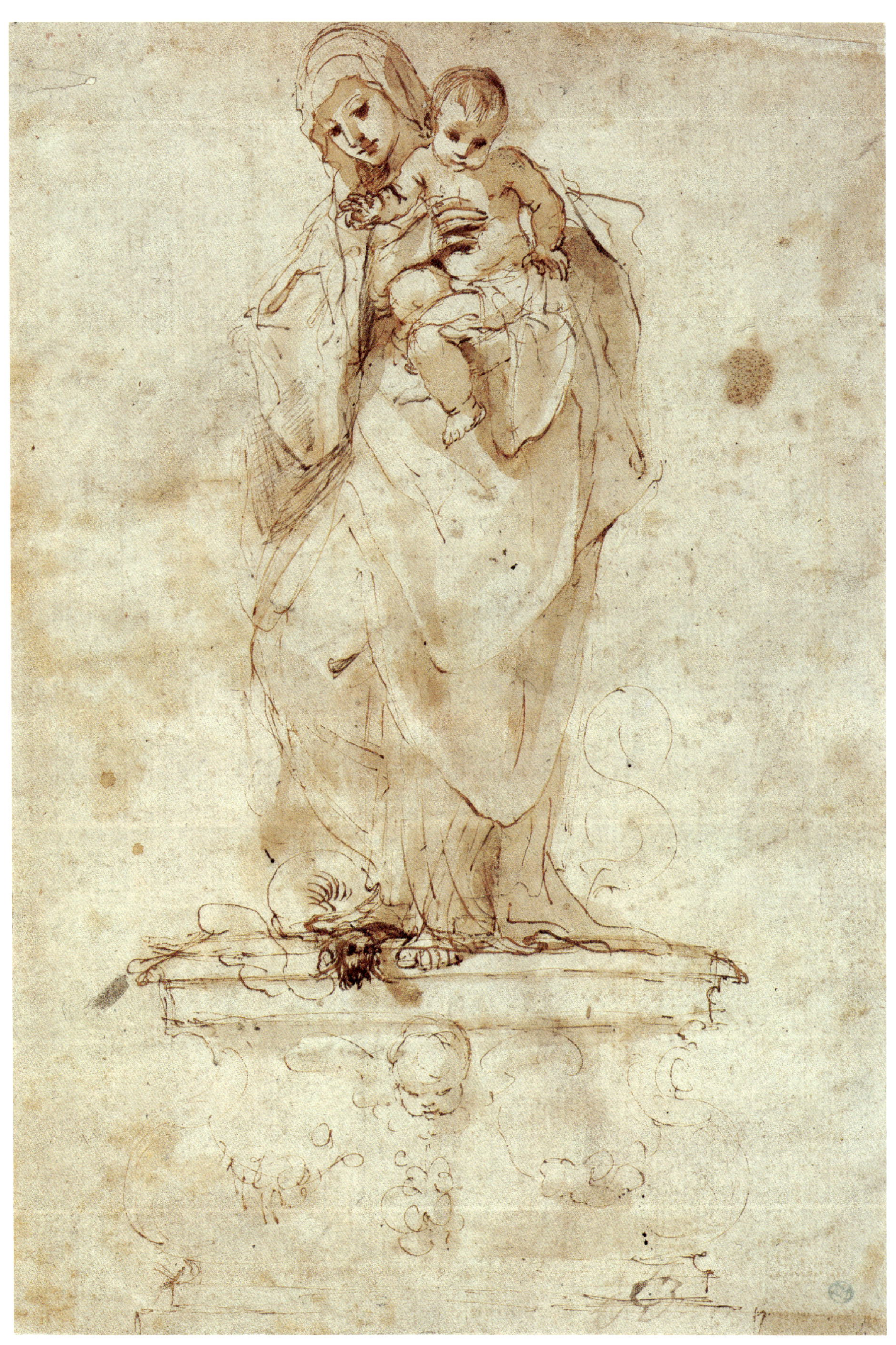

28

GIOVANNI BENEDETTO CASTIGLIONE, IL GRECHETTO (c. 1610-1663/65)

Angels Adoring the Child in the Arms of the Virgin

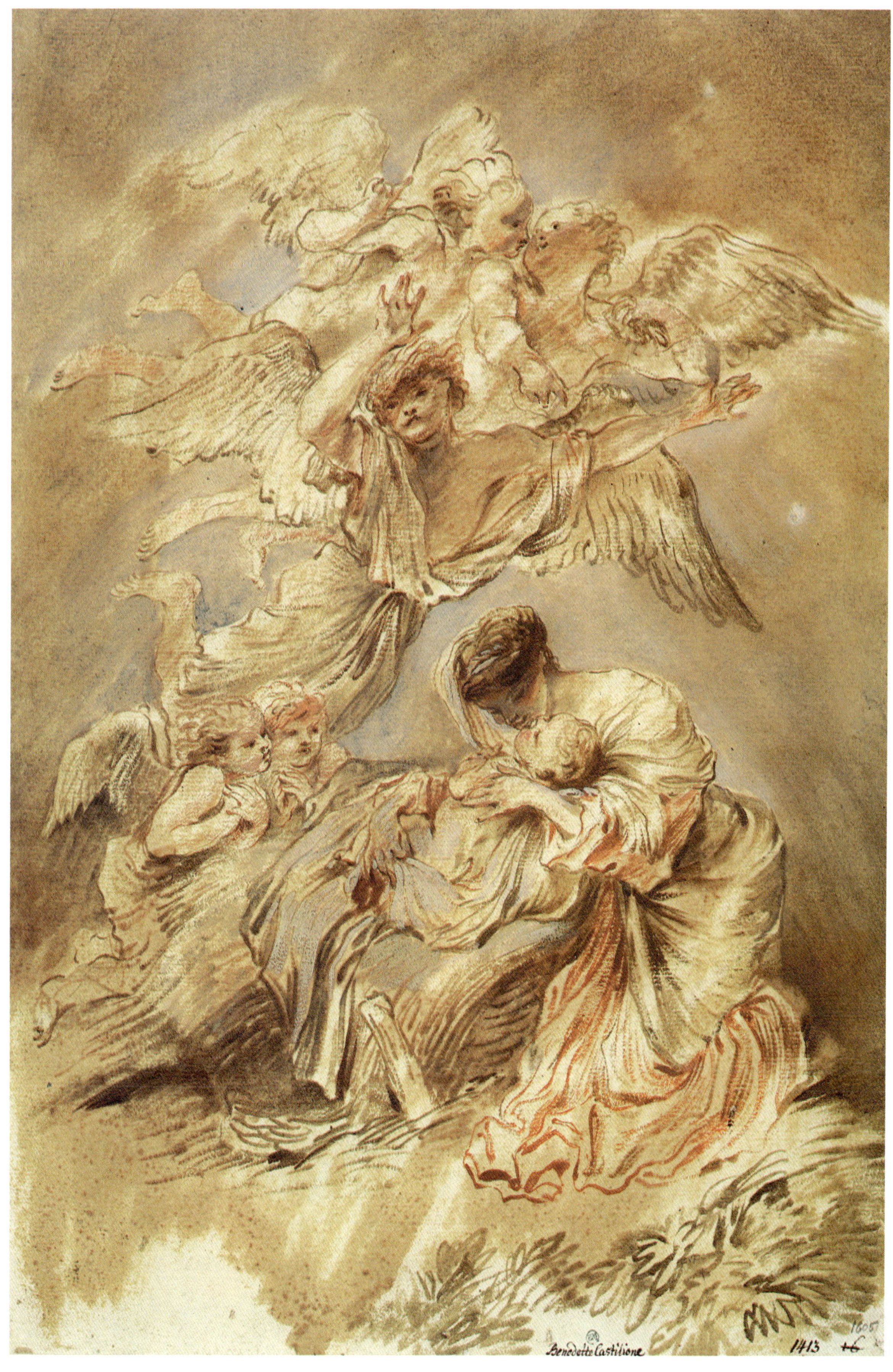

29

SEBASTIANO RICCI (1660-1734)

Head of a Young Girl, Facing Slightly Right

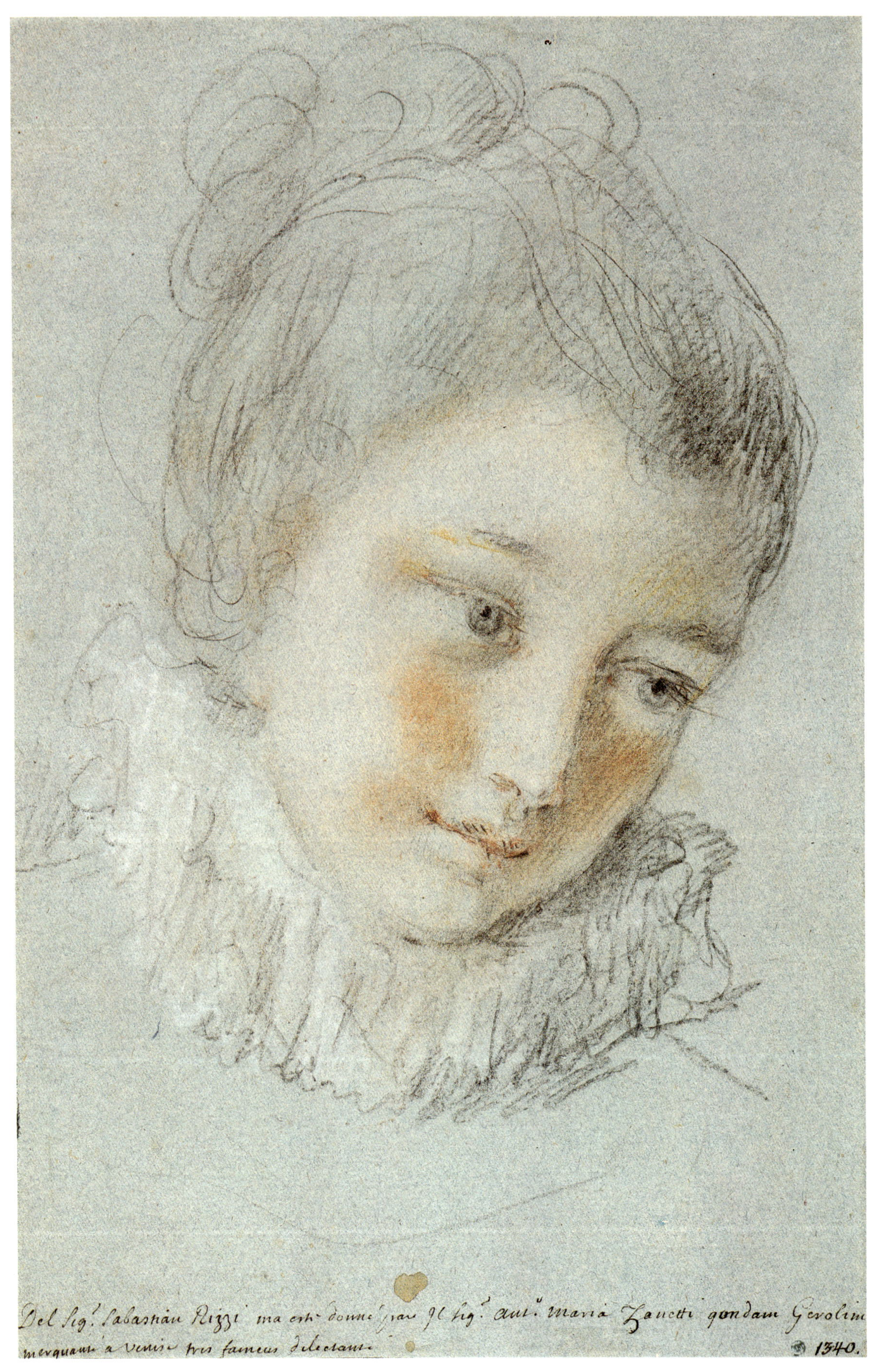

30

GIOVANNI BATTISTA TIEPOLO (1696-1770)

Variations on the Theme of Anthony and Cleopatra

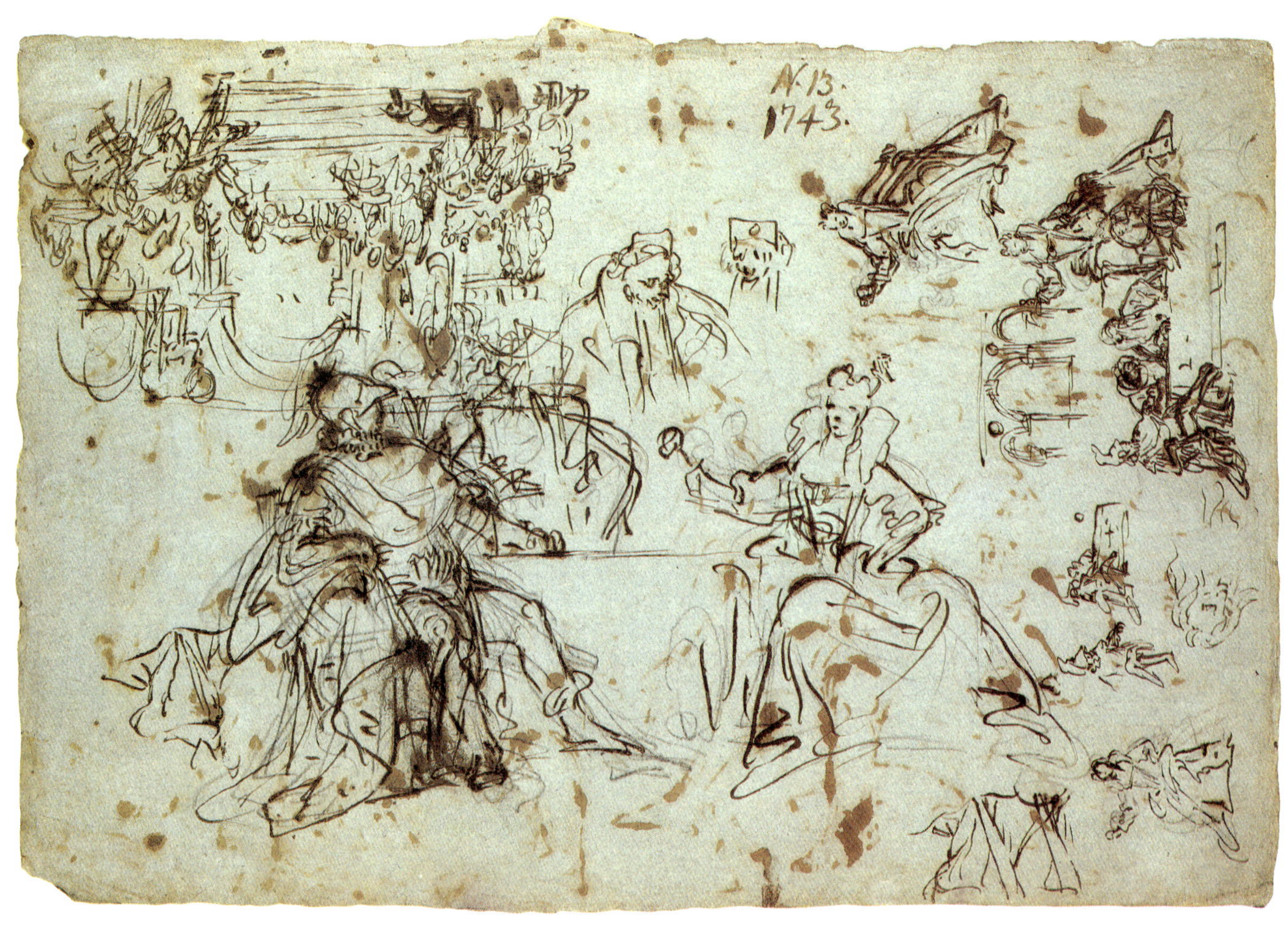

31

GIOVANNI BATTISTA PIRANESI (1720-1778)

A Two-storied Interior of a Temple

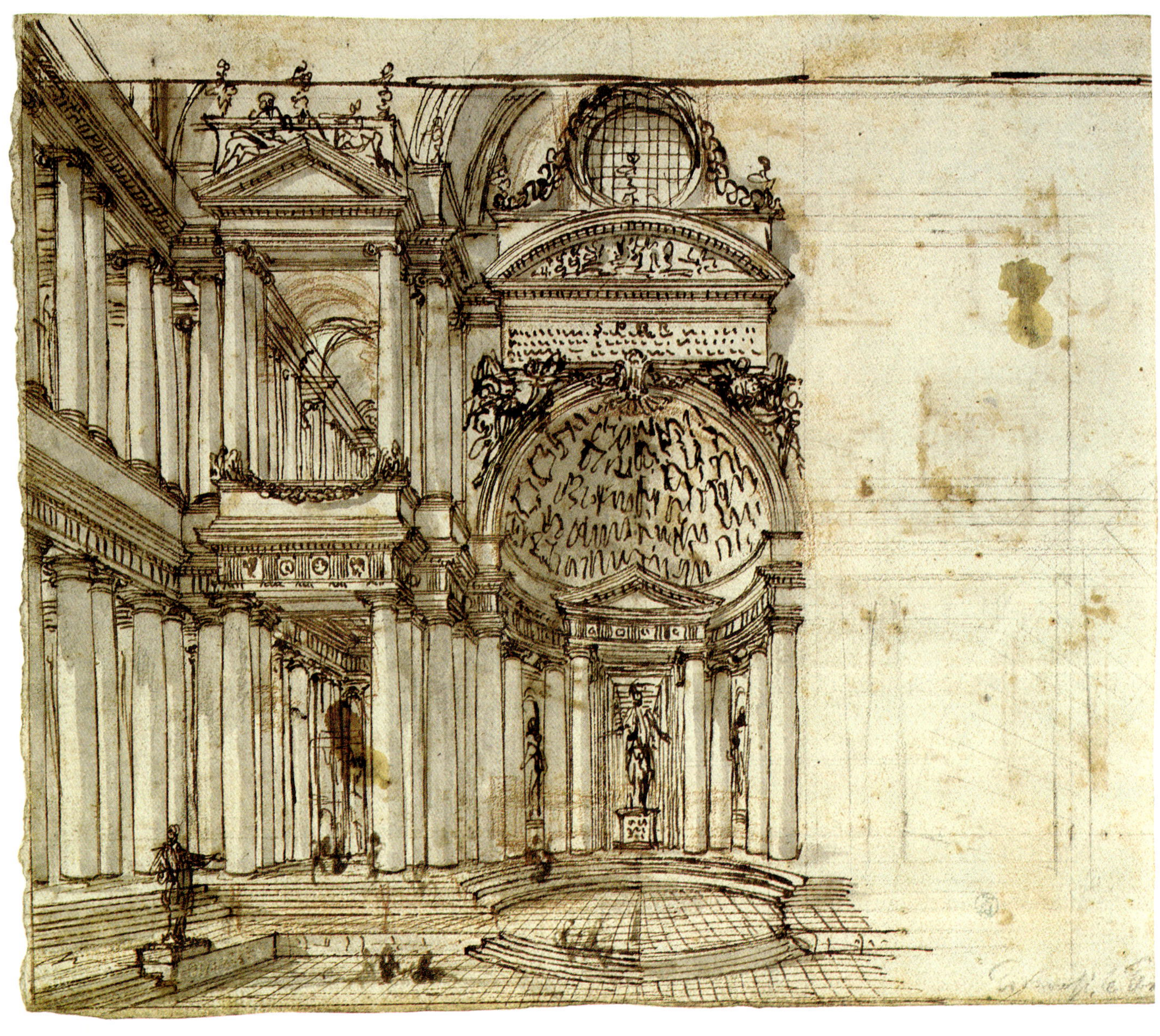

33

FRANCESCO PRIMATICCIO (1504-1570)

Minerva Beautifies Ulysses

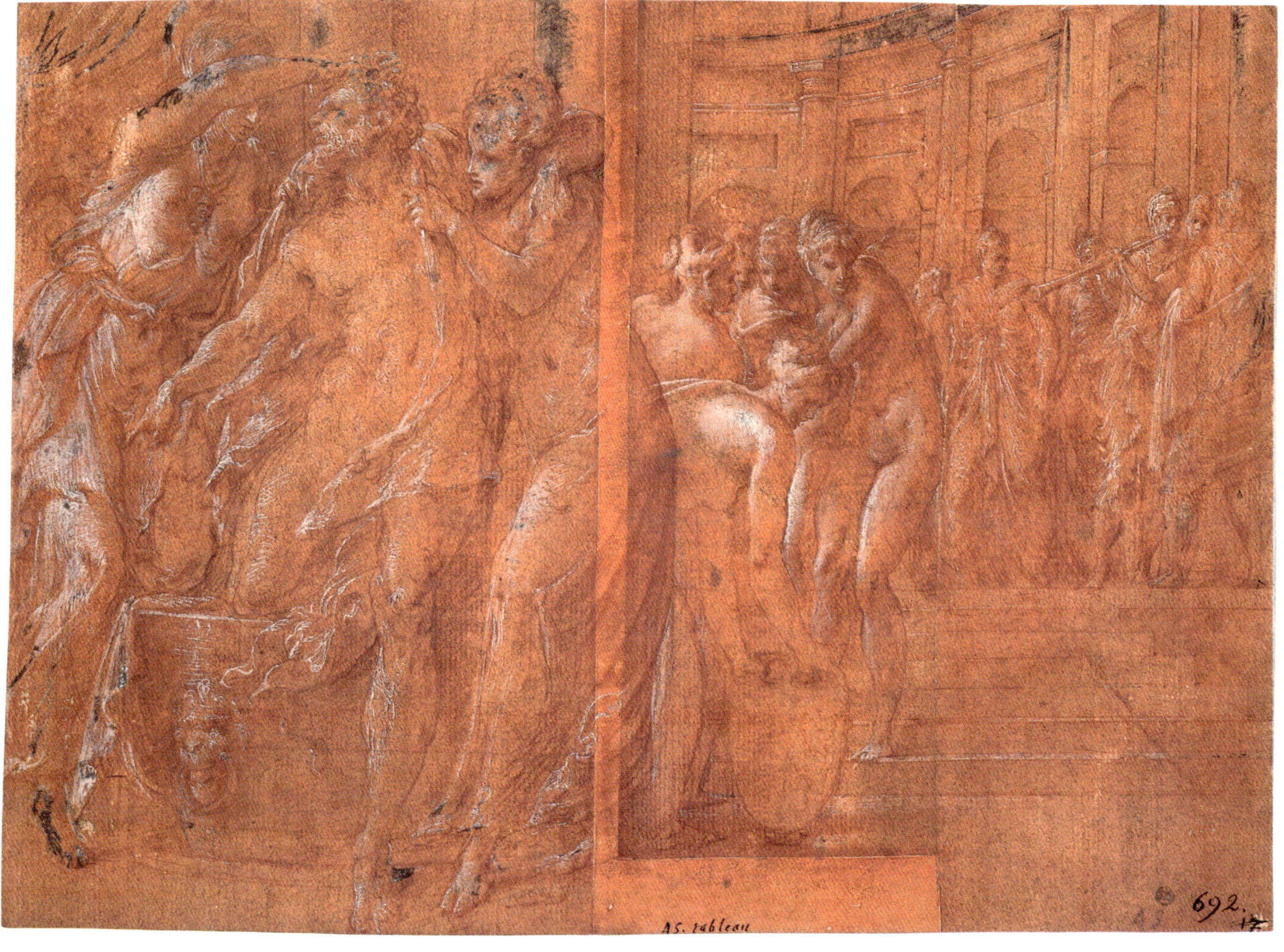

34

FRANCESCO PRIMATICCIO (1504-1570)

Alexander and Thalestris

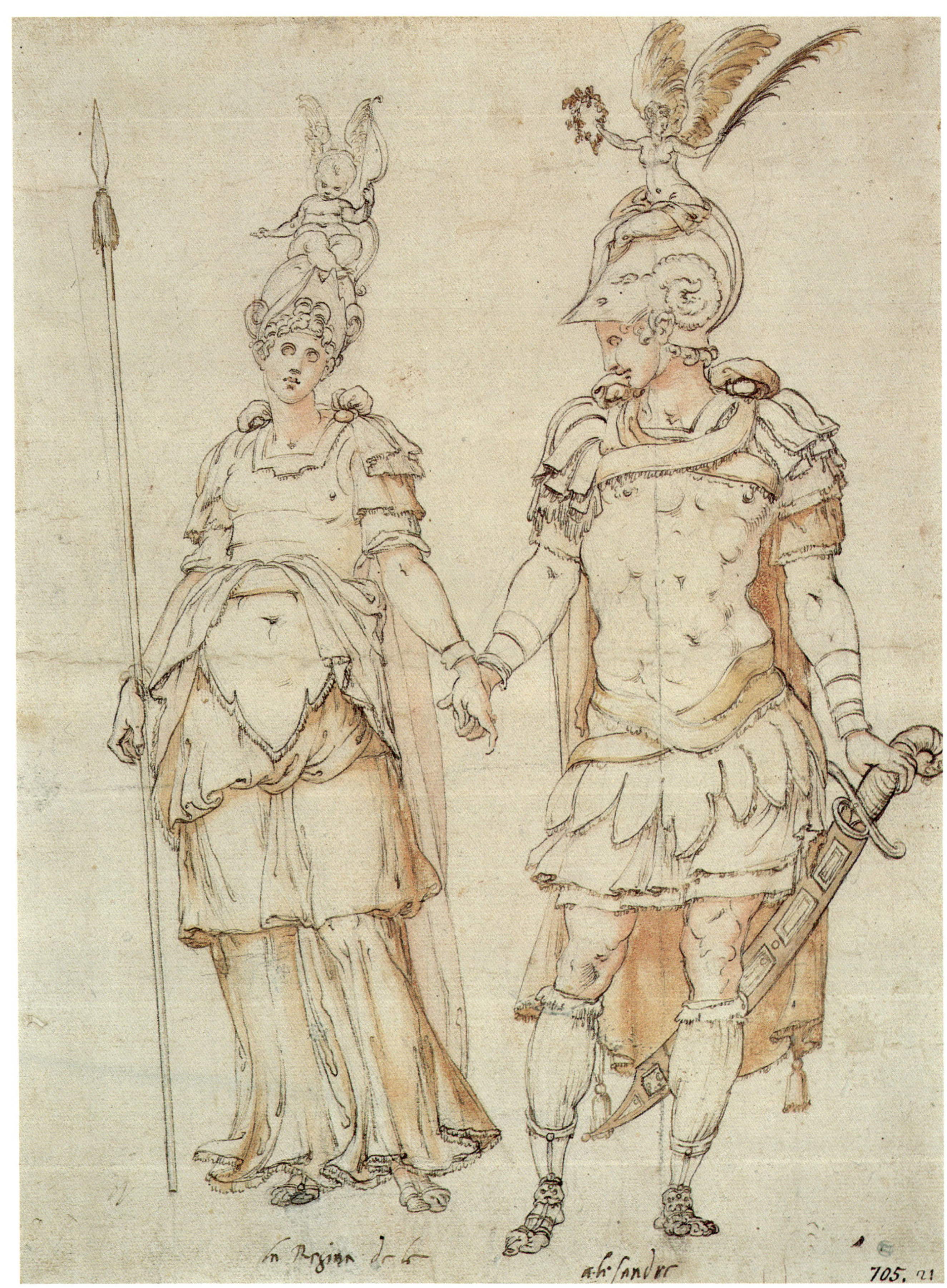

36

FRANÇOIS QUESNEL (1543-1617)

Portrait Said to be Christine of Lorraine, Grand Duchess of Tuscany

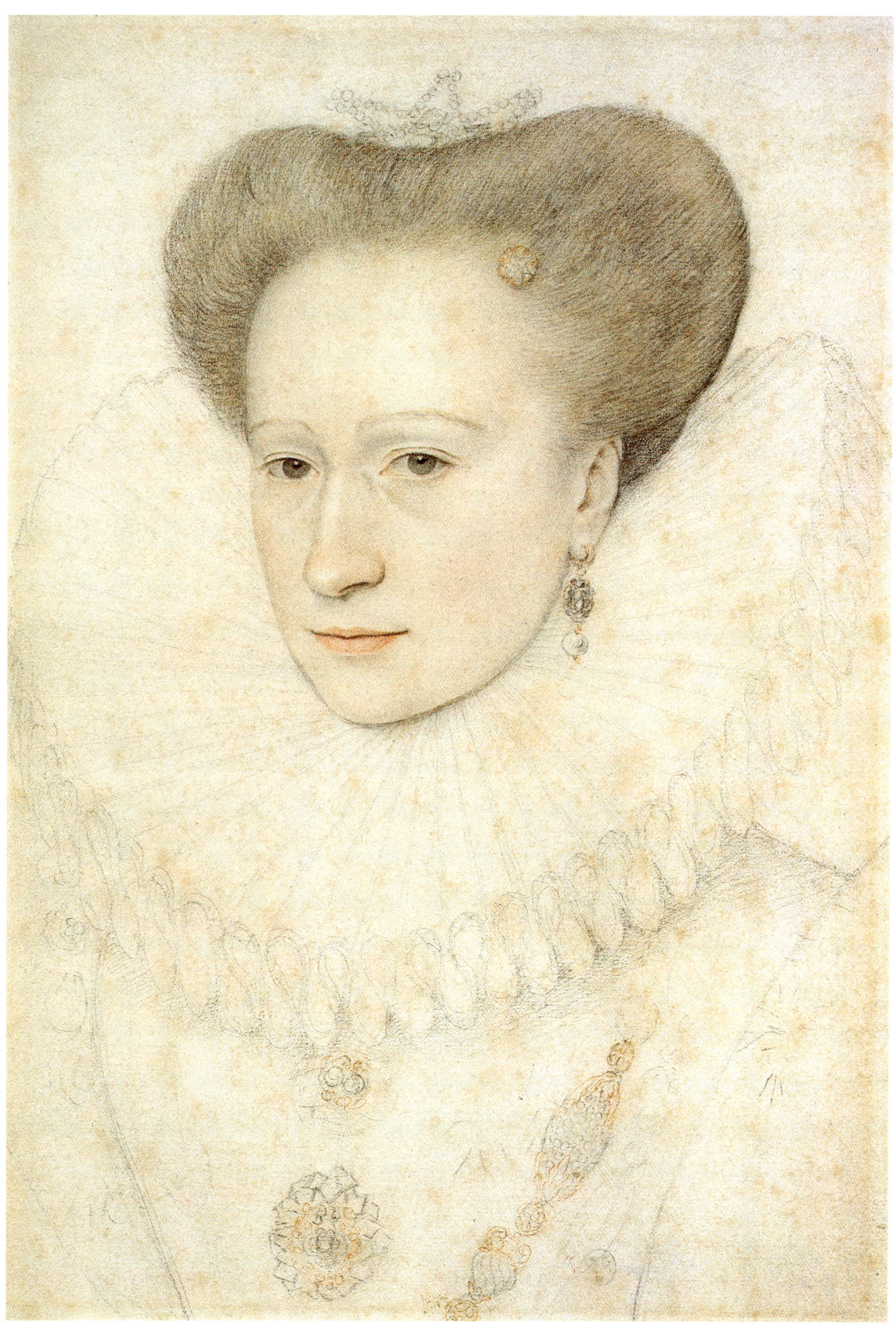

39

JACQUES CALLOT (1592-1635)

The Village Place

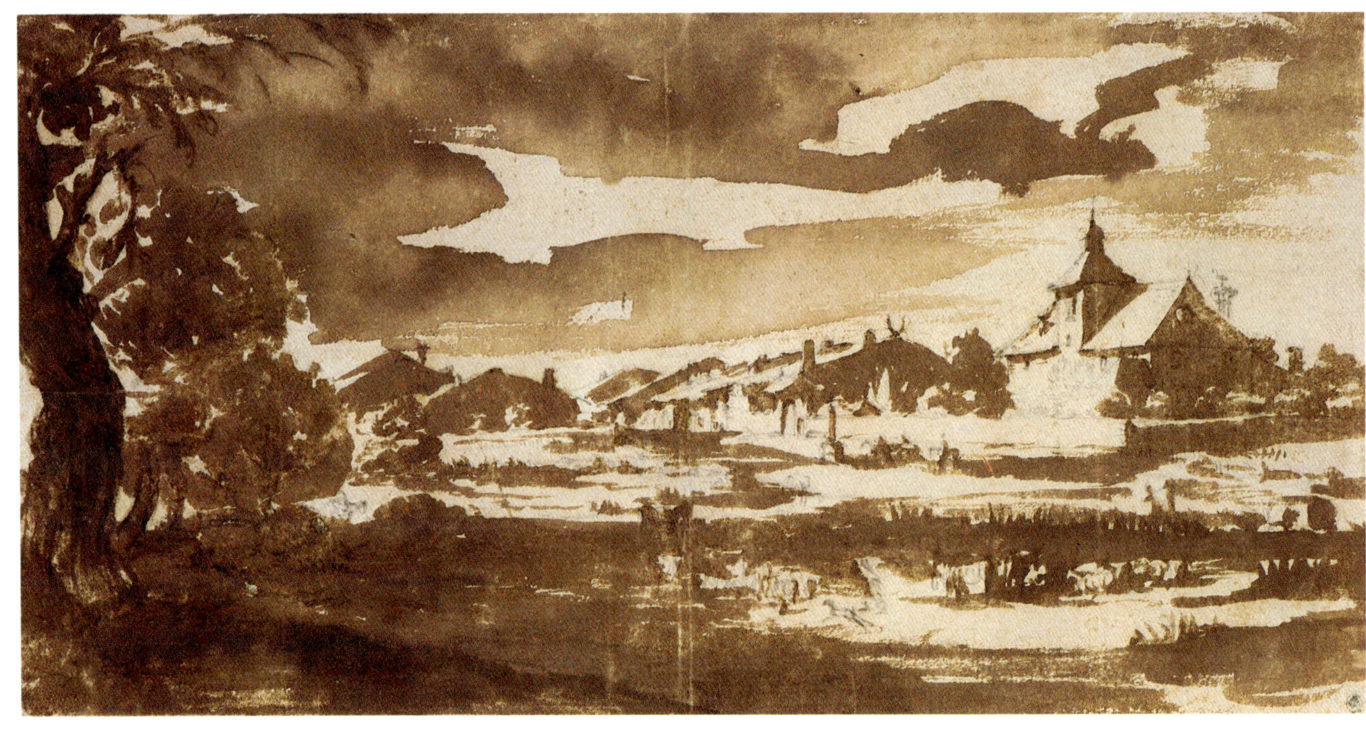

41

CLAUDE GELLÉE, called LORRAIN (1600-1682)

Landscape with the Landing of Aeneas in Latium

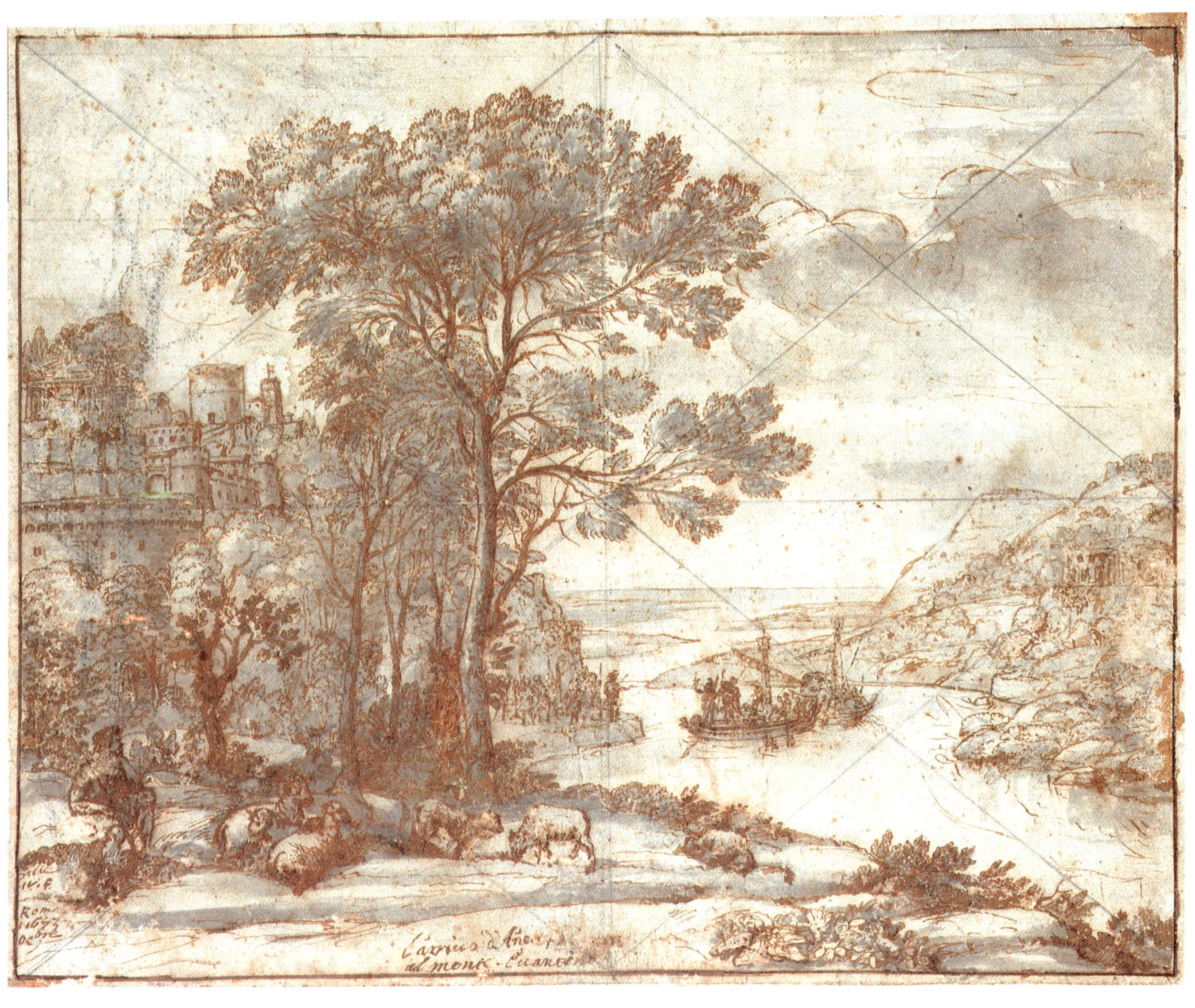

42

NICOLAS POUSSIN (1593/94-1665)

The Triumph of Galatea

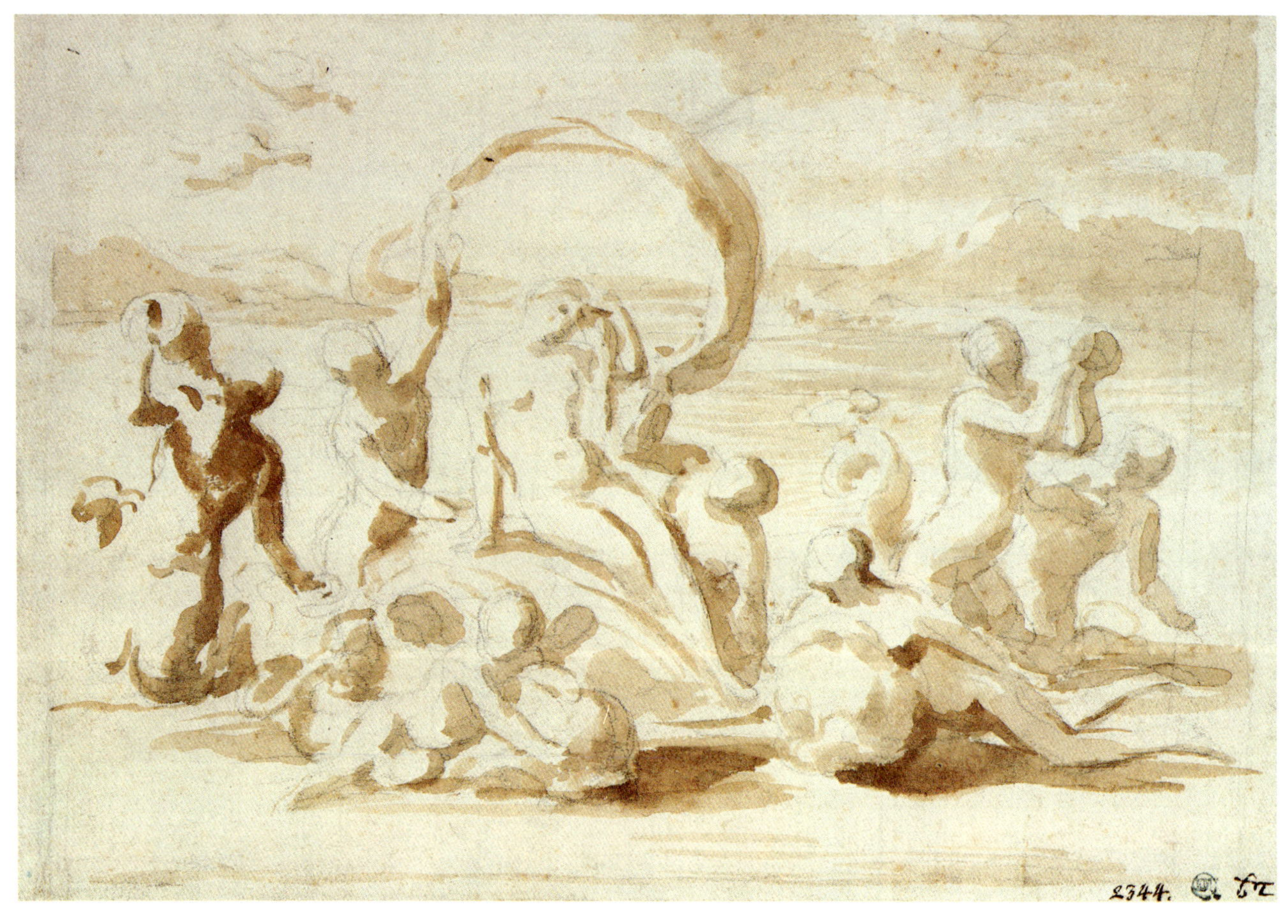

44

FRANÇOIS BOUCHER (1703-1770)

A Seduction

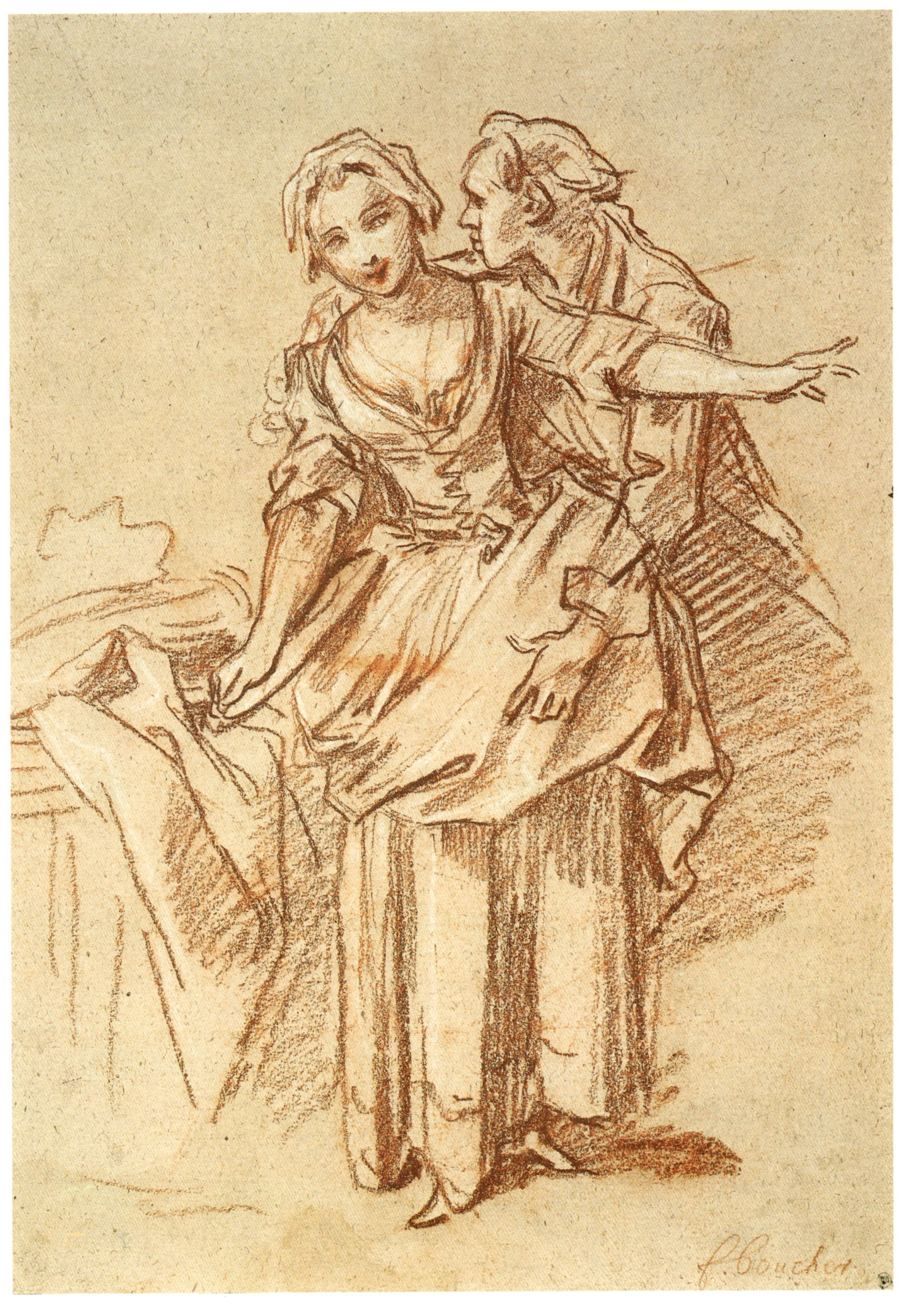

45

FRANÇOIS BOUCHER (1703-1770)

Male Nude Study

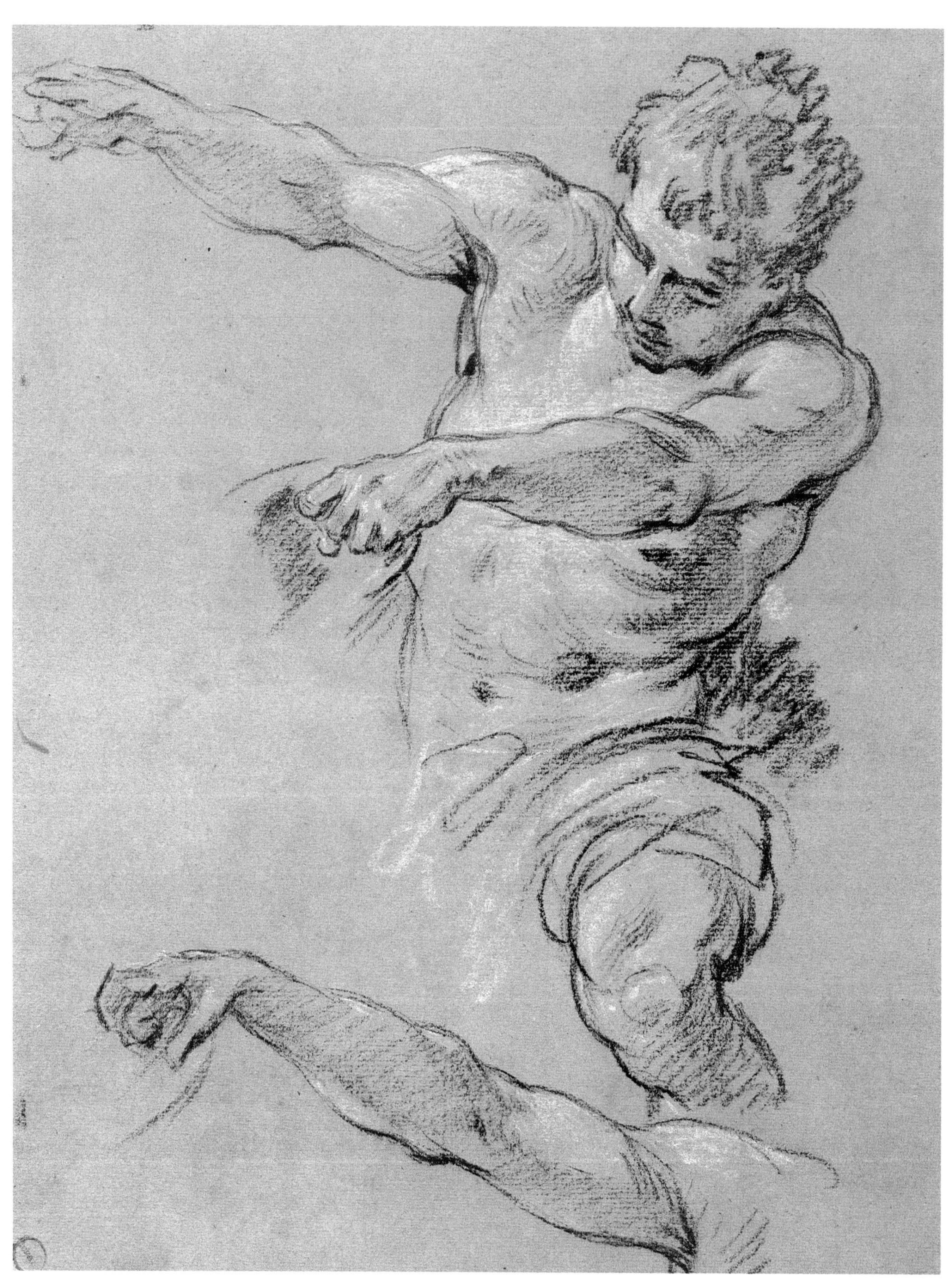

46
JEAN-BAPTISTE-SIMÉON CHARDIN (1699-1779)

Servant Pouring a Drink for a Billiard Player

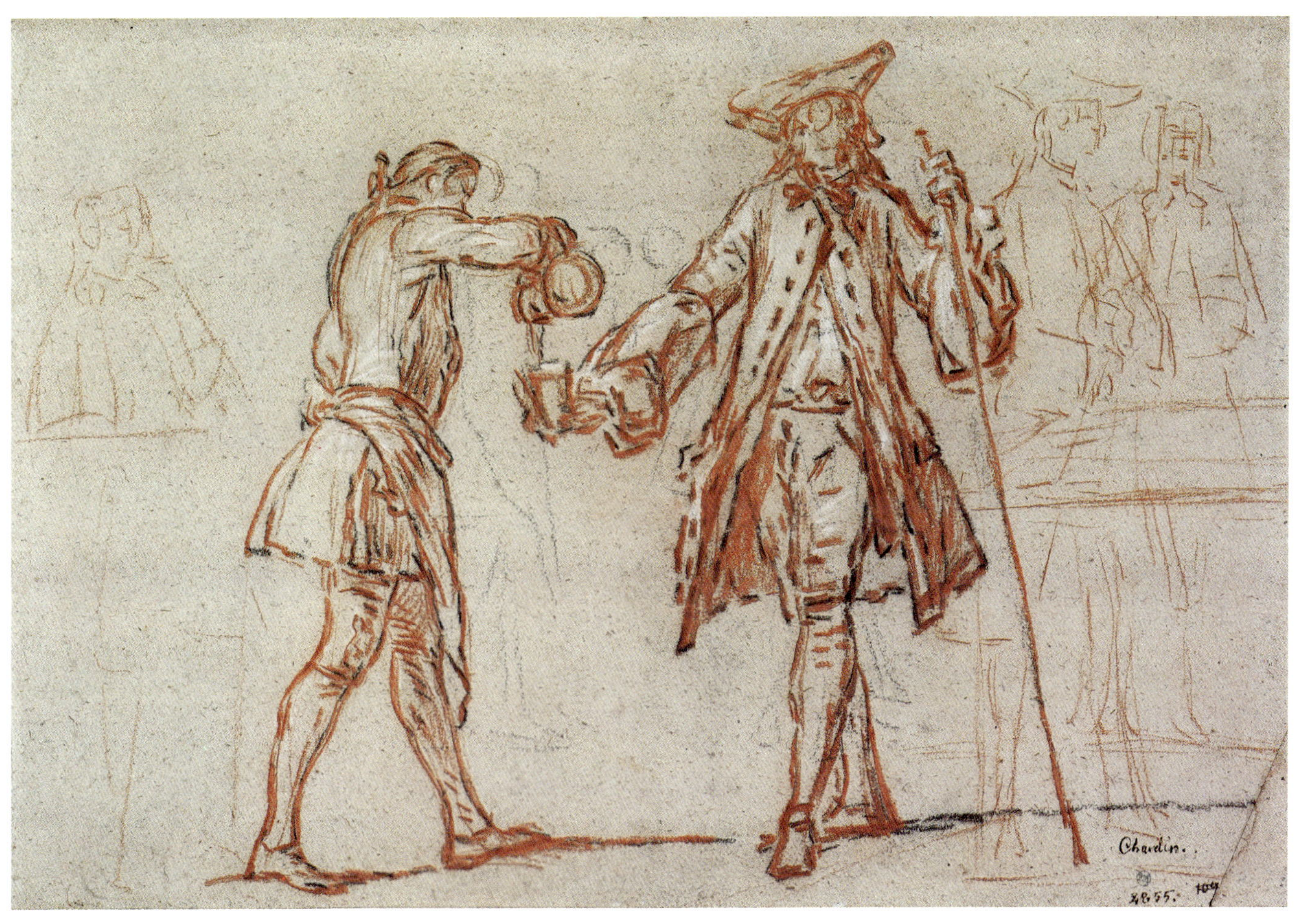

48

JEAN-HONORÉ FRAGONARD (1732-1806)

Italian Landscape

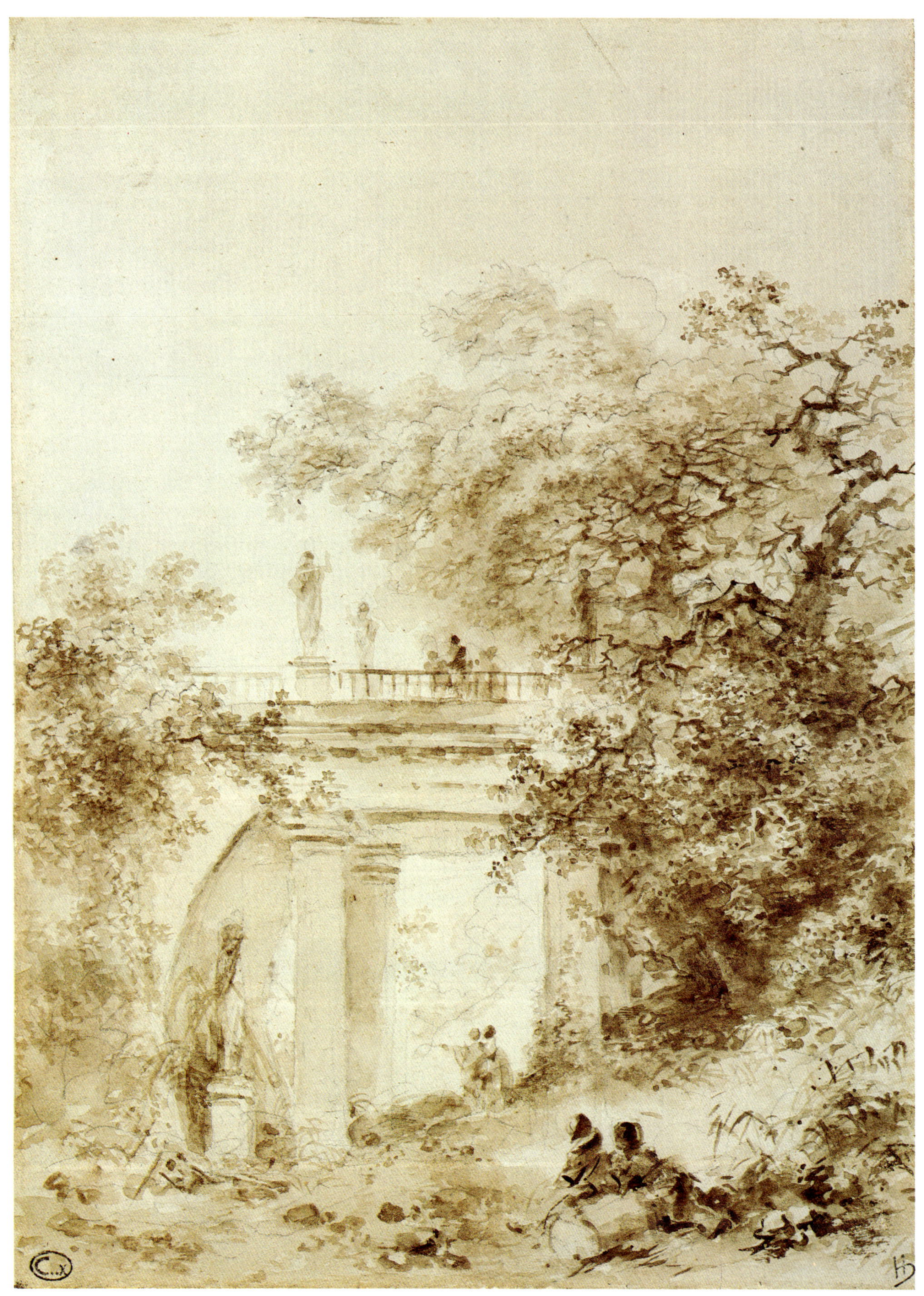

50

JEAN-BAPTISTE GREUZE (1725-1806)

Woman with a Child and a Dog on a Chaise-longue

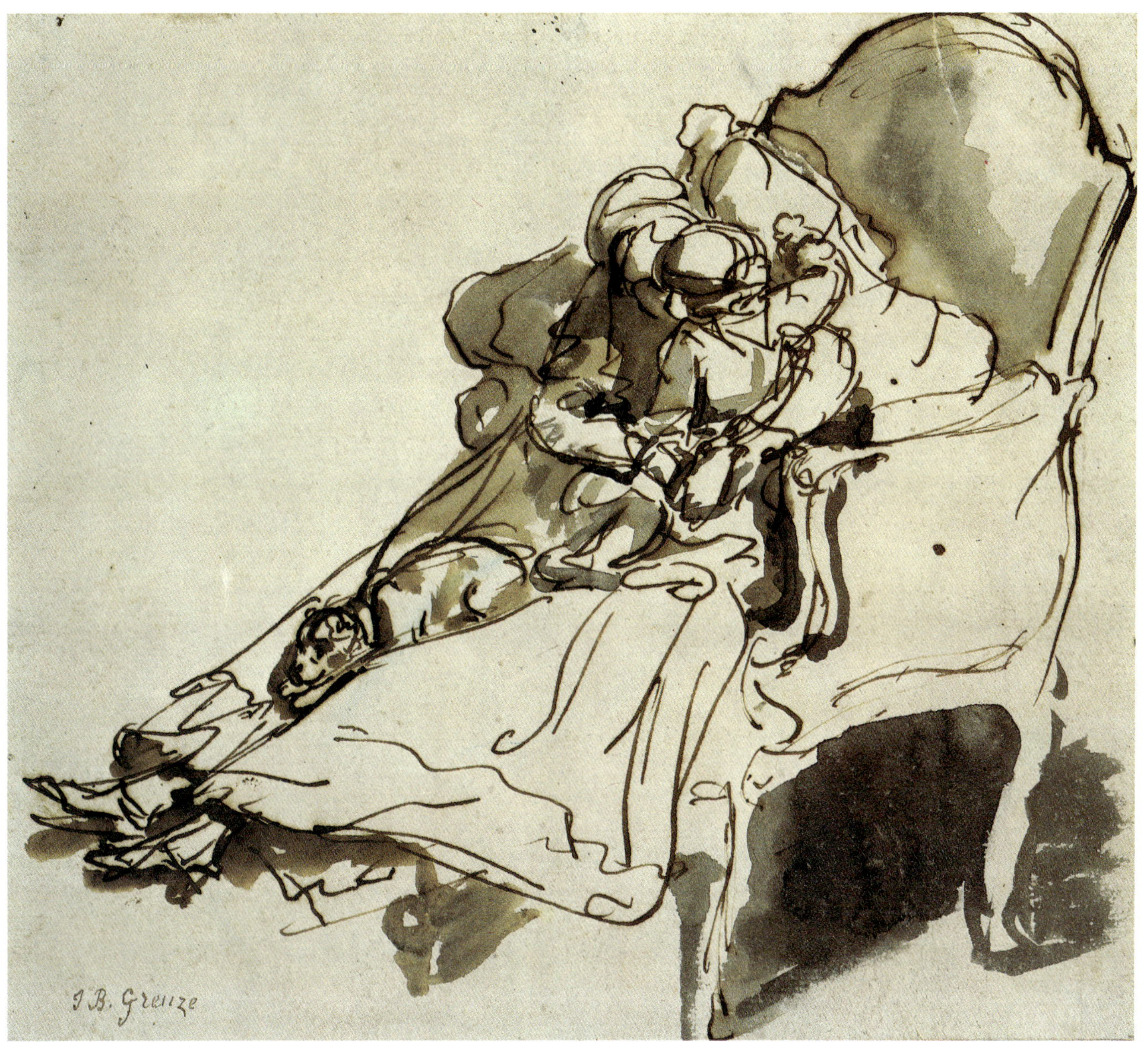

51

CHARLES-JOSEPH NATOIRE (1700-1777)

Calypso's Nymphs Set Fire to Telemachus' Ship

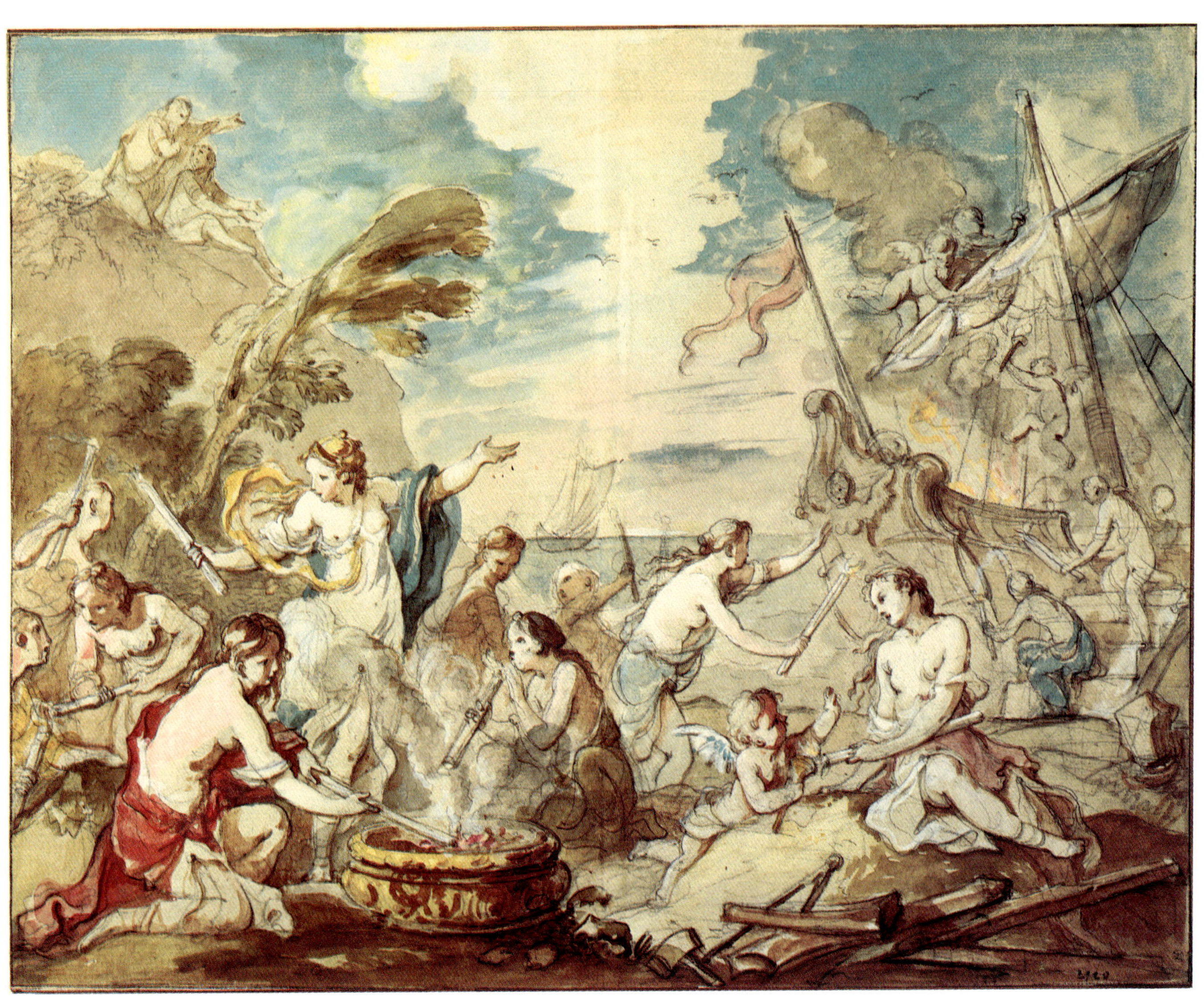

52

HUBERT ROBERT (1733-1808)

Antique Fragment in an Abandoned Garden

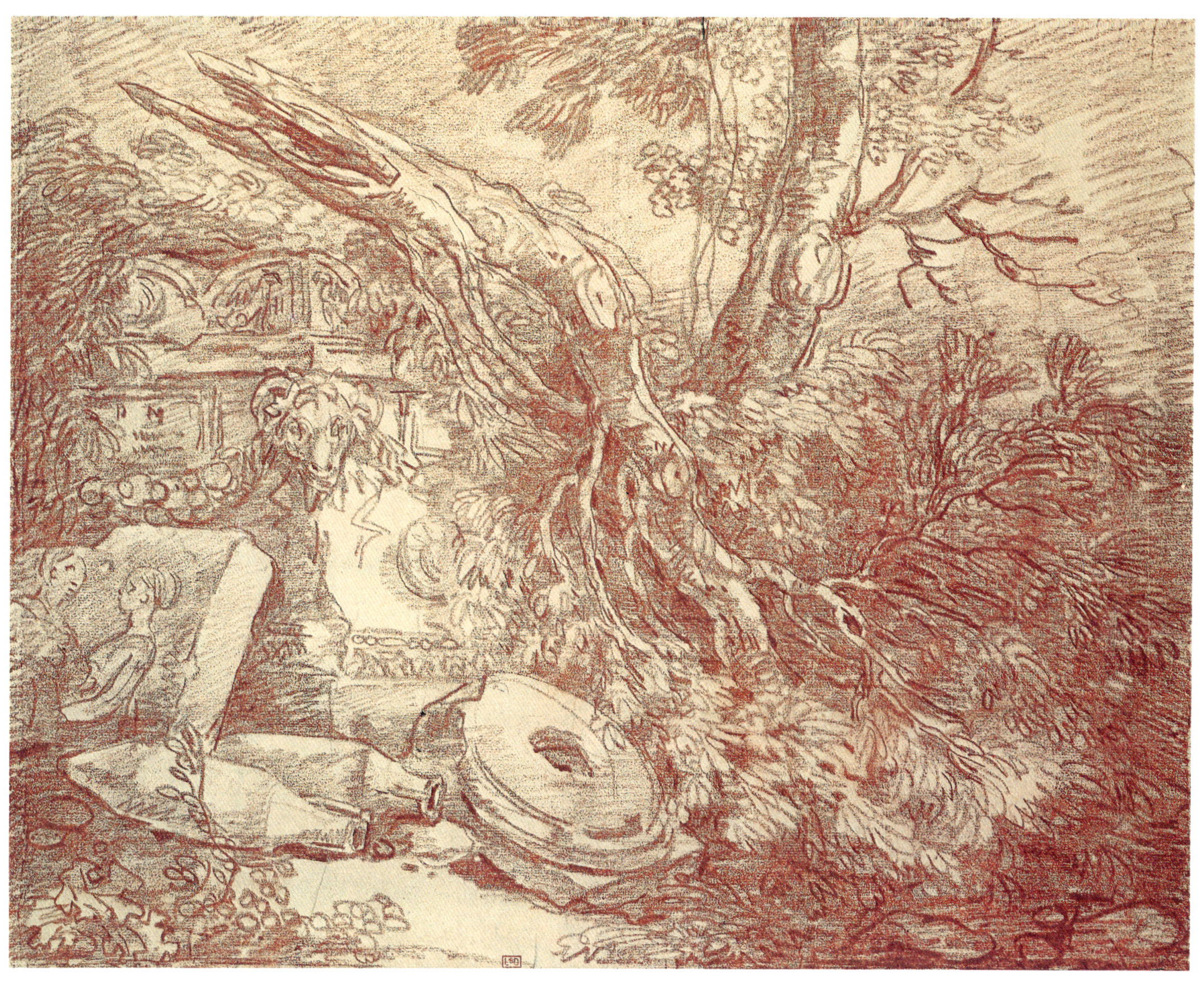

55

GABRIEL DE SAINT-AUBIN (1724-1780)

The South Transept of Notre-Dame

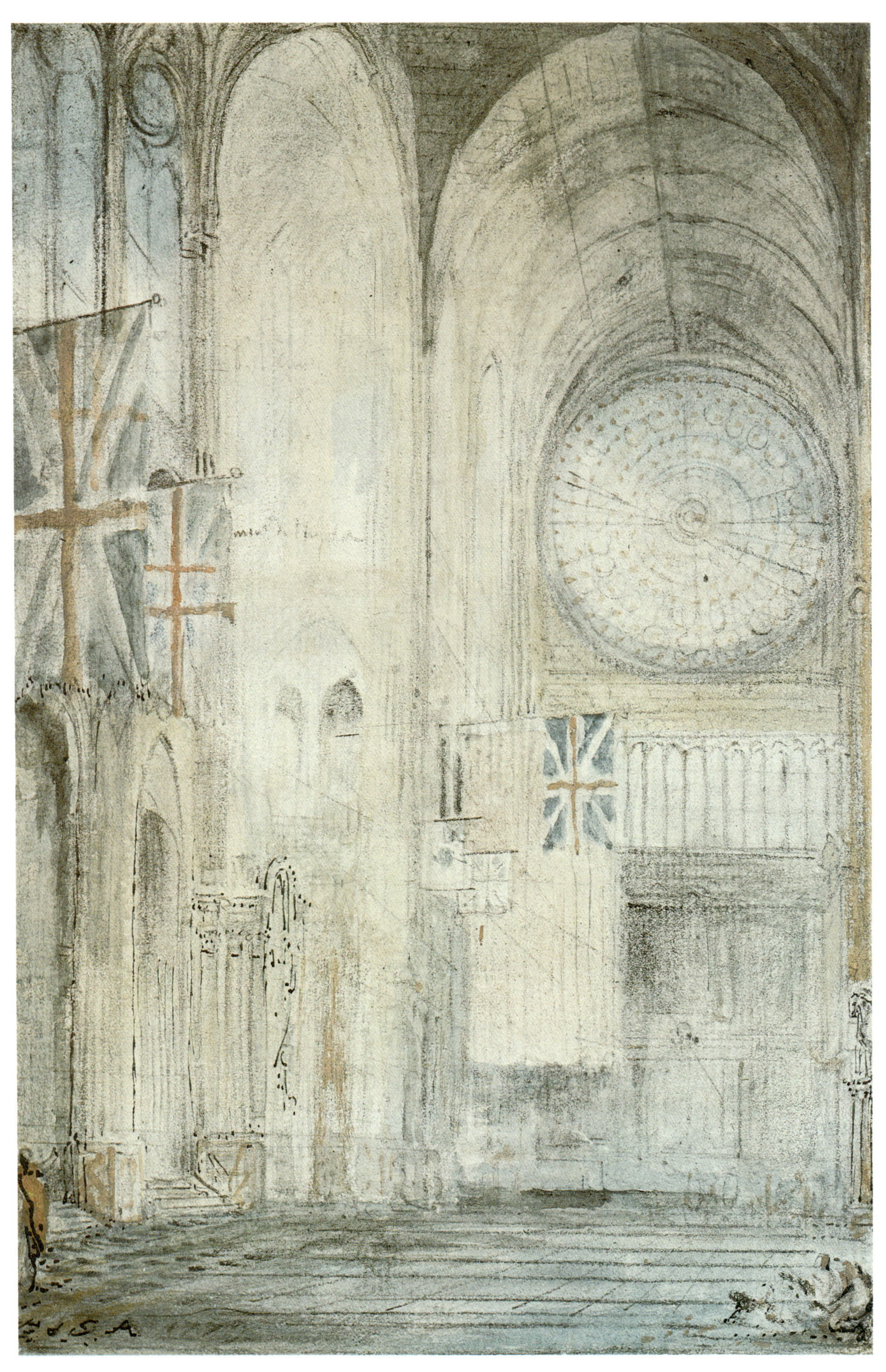

56
ANTOINE WATTEAU (1684-1721)
Portrait of a Young Man

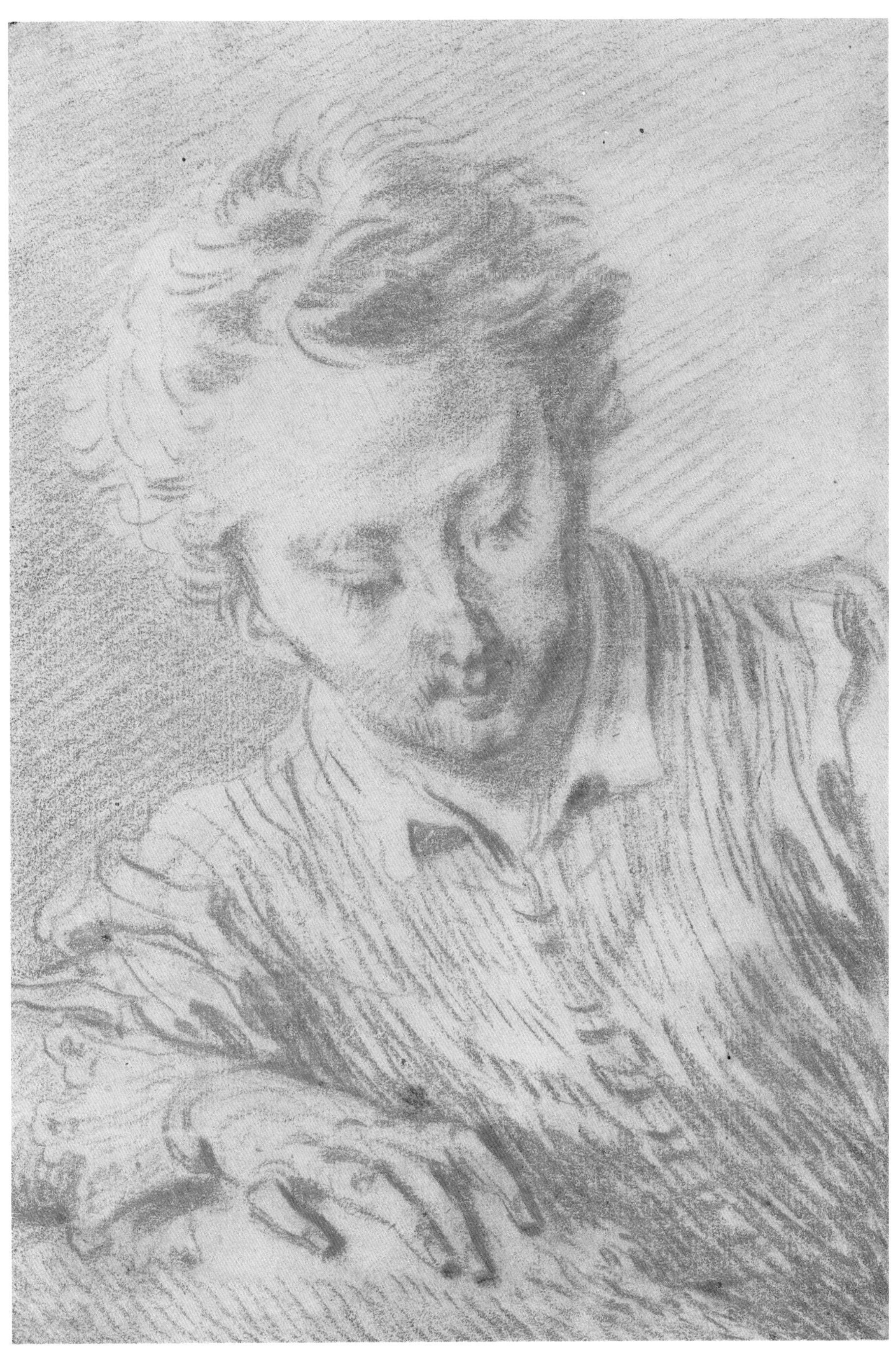

57

ANTOINE WATTEAU (1684-1721)

Singerie

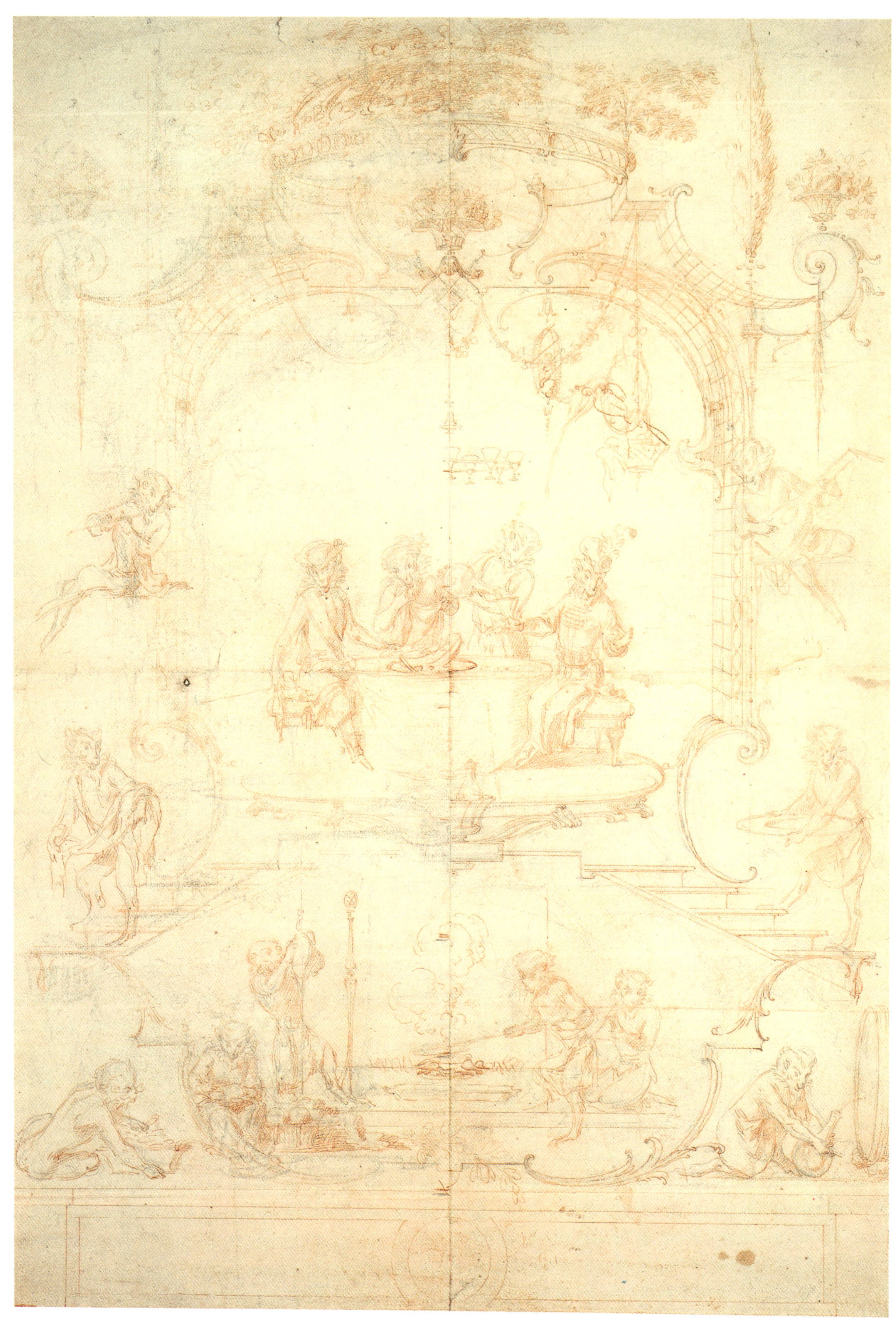

58

ANTOINE WATTEAU (1684-1721)

Two Studies of a Young Woman

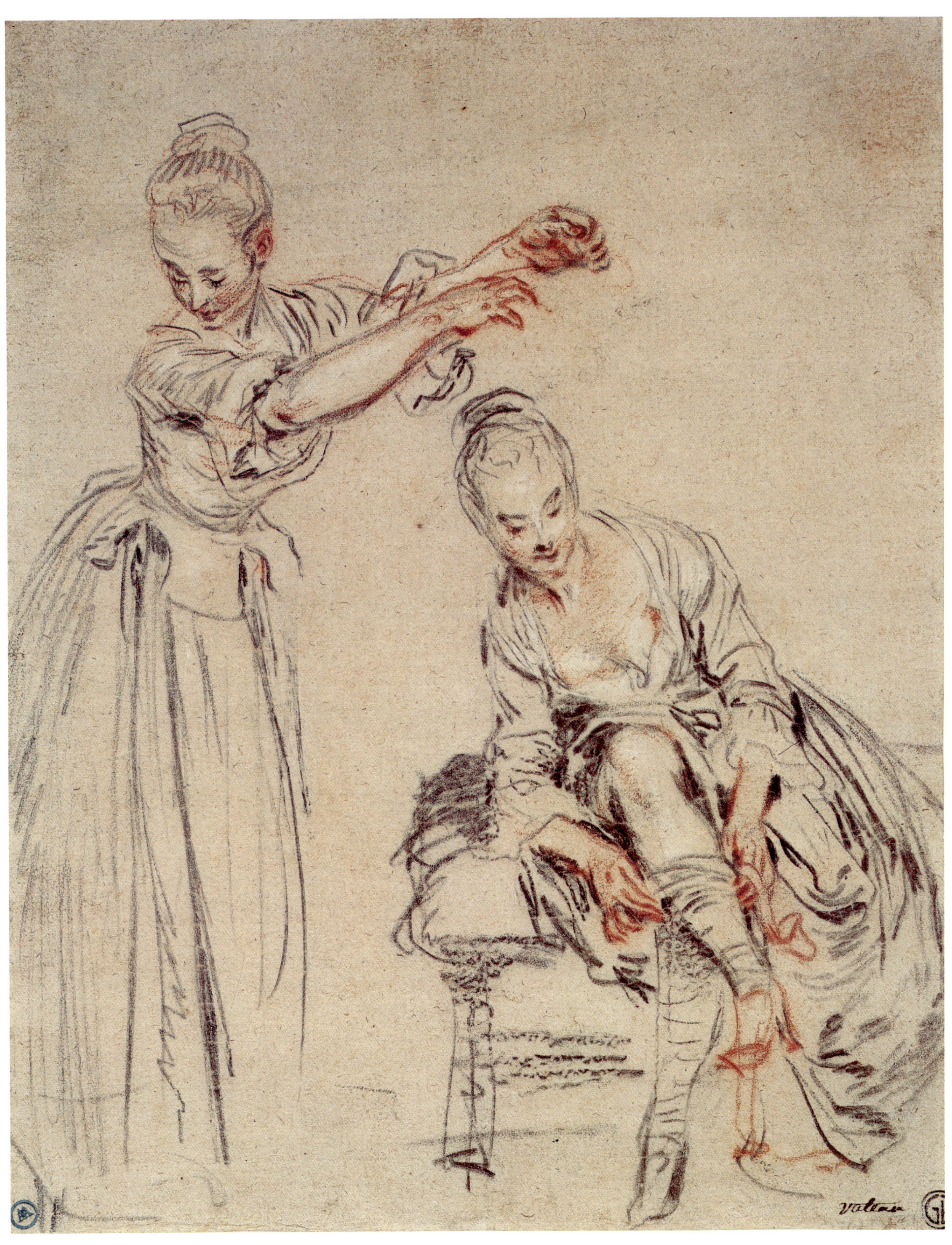

60

ANTOINE WATTEAU (1684-1721)

Man Seated Facing Left

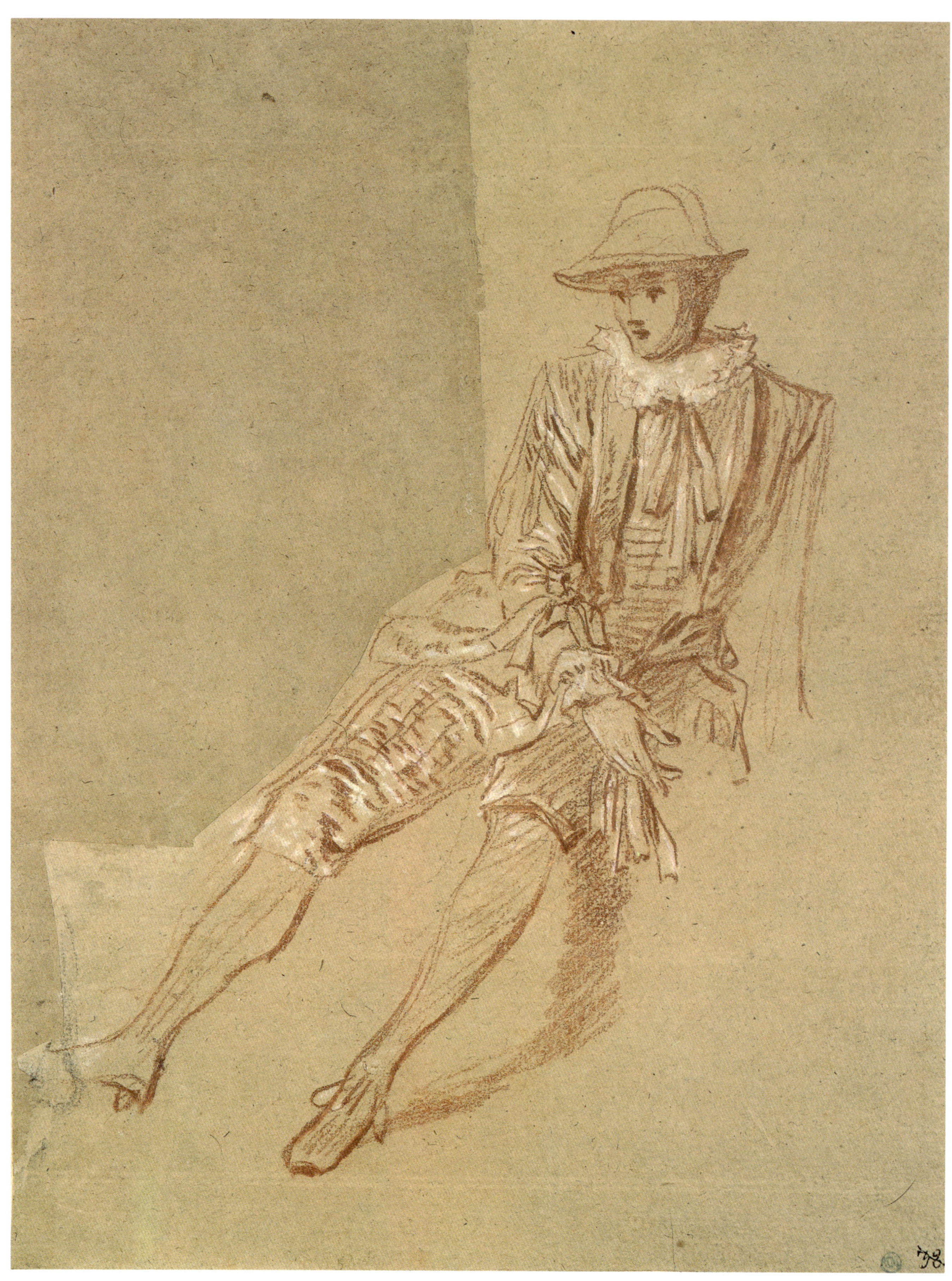

64
PIERRE-PAUL PRUD'HON (1758-1823)

Repentance

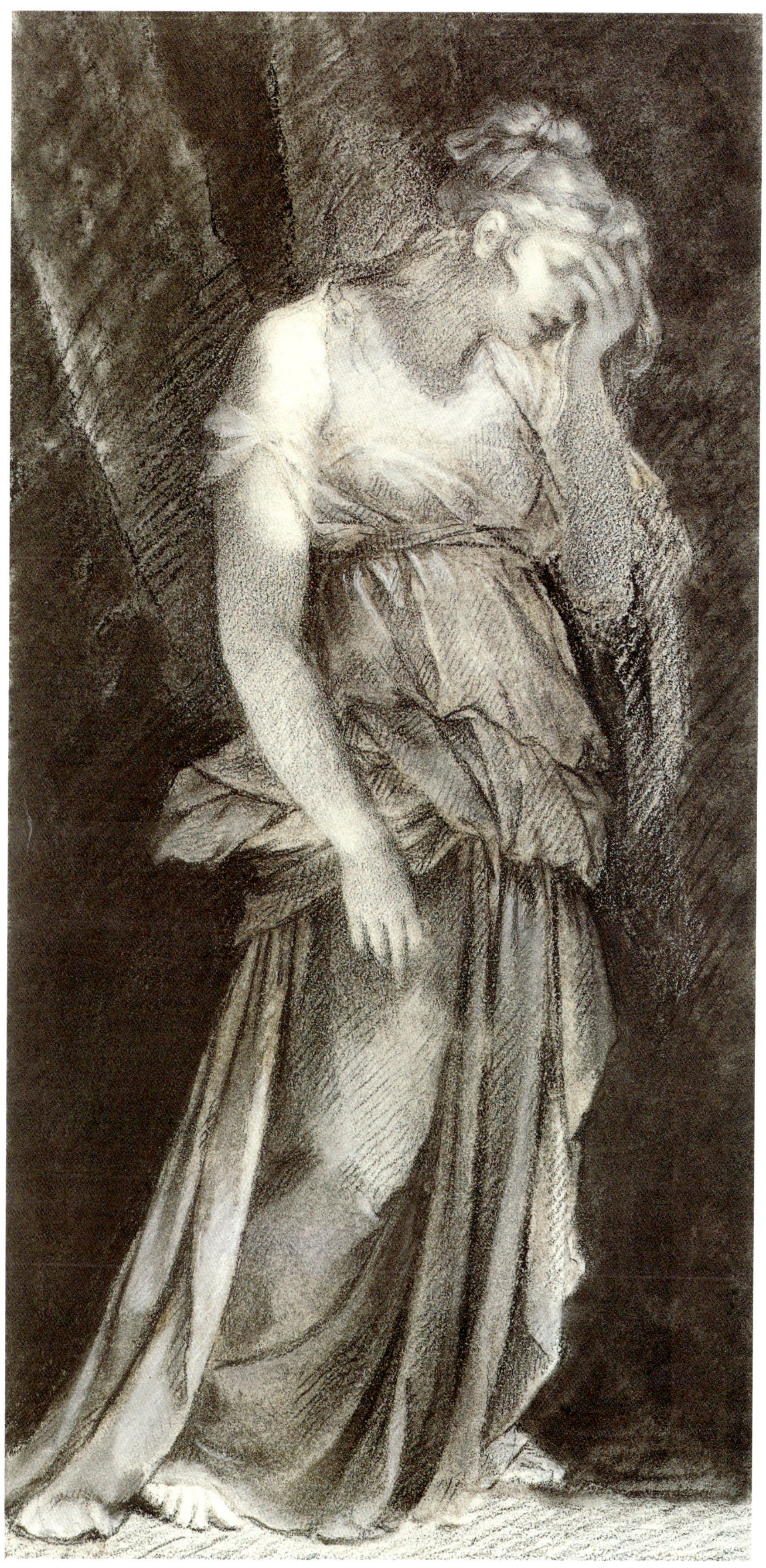

67

THÉODORE GÉRICAULT (1791-1824)

Stableboy Grooming a Horse

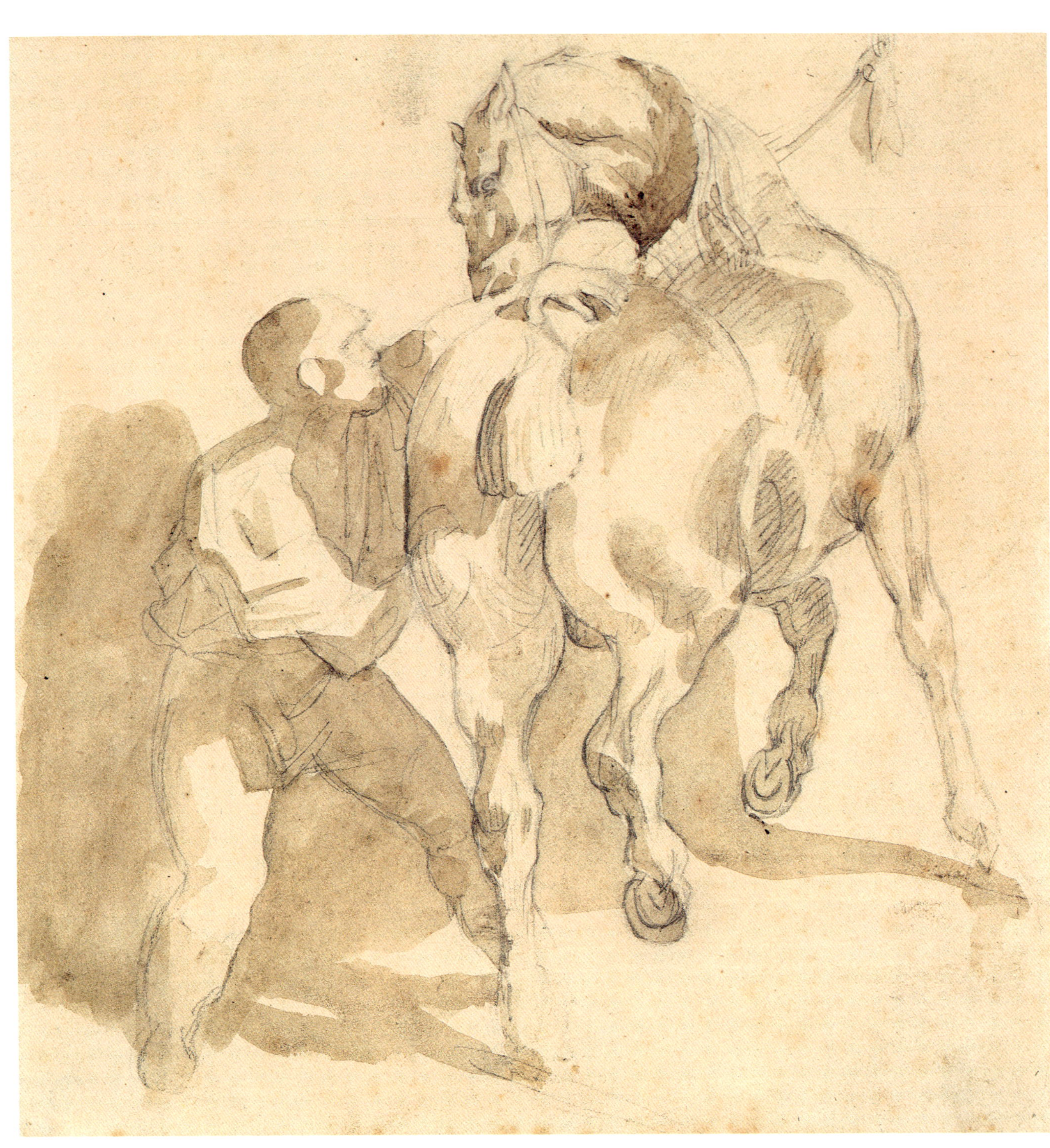

68

EUGÈNE DELACROIX (1798-1863)

Studies of Arabs on Horseback

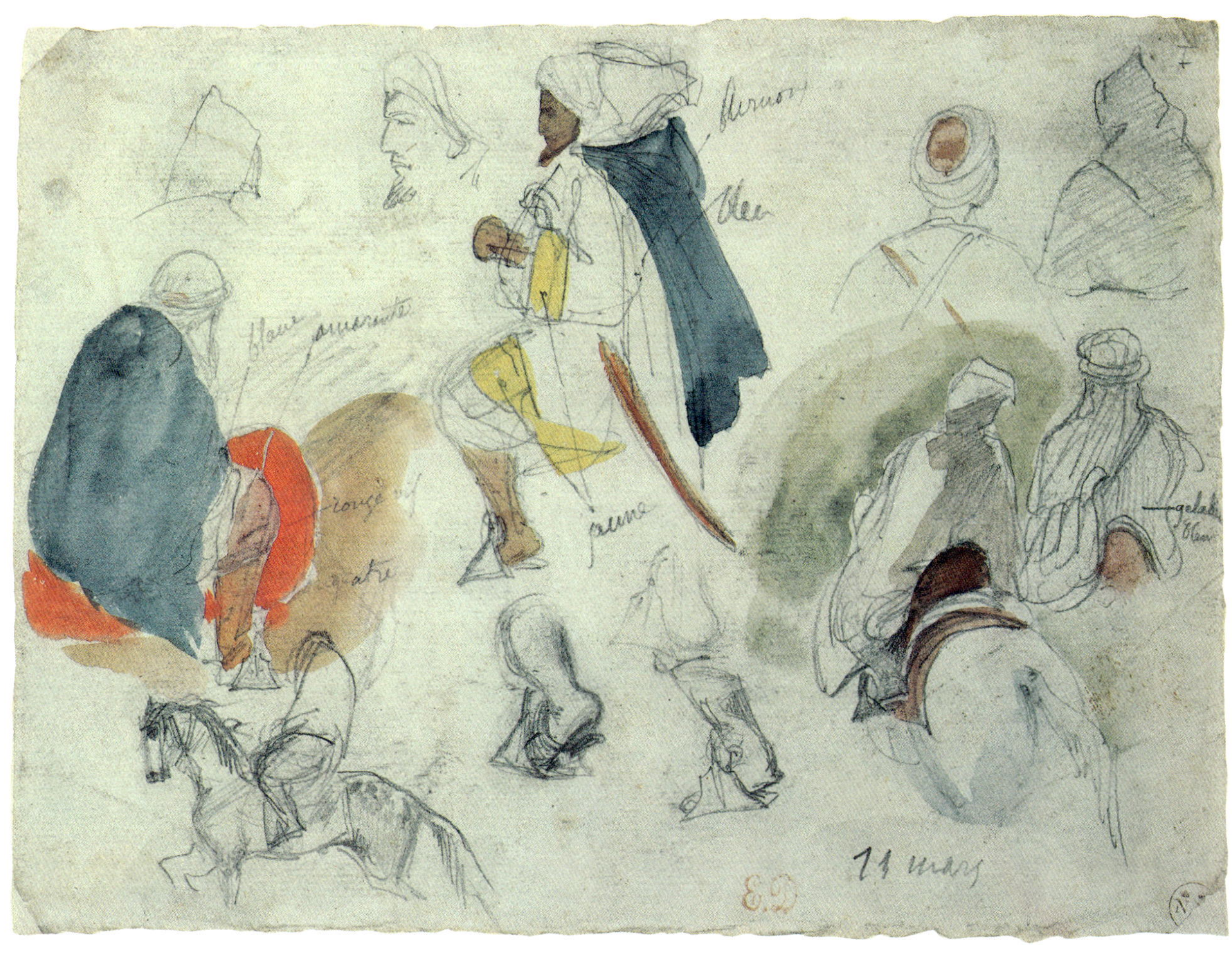

70

EUGÈNE DELACROIX (1798-1863)

A Seated Moor

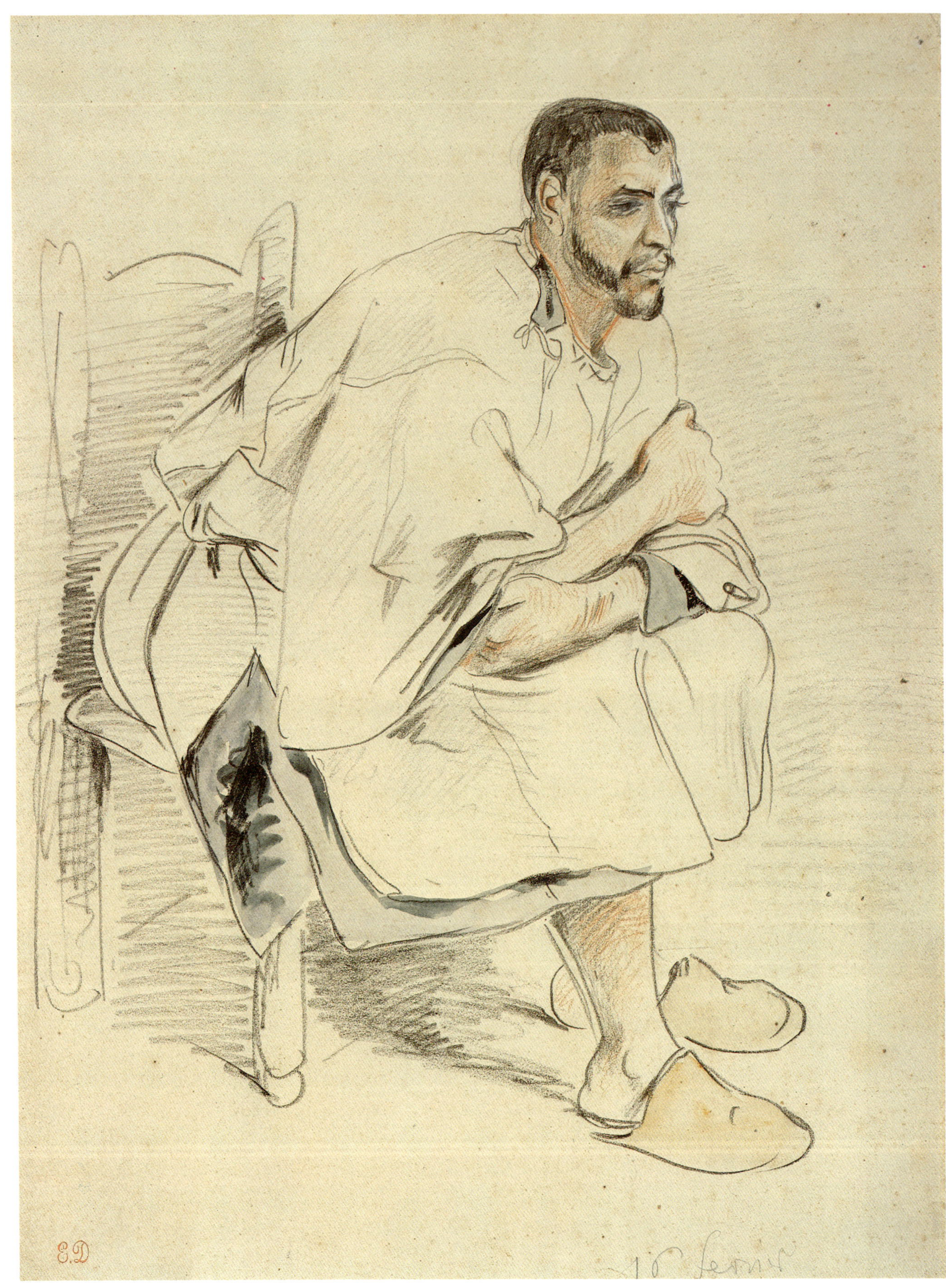

71

FRANCISCO GOYA (1746-1828)

Loco Picaro

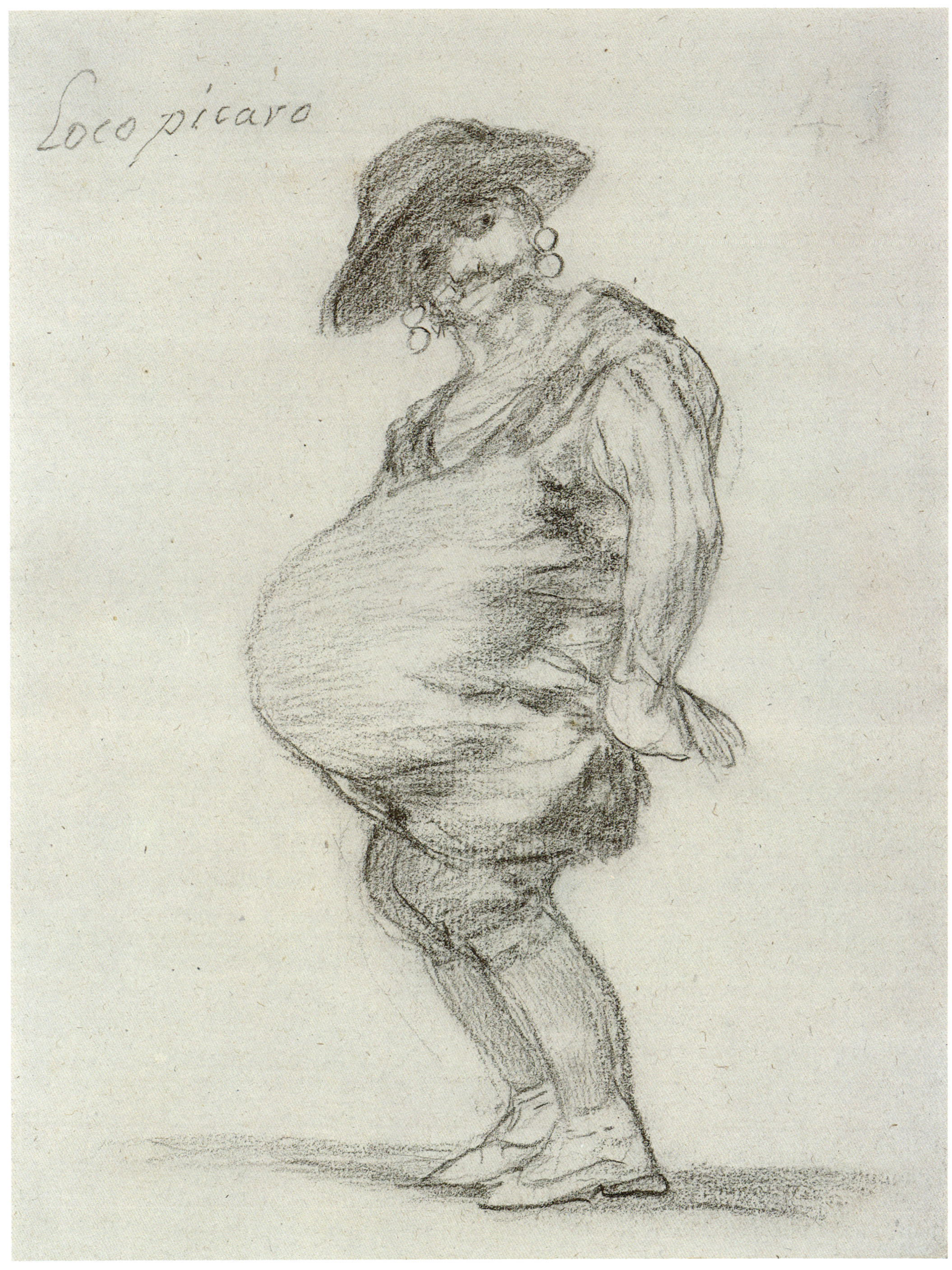

72

LUCAS VAN LEYDEN (1494-1533)

Portrait of a Young Man

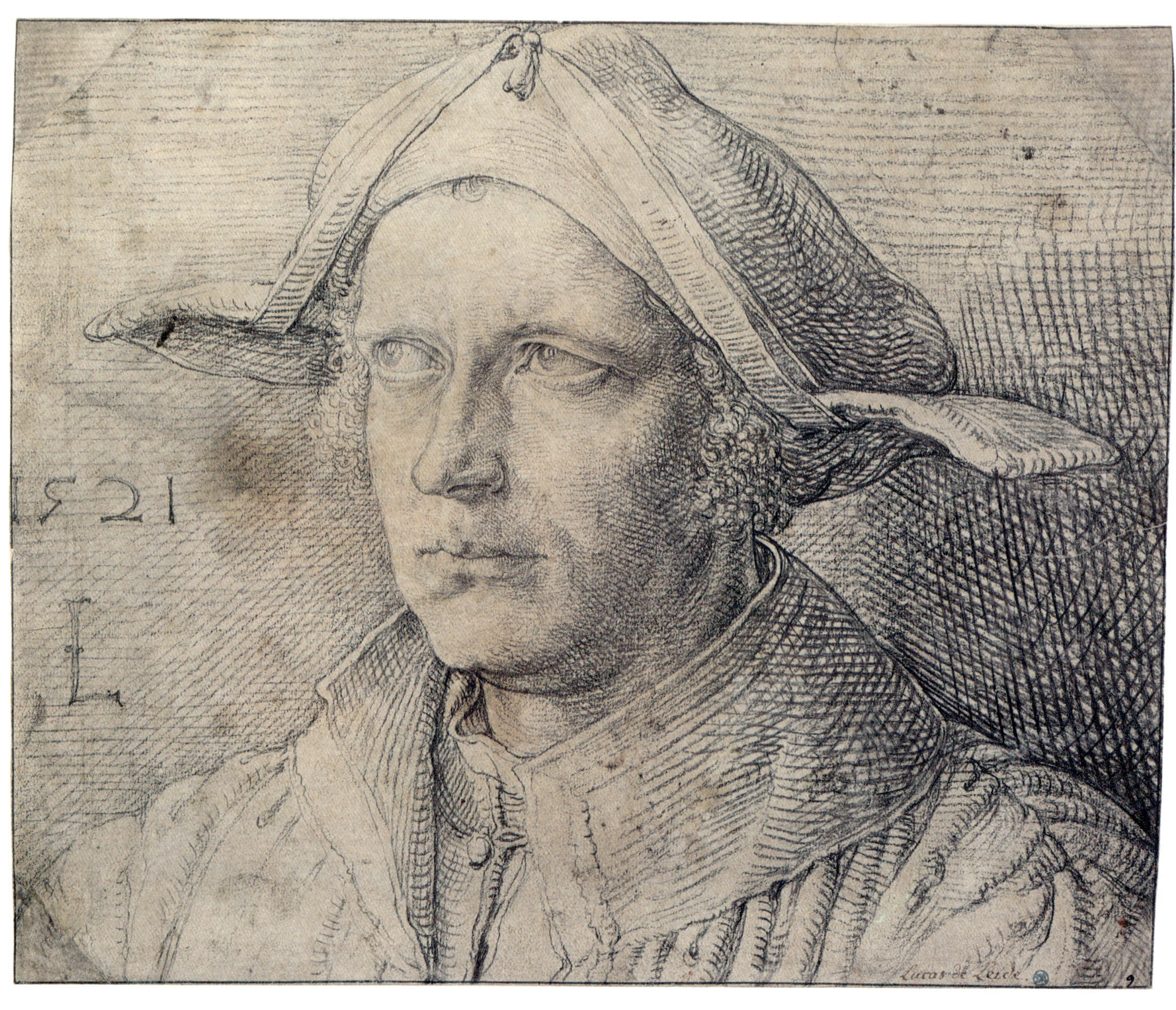

74

ROELANDT SAVERY (1576-1639)

Mountain Landscape with Travellers

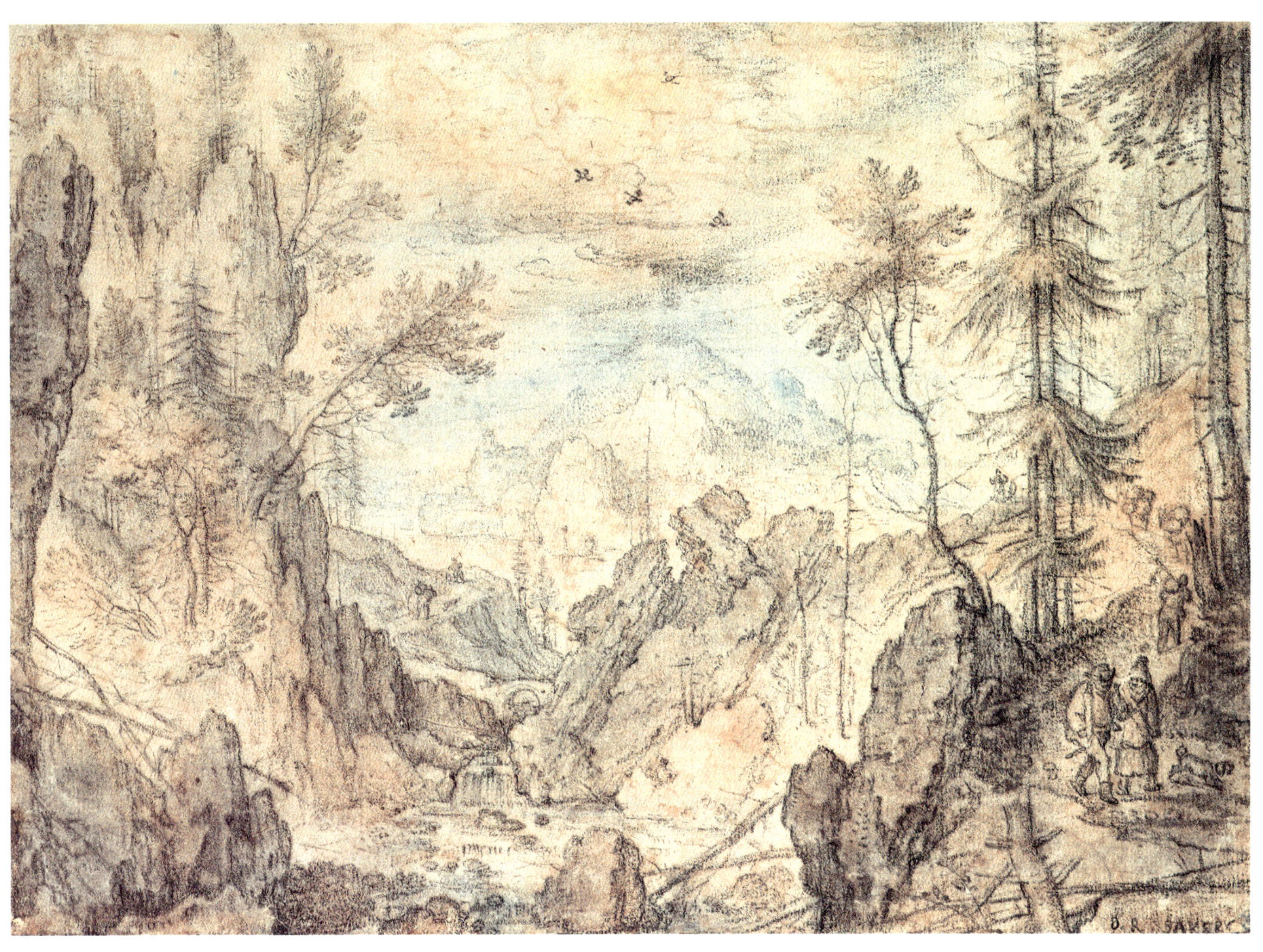

76

HENDRICK GOLTZIUS (1558-1616)

Three Fantastic Figures

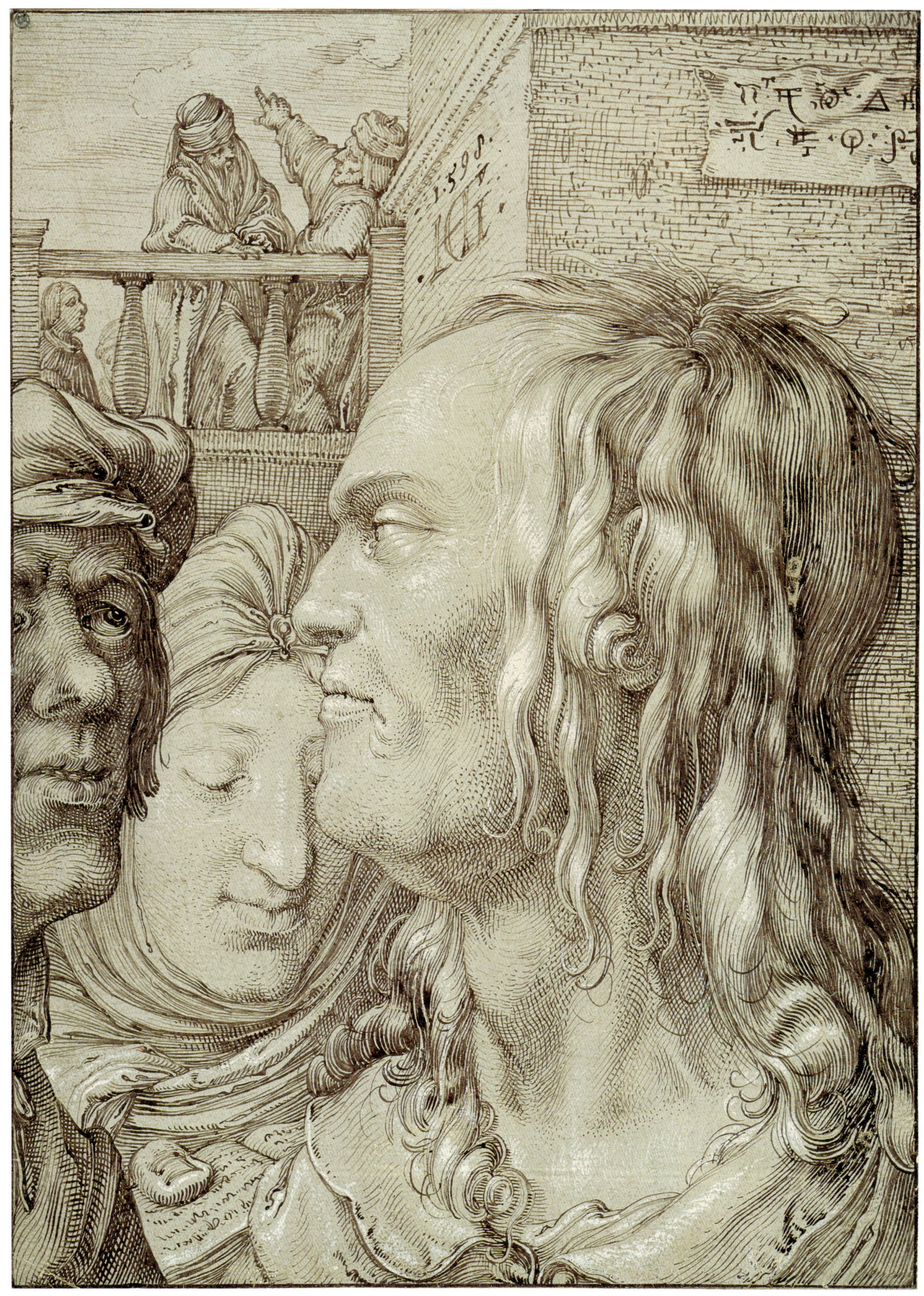

77

PETER PAUL RUBENS (1577-1640)
Head, Left Arm, and Right Hand of a Woman

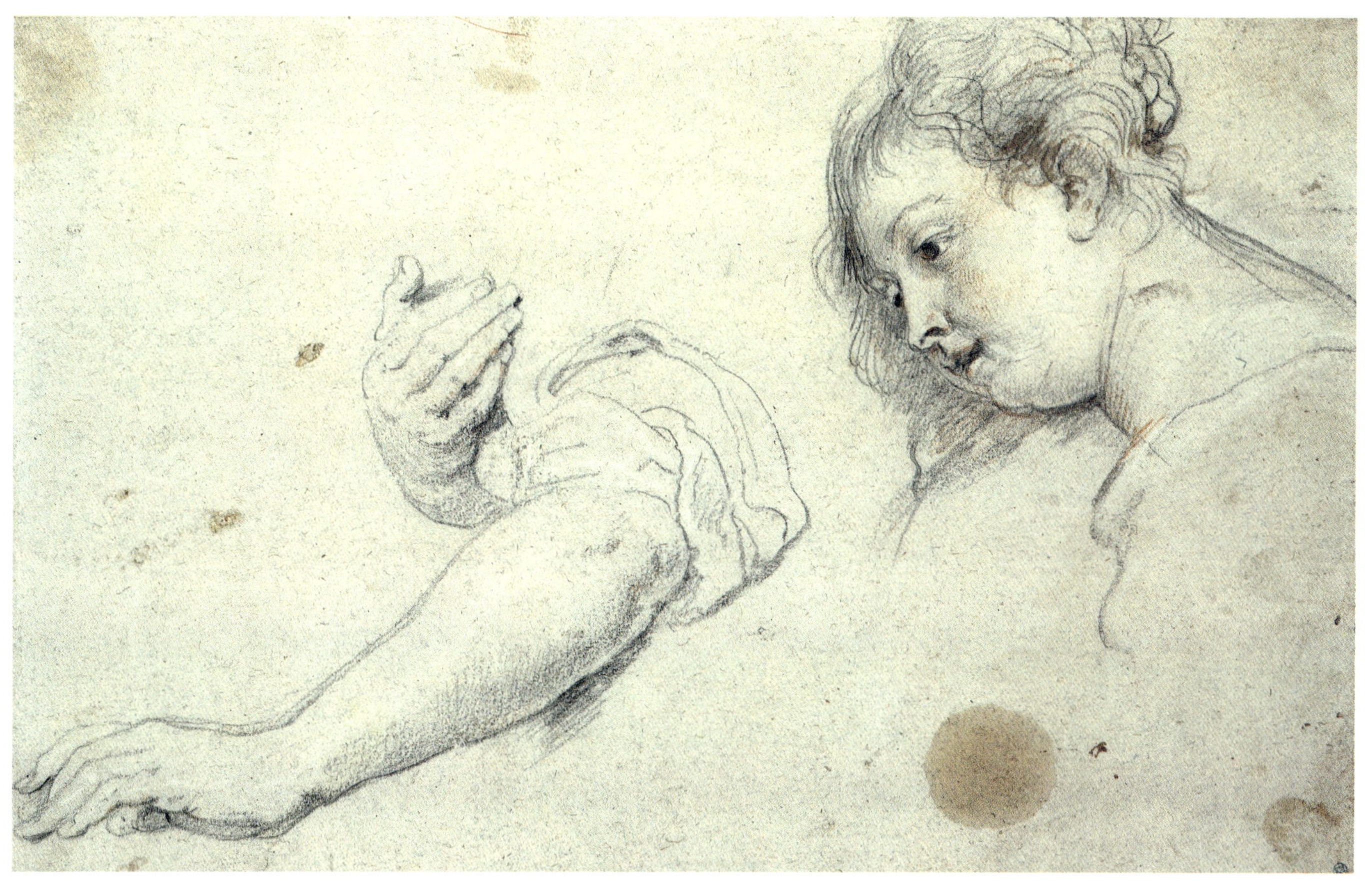

78

PETER PAUL RUBENS (1577-1640)

A Jesuit in a Chinese Dress

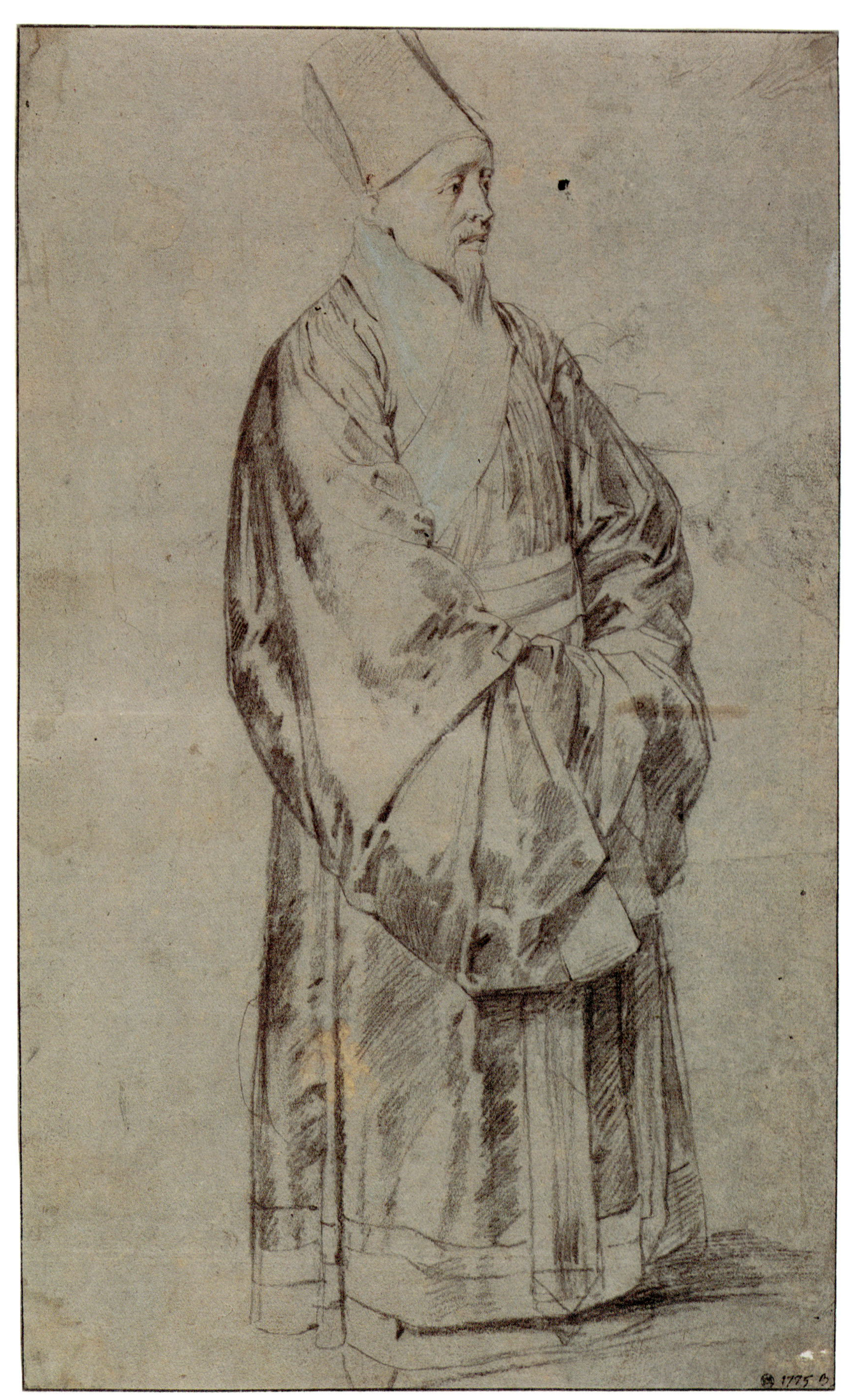

79

PETER PAUL RUBENS (1577-1640)

Studies of a Male Nude

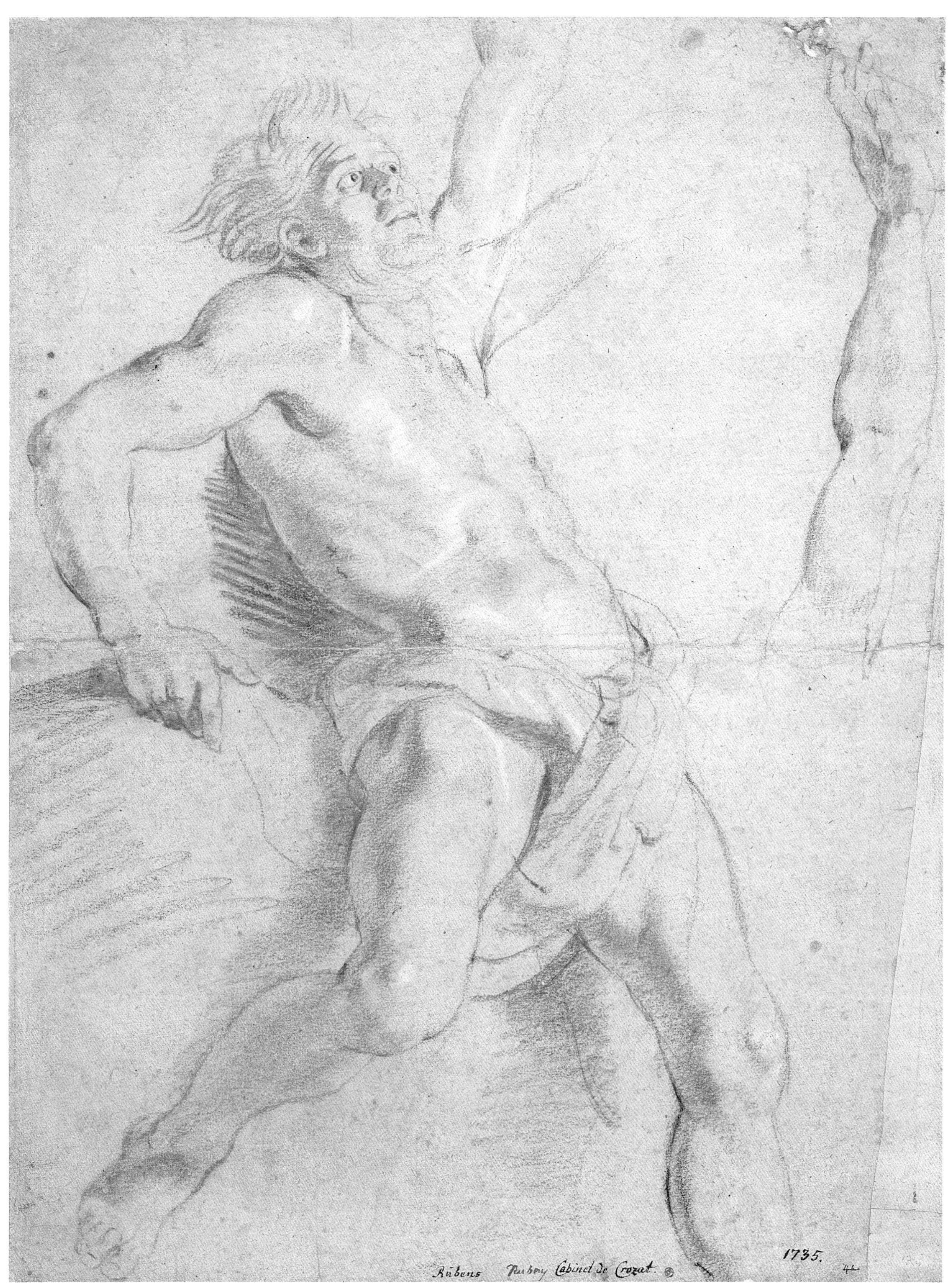

80

ANTONIS VAN DYCK (1599-1641)

Portrait of Cornelius van der Geest

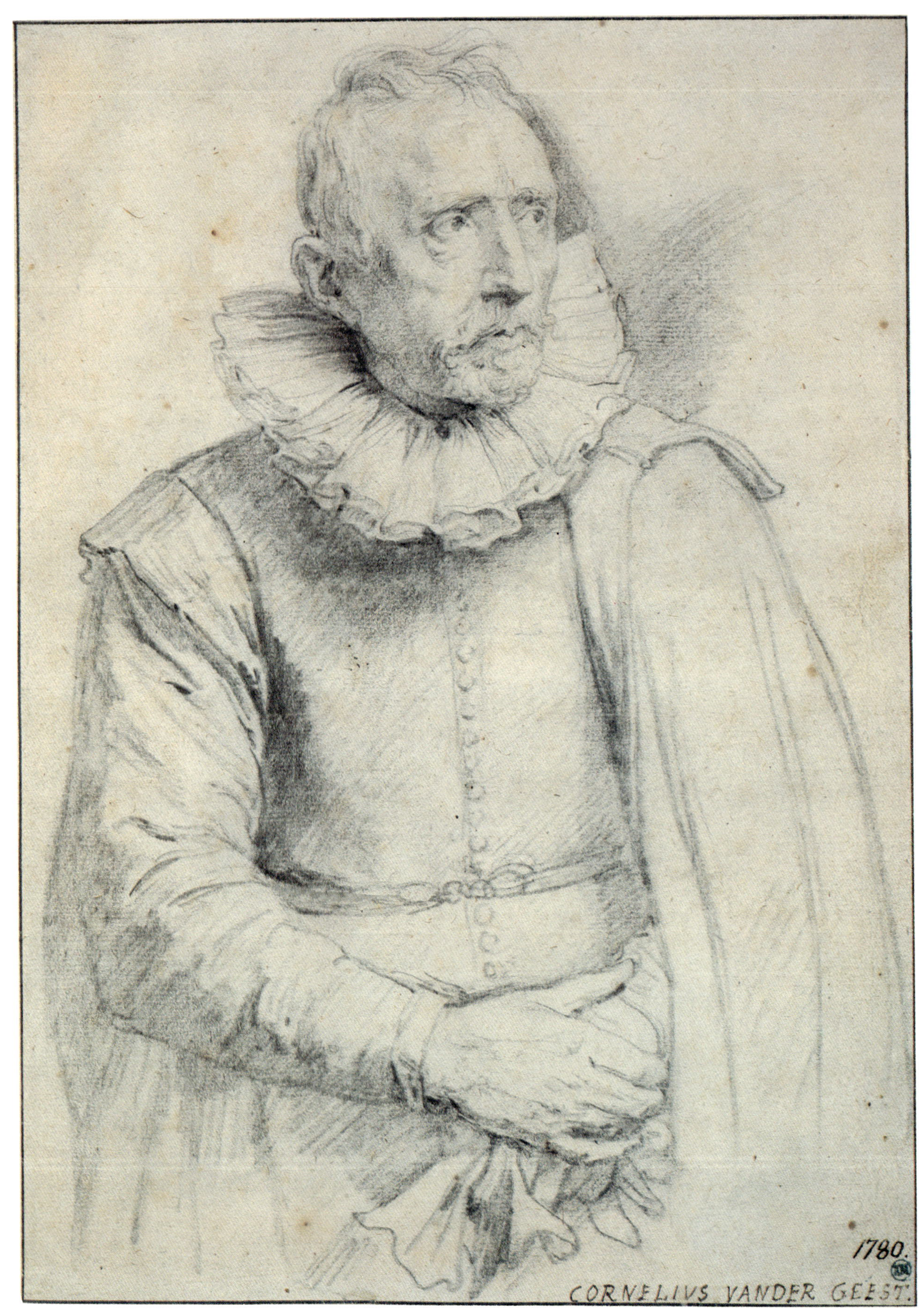

81

ANTONIS VAN DYCK (1599-1641)

Portrait of a Middle-Aged Man

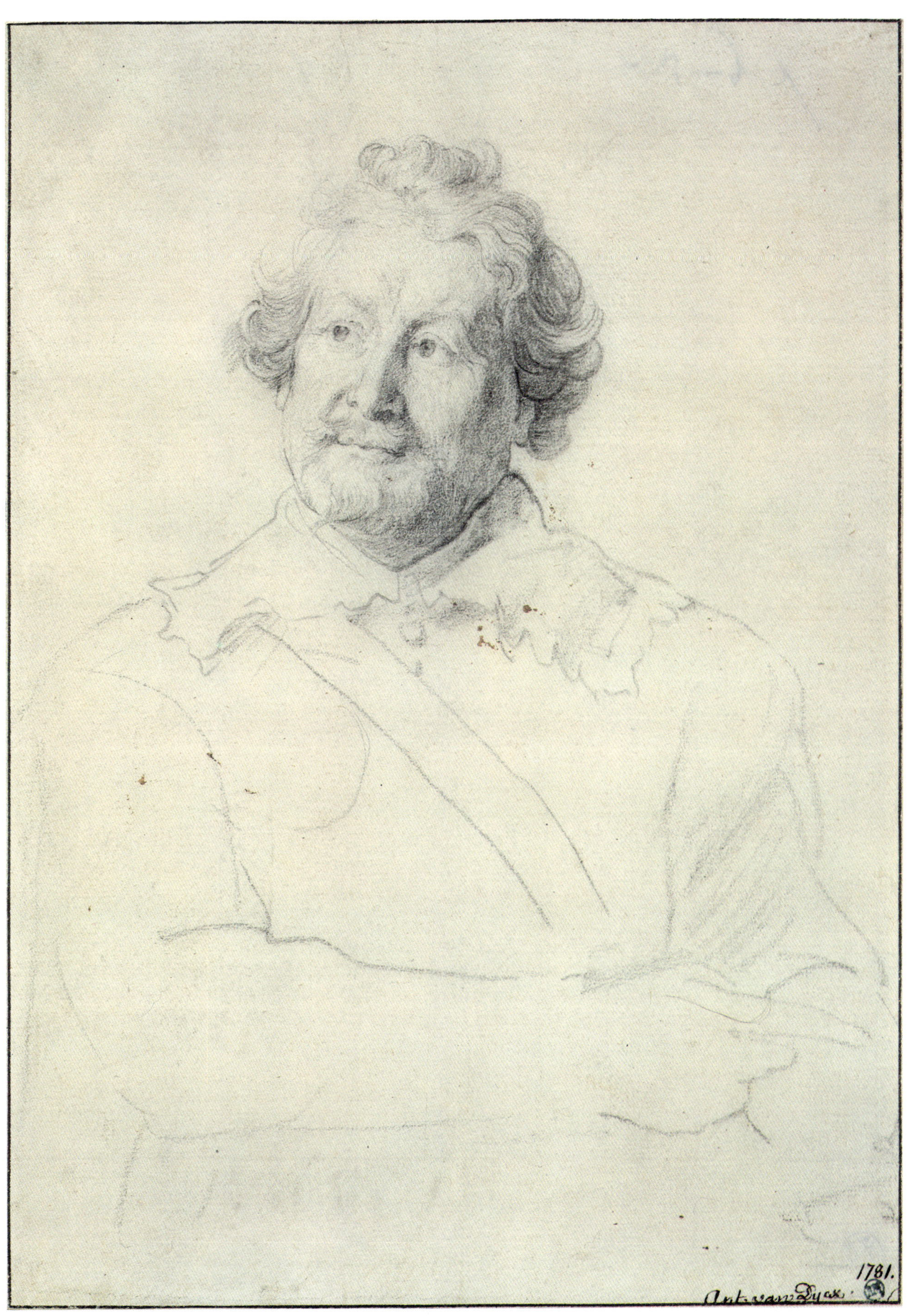

82

JACOB JORDAENS (1593-1678)

Telemachus Brings Theoclymenus Before his Mother Penelope

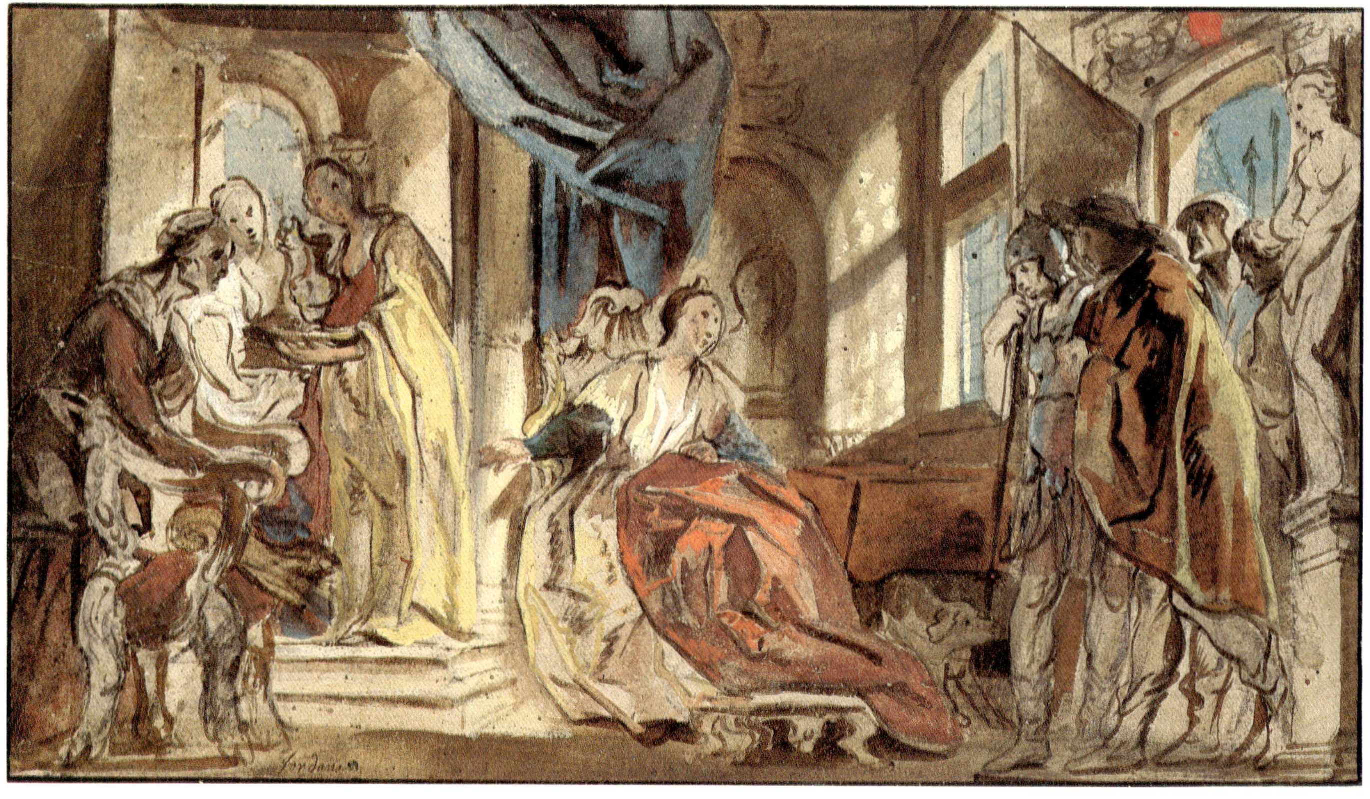

83

LUCAS VAN UDEN (1595-1672)

Landscape with a Setting Sun

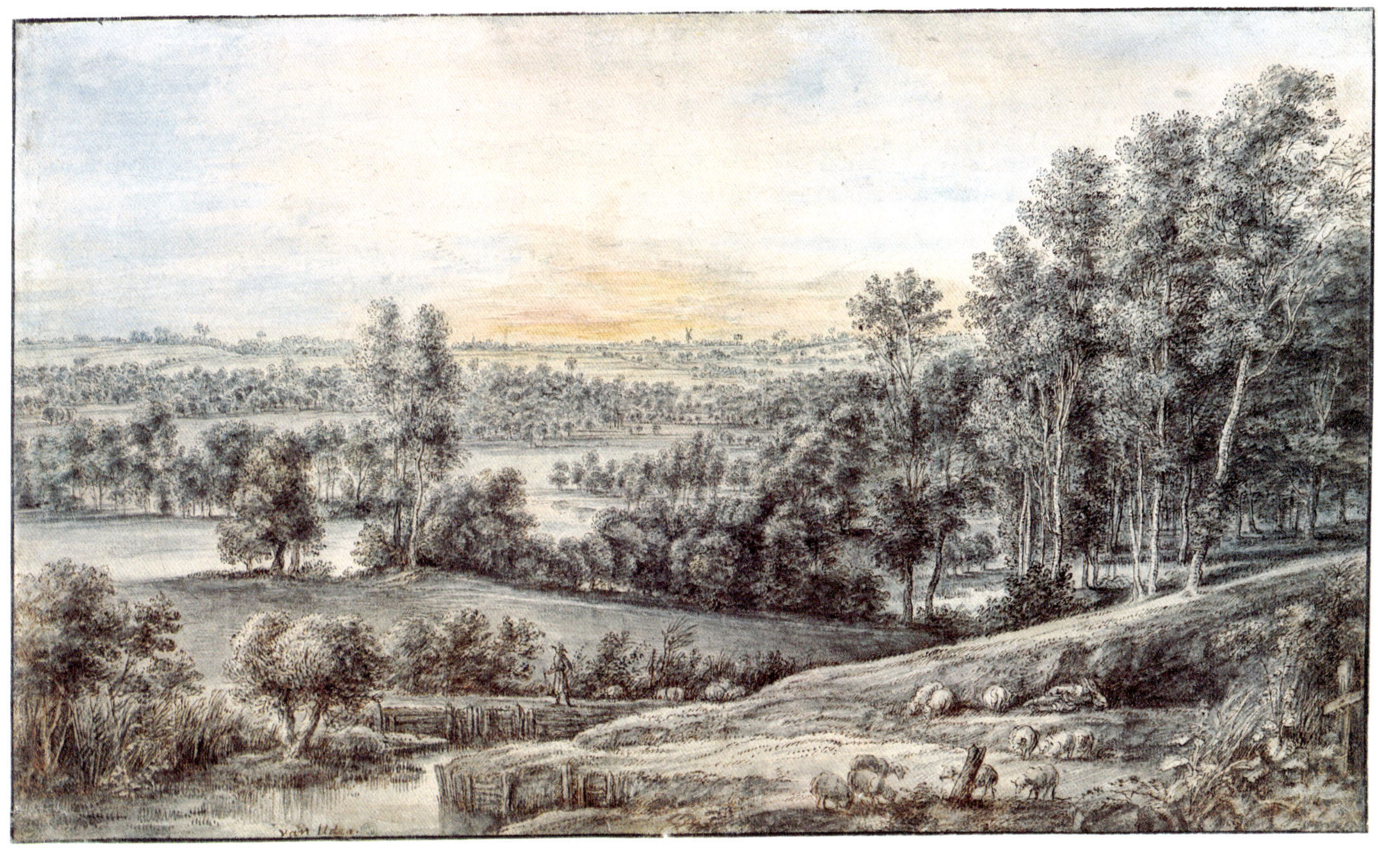

85

PHILIPS KONINCK (1619-1688)

Landscape with a Canal and a Town

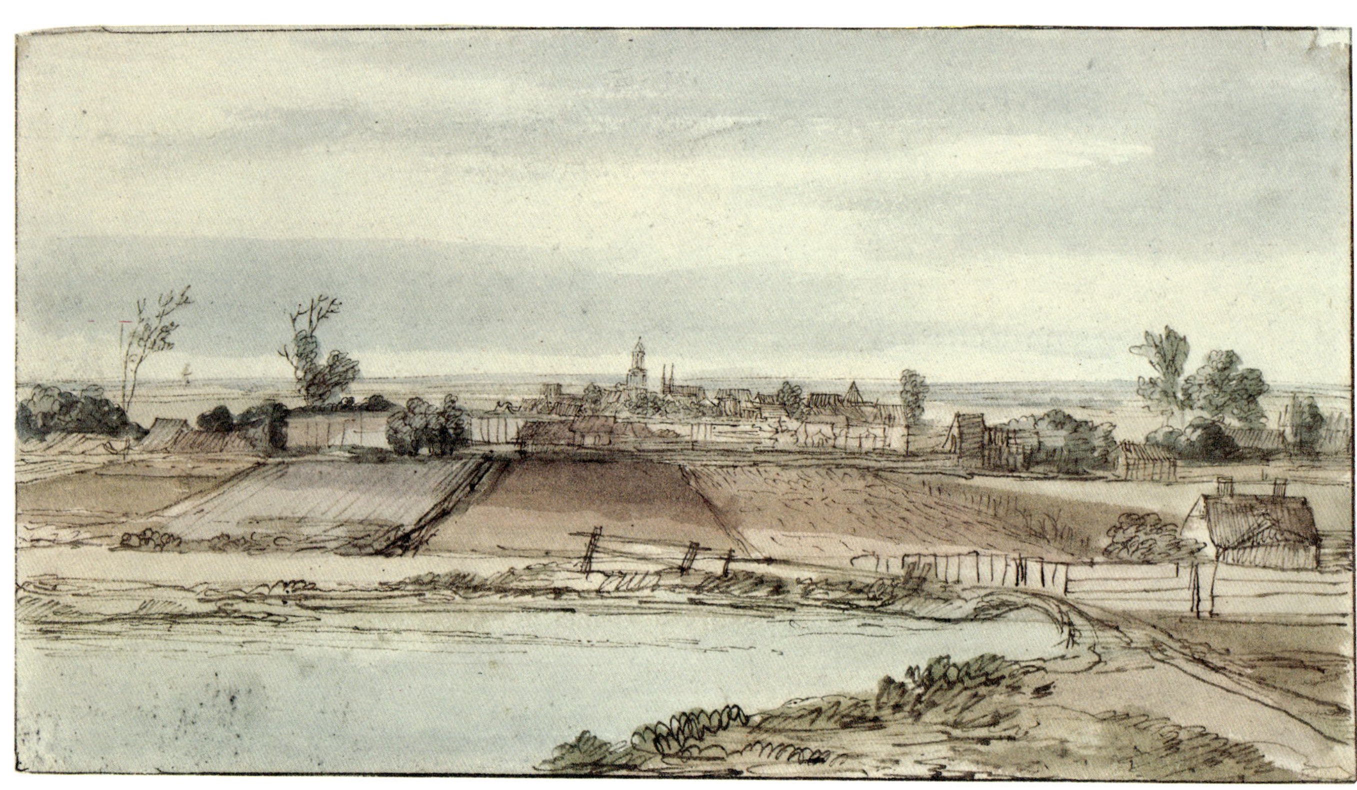

86

REMBRANDT VAN RIJN (1606-1669)

Seated Old Man

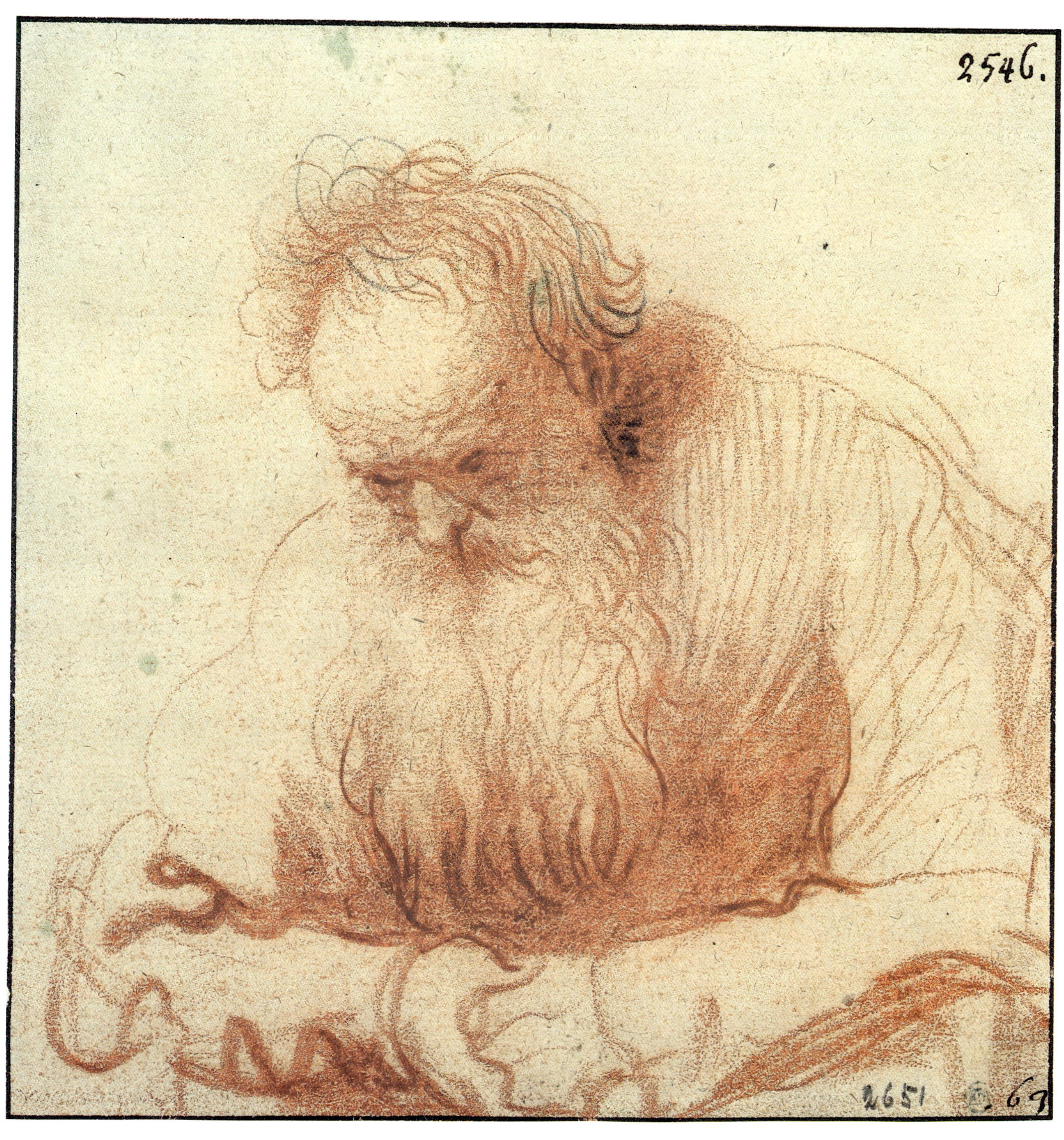

88

REMBRANDT VAN RIJN (1606-1669)

Esther

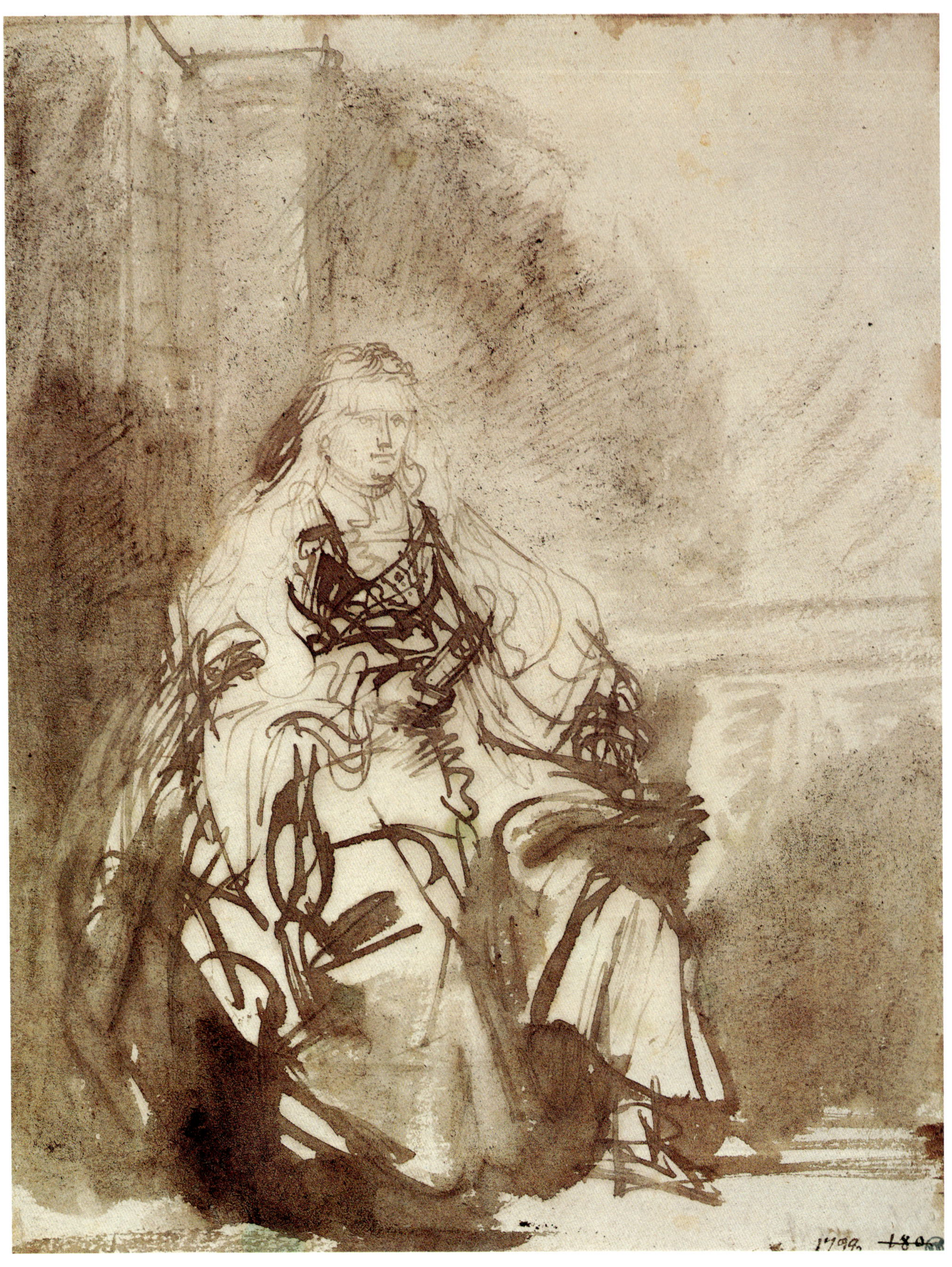

89

REMBRANDT VAN RIJN (1606-1669)

Portrait of Titia van Uylenburch

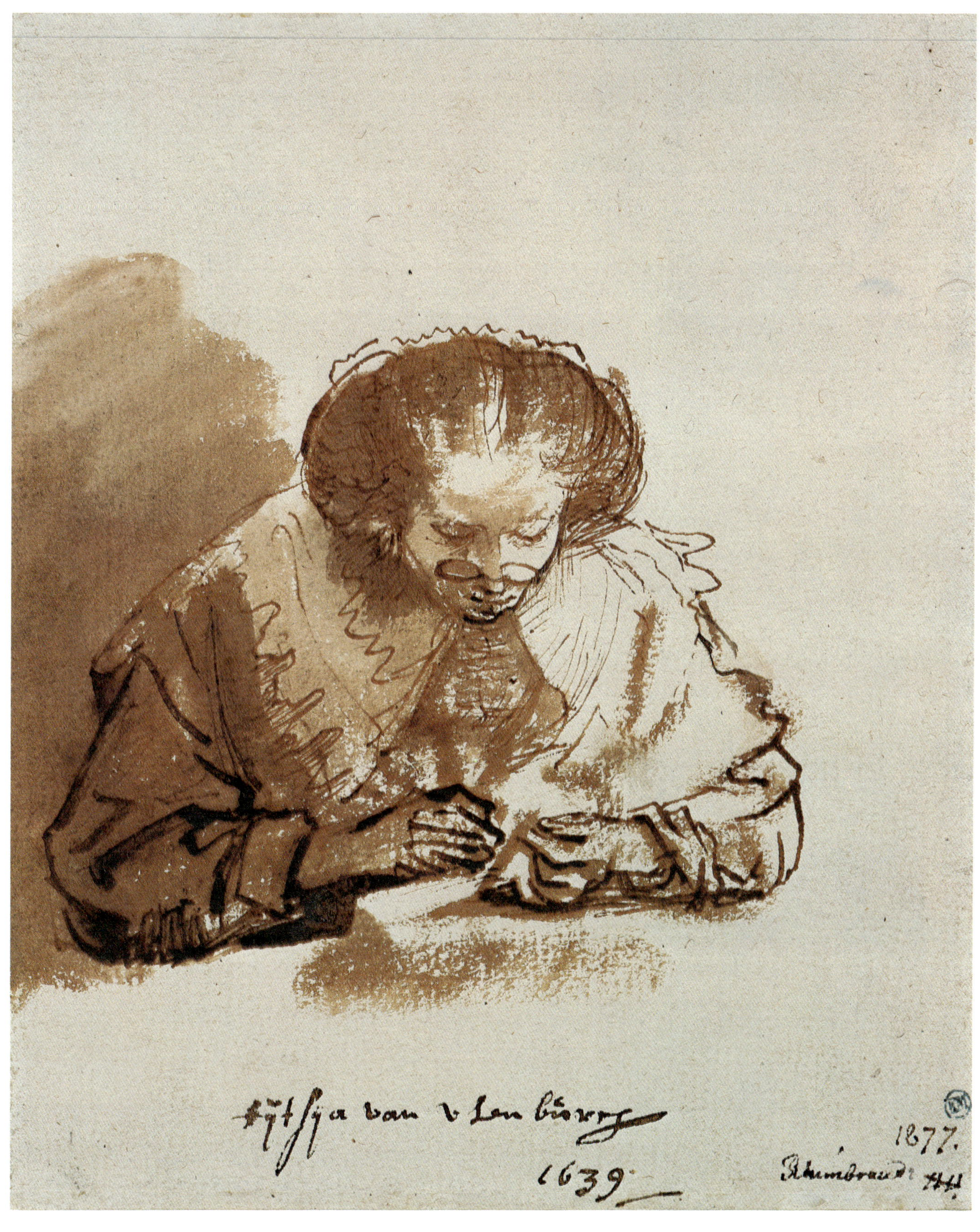

90

REMBRANDT VAN RIJN (1606-1669)

The Arrest of Christ

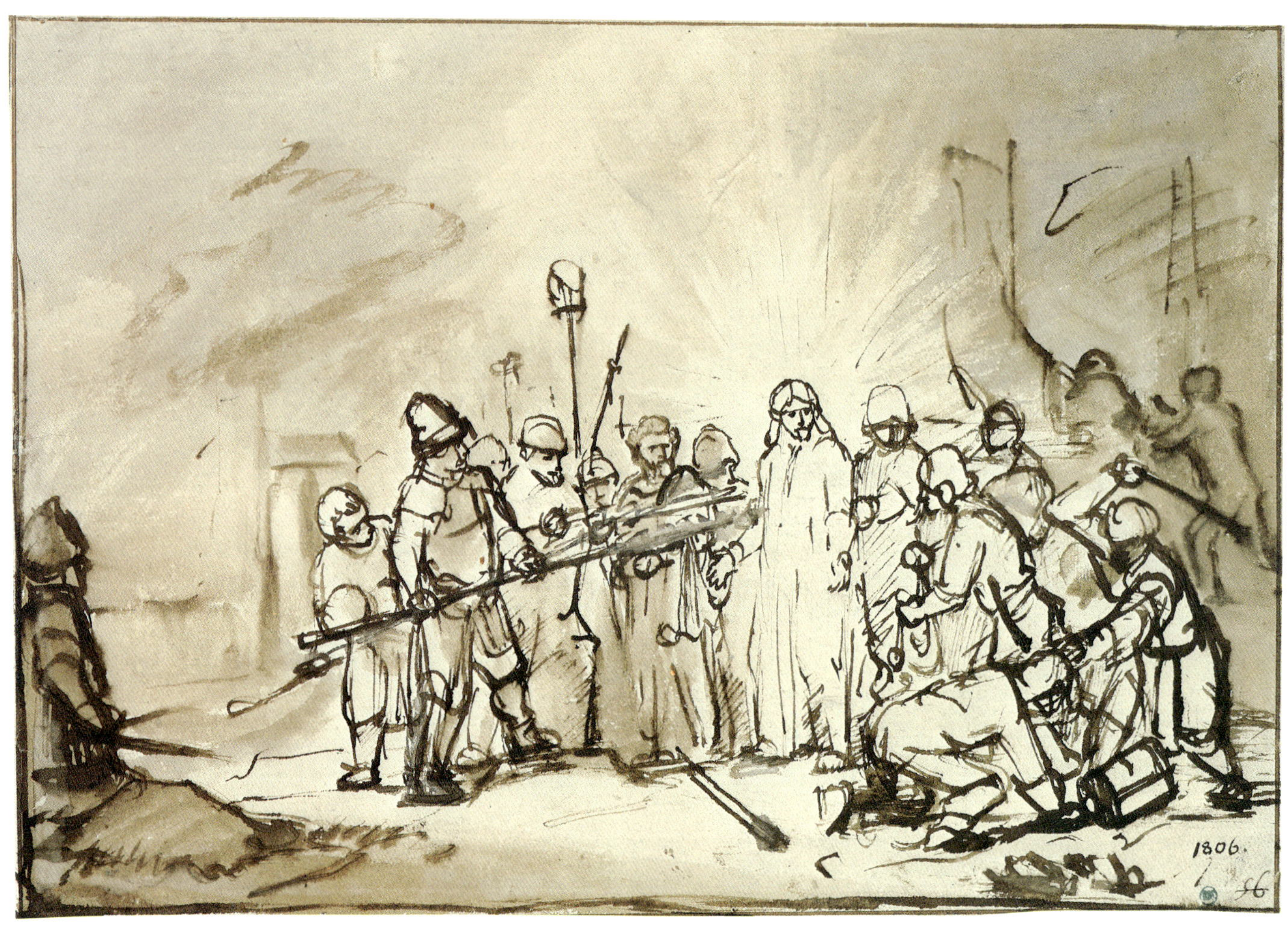

97
HANS BURGKMAIR THE ELDER (1473-1531)
Young Man with a Large Cap

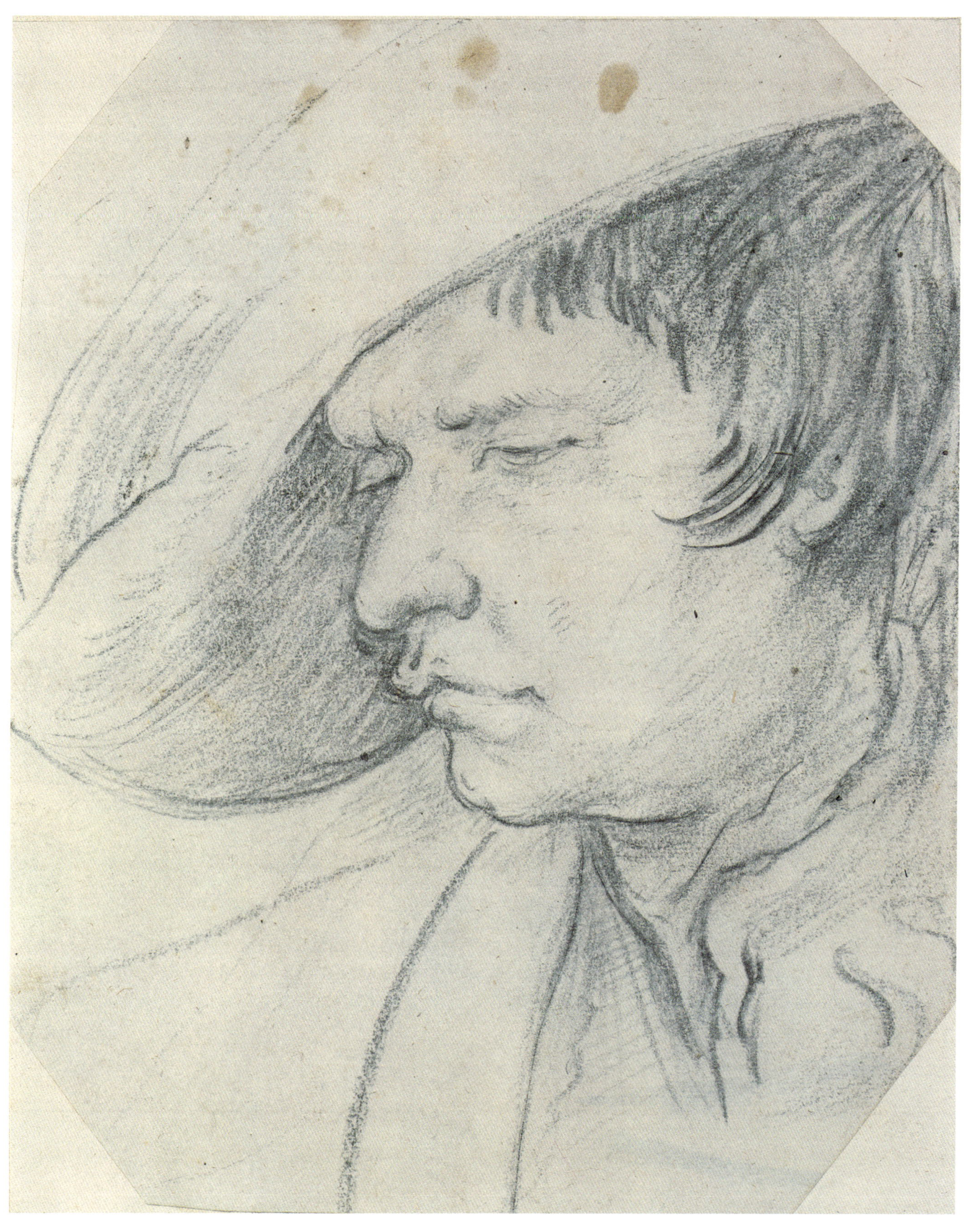

98

HANS BURGKMAIR THE ELDER (1473-1531)

Study of the Landscape for The Battle of Cannae

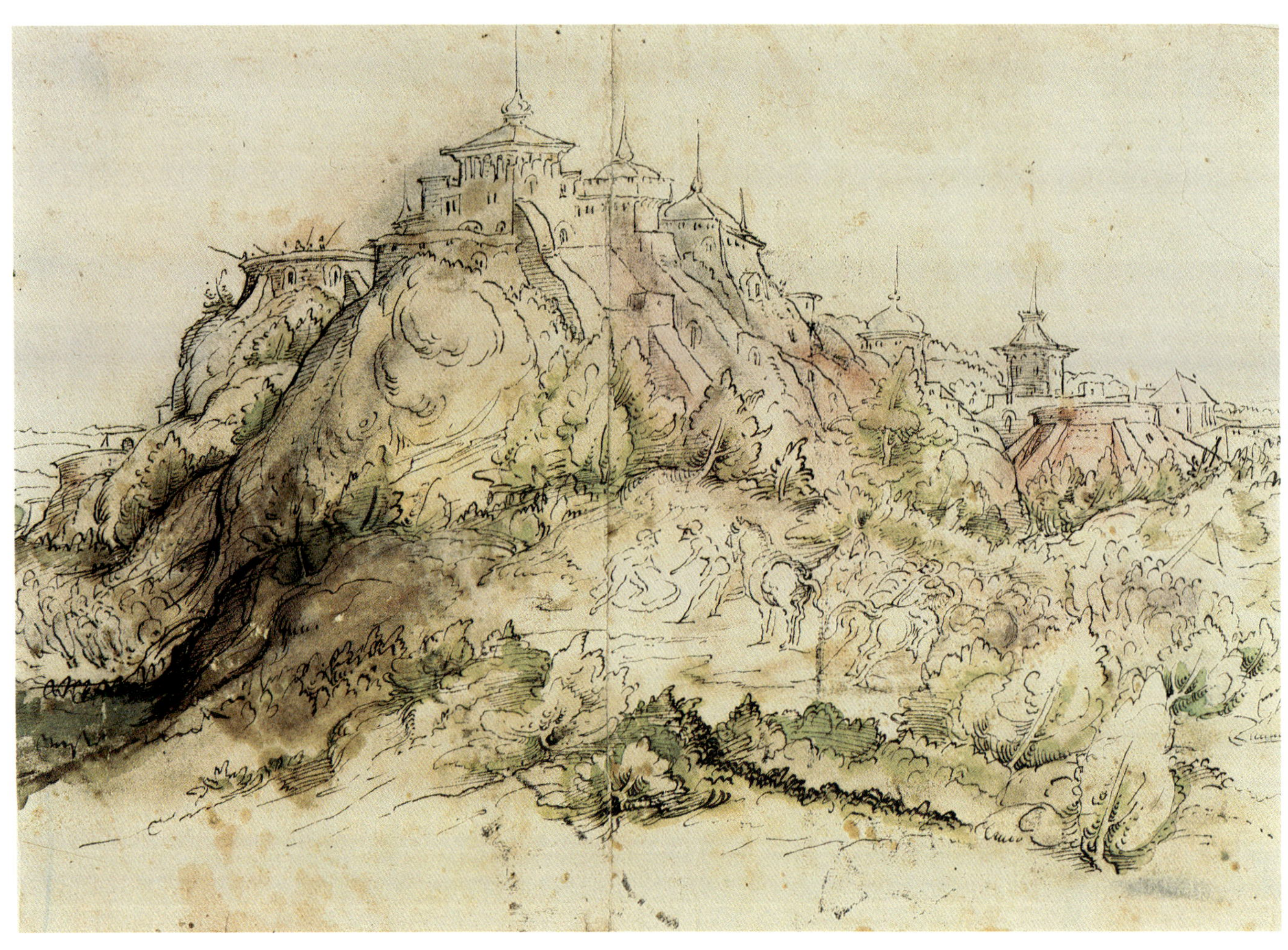

99

ALBRECHT DÜRER (1471-1528)

Portrait of a Girl

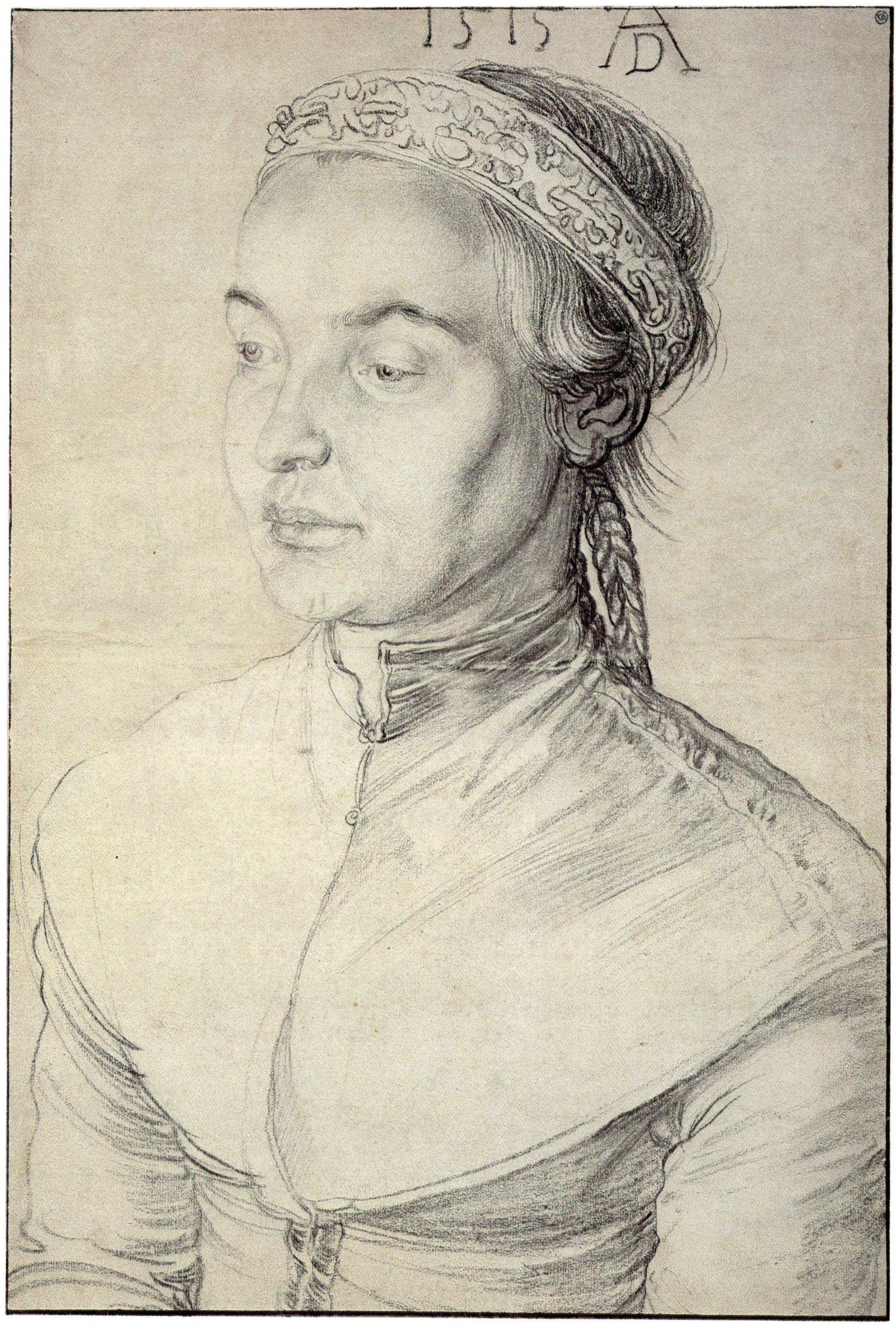

100

MATHIS GOTHART NITHART, called GRÜNEWALD (c. 1475/80-1528)

Head of a Beardless Old Man

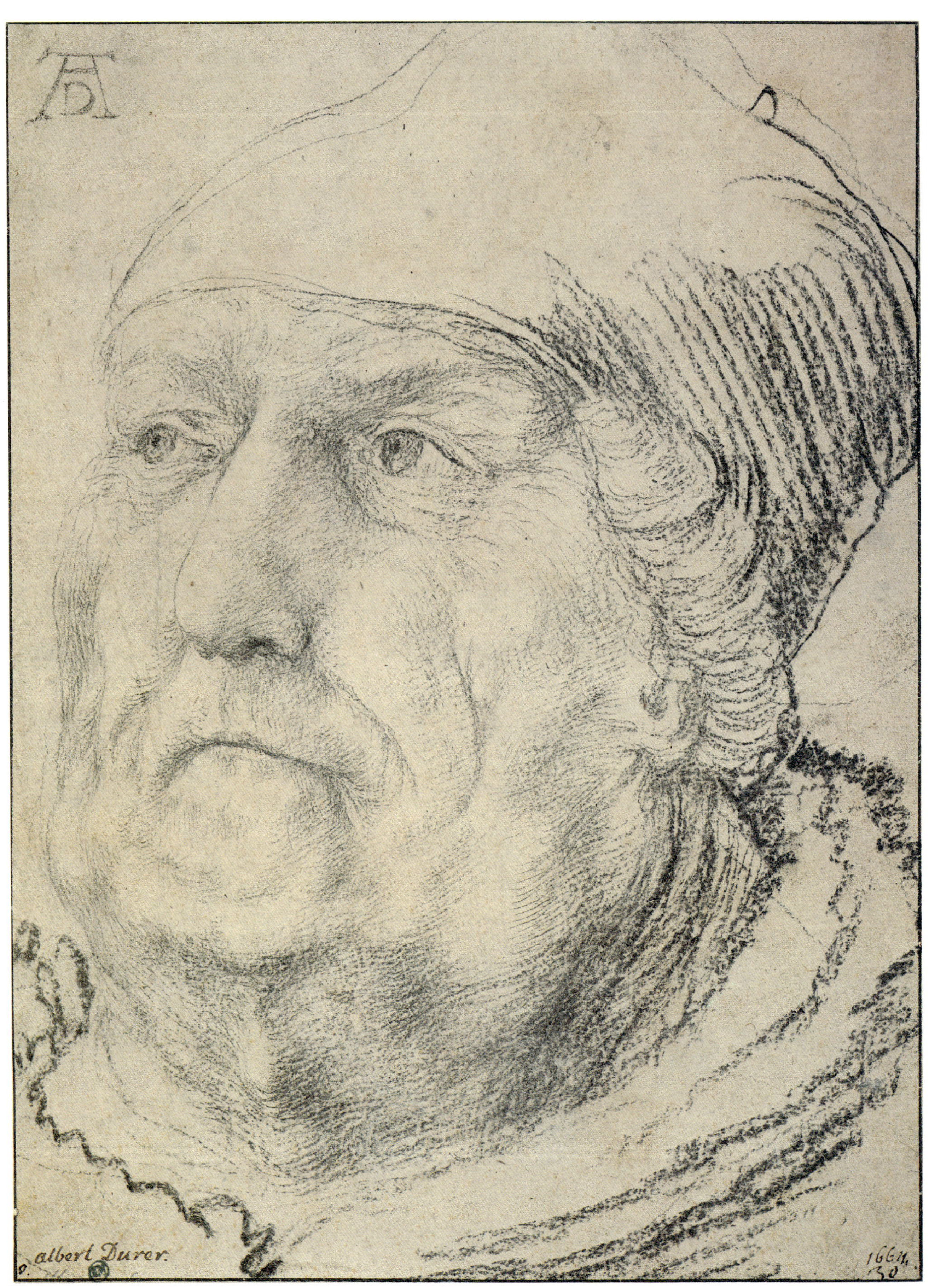

103

JOHANN HEINRICH FÜSSLI (FUSELI) (1741-1825)

Satan Flies at the Touch of Ithuriel's Spear

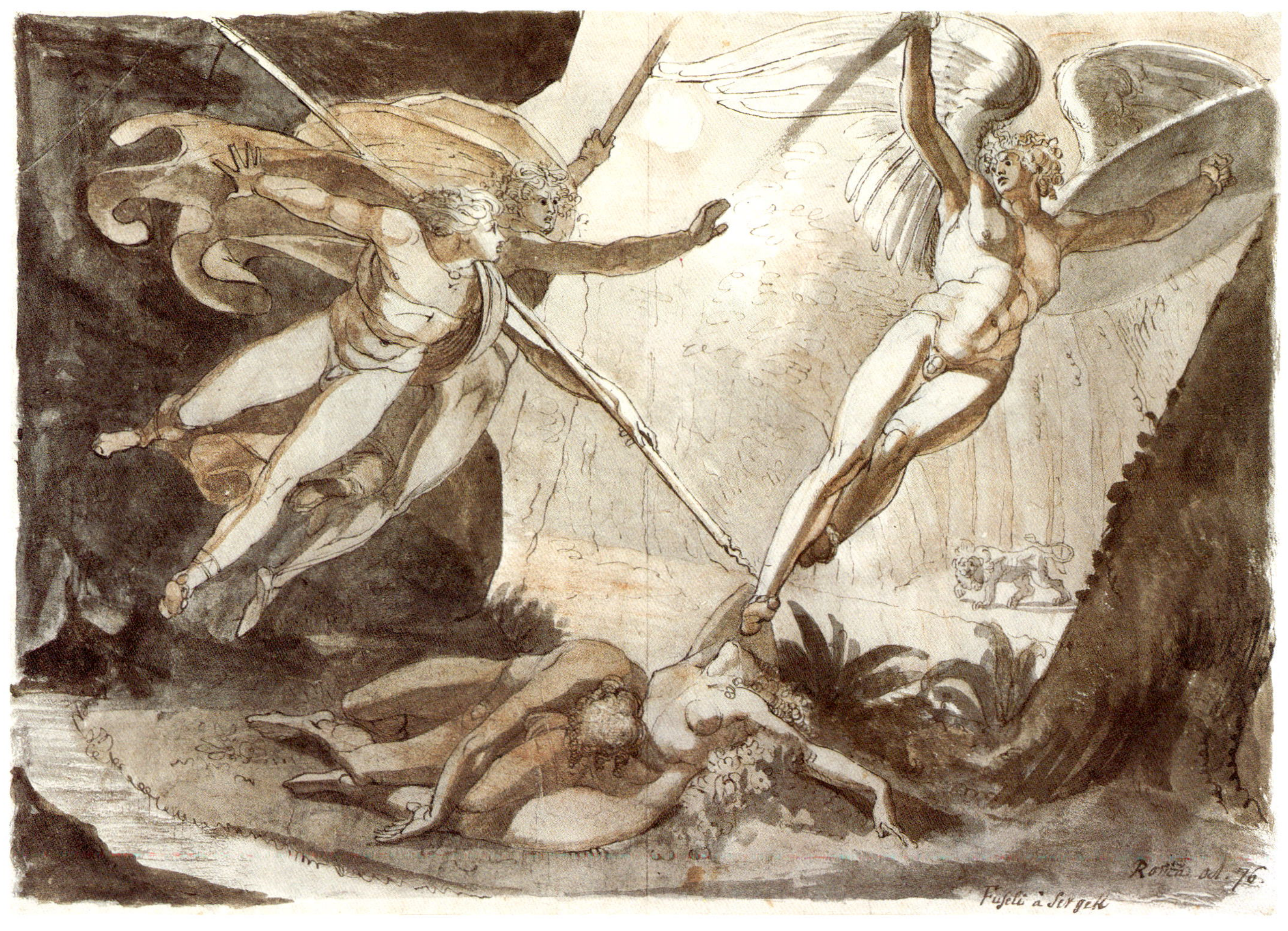

110

ELIAS MARTIN (1739-1818)

Romantic Mountain Landscape

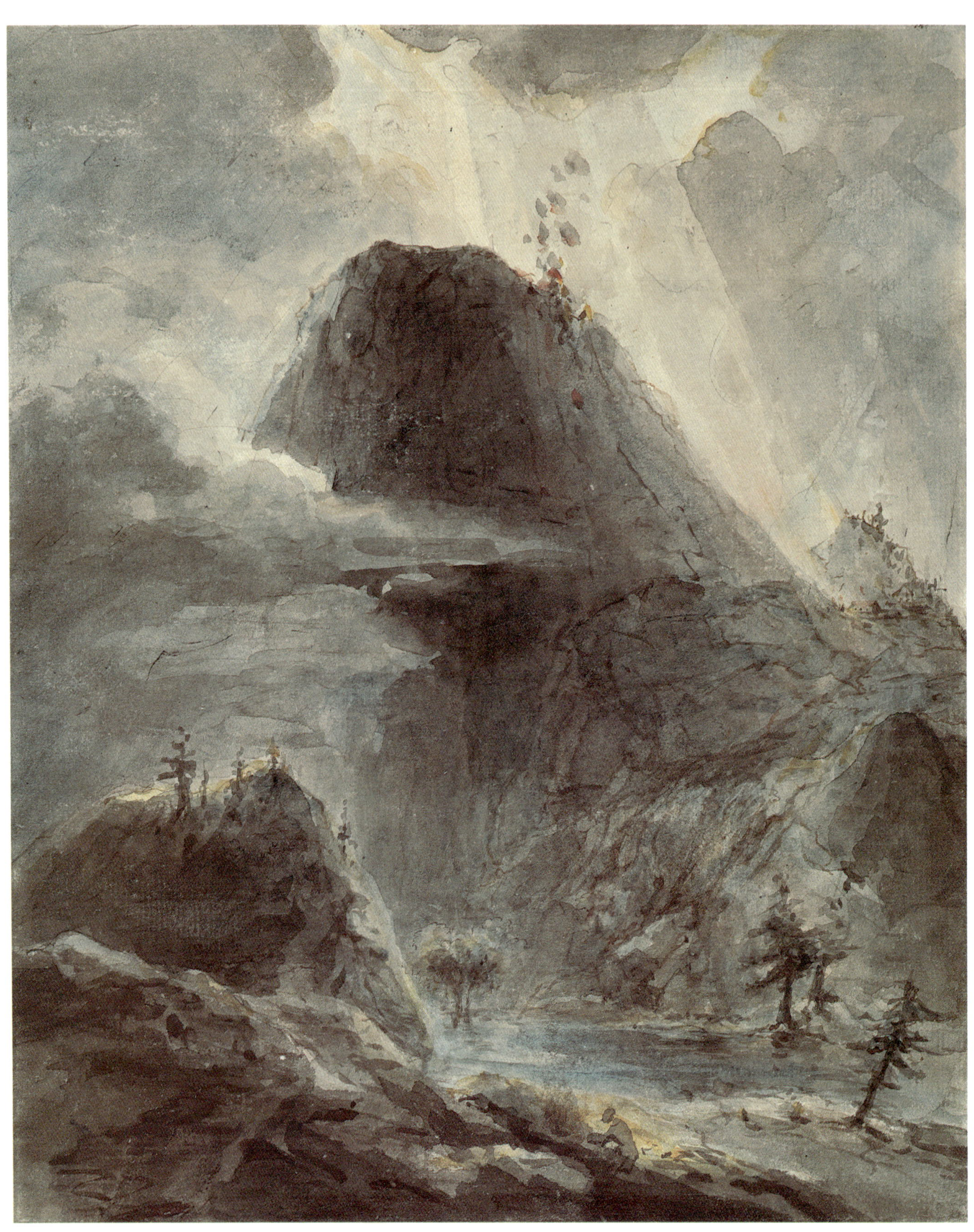

114

JOHAN TOBIAS SERGEL (1740-1814)

Passionate Lovers

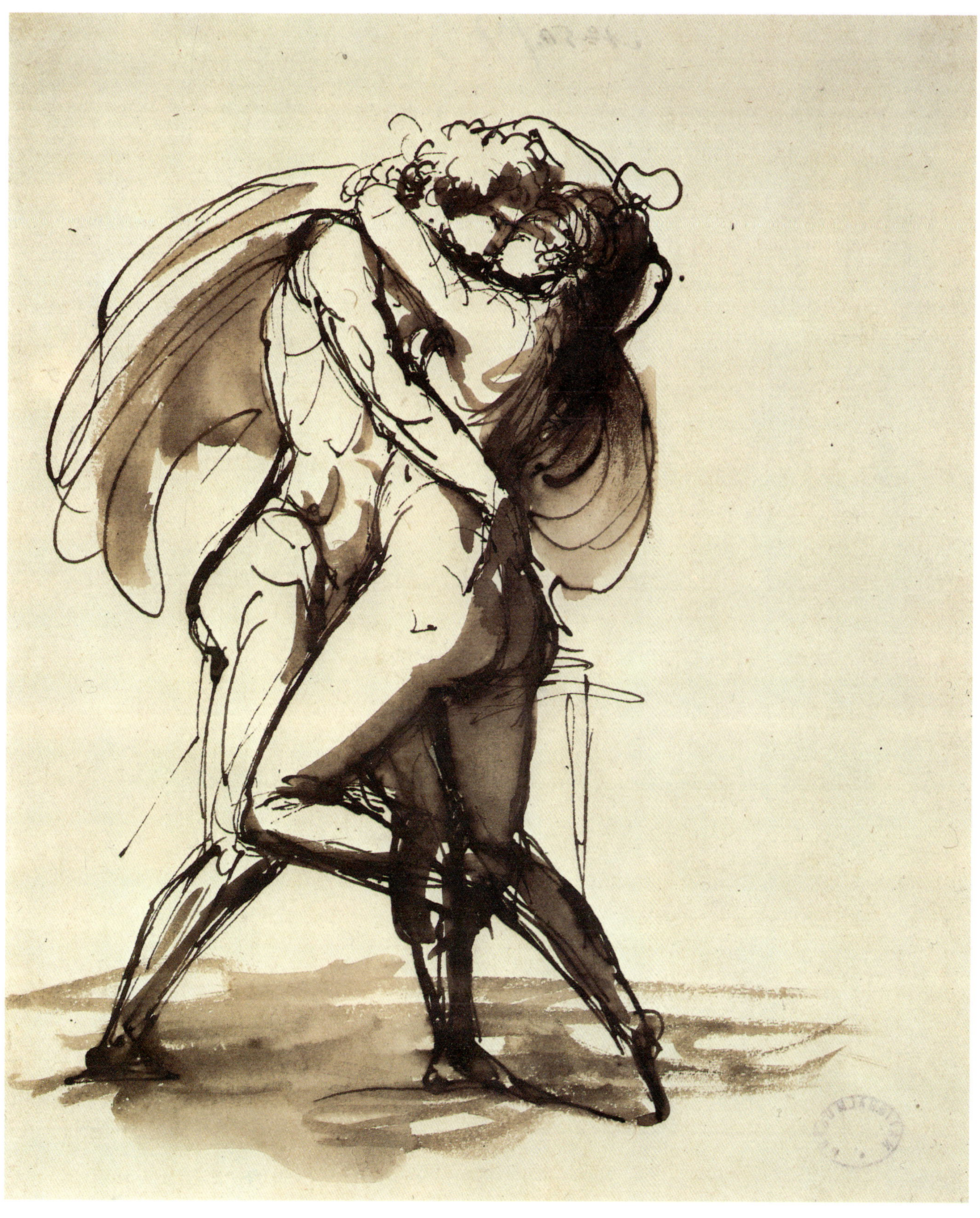

117

CARL AUGUST EHRENSVÄRD (1745-1800)

Scanian Peasant Girls

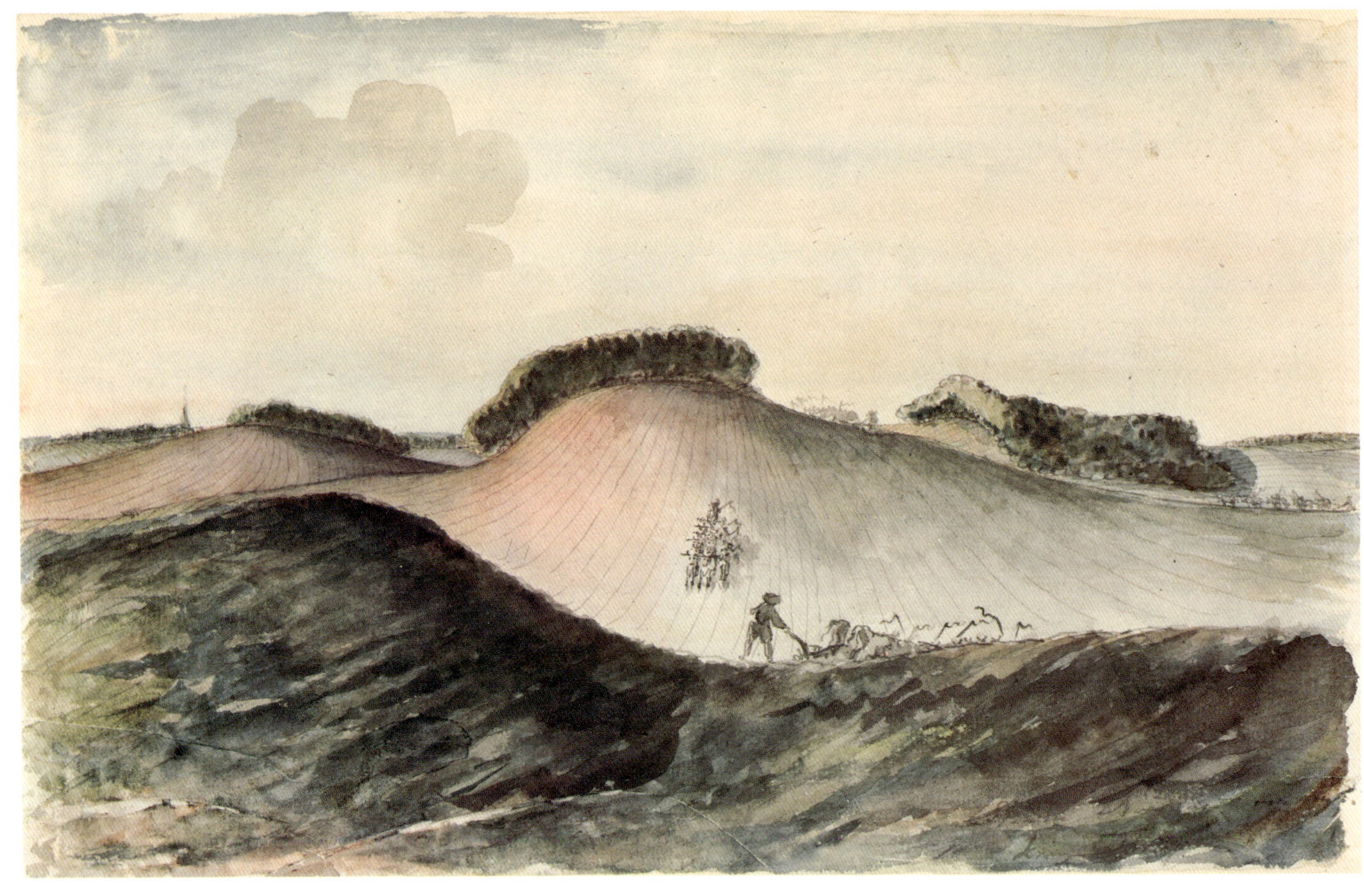

CATALOGUE OF DRAWINGS

1

ANONYMOUS FLORENTINE ARTIST
c. 1460

Reproduced in color.

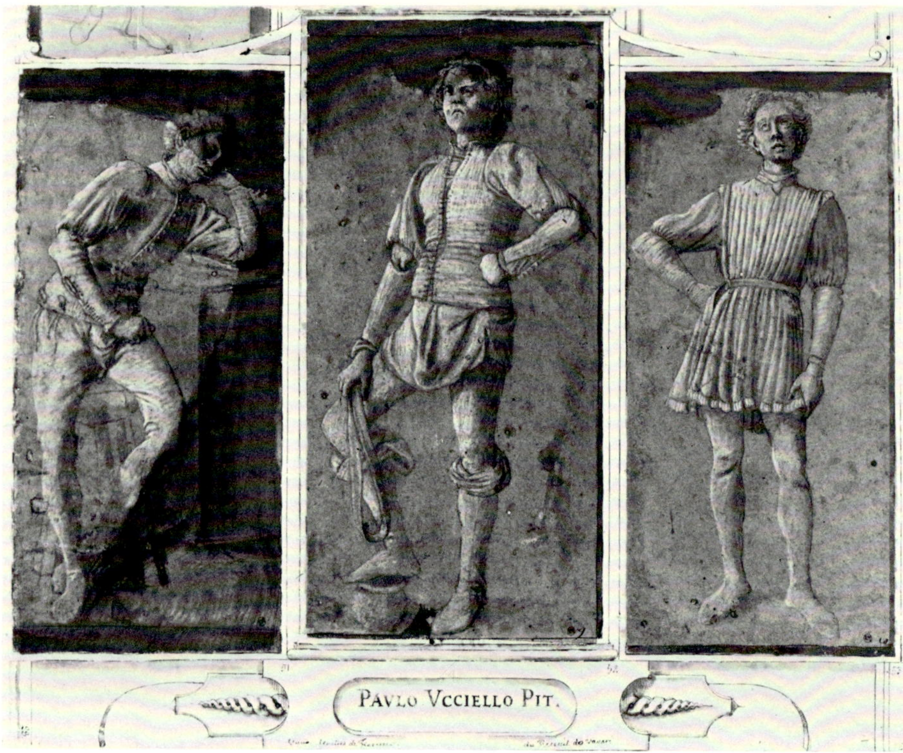

Three Figure Studies

Point of the brush in brown, heightened with white, on blue-gray paper. a) 27.4 x 13.4 cm; b) 29.3 x 14.8 cm; c) 26.5 x 13.5 cm. These rather fragmentary drawings have additions by Vasari (particularly the one on the right) and were mounted by him. NM 47, 48/1863. Inscribed on the old mount: PAVLO VCCIELO PIT in pen and brown ink (Vasari) and *Vieux maitres de Florence, du Recueil de Vasari* (Tessin) in pen and black ink. Numbered *8, 9, 10* at lower right and *51,52,53* (Tessin) on the mount, all in pen and black ink.

VERSO:
Two Nude Young Men. Point of the brush, brown wash, heightened with white on blue-gray paper. 19.2 x 20.8 cm. Inscribed on the old mount: PAVLO VCCIELLO PITT: FIORENTINO in pen and brown ink (Vasari). Numbered *11* at lower right in pen and black ink.

PROVENANCE:
Vasari □ Crozat (Mariette, no. 1 or 2) □ C. G. Tessin (List 1739-41, p. 53 v; Cat. 1749, livré 3, nos. 51-53; Paolo Uccello) □ Kongl. Biblioteket (Cat. 1790, no. 28; Paolo Uccello) □ Kongl. Museum (Lugt, 1638).

BIBLIOGRAPHY:
Sirén 1902, p. 22, nos. 12 and 13 (Uccello) □ Sirén 1917, nos. 11 and 12 (Uccello, his style) □ O. Sirén, *Italienska tavlor och teckningar i Nationalmuseum och andra svenska och finska samlingar*, Stockholm 1933, p. 34 (Uccello, his style) □ Schönbrunner and Meder, nos. 964 and 976 (circle of Uccello) □ B. Berenson, *The Drawings of the Florentine Painters*, Chicago 1938, no. 2779 I-J (School of Uccello) □ J. V. Schlosser, "Künstlerprobleme der Frührenaissance: Piero della Francesca, Paolo Uccello, Michelozzo und Alberti," *Sitzungsberichte der Akademie der Wissenschaften im Wien. Philosophisch- historische Klasse 214.5 Abhandlung* (1933), p. 38 □ W. Boeck, "Domenico Veneziano," *Pantheon*, 13 (1934), p. 85 (Domenico Veneziano) □ G. Gronau, "Piero della Francesca," *Old Master Drawings*, 4 (1929-30), p. 58 (Piero della Francesca) □ B. Degenhart, "Besprechung von W. Boeck: Paolo Uccello," *Zeitschrift für Kunstgeschichte*, 10 (1941-42), p. 82 f. □ Idem, "Domenico Veneziano als Zeichner," *Festschrift für Friedrich Winkler*, Berlin 1959, no. 101 (Domenico Veneziano, his style) □ Degenhart and Schmitt, nos. 505-507, 509 □ B. Berenson, *I Disegni dei pittori fiorentini*, Milan 1961, no. 2779 *I-J* (School of Uccello) □ L. Ragghianti Collobi, *Il Libro de Disegni del Vasari*, Florence 1974, pp. 46, 60, figs. 69-70.

EXHIBITIONS:
Paris, Brussels, Amsterdam 1970-71, no. 5.

These sheets and two in the Louvre (Inv. no. 1256 bis recto and verso) once belonged to Vasari and were attributed by him, as well as by subsequent writers, to Uccello or his immediate circle. A somewhat later date has been proposed by Degenhart and Schmitt, who detect strong similarities with the work of Pesellino, in particular his cassoni with subjects from the story of David (Coll. Lloyd). They therefore assign our sheets to an unknown hand in Pesellino's workshop.

In the three drawings the artist varies the positions of the figures, though Vasari's mount does, quite appropriately, accentuate the middle figure. The pose of the young man is derived from Donatello's *David Holding a Sling*; his appearance is very determined, and the jar under his right foot can be seen as an allusion to the head of Goliath.

2

DOMENICO GHIRLANDAIO
Florence 1449 - Florence 1494

Reproduced in color.

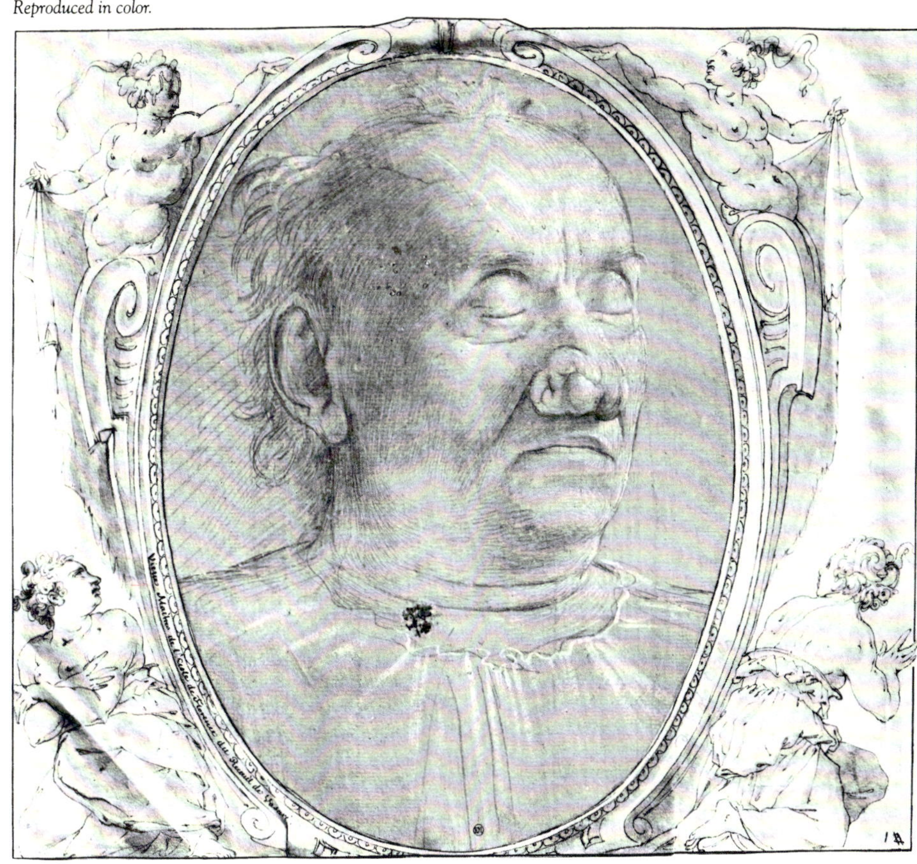

Head of an Old Man

Silverpoint and point of the brush, heightened with white on pink prepared paper. 28.2 x 21.4 cm without frame. Cut down to oval and framed with decorative Michelangelesque nudes by Vasari. Small stains on the model's temple, a large one on his throat. NM 1/1863. Inscribed in pen and black ink in the oval framing to the left *Vieux Maitres de l'école de Florence du Recueil de Vasari* (Tessin's handwriting), and to the right in the frame in black chalk, barely visible, *Di Paolo Ucello*. Numbered in pen and brown ink at lower right *1* and *2*, struck out.

VERSO:
FILIPPINO LIPPI, *Hercules and Nessus*, and inset below, a centaur downing a male nude, in the presence of a herm with hand extended. Pen and brown ink, brown wash, heightened with white. (Berenson 1938, no. 1366 C; Idem 1961, no 1366 D$^+$.)

PROVENANCE:
Vasari ☐ Crozat (Mariette, no. 1 or 2) ☐ C. G. Tessin (List 1739-41, p. 32; Cat. 1749, livré 17, no. 3) ☐ Kongl. Biblioteket (Cat. 1790, no. 1) ☐ Kongl. Museum (Lugt 1638).

BIBLIOGRAPHY:
Sirén 1902, p. 29, no. 26 ☐ Schönbrunner and Meder, no. 886 ☐ Sirén 1917, no. 28 ☐ H. S. Ede, *Florentine Drawings*, London 1926, pl. 33 ☐ R. van Marle, *The Development of the Italian Schools of Painting*, vol. 12, 1931, p. 101 ☐ B. Berenson, "Nova Ghirlandajana," *L'Arte* (1933), pp. 171, 175 ☐ O. Kurz, "Giorgio Vasari's 'Libro de' disegni,'" *Old Master Drawings*, 12 (June, 1937), p. 13 ☐ Berenson 1938, no. 890 B ☐ J. Lauts, *D. Ghirlandajo*, Vienna 1943, no. 112, p. 56 ☐ L. Grassi, *Il Disegno italiano*, Rome 1956, p. 66 ☐ Idem, *I Disegni italiani del' 300 e 400*, Venice 1962, no. 72 ☐ Berenson 1961, no. 890 ☐ B. R. Hausler and J. E. Schuler, *Meisterzeichnungen von der Welt bewundert*, Stuttgart 1962, no. 54 ☐ W. Ames in *Great Drawings of All Time* (Ira Moscowitz, ed.), New York 1962, Vol. I, Italian, no. 138 ☐ L. Ragghianti Collobi, *Il Libro de' Disegni del Vasari*, Florence 1974, pp. 76 and 181, fig. 201.

EXHIBITIONS:
Stockholm 1933, no. 6; New York, Boston, Chicago 1969, no. 4.

Ghirlandaio was the leading painter of pictures and frescoes in Florence in the final third of the fifteenth century. He is also remembered for the fact that he had Michelangelo as an apprentice in his studio.

This drawing, done in the traditional technique with silverpoint on pink prepared paper, depicts the same man illustrated in the Louvre's painting of an old man with his grandson.[1] Berenson asserts that the drawing must have been made when the subject was asleep or, more likely, had just died. In either case, it must have been done in a single, short sitting.

The sheet comes from the world's first systematic and perhaps most famous collection of drawings, assembled by Giorgio Vasari (1511-1574), who achieved renown for his biographies of artists, *Vite*, first published in 1550. Vasari arranged his collection in two volumes, and at least forty-odd sheets have found their way via Crozat and Tessin to the Nationalmuseum. He also embellished the drawings with frames, here consisting of four female guardians who are designed to heighten the effect of Ghirlandaio's composition. The wealth of decoration, unusually well preserved, suggests that Vasari set particular store by this sheet with its monumental format.

NOTE:
1. No. 1322; Van Marle *op. cit.*, vol. 13, p. 101.

3

SCHOOL OF
BERNARDINO PINTURICCHIO

Reproduced in color.

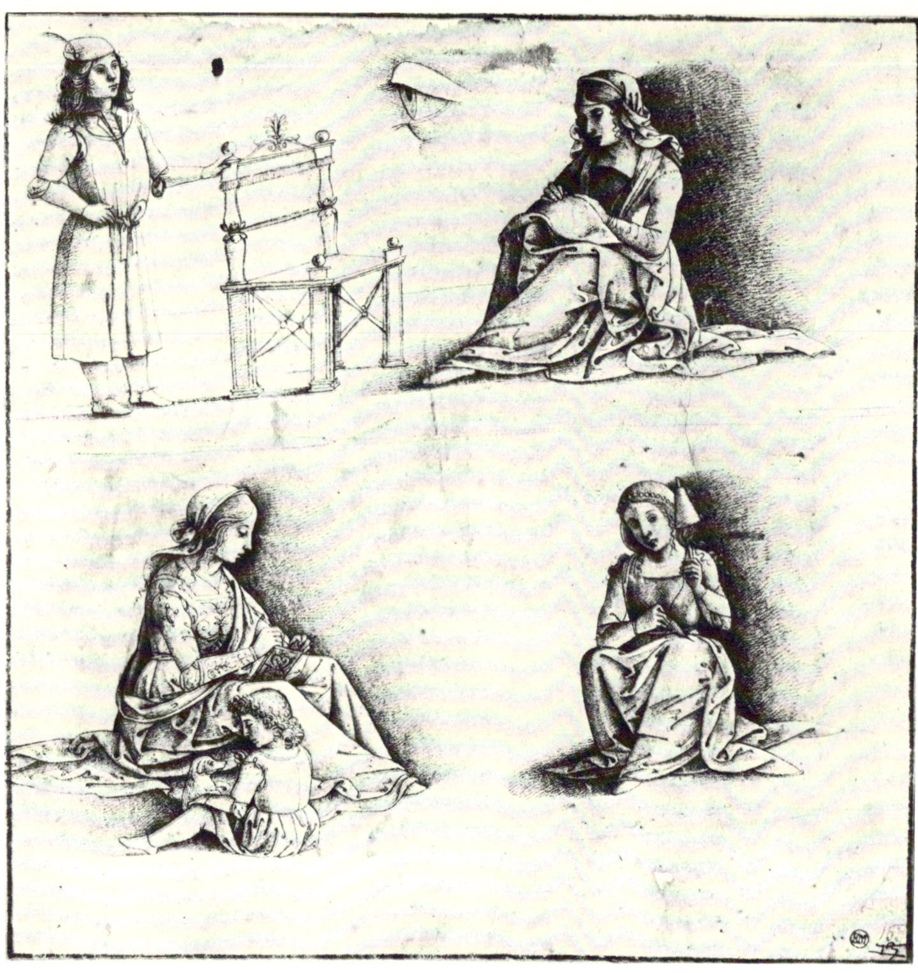

A Boy Standing by a Chair, an Eye, and Three Seated Women

Pen and brown ink. 20.5 x 20 cm. Repaired along the upper border, several small holes and tears. No watermark. NM 26/1863. Numbered in the lower right corner in pen and brown ink *13*, struck out, and, very faint, *15* (Sparre).

PROVENANCE:
Crozat? □ C. G. Tessin (List 1739-42, p. 43; Cat. 1749, livré 3, no. 3) □ Kongl. Biblioteket (Cat. 1790, no. 15) □ Kongl. Museum (Lugt 1638).

BIBLIOGRAPHY:
Sirén 1917, no. 157.

Compilations of figures, each meticulously rendered, are a typical kind of medieval and early Renaissance pattern sheet. They provided a storehouse of motifs which could be varied and incorporated in paintings, besides being copied by apprentices.

The boy playing with a dog (bottom) and the woman sewing (top right) occur in a Visitation fresco in the Vatican's Appartamento Borgia; the discrepancies between the drawing and frescoes, above all the finer garments in the drawing, are dictated by the composition. The fresco also shows less exact counterparts to the two female figures in the lower row of this sheet. The woman writing could be a more everyday prototype for the sibyls in paintings by Bernardino Pinturicchio (c. 1454-1513). The physiognomy of the standing boy bears a strong resemblance to the portrait of C. Bufalini's son in Pinturicchio's *Burial of St. Bernard* in S. Maria in Aracoeli, Rome.

Besides these parallels in subject matter, the drawing is linked to Pinturicchio or his circle by elements of style, such as the strict modelling of forms and the stiff, almost stylized folds of the drapery.

The frescoes in the Vatican Borgia suite were painted in 1493-96 and those in S. Maria in Aracoeli in c. 1486.

4

RAFFAELE BOTTICINI
Florence 1477 - Florence c. 1520

Reproduced in color.

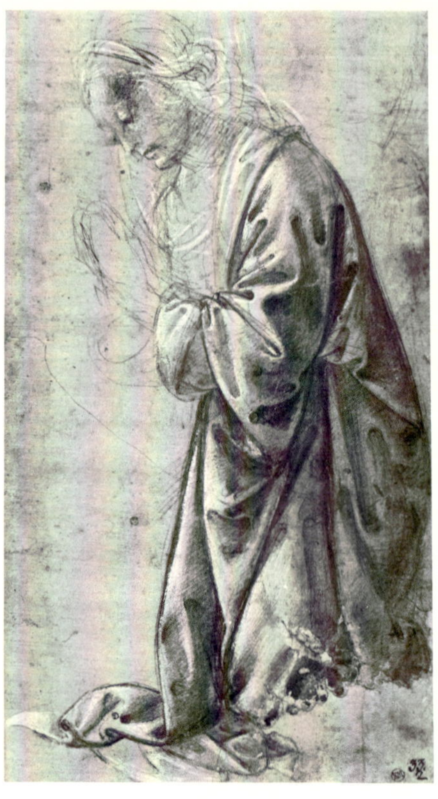

The Virgin Mary Kneeling, Study for a Nativity

Silverpoint, heightened with white, on pink prepared paper. 23.5 x 13.3 cm. Laid down. NM 54/1863. Numbered at lower right in pen and brown ink *33* and *2*. Inscribed on the old mount: *filippino*.

PROVENANCE:
Crozat (Mariette, no. 1 or 2) □ C. G. Tessin □ Kongl. Biblioteket (Cat. 1790, no. 33: Filippino Lippi) □ Kongl. Museum (Lugt 1638).

BIBLIOGRAPHY:
Sirén 1902, no. 34 (Filippino Lippi) □ Sirén 1917, no. 50 (pupil of Lorenzo di Credi) □ Schönbrunner and Meder, no. 1000 (Raffaele Botticini) □ Berenson 1938, no. 592 □ Idem 1961, no. 592 (Raffaele Botticini).

EXHIBITIONS:
Paris, Brussels, Amsterdam 1970-71, no. 7.

This is the only drawing that Berenson accepts as the work of Raffaele Botticini. In Berenson's opinion, only two paintings are by Botticini: the *Pietà* from 1508 in the Uffizi and the *Nativity* from 1512 in the Hermitage, Leningrad.

Raffaele Botticini, son of the much better-known Francesco, was evidently influenced by Lorenzo di Credi, as pointed out by Sirén.

5

LEONARDO DA VINCI ?
Vinci 1452 - Amboise 1519

Reproduced in color.

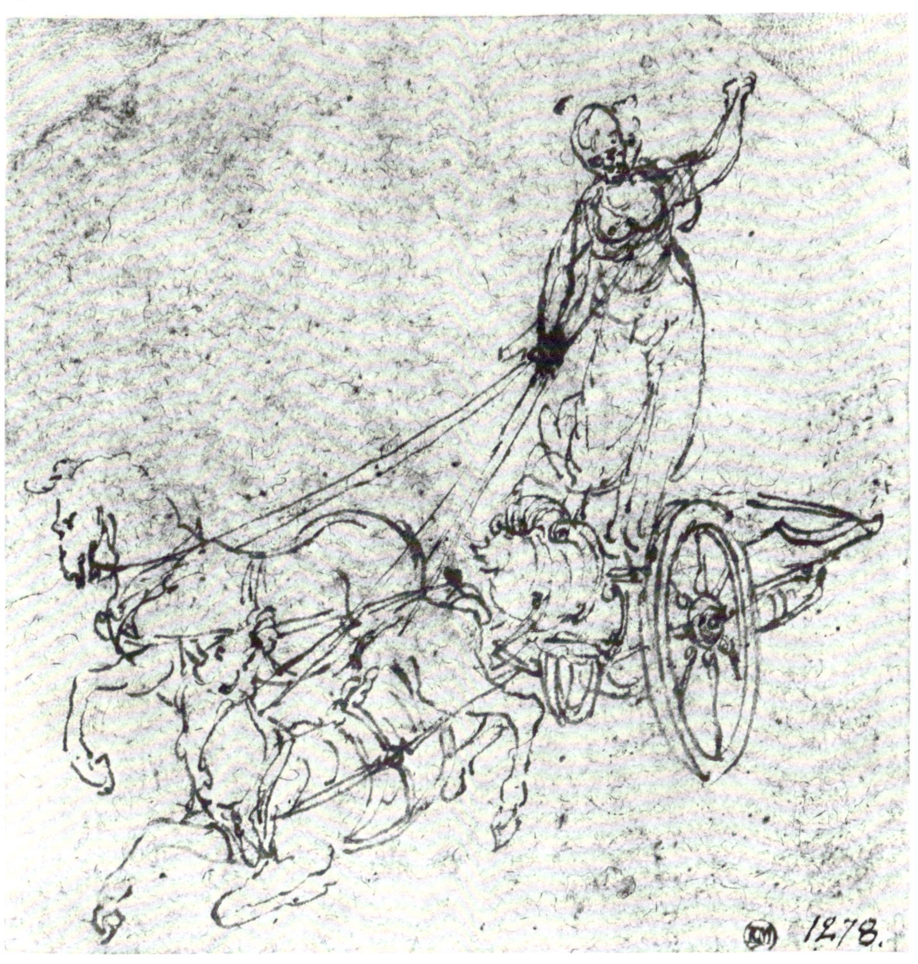

Goddess Standing in a Chariot Drawn by Two Horses, of Which One is Falling

Pen and brown ink on gray paper. 11.5 x 11 cm. No watermark. NM 1462/1863. Numbered at lower right in pen and black ink: *1278* (Sparre).

PROVENANCE:
Crozat (Mariette, no. 690 or 691) □ C. G. Tessin (List 1739-42, p. 48, v.; Cat. 1749, livré 10, no. 16) □ Kongl. Biblioteket (Cat. 1790, no. 1278) □ Kongl. Museum (Lugt 1638).

BIBLIOGRAPHY:
Sirén 1917, no. 476 □ Bjurström 1979, no. 126 (as Zelotti).

EXHIBITIONS:
Stockholm 1962, no. 236 □ Venice, Fondazione Giorgio Cini, *Disegni veronesi del cinquecento*, 1971, no. 62.

This drawing was listed under Veronese by Crozat and Tessin, but Sirén was doubtful and regarded it as belonging to Veronese's circle, certainly Venetian but probably later than Paolo Veronese. Zelotti was suggested tentatively by Fiocco; Terrence Mullaly supported this authorship in the catalogue for an exhibition at the Fondazione Cini in 1971, comparing our sheet with two other pen drawings by Zelotti at the same exhibition[1] and arguing that the three together provide a basis for assessing Zelotti's manner of drawing with the pen.

The whole question concerning the attribution of this drawing has changed after Bengt Dahlbäck in 1979 suggested that the drawing might be a work by Leonardo da Vinci, describing the sheet as an emblematic drawing of a carriage and two horses, one of which has fallen to the ground, with a standing female figure pulling the reins.

In 1983, Carlo Pedretti affirmed that the drawing is quite possibly by Leonardo, done very late, perhaps in France after 1517. The drawing is executed on coarse brown paper, as in Leonardo's latest drawings and manuscripts. Pedretti further notes that the untidy touch of the pen and careless perspective are very similar to Leonardo's latest drawings. The subject might have something to do with Leonardo's studies for a Rape of Proserpina or the "cavalli per il re Valesio" known to have been done in France.

Perhaps the fragment was at one time part of a sheet in the Codex Atlanticus.[2]

NOTES:

1. Exh. cat. Venice 1971, nos. 59 (Coll. McCrindle, New York) and 56 (Christ Church, Oxford).

2. Letter from Carlo Pedretti, 5 September 1983.

6

VITTORE CARPACCIO
Venice c. 1455 - Venice 1526

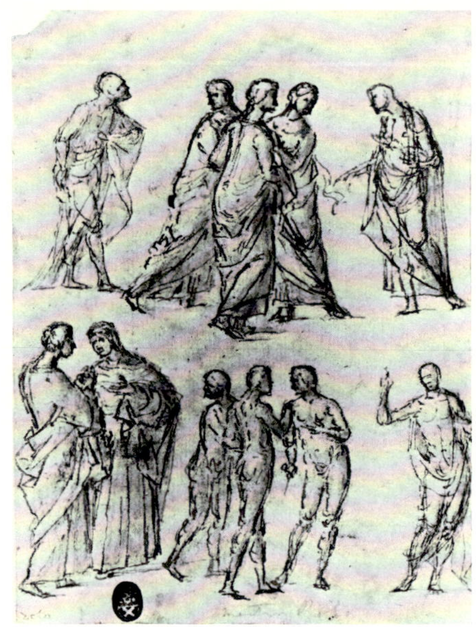

Figure Studies

Pen and brown ink, gray wash. 15.5 x 11.8 cm. Laid down. NM 31/1973.

VERSO:
The Circumcision. Red chalk. Inscribed verso in pen and brown ink: *Carpac*.

PROVENANCE:
Prince Charles de Ligne (Bartsch 1794, p. 72, no. 4, "Martin Rota") ☐ Herzog Albert von Sachsen-Teschen ☐ Count J. G. De la Gardie (Lugt 2722a) ☐ Gift to the museum in 1973 (bequest).

BIBLIOGRAPHY:
H. Tietze, "Unknown Venetian Renaissance drawings in Swedish collections," *Gazette des Beaux-Arts*, 6:30 (1949), pp. 185 f. ☐ E. Arslan, "Due disegni e un dipinto di Carpaccio," *Emporium*, 116 (1952), p. 109 f. ☐ J. Lauts, *Carpaccio*, London 1962, pp. 232, 236, 265 (drawing no. 3), pl. 164 ☐ M. Cancogni and G. Perocca, *L'opera completa del Carpaccio*, Milan 1967, p. 107 ☐ M. Muraro, *I disegni di Vittore Carpaccio*, Florence 1977, p. 78, fig. 37 ☐ Bjurström 1979, no. 31.

EXHIBITIONS:
Stockholm 1962, no. 209 ☐ Venice 1974, no. 1.

This sheet, filled with separate figure studies, belongs to a category of drawings which Carpaccio used as a starting point when working out his compositions. The number of such sheets extant is small. The closest examples are one in the Uffizi, Florence, *Five Figure Studies*, dated by Lauts to about 1505,[1] and a *Study for the Listeners in the Sermon of St. Stephen*, from 1513-14.[2] The former is also close to our sheet stylistically.

Lauts has managed to identify practically all the figures, with minor changes, in works by Carpaccio from around 1511: the group of three women, top center, appears with slight alterations in the *Ordination of St. Stephen* from 1511[3] and also in the drawing of the *Presentation of the Virgin in the Temple*.[4] The male figure, top right, appears almost unchanged in the same painting (as St. Peter) and in *St. Vitalis on Horseback and Other Saints*.[5] The two women, bottom left, in different costumes and slightly changed, appear as spectators in the *Ordination of St. Stephen*. One of them, moreover, occurs in a sheet with *Five Figure Studies* in the Uffizi.[6] Christ blessing, bottom right, is closely related to the altar figure in the *Vision of St. Augustine* in the Scuola di San Giorgio degli Schiavoni.[7]

Lauts considers that the many connections with the *Ordination of St. Stephen* from 1511 make it probable that our sheet was done during the preparation for the composition and therefore dates around 1510-11.

For the verso drawing, see sheet no. 1691 F in the Uffizi. Red chalk drawings are rare in this artist's oeuvre.

NOTES:
1. Lauts, *op. cit.*, p. 268, no. 14, pl. 121; Cancogni & Perocca, *op. cit.*, p. 113 (Florence, Uffizi).
2. Lauts, *op. cit.*, p. 265, no. 1, pl. vii-b; Cancogni & Perocca, *op. cit.*, p. 107 (Basel, R. von Hirsch coll.).
3. Lauts, *op. cit.*, p. 236, no. 26, pl. 160; Cancogni & Perocca, *op. cit.*, p. 107, no. 56A (Berlin, Staatliche Museen).
4. Lauts, *op. cit.*, p. 270, no. 21, pl. 199; Cancogni & Perocca, *op. cit.*, p. 103 (Florence, Uffizi).
5. Lauts, *op. cit.*, p. 249, no. 76, pl. 177; Cancogni & Perocca, *op. cit.*, pp. 108-09, no. 57 (Venice, San Vitale).
6. Tietze 1944, no. 603.
7. Lauts, *op. cit.*, p. 268, no. 14, pl. 121; Cancogni & Perocca, *op. cit.*, p. 113 (Florence, Uffizi).

Verso

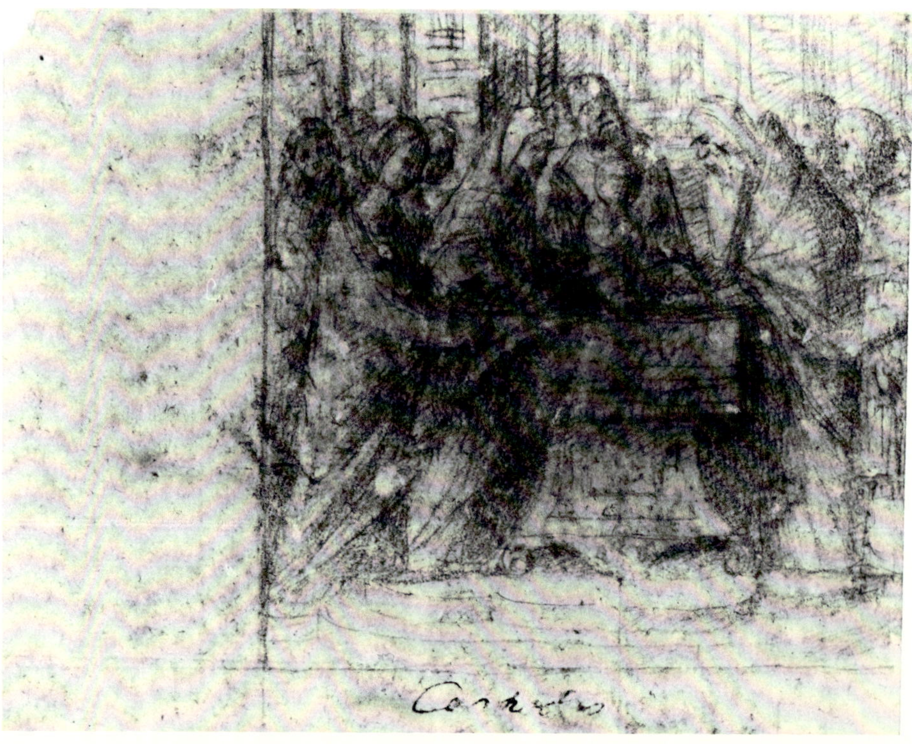

7

GIROLAMO GENGA
Urbino 1467 - Urbino 1551

Battle in Front of a Castle

Pen and brown ink. 18.8 x 27.5 cm. Watermark: Letter A (close to Briquet 1919: Venice 1503). NM 1384/1863. Inscribed at lower left in pen and brown ink: TICIAN (Antonio Santa Croce?). Numbered at lower center: 1205.

PROVENANCE:
Cardinale Antonio Santa Croce (1589-1641) ☐ Crozat (Mariette, no. 655 or 664: Deux desseins differens pour celui (le tableau) de la Bataille de Ghiaradadda) ☐ C. G. Tessin (List 1739-42, p. 60, v.; Cat. 1749, livré 10, no. 2) ☐ Kongl. Biblioteket (Cat. 1790, no. 1205) ☐ Kongl. Museum (Lugt 1638). Traditionally attributed to Titian.

BIBLIOGRAPHY:
Sirén 1902, pp. 64, 134 (Titian) ☐ Schönbrunner and Meder, no. 1075 (Titian) ☐ Sirén 1917, no. 455 (Romanino) ☐ G. Nicodemi, *Girolamo Romanino*, Brescia 1925, p. 202 ☐ L. Fröhlich-Bum, "Studien zu Handzeichnungen der italienischen Renaissance," *Jahrbuch der Kunsthistorischen Sammlungen in Wien*, N.F. 2, (1928), p. 187 (Paris Bordone) ☐ Sirén 1933, reprod. 95 ☐ W. Suida, "Romanino," *Thieme-Becker* 1934, 28, pp. 549-550 ☐ Tietze 1944, no. A 1968 (Tizian) ☐ A. Morassi, "Alcuni disegni inediti del Romanino," *Festschrift Karl M. Swoboda zum 28. Januar 1959*, Vienna 1959, p. 192 ☐ J. Bean, "Review of Drawings from Stockholm," *Master Drawings*, 7 (1969), 2, p. 170 ☐ Bjurström 1979, no. 120 (as Titian).

EXHIBITIONS:
Brescia, Palazzo della Pinacoteca Comunale, *La pittura bresciana del Rinascimento*, 1939, p. 342 (F. Lechi-G. Panazza) ☐ Stockholm 1962, no. 216 ☐ Brescia, Duomo Vecchio, *Girolamo Romanino*, 1965, no. 129 (G. Panazza) ☐ New York, Boston, Chicago 1969, no. 12 ☐ Venice 1974, no. 11.

Reproduced in color.

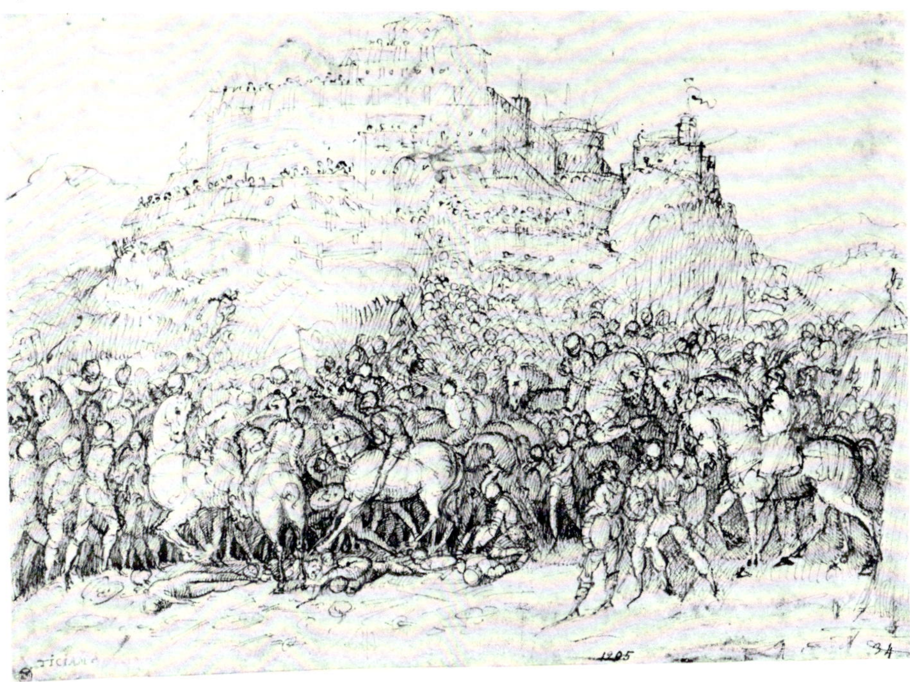

This drawing was given to Titian by Antonio Santa Croce, Crozat, and Tessin, an attribution accepted by Sirén in 1902. In 1917, however, Sirén suggested Romanino on the basis of a drawing in the Uffizi, Florence, "which displays the same stylistic peculiarities."[1] This was subsequently affirmed by G. Nicodemi, W. Suida, F. Lechi and G. Panazzo, A. Morassi, F. Kossoff, and F. Heinemann (the last two in personal communications). Paris Bordone has been proposed by L. Fröhlich-Bum. While arguing in favor of a link with Titian, the Tietzes also compare our drawing with another sheet, in Budapest,[2] which they attribute to Romanino.[3]

There are unquestionably likenesses between our drawing and the one in Budapest, but a general comparison with Romanino's drawn oeuvre is unconvincing. Romanino's figures are constructed by adding the components: trunk, legs, arms, head. Correct anatomical proportions are often lost. He shades with parallel lines in groups as well as with short, comma-like strokes and dots.

None of these characteristics is present in our drawing. On the contrary, each figure is a well-proportioned whole and the foreground figural groups, although they stand out, are tied in with the mid- and background. In Romanino's drawings with many figures, the composition tends to break down into distinct layers.

Our drawing has also been connected with one of the paintings belonging to the series of twenty-two compositions in the Sala del Gran Consiglio in the Palazzo Ducale in Venice, executed by Titian between 1513 and 1537. This identification is, however, questionable. Moreover, the drawing differs considerably from a sheet in the Louvre which has been mentioned in connection with the same composition.

An attribution to Girolamo Genga seems likely on the basis of similarities with two sheets of similar battle scenes in the British Museum[4] and the Louvre.[5] Common to all three works is the drawing of the horses and the small muscular figures in the midst of dense crowds. The technique of backing up detailed foreground figures with more distant fragmentary renderings, overdrawn with a close network of shading, also appears in the works under discussion. The British Museum and Louvre sheets, together with one in the Fondazione Horne, Florence (5951), have been connected by Pouncey with the decoration of the Villa Imperiale at Pesaro. Genga was employed by the Duke of Urbino, Francesco Maria della Rovere, to restore, enlarge, and embellish his residence from 1522-23.

NOTES:

1. No. 683, Exh. cat. Brescia 1965, no. 118.
2. Tietze 1944, no. A 307.
3. Exh. cat. Venice 1965, no. 14. The sheet is accepted as a work of Romanino by Morassi, who dates it c. 1530 and connects it with the frescoes in Trento.
4. P. Pouncey and J. A. Gere, *Italian Drawings in the Department of Prints and Drawings in the British Museum*, London 1962, no. 271, pl. 253.
5. R. Bacou, *Autour de Raphael, Dessins et peintures du Musée du Louvre*, 80e exposition du Cabinet des Dessins, Paris 1984, p. 14, no. 7 (ill.).

8

TIZIANO VECELLI
Cadore 1485/88 - Venice 1576

Reproduced in color.

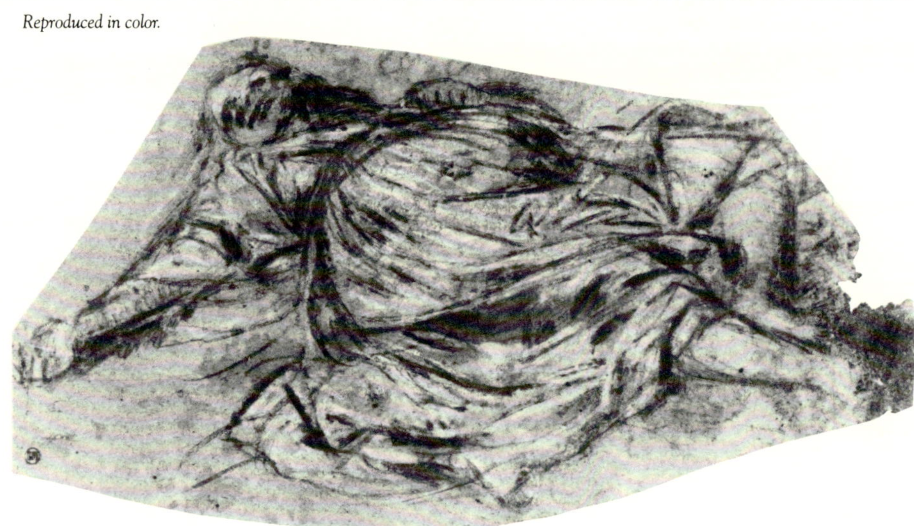

Girl Lying on Her Back with One Arm Outstretched

Black chalk, heightened with white on grayish blue paper. 24 x 12.5 cm. Cut irregularly close to the motif. Far right, a patch of oil that has partly destroyed the paper. Laid down. NM 1385/1863. Inscribed on the old mount at lower right in pen and brown ink: *TICIANO* (Antonio Santa Croce?). Numbered at lower right: *1206* (Sparre), *35* and *21* (struck out).

PROVENANCE:
Cardinal Antonio Santa Croce (1589-1641) □ Crozat (Mariette, no. 664?) □ C. G. Tessin (List 1739-42, p. 60, v.; Cat. 1749, livré 10, no. 3) □ Kongl. Biblioteket (Cat. 1790, no. 1260) □ Kongl. Museum (Lugt 1638).

BIBLIOGRAPHY:
Sirén 1902, p. 65, no. 156 (Tintoretto) □ Sirén 1917, no. 464 (school of Tintoretto) □ Tietze 1944, no. A 1967 (Titian, circle of) □ H. Tietze, "Studies from nature by Titian," *Nationalmusei Årsbok*, 19-20 (1949-50), p. 27, fig. 4 □ J. Bean 1969, p. 170 □ Bjurström 1979, no. 119.

EXHIBITIONS:
Stockholm 1962, no. 221 □ Paris, Brussels, Amsterdam 1970-71, no. 10 □ Venice 1974, no. 12.

This drawing was acquired by Tessin together with the previous number. Both works probably came from the collection of Antonio Santa Croce, where they were attributed to Titian. This authorship was accepted until 1902, when Sirén linked the drawings with Tintoretto. In 1944, the Tietzes listed the sheet as a work from Titian's circle but after seeing the original in 1952, Hans Tietze published it as by Titian, comparing it with the *St. Peter* in London, dated about 1516-18,[1] and the *Study for St. Bernard* in the votive painting for the Doge Gritti in the Uffizi, dated about 1531.[2]

As Tietze points out, there is a clear likeness between the motif of the girl lying on her back with outstretched arm and the *Miracle of the Jealous Husband* in the Scuola del Santo in Padua, from 1510-11, with the same strongly foreshortened woman.[3] He hesitates, however, to date the drawing as early as this, arguing that "it is an independent treatment of a similar motive, not invented by the artist, but forced upon him by some visual experience that broke through his artistic defences."[4]

The character of the drawing admittedly makes it reasonable to consider a date in the 1540s or 1550s, but there is also so much agreement with the study of St. Peter for *The Assumption of the Virgin* in Santa Maria dei Frari, Venice, from 1516-18, that the drawing could conceivably be connected directly with the Padua fresco. This view is also expressed by Bert W. Meijer:

> When considered along with the early dating, the similarities between the drawing and the fresco prove to be more convincing than the differences, which are admittedly considerable. The woman's garments are virtually identical in the two works, and corresponding no less decisively is her position on the ground. Whereas a nude Venus(-like) figure reclining parallel to the picture plane occurs rather frequently in Titian's *oeuvre*, a fully dressed woman lying on her back in a more or less diagonal position is extremely rare. It would therefore be highly illogical to assume that this same exceptional motive happened only by coincidence in the contemporaneous drawing and a scene that formed part of the fresco cycle at Padua, Titian's first major independent commission.[5]

NOTES:

1. Tietze 1944, no. 1929.
2. Tietze 1944, no. 1904.
3. Cf. H. E. Wethey, *The Paintings of Titian*, 1, London 1969, p. 128, no. 95, fig. 141.
4. Tietze, *op. cit.* 1952, p. 37.
5. B. W. Meijer, "Early drawings by Titian: Some attributions," *Arte Veneta*, 28 (1974), pp. 85 f.

9

GIROLAMO ROMANINO?
Brescia 1484/87 - Brescia 1562?

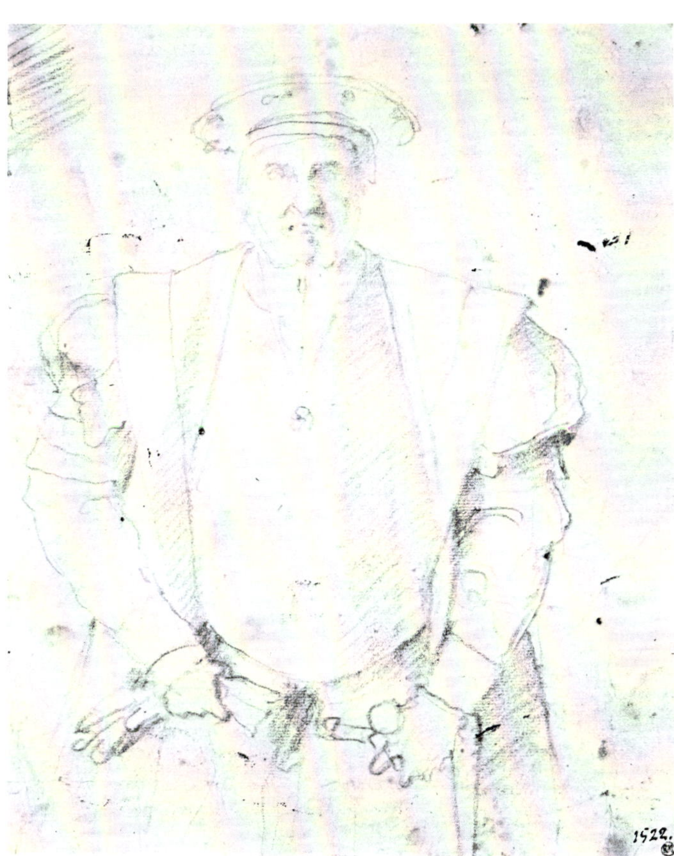

Verso

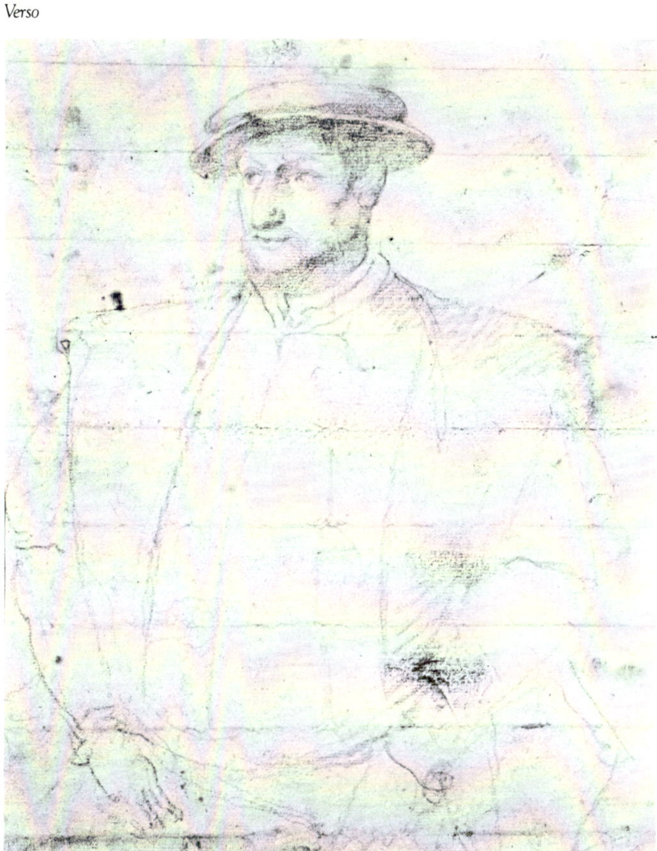

Frontal Study of a Man in Sumptuous Costume

Red chalk. 14.2 x 19.5 cm. No watermark. NM 1716-1717/1863. Numbered at lower right in pen and brown ink: *1522*.

VERSO:
Portrait of a Man. Red chalk.

PROVENANCE:
C. G. Tessin (Cat. 1749, livré 25, no. 52-209?) □ Kongl. Biblioteket (Cat. 1790, no. 1522) □ Kongl. Museum (Lugt 1638).

BIBLIOGRAPHY:
Bjurström 1979, no. 243.

This drawing probably was part of Tessin's collection, although it lacks a traditional attribution. It is an accomplished work with obvious similarities to the few extant sheets by Romanino done in red chalk: one of a man in prayer,[1] another of a German lansquenet,[2] and a third of the Virgin with St. Anthony and St. Francis.[3] All display relatively schematic hatching and a nervous, almost rotating outline. The drawing of hands is particularly characteristic and is a detail common to all the above mentioned sheets as well as to sheets done with a pen.

These two figures have not been identified in paintings by Romanino but they recall the frescoes in the Cremona cathedral from the early 1520s. The costumes, of North Italian type, are consistent with such a date.

NOTES:
1. Gabinetto dei Disegni e Stampe, Uffizi, Florence. Cf. G. Panazza, *Mostra di Girolamo Romanino*, exh. cat., Brescia 1965, no. 119.
2. Collection Janos Scholz, New York. Cf. G. Panazza, *op. cit.*, no. 123.
3. Collection Rasini, Milan. Cf. G. Panazza, *op. cit.*, no. 122.

10

GIOVANNI GIROLAMO SAVOLDO
Brescia c. 1480 - Brescia after 1548

Reproduced in color.

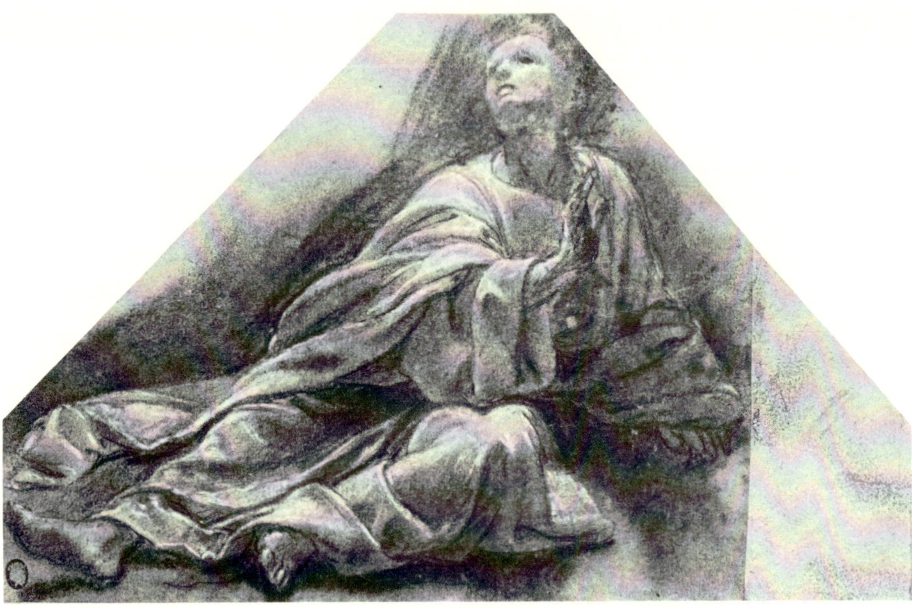

St. John the Evangelist

Black and white chalk on blue paper. 19.7 x 26.1 cm. Irregularly cut; a large section of the upper left-hand corner and a smaller part of the upper right cut away. Laid down. NM 375/1973.

PROVENANCE:
Prince Charles de Ligne (Bartsch 1794, p. 454, no. 95: unknown) □ Herzog Albert von Sachsen-Teschen □ Count J. G. De la Gardie (Lugt 2722a) □ Gift to the museum in 1973 (bequest).

BIBLIOGRAPHY:
H. Tietze, "Unknown Venetian Renaissance drawings in Swedish collection," *Gazette des Beaux-Arts*, 6:30 (1949), pp. 186 f. □ C. Gilbert, "Savoldo's drawings put to use," *Gazette des Beaux-Arts*, 6:41 (1953), pp. 5 ff. (Published also in *Essays in Honor of Hans Tietze 1880-1954*, New York 1958, pp. 95 ff.) □ Bjurström 1979, no. 246.

EXHIBITIONS:
Venice 1974, no. 5.

This drawing was identified in 1949 by Tietze as a preparatory study for St. John the Evangelist in Savoldo's painting of *The Transfiguration* in the Pitti Gallery (temporarily exhibited in the Uffizi), Florence. The sheet gives a good impression of the monumentality in this artist's style and his command of the anatomical structure behind the rich folds of the dress.

It is important as one of three drawings with direct links to Savoldo's paintings.[1] Creighton Gilbert considers that they were done after the artist had executed an initial painted version of the composition; he notes its revisionist quality and asserts it served as a basis for the workshop copy of *The Transfiguration* in the Ambrosiana, Milan. The figure of the Baptist is indeed closer to our sheet than this is to the earlier version.

The same applies to another study that is connected directly with this composition, the *Head of an Apostle* in the Uffizi,[2] which Gilbert interprets as supporting his theory about our drawing. The copy is faithful throughout and presupposes that the artist had access to Savoldo's original painting. But at times the copy departs from the model and therefore, he argues, the drawings were revisions of the painting.

But the workshop copy is a small painting, 21 x 27 cm, the whole composition being no bigger than our study of a detail. It seems conceivable that the copyist felt more tied to the drawn sketches at his disposal than Savoldo did when he started work on his large canvas. This would suffice to explain the discrepancies noted by Gilbert and would place our drawing earlier than the original version.

NOTES:
1. Tietze 1944, no. 1405, *St. John the Evangelist* (Berlin), *Study for a Pietà*, regarded by Gilbert as a condensation by Savoldo himself in connection with *The Deposition*, formerly Kaiser Friedrich Museum, burnt in 1945; Tietze 1944, no. 1415, *Head of St. Jerome* (Paris, Louvre). It is connected with a painting of the same subject in the National Gallery, London.
2. Tietze 1944, no. 1408.

11

PARIS BORDONE
Treviso 1500 - Treviso 1570

Reproduced in color.

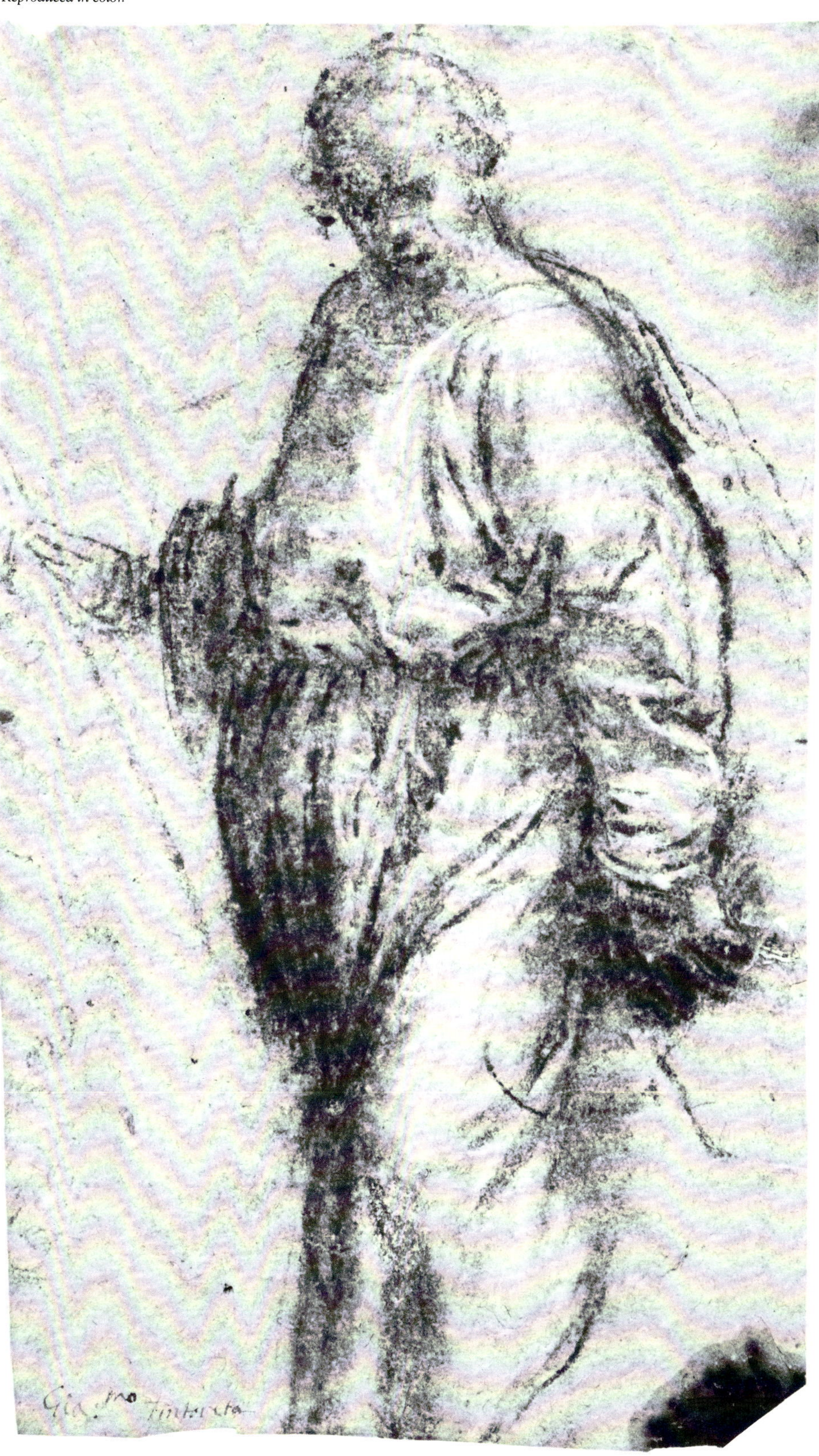

Walking Male Figure

Black chalk heightened with white on bluish paper. 30.4 x 17.5 cm. Oil patches on upper right; lower right corner cut, darkened patch of oil. Laid down. NM 1606/1875. Inscribed at lower left in pen and brown ink: *Gia. mo Tintoreto.*

PROVENANCE:
J. T. Sergel (Lugt 2339b).

BIBLIOGRAPHY:
Bjurström 1979, no. 6.

EXHIBITIONS:
Stockholm 1962, no. 225 □ Venice 1974, no. 16.

An attempt to trace the activities of Paris Bordone as a draughtsman was made by Tietze in 1944.[1] Already Vasari noted that Bordone imitated Titian, especially in his drawings. Bordone probably worked for Titian in the early 1520s, when he adopted a manner of drawing which is very close to that of the master. During the next few decades he kept to this manner on the whole, though his work acquired a more personal stamp.

As a starting point for the drawing, Tietze posited a study for the fisherboy in the foreground of *The Fisherman Delivering the Ring to the Doge*, from 1534.[2] Our drawing has a purely technical affinity with this sheet in the wealth of short, sharp folds and the contrast between light and dark parts of the costume.

Stylistically, however, there are closer parallels in drawings that have been dated to Bordone's later works, for instance *The Draped Figure* in the Uffizi, Florence,[3] which has the same loose form as our sheet. Rearick is inclined to date that drawing to the 1550s and emphasizes its representativeness for the artist's late work "con il suo gioco luministico nervoso e franto sul panneggio svolazzante e la sua tendenza a evitare brani anatomici difficoltosi come ad esempio la mano."[4] This description is equally applicable to our sheet, which no doubt also belongs to Bordone's later years.

NOTES:
1. Tietze 1944, pp. 118 f.
2. Tietze 1944, p. 121, no. 405, in Ashmolean Museum. K. T. Parker, *Disegni veneti di Oxford* (exh. cat.) Fondazione Giorgio Cini, Venice 1958, no. 24; cf. also G. Canova, *Paris Bordon*, Venice 1964, pp. 93 f., figs. 37-42.
3. Inv. no. 15020 F; D. von Hadeln, *Venezianische Zeichnungen der Hochrenaissance*, Berlin 1925, p. 30, fig. 61; Tietze 1944, no. 397.
4. W. R. Rearick, *Tiziano e il disegno veneziano del suo tempo*, Cat. Gabinetto disegni e stampe degli Uffizi, 45, Florence 1976, p. 85, no. 45.

12

RAFFAELLO SANTI
called RAPHAEL
Urbino 1483 - Rome 1520

Reproduced in color.

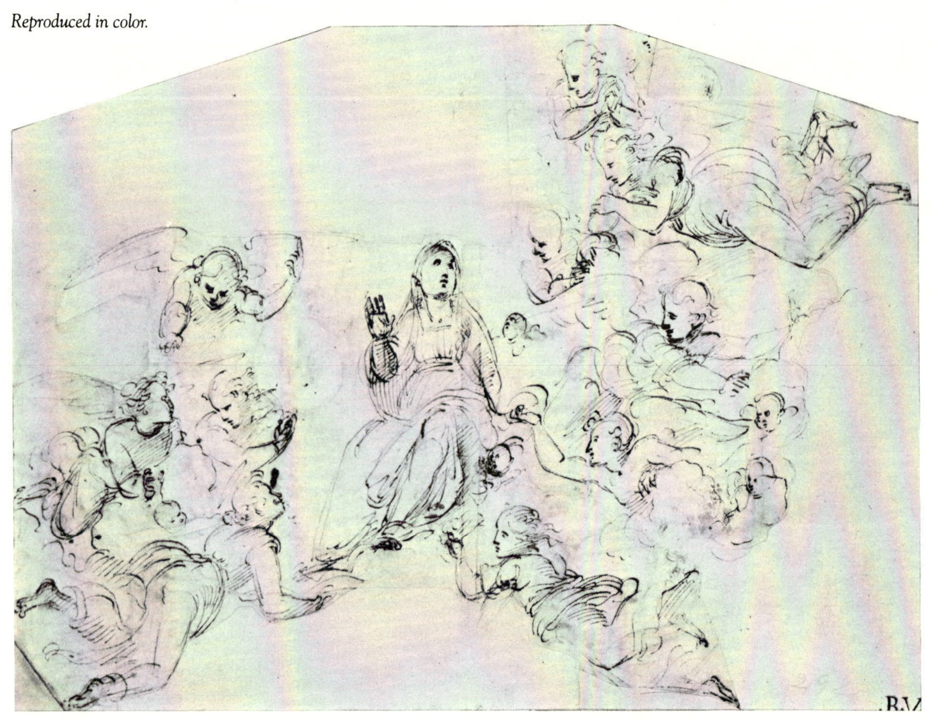

The Ascension of the Virgin

Traces of black chalk, pen and brown ink. 23.5 x 32.4 cm. No watermark. Pieces of paper glued secondarily around the motif. Central vertical fold. Mendings with small strips of paper in the middle, at lower right, and at lower and upper left. NM 292/1863. Inscribed at lower right in pen and brown ink: *.R.V.* (Lugt 2245).

VERSO:
The Annunciation. Traces of black chalk, pen and brown ink. 43.1 x 27.2 cm. NM 291/1863. Inscribed at lower right in pen and brown ink: 48, 240 (Sparre) and *.R.V.* (Lugt 2245).

PROVENANCE:
Collection Viti-Antaldi (Lugt 2245) □ Acquired by Crozat in 1714 (Mariette 1741, no. 127, "l'Annonciation de la sainte Vierge, et au revers son Assomption") □ C. G. Tessin (List 1739-42, p. 39 v., Cat. 1749, livré 16, no. 13) □ Kongl. Biblioteket (Cat. 1790, no. 240) □ Kongl. Museum (Lugt 1638).

BIBLIOGRAPHY:

J. D. Passavant, *Raphael von Urbino und sein Vater*, Leipzig 1839-58, II, p. 463 b □ J. C. Robinson, *Critical Account of the Drawings of Michel Ange and Raffaello in the University Galleries at Oxford*, Oxford 1870, no. 16 □ Sirén 1902, nos. 95-96 (Gianfrancesco Penni) □ Sirén 1917, nos. 302-303 □ Schönbrunner and Meder 1896-1908, nos. 919 and 1054 (Penni) □ O. Fischel, *Raphaels Zeichnungen*, 5, Berlin 1924, no. 215 (The Annunciation), 8, Berlin 1941, no. 381 (The Ascension) □ J. Shearman, "The Chigi Chapel in S. Maria del Popolo," *Journal of the Warburg and Courtauld Institutes*, 24 (1961), pp. 142 and 155 □ J. Shearman, "Raphael, Rome and the Codex Excurialensis," *Master Drawings*, 15 (1977), p. 134 (The Annunciation) □ M. Salmi (ed.), *Raffaello, l'opera, le fonti, la fortuna*, Novara 1968, p. 397 □ E. Knab, E. Mitsch, and K. Oberhuber, *Raphael - Die Zeichnungen*, Stuttgart 1983, no. 213 (The Annunciation), no. 331 (The Ascension) □ P. Joannides, *The Drawings of Raphael*, Oxford 1983, no. 317.

EXHIBITIONS:
Paris, Brussels, Amsterdam 1970-71, no. 9.

Fischel established, in his authoritative catalogue of drawings by Raphael, that our *Ascension* is an original work and not, as asserted earlier, a workshop product by Francesco Penni. Fischel dated the drawing to the beginning of Raphael's time in Rome and linked it with a similar sheet in the Oxford Ashmolean (Fischel 380) which relates to a commission, obtained in 1503 and renewed in 1505, for an altar painting with an Ascension for the nuns at Monteluce, near Perugia. In the interval between the contracts the commission was enlarged to include the scene of the Coronation of the Virgin. Research has shown that Raphael never completed the undertaking; this was left to his pupils, Penni and Giulio Romano, who followed his intentions twenty years later. The altar painting is now in the Vatican (for the complicated story and fate of the painting see *Rafaello in Vaticano*, Exh. cat., Città del Vaticano 1984-85, nos. 108-114.)

An alternative purpose for both drawings was put forward by Shearman in 1961. He found iconographic evidence that the works were part of Raphael's program for the Chigi Chapel in S. Maria del Popolo, Rome, namely sketches for an altar painting, never executed, which was intended for the burial chapel. This would date the sheets to shortly after 1510, as work on the building is generally considered to have started around 1512.

The *Annunciation* on the verso of our sheet is done on the same paper as the recto; the difference in size has to do with the mount. Here the whole of the sheet is exposed. The drawing is catalogued by Fischel as a skillful but dependent work by a pupil in the circle around Raphael. More recent compilers (Knab, Mitsch, and Oberhuber 1983, Joannides 1983) are more inclined to classify it as an original drawing, datable around 1506-08 when Raphael was in Florence. The characteristic background architecture displays certain similarities with an *Annunciation* painted by Mariotto Albertinelli, signed and dated 1510 (Accademia, Florence). This has prompted the suggestion that Raphael's drawing was intended for the same project as the Florentine's.

13

UNKNOWN ARTIST
NORTHERN ITALY
Second half of the 16th century

Three Singers Accompanied by a Lutanist

Black chalk, heightened with white on blue paper. Squared in red chalk. 40.6 x 35 cm. Upper left corner cut and restored. Watermark: Fleur de lis (primitive). NM 1389/1863. Inscribed at lower left in pen and black ink: *Cabinet de Crozat* (Tessin), further right in pen and brown ink: *TICIAN* (Santa Croce?). Numbered *1208* (Sparre) and *29* (struck out).

PROVENANCE:
Cardinal Antonio Santa Croce (1589-1641) ☐ Crozat (Mariette, no. 655) ☐ C. G. Tessin (List 1739-42, p. 48 r,; Cat. 1749, livré 10, no. 5) ☐ Kongl. Biblioteket (Cat. 1790, no. 1208) ☐ Kongl. Museum (Lugt 1638). Traditionally attributed to Titian.

BIBLIOGRAPHY:
Sirén 1917, no. 458 (Veronese artist) ☐ Bjurström 1979, no. 372.

EXHIBITIONS:
Venice 1974, no. 38 (North Italian artist).

The drawing has had a roving attribution. It was given to Titian from the early seventeenth century (Cardinal Santa Croce) until Sirén placed the sheet in the circle of Paolo Veronese. Ugo Ruggeri agreed with Rodolfo Pallucchini's opinion that the artist is to be sought in the circle around Parmigianino[1] while Creighton Gilbert (personal communication) preferred a Cremonese artist, possibly in the group of Bernadino Campi.

The drawing cannot be connected with the style of drawing in Parma, nor are there any pegs on which to hang an attribution to Campi.

Another drawing formerly associated with Veronese, *Study of a Bearded Man with His Right Arm Raised*, in the Gathorne-Hardy collection, has proved to be a study by Giuseppe Porta il Salviati for the fresco of *The Reconciliation between Alessandro III and Fredric Barbarossa*, in the Sala Regia in the Vatican, datable c. 1564. Certain likenesses with the present sheet are not without interest. Instead of a certain slender refinement in the picture of a bearded man, our sheet has squatter proportions. The most noteworthy aspect of the present drawing is the four figures' obvious musical experience and involvement. They are drawn frontally but their gazes seem to be directed, not at the viewer, but at some distant object as if they were enchanted by music.

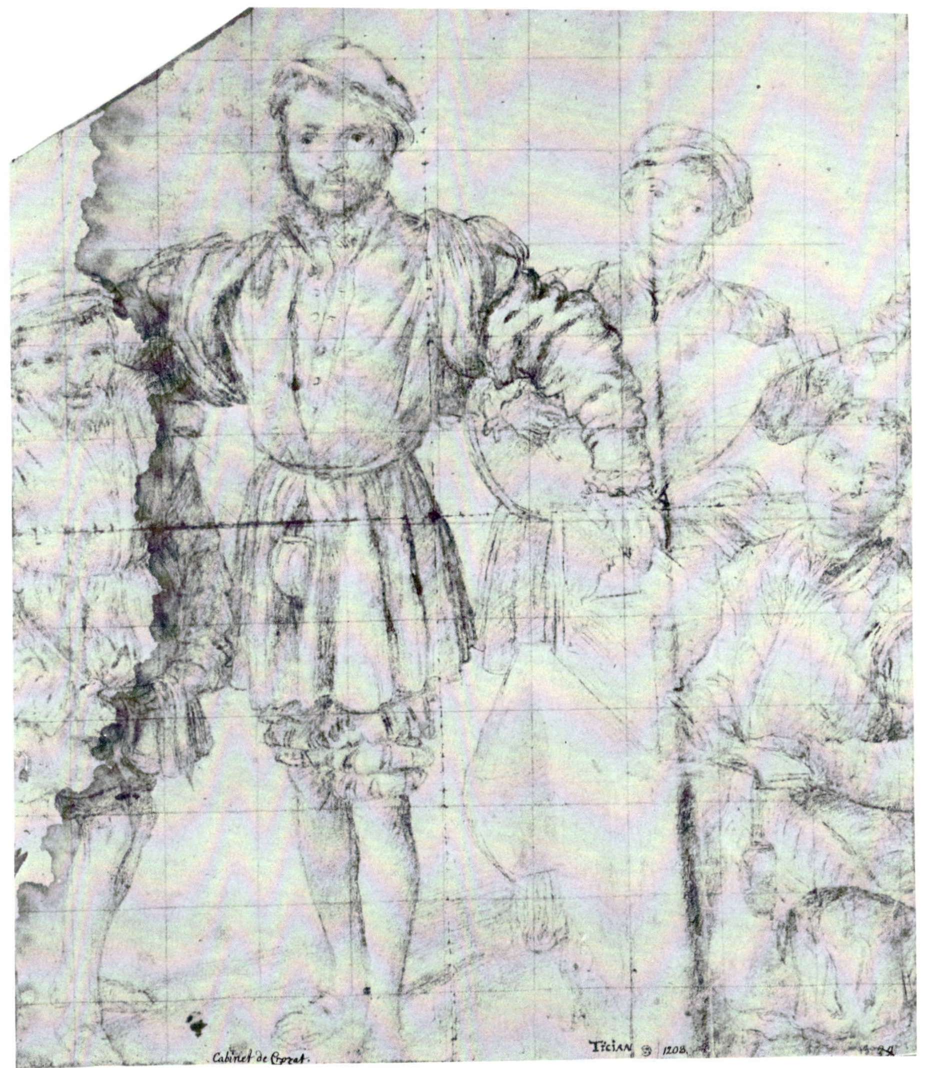

NOTES:
1. U. Ruggeri, "Disegni veneti del museo di Stoccolma esposti alla Fondazione Cini," *Arte Veneta*, 28 (1974), p. 329.
2. (J. Stock), *Loan Exhibition of Drawings by Old Masters from the Collection of Mr. Geoffrey Gathorne-Hardy*, P & D. Colnaghi & Co., London 1971-72, no. 30. Sotheby's Auction catalogue, Gathorne-Hardy Collection, 28 April 1976, no. 11.

14

POLIDORO
DA CARAVAGGIO
Caravaggio 1490/1500 - Messina 1543

Reproduced in color.

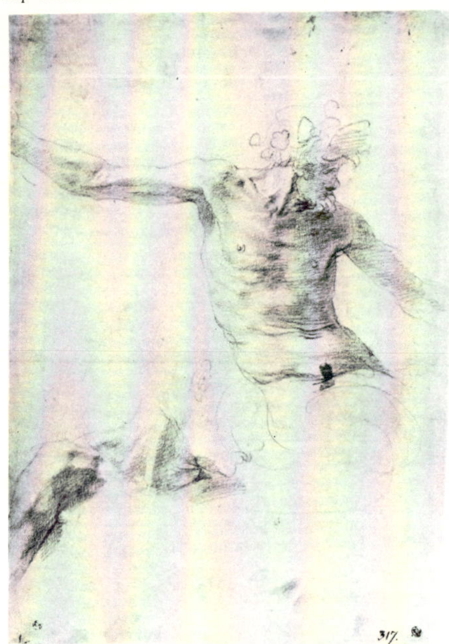

Verso

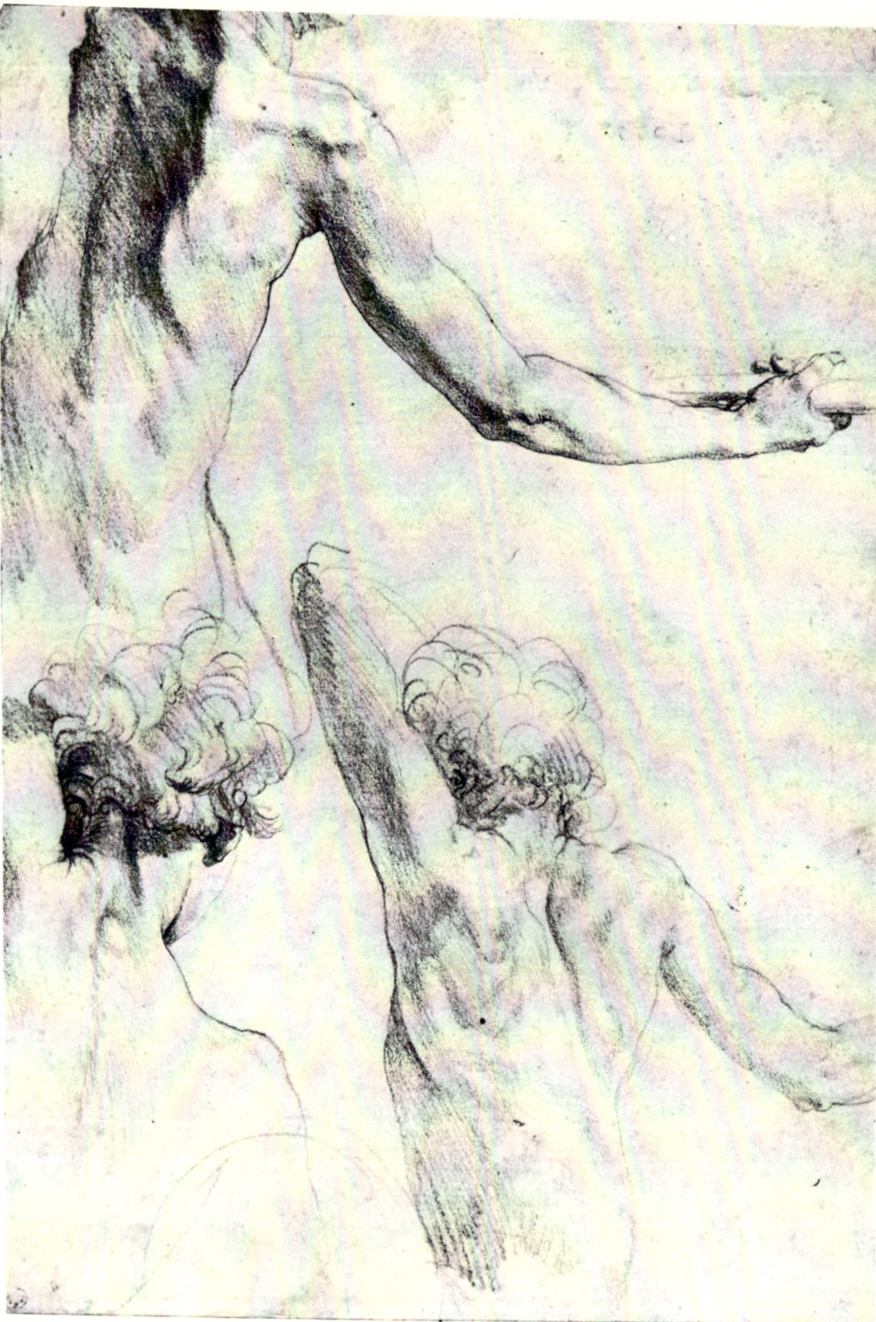

Figure Studies, Possibly for a Triton

Red chalk. 27.5 x 18.6 cm. No watermark. NM 377-378/1863. Numbered in the lower right corner in pen and brown ink: *317* (Sparre).

VERSO:
Three Studies of the Back and Shoulders of a Male Nude. Red chalk.

PROVENANCE:
C. G. Tessin? □ Kongl. Biblioteket (Cat. 1790, no. 317) □ Kongl. Museum (Lugt 1638).

Both sides of the sheet are filled with studies after models. The attributes of the principal recto figure suggest that this could be a draft for a particular composition. The features are slightly grotesque, the head is wreathed with leaves and the lower part of the body ends with some loose strokes of the chalk in a way that brings to mind mythological sea creatures. A conceivable use of the study is a frieze of the type that Polidoro employed when composing compositions for painted facades.

The verso contains three studies of a skinny youth seen from behind with one arm outstretched backwards and the other raised above his head. The model is almost certainly the same as in a drawing in the Berlin Kupferstichkabinett, also with a markedly twisted back and a raised arm, seen there from the front view. Our sheet can accordingly be assigned to a group of red chalk figure studies with a probable date in the mid-1530s.

15

GIULIO PIPPI
called GIULIO ROMANO
Rome 1493 - Mantua 1546

Reproduced in color.

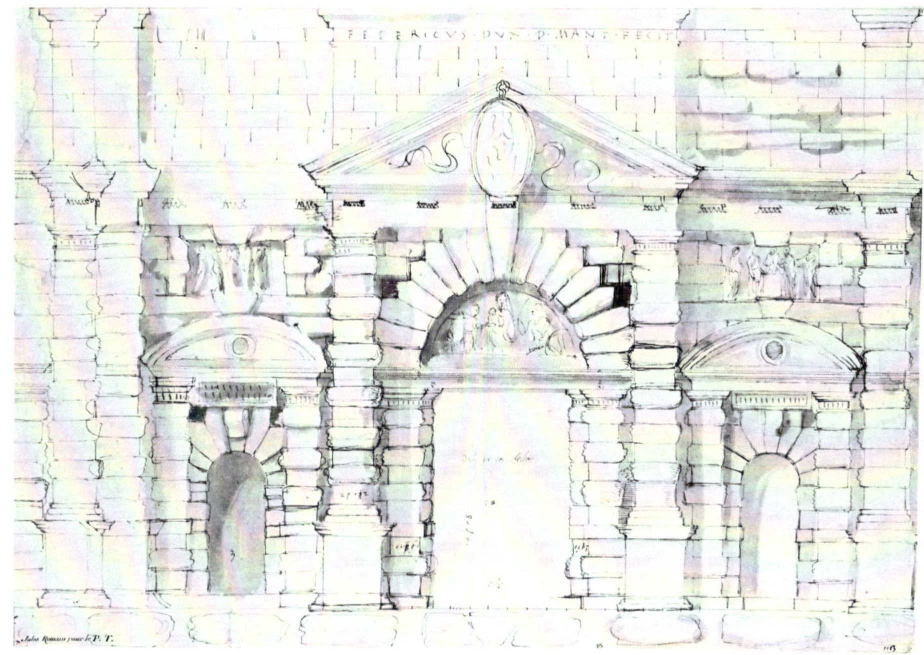

Study for Porta della Cittadèlla in Mantua

Pen and brown ink, brown wash 37.0 x 55.2 cm. Lined. A small strip of paper (8.5 x 1.5 cm) missing in upper left corner. Scratches in upper left margin. Central vertical folds. NM 360/1863. Inscribed in upper part of the portico in brown ink: *FEDERICUS DUX. P. MANT. FECIT.* In the archway in brown ink and Romano's own handwriting: *Dela porta deCta.* At lower left in black ink: *Jules Romain pour le P. T.* (for the handwriting see comments in catalogue *Disegni di una collezione veneziana del Settecento*, Venice 1966, p. 14). Measurements in brown ink.

PROVENANCE:
Anonymous eighteenth century collector (see catalogue *Disegni di una collezione veneziana del Settecento*, Venice 1966, p. 14) ☐ Crozat (?) ☐ C. G. Tessin (List 1739-42, p. 59 r.; Cat. 1749, livré 16, no. 14) ☐ Kongl. Biblioteket (Cat. 1790, no. 240) ☐ Kongl. Museum (Lugt 1638).

BIBLIOGRAPHY:
Sirén 1902, no. 118 ☐ Sirén 1917, no. 320 ☐ F. Hartt, "Drawings by Giulio Romano in the National Museum in Stockholm," *Nationalmusei Årsbok* (1939), p. 51, fig. 25 ☐ Idem, *Giulio Romano, I-II*, New Haven 1958, pp. 194f, fig. 416.

This drawing was interpreted as a project for the Palazzo del Té, but Hartt has shown that it has to do with the fortifications in Mantua. An authentic inscription in the central gateway of the drawing can be deciphered as "Dela porta deCta," indicating that the draft was for the still extant Porta della Citadella. From this gateway one can pass from the city to a small moated fortress overlooking the approaches from Verona and Brescia via the important Ponte dei Molini. The work of strengthening Mantua's defenses had been started by Duke Federigo of Gonzaga in 1533, three years after he had been given this title by the Emperor Charles V.

The Albertina, Vienna, has another two drafts, somewhat more finished, by Giulio for the same project (inv. nos. 14203 and 14204). All three vary the same architectural scheme, largely derived from Rome's tripartite triumphal arches and the highly rusticated Porta Maggiore. In Giulio's proposal only the central arch is a proper gateway; the smaller, flanking arches are envisaged as niches.

Our drawing is a preliminary sketch for Albertina no. 14204. The edifice stands on a robust stylobate that the first draft (no. 14203) does not have. The right and left parts differ in matters of detail, which accordingly represent alternative proposals. The rustication of the columns, pilasters, and wall surfaces meshes in an intricate pattern. As a sketch this is one of Giulio Romano's freest and most brilliant architectural sheets. It should be dated in the 1530s.

16

TADDEO ZUCCARO
S. Agnolo in Vado 1529 - Rome 1566

Reproduced in color.

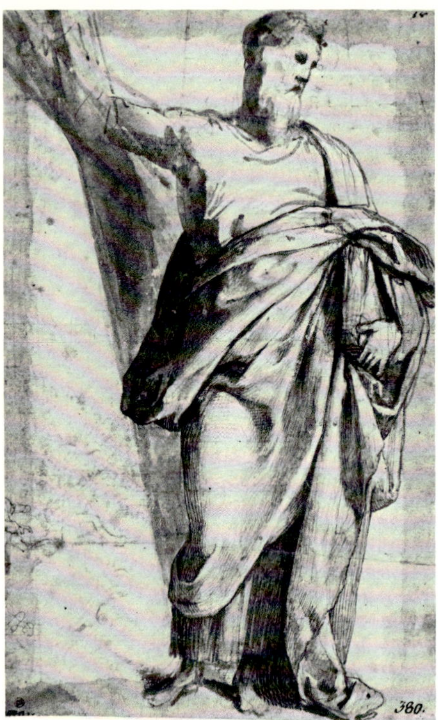

St. Paul or St. Andrew

Brush and red ink, red wash, white body color. Traces of underdrawing in black chalk. The book outlined in pen. 28.7 x 17.6 cm. No watermark. Vertical and horizontal folds. NM 452/1863. Inscribed in upper right in brown ink: 38, in lower right in brown ink: 380 (Sparre).

VERSO:
Design for the stucco decoration of a ceiling. Pen and brown ink. Traces of underdrawing in red chalk.

PROVENANCE:
C. G. Tessin (List 1739-42, p. 51 r.; Cat. 1749, livré 8, no. 64) □ Kongl. Biblioteket (Cat. 1790, no. 380) □ Kongl. Museum (Lugt 1638).

BIBLIOGRAPHY:
Sirén 1917, no. 385 □ J. A. Gere, *Taddeo Zuccaro. His Development Studied in his Drawings*, London 1969, no. 223, pl. 100.

The attribution to Taddeo Zuccaro is traditional. The presence of a cross caused Sirén to interpret the drawing as a study for St. Andrew, but Gere has drawn attention to other possibilities, juxtaposing our sheet with similar drawings by this artist in The Art Institute of Chicago, Windsor Library, the Louvre, and the Albertina. They all show a bearded man dressed in garments with many folds holding his arm round a weighty volume. In all these drawings the technique is the same as is the chiselled representation of the figure as a solitary sculpture on an otherwise empty sheet.

Gere considers that all these studies are done after wax models, clothed in proper garments made of thin fabric soaked in an emulsion so that it stiffens in the appropriate folds when dry. Most of the studies are clearly work for the fresco of *Paul Healing a Cripple* in the Frangipani Chapel in S. Marcello al Corso, Rome, a project that Taddeo started about 1558-59, but had not completed when he died in 1566.

The Stockholm study could thus have originally been done for the figure of Paul in the Frangipani Chapel and subsequently been transformed by the artist into a St. Andrew through the addition of a cross.

The verso drawing is a schematic representation of a stucco ceiling consisting of four elongated ovals surrounding a central rectangular field, bordered with downward, ornamental ribs ending in cartouches.

This ceiling scheme is equally applicable, according to Gere, to the Camera di Isabella in the Castello Orsini (now Odescalchi) and to the two rooms which Taddeo decorated in the Palazzo Caetani, Rome. Gere dates both alternatives to c. 1559-60.

17

TADDEO ZUCCARO

The Virgin and St. Joseph and Other Figures on the Right of an Adoration of the Magi

Black chalk, touched in places with white chalk. 65.8 x 41.0 cm. No watermark. The sheet is made up of four pieces of paper, the horizontal join being just above the Virgin's elbow. The vertical join close to the left hand edge. Strip of paper (16.0 x 1.5 cm) glued on the sheet in the middle part to the left. NM 1361/1863. Inscribed in lower left in black chalk: *Muciano*, in lower right in pen and brown ink: *1181* (Sparre).

VERSO:
The Virgin and Other Figures on the Right of an Adoration of the Shepherds. Black chalk. NM 1360/1863.

PROVENANCE:
C. G. Tessin (List 1739-42, p. 59 v.; Cat. 1749, livré 16, no. 63) ☐ Kongl. Biblioteket (Cat. 1790, no. 1181) ☐ Kongl. Museum (Lugt 1638).

BIBLIOGRAPHY:
J. A. Gere, "Two panel-pictures by Taddeo Zuccaro, and some related compositions - I: The 'Adoration of the Magi' in the Fitzwilliam Museum," *The Burlington Magazine*, 15 (1963), p. 363, figs. 28 and 29 ☐ Gere 1969, no. 227, pl. 77.

In the Tessin inventories this and another sheet (NM 1362/1863) are listed under the name Girolami Muziano. Sirén did not include either of them in his catalogue of the Italian drawings in the Nationalmuseum. Nils Lindhagen, who first attributed them to Taddeo Zuccaro, also demonstrated that they were both fragments of larger representations, on several sheets pasted together, of an *Adoration of the Magi* (NM 1361 and 1362 verso) and an *Adoration of the Shepherds* (NM 1360 and 1362 recto).

Later it was shown by Gere (1963) that the *Adoration of the Magi* in Stockholm is a sketch, or rather an unfinished cartoon, for a panel painting that Philip Pouncey had attributed to Taddeo (Fitzwilliam, Cambridge).

The *Adoration of the Shepherds*, according to Gere, closely resembles two other drawings (Chatsworth and the Uffizi). In his 1969 oeuvre catalogue, he links them with the first (rejected) program for Taddeo's principle work, the frescoes in the Matthew Chapel in S. Maria della Consolazione, Rome, begun in about 1553.

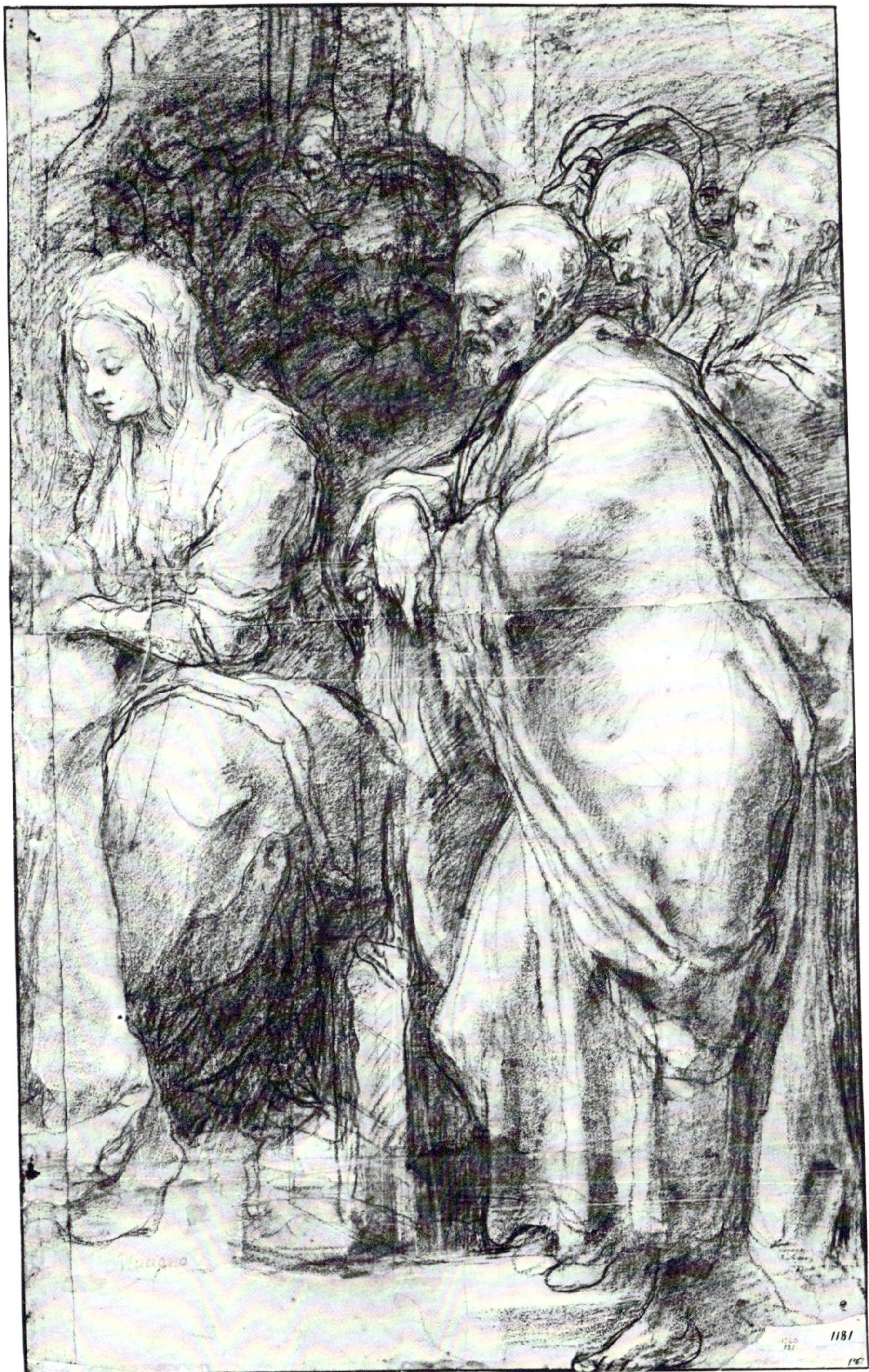

The Stockholm version, however, is a vertical composition, while the other two are broader than they are tall. Gere's explanation is that our motif has been taken from the uncompleted Matthew program and adapted to serve as an alternative proposal when Taddeo was negotiating the commission for the painting in the Fitzwilliam.

18

FEDERICO ZUCCARO
S. Agnolo in Vado 1540/1 - Rome 1609

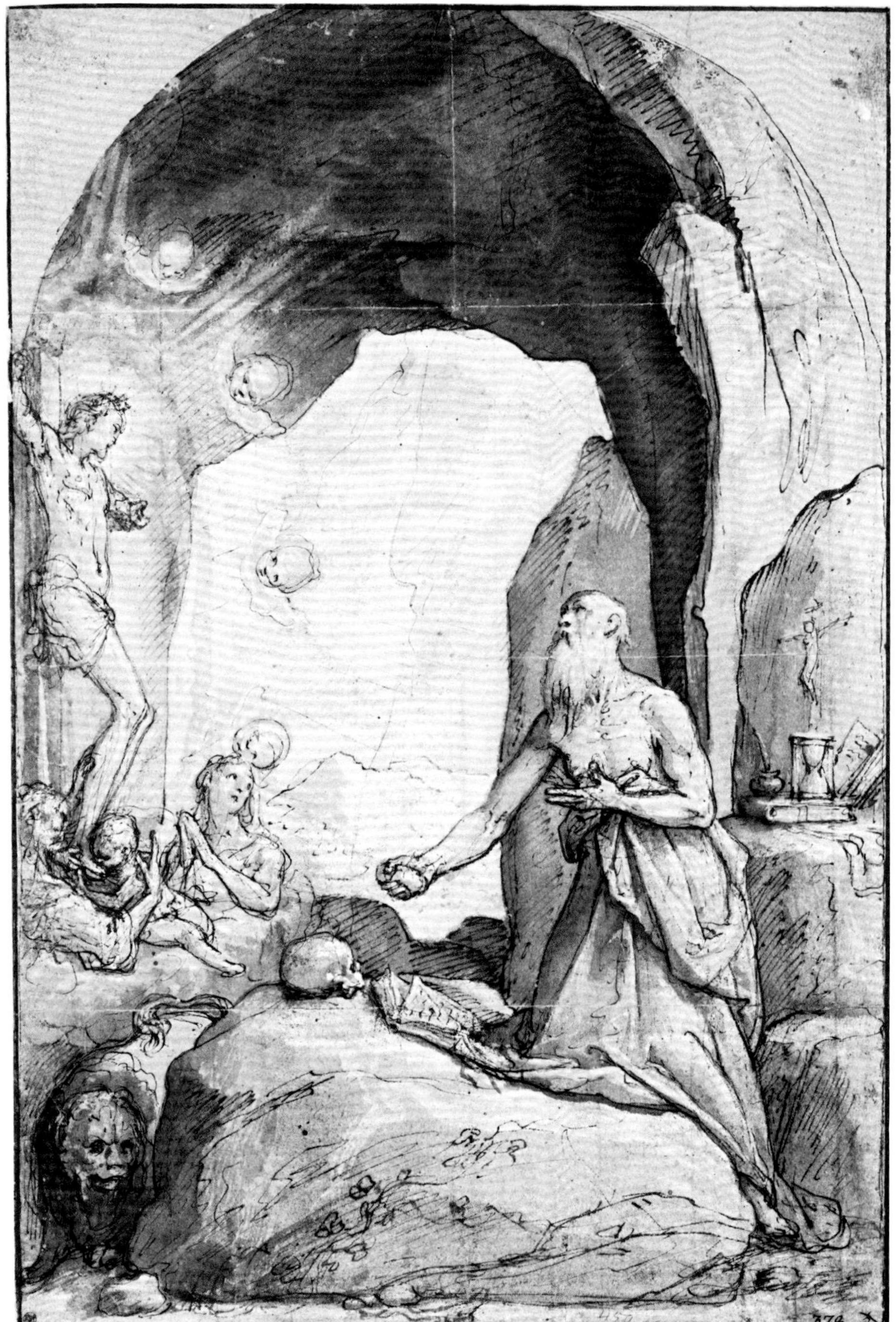

St. Jerome

Pen and brown ink, brownish gray wash, white body color on blue-green paper. 39.2 x 26.1 cm. No watermark. Three vertical and three horizontal folds. NM 450/1863. Inscribed in lower right in brown ink: *378* (Sparre), at verso in brown ink: *in spagnia nel Escurialo anno 1587*.

PROVENANCE:
C. G. Tessin (List 1739-43, p. 51 v.; Cat. 1749, livré 8, no. 62) ☐ Kongl. Biblioteket (Cat. 1790, no. 378) ☐ Kongl. Museum (Lugt 1638).

BIBLIOGRAPHY:
Sirén 1917, no. 383.

In the Tessin inventories this drawing has a joint attribution to Taddeo and Federico Zuccaro, with the appreciative comment "beau dessin." The 1790 catalogue of the Royal Library lists Taddeo alone, but Sirén questioned this, noting succinctly in his 1917 catalogue, "Weak drawing, hardly worthy of Taddeo."

The recent removal of the eighteenth-century mount revealed an interesting inscription on the verso possibly contemporary with the drawing, which mentions the Escorial outside Madrid.

Federico Zuccaro was summoned to Spain by Philip II in 1585 or 1586 to execute the high altar in the Escorial church of S. Lorenzo. Failing to please the monarch, Federico was obliged to return to Italy in 1588, but he still managed to produce ten or so large paintings, including the wings of an altarpiece with *St. Jerome in the Desert* (cf. *Pintores Italianos en San Lorenzo el Real de el Escorial (1575-1613)*, Madrid 1951, p. 200, no. 10, fig. after p. 208).

The painted version is largely the same as our drawing, the main discrepancies being that the left-hand group with the crucifix has been omitted, bodies have been added to the angels' heads, and their number has been increased so that they almost fill the width of the painting just above the view of the landscape.

The drawing has been folded on some occasion, possibly to be sent through the post.

19

FEDERIGO BAROCCI
Urbino 1526 - Urbino 1612

Reproduced in color.

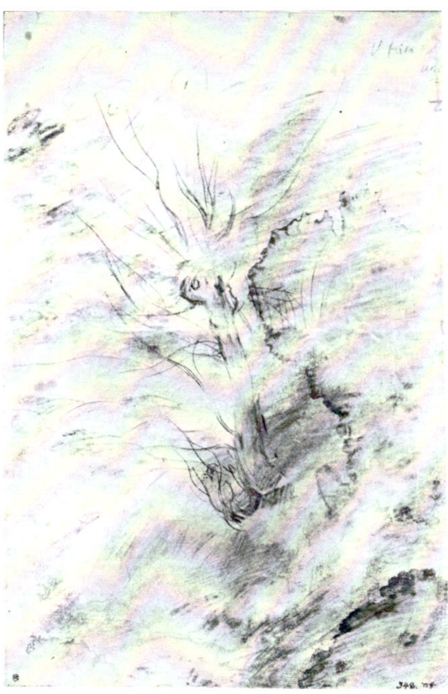

Study of a Tree

Black, green, and brown chalk. 40.4 x 26.4 cm. Stained. Old horizontal fold. No watermark. NM 410/1863. Inscribed in black chalk at upper right, *Il Tuto . . . uno.* Numbered in pen and brown ink *348* (Sparre) and *23* struck out.

VERSO:
Study of a Landscape, fragmentary. Black chalk.

PROVENANCE:
Crozat (Mariette, no. 224) ☐ C. G. Tessin (List 1739-41, p. 32 r.; Cat. 1749, livré 12, no. 34) ☐ Kongl. Biblioteket (Cat. 1790, no. 348) ☐ Kongl. Museum (Lugt 1638).

BIBLIOGRAPHY:
A. Schmarsow, "Federigo Baroccis Zeichnungen, 3, Die Zeichnungen in den Sammlungen ausserhalb Italien, B: Östliche Hälfte Europas," *Abbandlungen der Philologisch-Historischen Klasse der Königlichen Sächsischen Gesellshaft der Wissenschaften*, Leipzig 1914, p. 27 ☐ Sirén 1917, no. 173 ☐ H. Olsen, *Federico Barocci*, Uppsala 1955, p. 182 ☐ Idem., *Federico Barocci*, Copenhagen 1962, p. 234.

EXHIBITIONS:
New York, Boston, Chicago 1969, no. 19.

This fresh and spontaneous study after nature might be connected with other drawings of the same kind, for example, the study of a slope with a bush in the British Museum (P. 3-202) which Harold Olsen associates with the etching, *Stigmatization of St. Francis* (Bartsch 3). Other drawings in this very limited group of studies of trees are in the Louvre, Paris (2), the Albertina, Vienna, the Uffizi, Florence, Biblioteca Communale, Urbino, and the collection of Frits Lugt, Institut Néerlandais, Paris.

20

FEDERIGO BAROCCI

Reproduced in color.

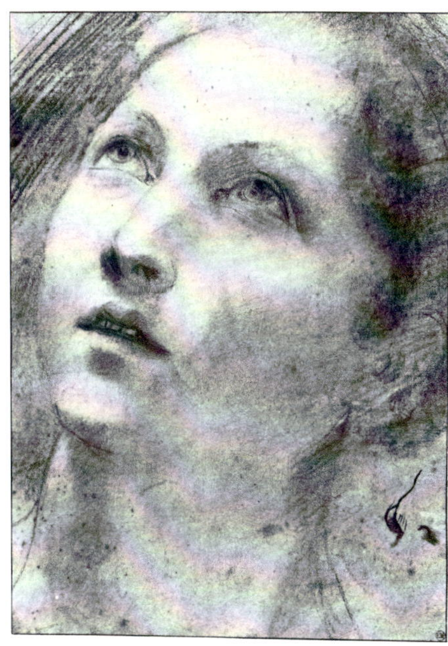

Head of a Woman

Black and red chalk, pastel, pen and brown ink on blue paper. 25.3 x 17.7 cm. Watermark: Star in ring. NM 407/1863.

PROVENANCE:
Crozat (Mariette, no. 238) ☐ C. G. Tessin (Cat. 1749, livré 17, no. 70) ☐ Kongl. Biblioteket (Cat. 1790, no. 345) ☐ Kongl. Museum (Lugt 1638).

BIBLIOGRAPHY:
Schmarsow 1914, p. 26 ☐ Sirén 1917, no. 170 ☐ Olsen 1955, p. 227 ☐ Idem, 1962, pp. 212 f., pl. 107b and 111.

The drawing is a study of a head for the Virgin in the *Assumption* that Orazio Albani may have commissioned and that remains in the same family collection. The painting was left unfinished and must, according to Olsen, have been painted in Barocci's last years (1610-12), being very close to the *Last Supper* in Rome.

Almost thirty drawn studies for the *Assumption* are extant, most of them concerned with details — individual figures, faces, hands. They are done after models in black, white, and occasionally also red chalk, predominantly on blue paper. Besides these studies there is a larger compositional sheet executed, as was Barocci's custom, with pen and brush (Chatsworth). In its strong expression as well as its considerable size, our drawing is one of the more impressive of its kind by Barocci.

21

AGOSTINO TASSI
Rome 1580 - Rome 1644

Galleys

Pen and brown ink, brown wash. 32.5 x 22.6 cm. Laid down. NM 103/1970.

PROVENANCE:
Carl Gustaf Tessin (Cat. 1785, no. 102) □ Einar Perman.

Tassi's chief claim to fame is based on the fact he was the first master of Claude Lorrain. His career as an artist started in 1595, when he left Rome for an apprenticeship in Florence, probably with Giulio Parigi. At the turn of the century, however, he served a sentence for some unknown crime in the Tuscan galleys, which later provided one of the most frequent motifs in his art.

Tassi was back in Rome around 1610, some five years before the adolescent Claude, subsequently his assistant, joined his household as a servant. Claude's first task concerned the decoration of Cardinal Montalto's Villa Lante at Bagnaia, near Viterbo. The paintings consisted largely of landscapes and marine subjects, with Tassi continuing in the mannerist tradition exemplified by the Netherlandish artist Paul Bril, who was active in Rome at this time. It can be mentioned that galleys also feature in the art of Claude.

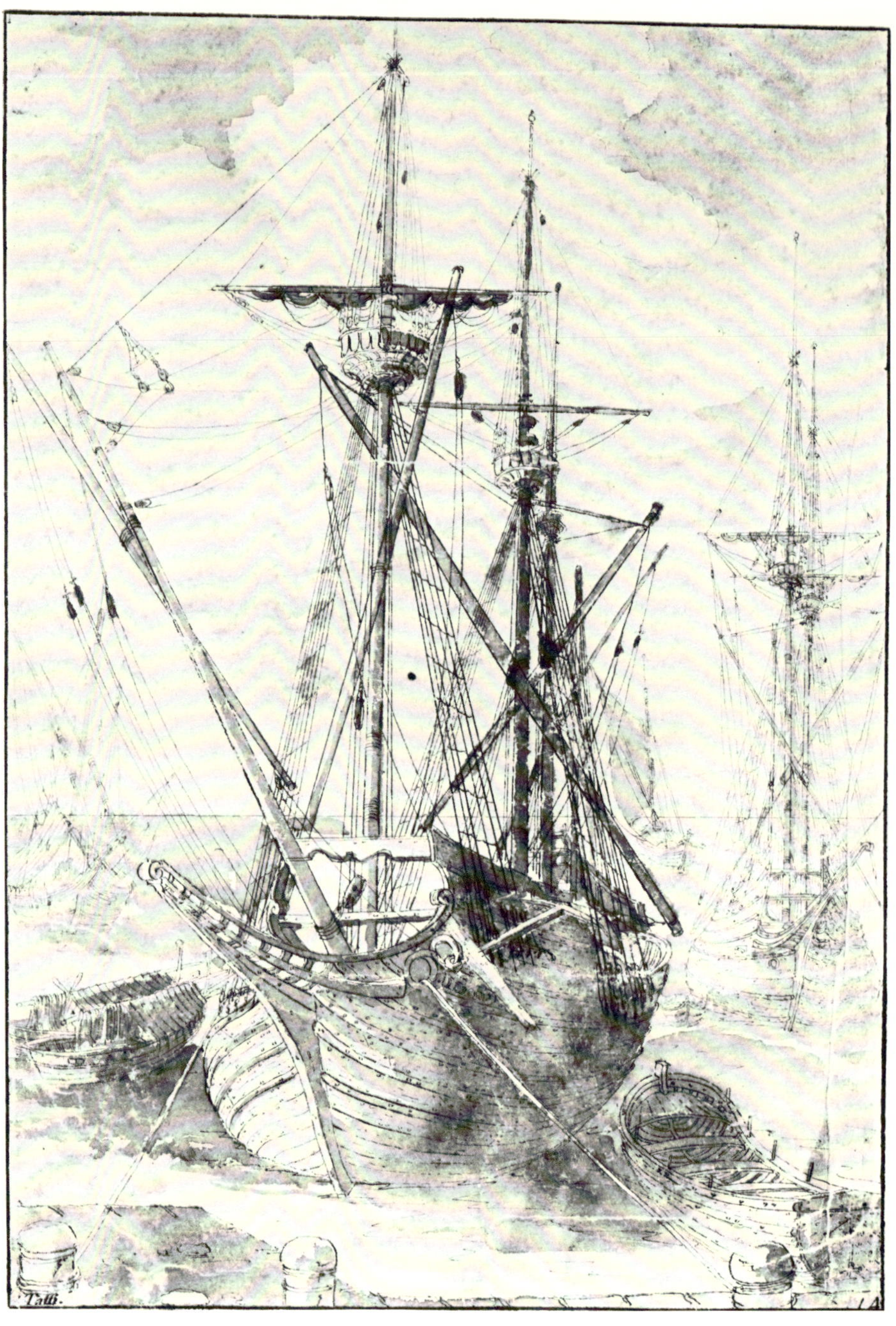

22

PIETRO DA CORTONA
Cortona 1596 - Rome 1669

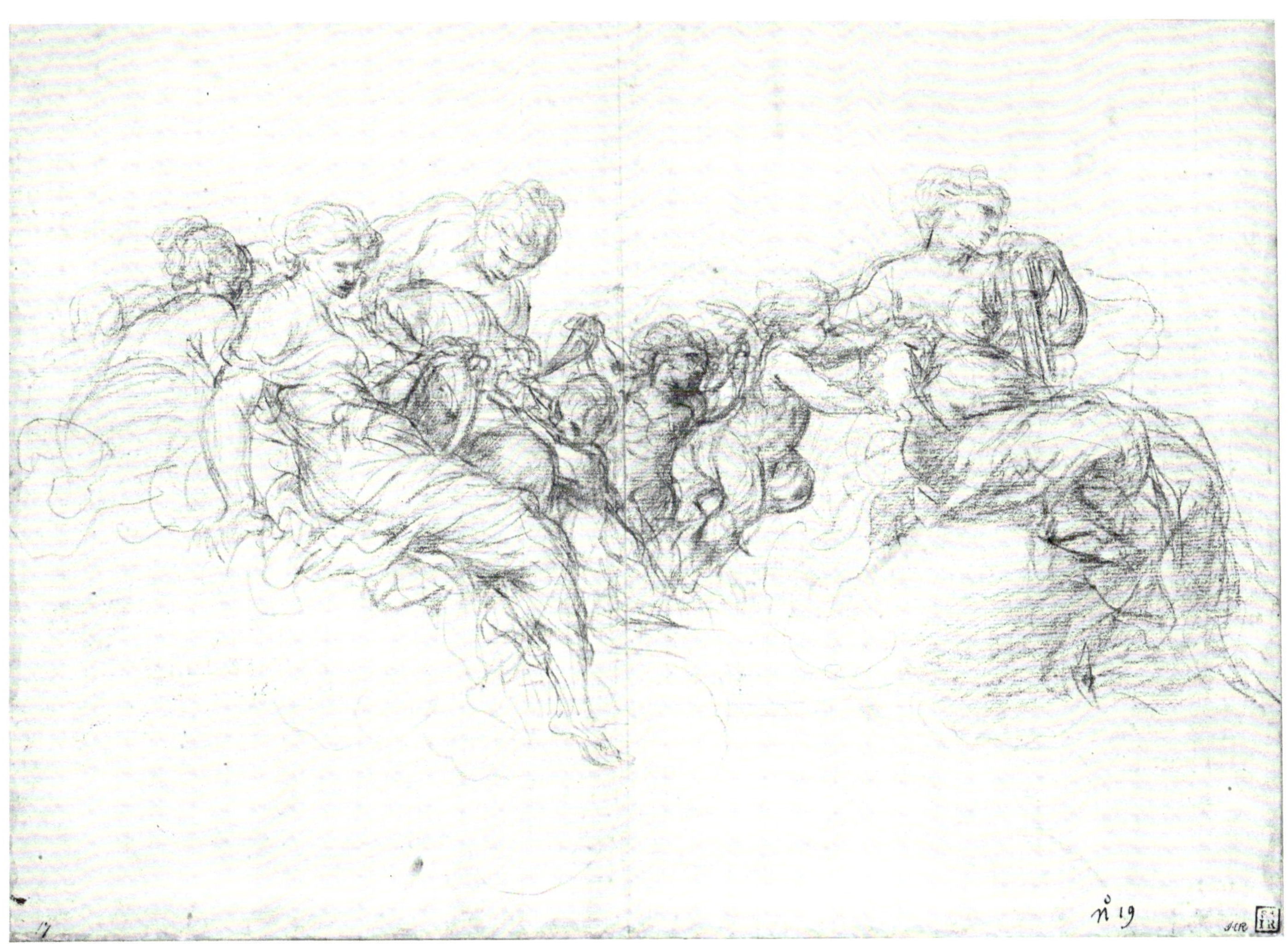

Study of Justice, Honor, and Generosity

Black chalk. 31.7 x 46 cm. NM 170/1969. Inscribed at lower left: *17*, at lower right: *no. 19*; verso: *from Sir J.. Reynolds collection*, at lower right: *D 30 701*.

PROVENANCE:
Sir J. Reynolds (Lugt 2364) ☐ J. C. Robinson (Lugt 1433) ☐ Christie's sale 26 November 1968, no. 149 ☐ P. & D. Colnaghi & Co.

When he had finished painting the ceiling in the Barberini Palace in Rome, Pietro da Cortona was commissioned in 1640 to decorate seven stanze on the first floor of the Pitti Palace in Florence, following a program drawn up by Francesco Rondinelli. These frescoes amount to an astro-mythological record of the life and exploits of Cosimo I, represented allegorically in the context of the characteristics of the seven planets, one per room.

Cortona started the Pitti project in 1641 with the room devoted to Venus and continued in 1643 with the Sala di Giove (Jupiter Room), which occupied him until 1645. The three female personifications—Justice, Honor, and Generosity—in our compositional drawing are positioned just behind Jupiter, who is receiving the young prince.[1] The sheet is a characteristic example of Cortona's mature style and undoubtedly the most important of the known drawings for the Jupiter fresco.[2]

The ceiling in the Sala di Giove is an excellent demonstration of Cortona's concept of a great allegorical fresco as an application of the theory of poetry — the painted composition could be likened to an epic, where the main theme is backed up by numerous secondary episodes.

NOTES:
1. G. Briganti, *Pietro da Cortona*, Florence 1862, p. 235, no. 95.
2. The Uffizi, Florence, also has a number of drawings (11682, 11695, 11697) connected with the Jupiter fresco.

23

PIER FRANCESCO MOLA
Caldrerio 1612 - Rome 1666

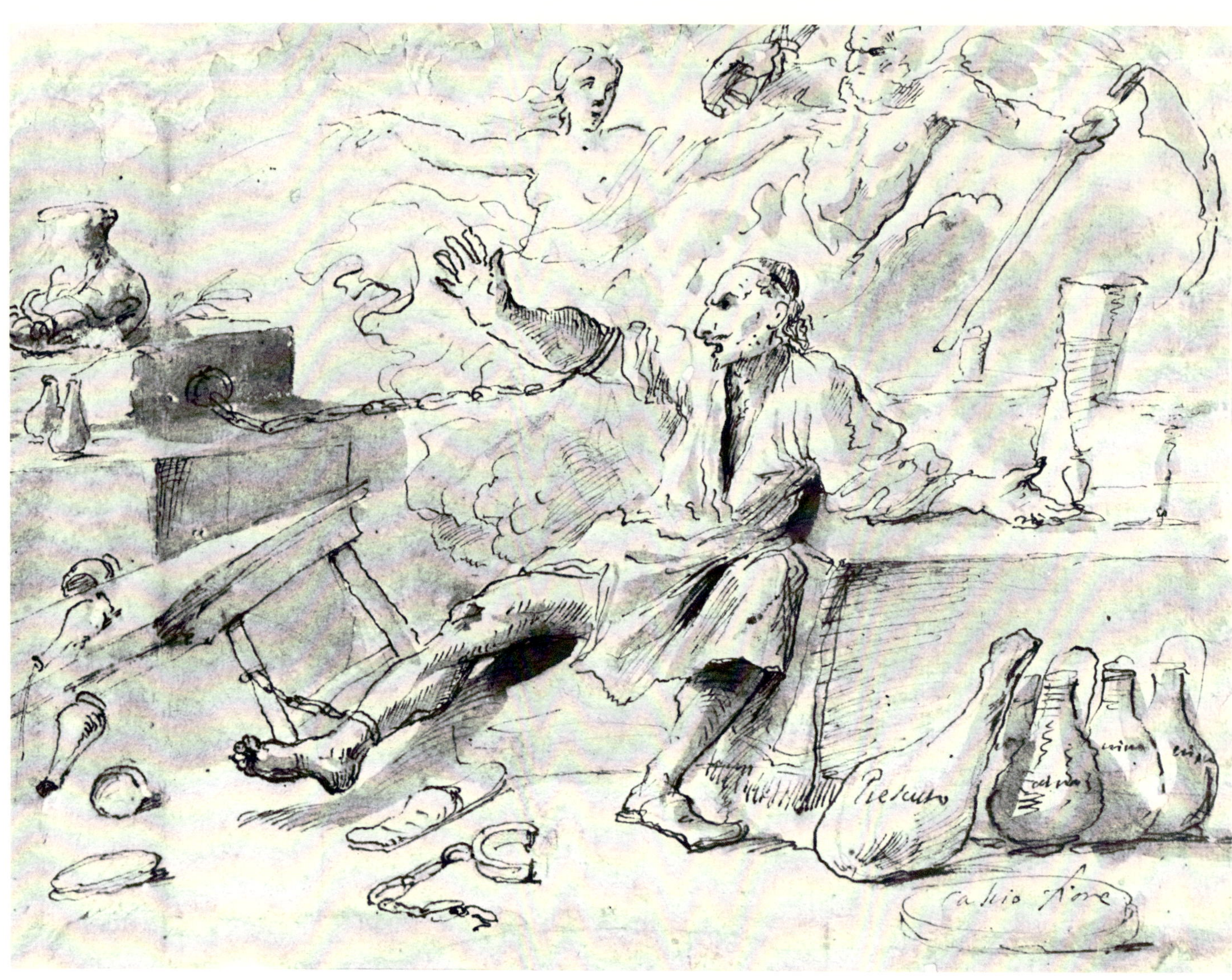

Self-portrait as an Alchemist

Pen and brown ink, brown wash over red chalk. 18.7 x 25.5 cm. NM 116/1970. Inscribed at lower right: *Prosciuto - vino vino vino cascio fiore*.

PROVENANCE:
Queen Christina? ☐ Decio Azzolino? ☐ Pompeo Azzolino? ☐ Livio Odescalchi ☐ Einar Perman.

BIBLIOGRAPHY:
J. Q. van Regteren Altena, *Les dessins italiens de la reine Christine de Suède*, Analecta reginensia II, Stockholm 1966, p. 30.

Mola represents a semi-romantic trend in Roman baroque art, and it is characteristic that he served his apprenticeship in Venice. His Venetian experience is particularly evident in his paintings, many of which are primarily landscapes. His drawings have an expressive wash and a painterly breadth.

Our sheet is of particular interest because it can almost certainly be identified in Odescalchi's inventory of 1713[1] along with another Mola drawing in our collection[2] that bears an inscription in Tessin's hand, "Vien du Prince dom Livio." It is tempting to assume a link to Queen Christina in view of Mola's close relationship with members of her court and the account of how the Queen invited Mola to ride in her coach.[3]

This self-portrait symbolizes the artist as the prisoner of his own occult powers. The right hand and foot are chained to a pedestal and a table, respectively. A bowl of snakes and various other vessels placed on the table allude to the metaphysical context. A table on the right, with a large ham and some wine jars, provides more trivial associations. In the background is a composition with Truth and Time.

NOTES:

1. van Regteren Altena, *op. cit.*, p. 30 "un chimico prigione(!) originale per caricatura del Mola."
2. *Christina*, (exh.) Nationalmuseum, Stockholm 1966, no. 1129. Cf. van Regteren Altena, *op. cit.*, p. 18.
3. L. Pascoli, *Vite, etc.*, Rome 1730, p. 122.

24

SALVATOR ROSA
Arenella 1615 - Rome 1673

Reproduced in color.

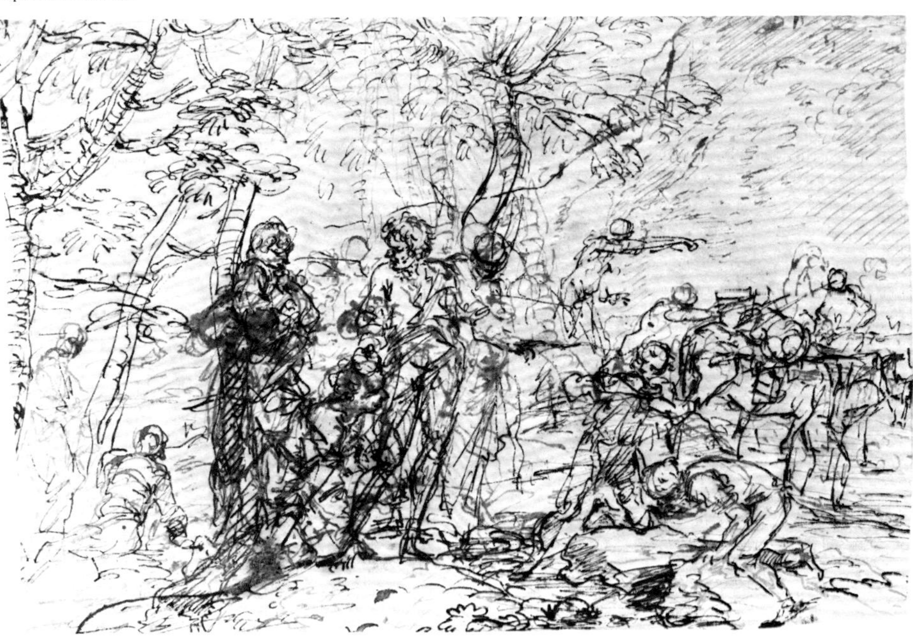

Study for The Philosophers' Grove

Pen and brown ink. 20.5 x 31.7 cm. NM 235/1975.

PROVENANCE:
Queen Christina? □ Decio Azzolino? □ Pompeo Azzolino? □ Livio Odescalchi and then by descent to Prince Ladislao Odeschalchi □ Galerie Gerda Bassenge, Berlin.

BIBLIOGRAPHY:
L. Salerno, "Il disegno nella pittura," *Storia dell'Arte*, 7 (1970), fig. 30 □ *Salvator Rosa*, Exh. cat., Arts Council of Great Britain, Hayward Gallery, London 1973, under no. 58 □ L. Salerno, *L'opera completa di Salvator Rosa*, Milan 1975, under no. 85 □ M. Mahoney, *The Drawings of Salvator Rosa*, New York and London 1977, p. 315, no. 26.1.

This is a compositional drawing for a painting, *The Philosophers' Grove*, in the Pitti Palace in Florence. It shows the encounter between Diogenes and a youth who is drinking water from a stream, from which the philosopher concludes that even his drinking bowl is an unnecessary encumbrance.[1]

The painting is undated, but the advanced style of the drawing indicates that the composition stems from the latter half of the 1640s. This date also agrees with the chronology of Rosa's Florentine painting.

It is notable that a dense screen of trees behind the figures almost completely separates the foreground from the background in this composition. This device provides a contrast between the shaded scene and the bright light that penetrates from behind. Such a landscape construction is reminiscent of early sixteenth-century Venetian painting, a good example being Bellini/Titian's *Feast of the Gods* (National Gallery, Washington). Rosa had in fact visited Venice some time before 1649,[2] and it is reasonable to suppose that this influenced his style.

The Philosophers' Grove seems to have had a companion piece with a similar subject: *Crates the Cynic Throwing Money into the Sea* (now in an English private collection). Crates was a pupil of Diogenes, and the pair of paintings is evidence of Rosa's feeling for the cynic philosophy, which minimizes the importance of external pleasure and restricts life's preoccupation to absolute necessities by keeping worldly needs in check and maintaining a balanced composure.

NOTES:
1. Diogenes Laertius, vi, 36.
2. U. Limentani, *Poesie e Lettere inedite di Salvator Rosa*, Florence 1950, p. 21, letters i xxxix and xl.

25

GUIDO RENI
Bologna 1575 - Bologna 1642

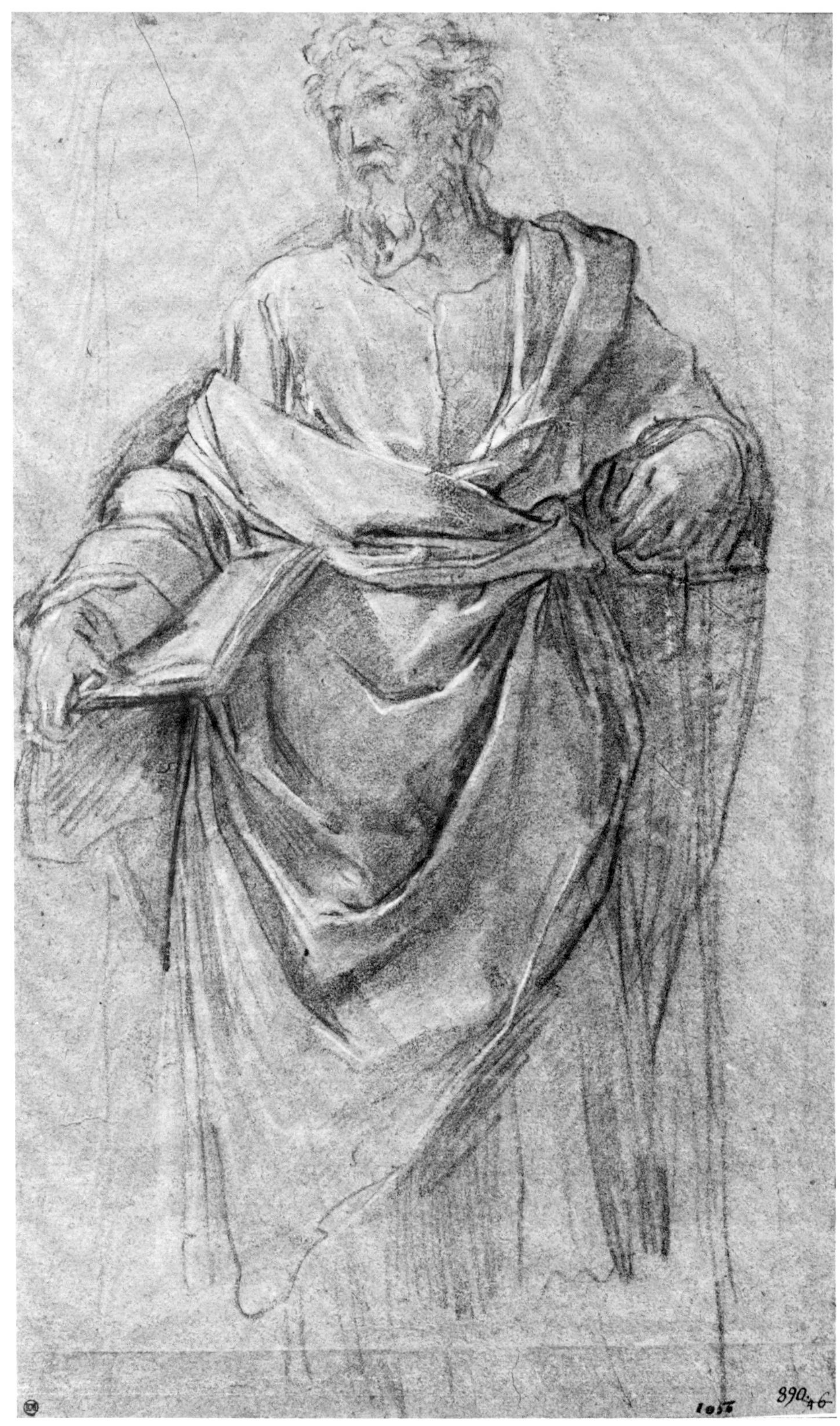

Study for St. Paul

Black and white chalk on blue paper. 39.1 x 23.1 cm. Watermark: Bird in an oval. NM 1056/1863. Numbered in the lower right corner in pen and brown ink: 890 (Sparre) and 46, struck out. Formerly glued to the verso of the drawing an etched cartouche inscribed in pen and brown ink: *Di Guido Reno sono tanto note l'opere sue famose, che in 67 anni di sua vita diede alla luce, o pr essere descritti da scrittori, o celebrate da Poeti, o dati alle stampe, o aclamati dalla tromba della fama, che solo si restringe il celebrar' il presente disegno, qte servi per la Cupola del Duomo di Ravena, ordinatali dal Cardinale Aldobrandini Arcives: o di qta Cated:le.*

PROVENANCE:
Crozat (Mariette, no. 526 or 527) □ C. G. Tessin (List 1739-42, p. 56; Cat. 1749, livré 6, no. 5) □ Kongl. Biblioteket (Cat. 1790, no. 890) □ Kongl. Museum (Lugt 1638).

EXHIBITIONS:
Italienska barockteckningar. Nationalmuseum, Stockholm 1965, no. 125.

While this is primarily a study of drapery, the book and sword indicate that the subject is St. Paul. The early inscription in the cartouche on the reverse of the sheet states that this is a preliminary study for the Aldobrandini Chapel in the Ravenna cathedral. The chapel was decorated, largely by assistants working from drafts by Reni, in 1615-16; the style of the drapery is similar to that of other studies of clothing from the mid-1610s. At Windsor Castle there is a chalk study for the archangel Raphael who appears in the chapel's cupola.[1]

NOTE:
1. O. Kurz, *Bolognese drawings ... at Windsor Castle*, London 1955, no. 342.

26

GIOVANNI FRANCESCO BARBIERI
called IL GUERCINO
Cento 1591 - Bologna 1666

Reproduced in color.

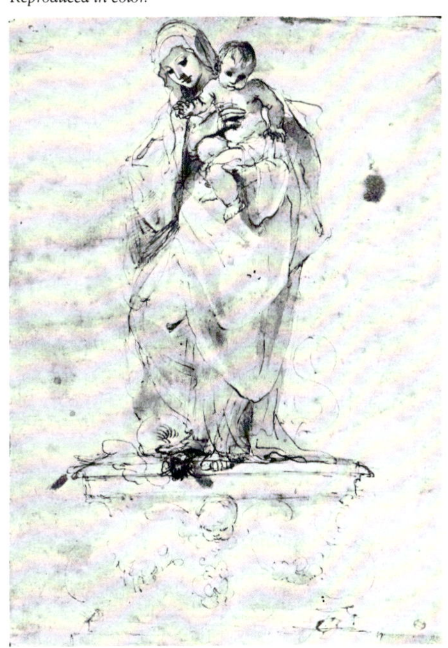

Virgin and Child on a Pedestal

Pen and brown ink, brown wash. The folds on the Virgin's right partly reworked in grayish ink. 24 x 16.7 cm. Oil stains. No watermark. NM 898/1863.

VERSO:
Sketch of a Seated Angel, pen and brown ink (faint).

PROVENANCE:
Crozat (Mariette, no. 545 or 546) □ C. G. Tessin (List 1739-42, p. 60 v.; Cat. 1749, livré 21, no. 39 [as Lodovico Caracci]) □ Kongl. Biblioteket (Cat. 1790, no. 755 [as Lodovico Caracci]) □ Kongl. Museum (Lugt 1638).

The devotional nature of the work suggests that this is a composition for a church altar. The pedestal, only sketched in and decorated with winged genii and garlands, was presumably to be represented as painted sculpture.

A similar conception is evident in a painting for the Falconbelli chapel in S. Giuseppe dei Gesuiti, Pinerolo, dated 1651, now in the Galleria Sabauda, Turin. There the Madonna is placed in a room in front of a painted relief, with a view of a landscape in the background, but the monumental figure, seen from slightly below, is similar.

27

STEFANO DELLA BELLA
Florence 1610 - Florence 1664

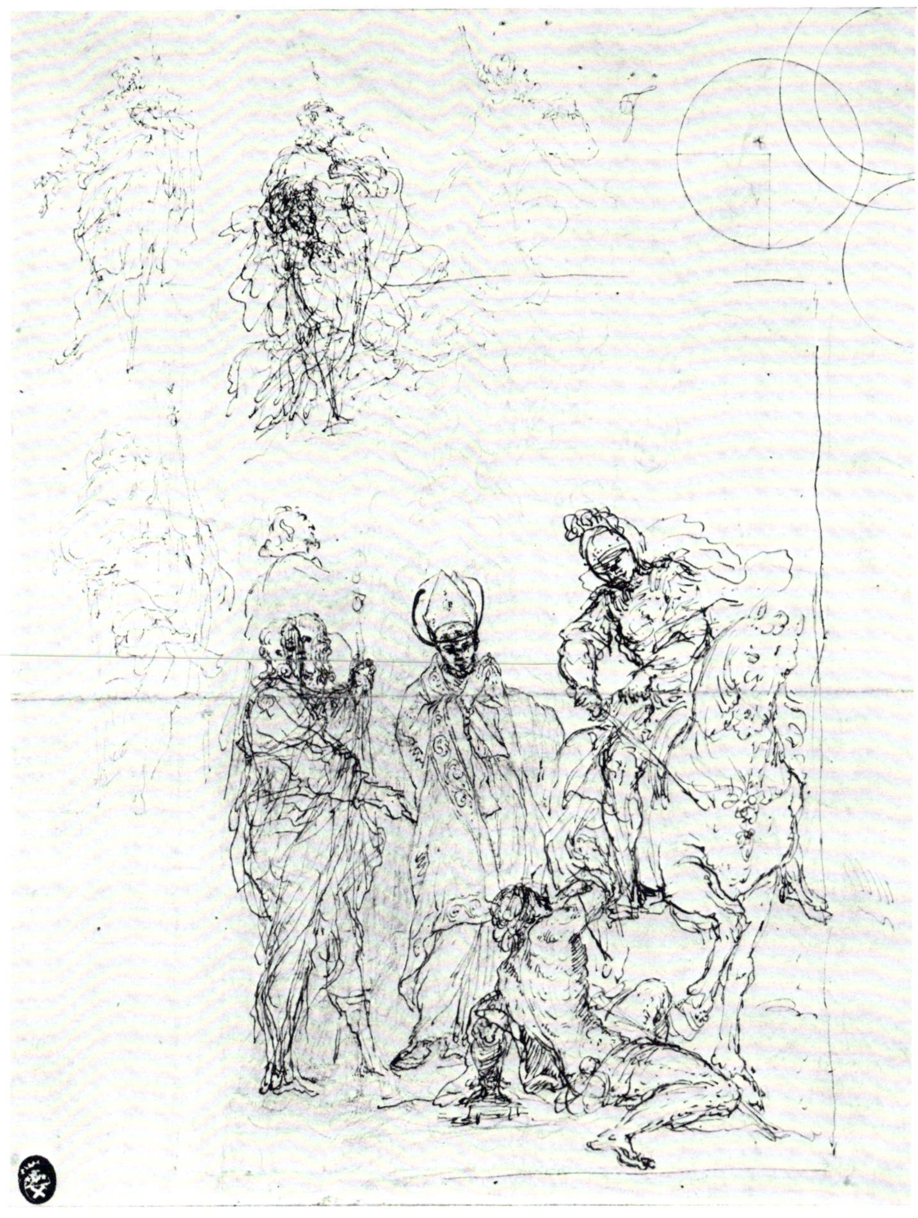

St. James, a Bishop Saint, and St. Martin

Black chalk, pen and brown ink. 25 x 19.5 cm. Laid down. NM 289/1973.

PROVENANCE:
Prince Charles de Ligne (Bartsch 1794, p. 405, no. 31, maître inconnu) □ Herzog Albert von Sachsen-Teschen □ Count J. G. De la Gardie (Lugt 2722a) □ Gift to the museum in 1973 (bequest).

The nervous line and open construction of this drawing match the artist's late style, following his return to Italy in 1650. The subject has no counterpart in his known oeuvre of paintings or graphic art.

The drawing also offers insights into della Bella's working method. The main composition with the three saints is accompanied by a number of sketched variants of St. James.

28

GIOVANNI BENEDETTO CASTIGLIONE (IL GRECHETTO)

Genoa c. 1610 - Mantua 1663/65

Reproduced in color.

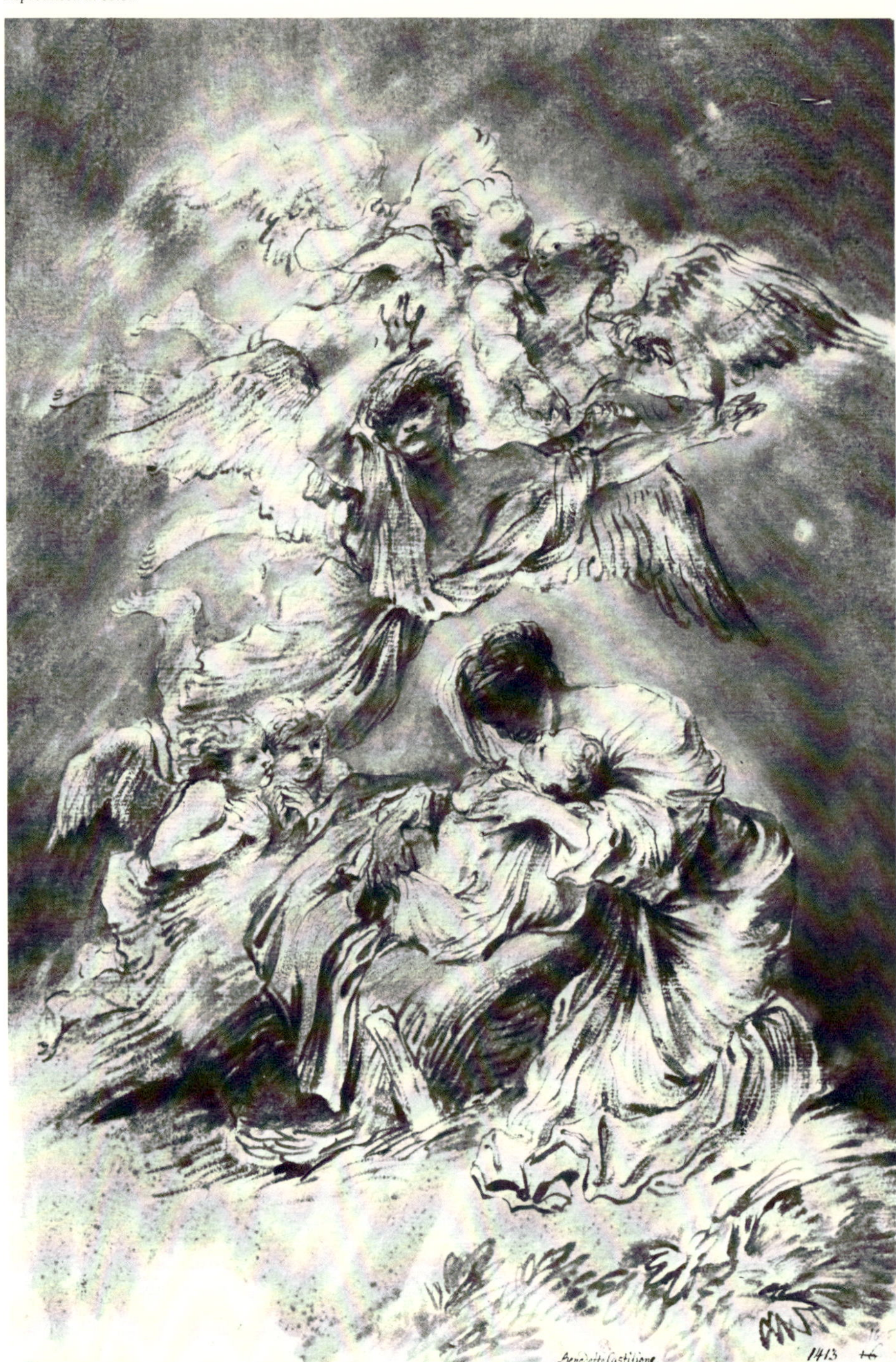

Angels Adoring the Child in the Arms of the Virgin

Brush drawing, brown paint with touches of red, heightened with white. 41.8 x 28.1 cm. Small tear bottom right. No watermark. NM 1605/1863. Inscribed at lower right in pen and brown ink: *Benedetto Castilione*. Numbered. *1413* (Sparre) and *16* (struck out).

PROVENANCE:
Crozat (Mariette, no. 752, described) □ C. G. Tessin (List 1739-42, p. 58 v.; Cat. 1749, livré 11, no. 53) □ Kongl. Biblioteket (Cat. 1790, no. 1413) □ Kongl. Museum (Lugt. 1638).

BIBLIOGRAPHY:
Bjurström 1979, no. 363.

EXHIBITIONS:
Stockholm 1965, no. 60 □ Paris, Brussels, Amsterdam 1970-71, no. 25 □ Philadelphia, Philadelphia Museum of Art, *Giovanni Bennedetto Castiglione Master Draughtsman of the Italian Baroque*, 1971, no. 48 (A. Percy).

Castiglione's drawings are characterized by his technical skill and stylistic eclecticism. In fact he invented the technique used in this sheet. In many ways the technique is an equivalent on paper to Rubens' rapid oil sketches on wooden panels in which oil was mixed in the pigment to achieve a stronger coloristic effect and expressiveness. This drawing was executed after Castiglione's second stay in Rome (1647-51), where he had been strongly influenced both by Poussin and, as in this case, by Bernini and Rembrandt. Rembrandt was fairly well known in Italy through his etchings, and already in the late 1630s a Rembrantesque chiaroscuro characterizes many of Castiglione's own etchings.

This drawing served as a model for an unfinished etching of the subject,[1] although in the etching two of the flying angels are missing. Both drawing and etching can be dated to the early 1650s, supposedly executed in Mantua where the artist spent the last years of his life and where his art took on a baroque magnificence.

A copy of the drawing is in the Hessisches Landesmuseum, Darmstadt,[2] while a studio version of a variant composition is in the Metropolitan Museum, New York.[3]

NOTES:
1. Bartsch 21, p. 14, no. 8.
2. Inv. no. AE 1856.
3. Inv. no. 80.3.458.

29

SEBASTIANO RICCI
Belluno 1660 - Venice 1734

Reproduced in color.

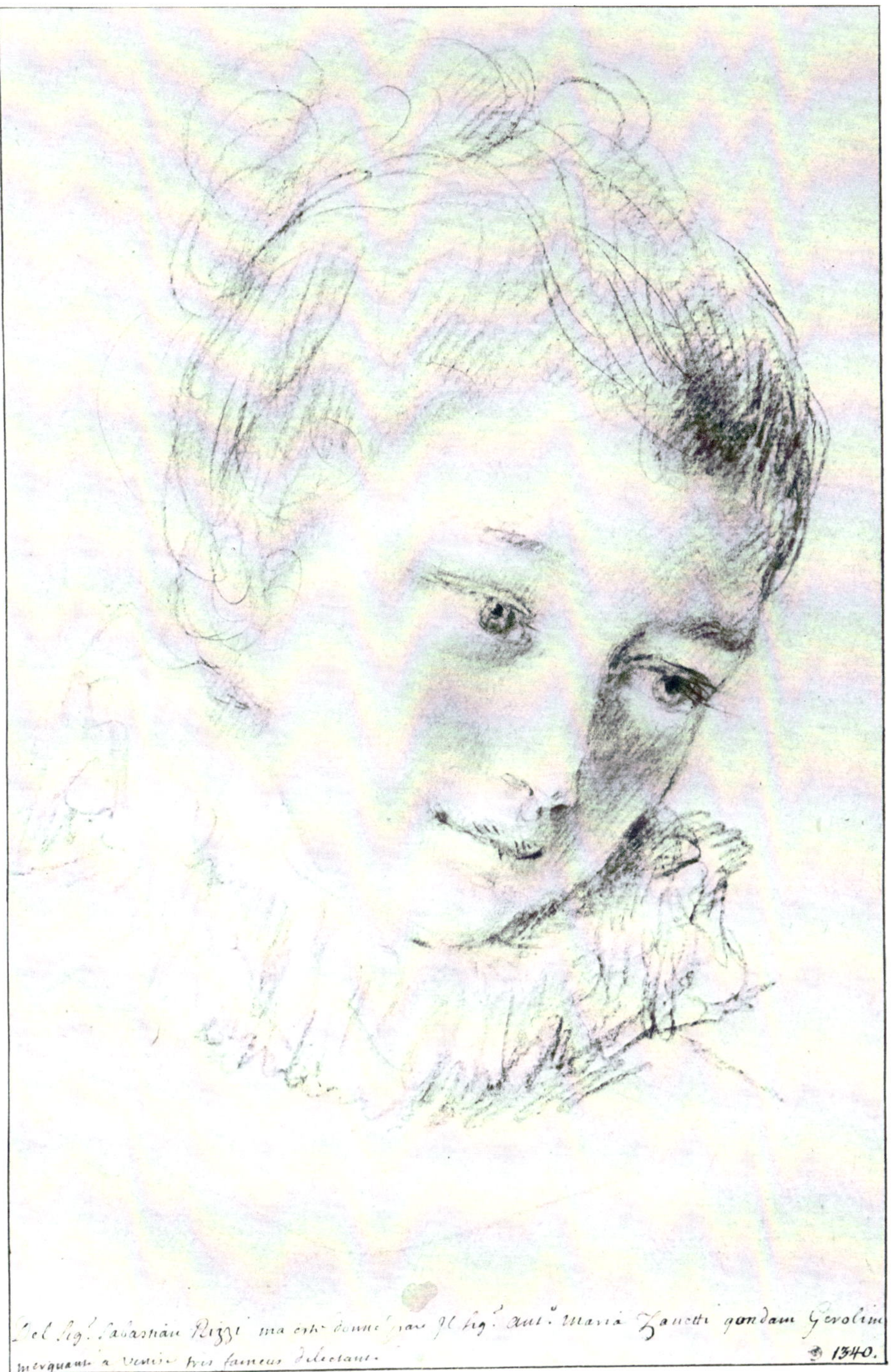

Head of a Young Girl, Facing Slightly Right

Black chalk, pastels, heightened with white on grayish blue paper. 38.4 x 25.3 cm. Laid down. NM 1530/1863. Inscribed in lower margin in pen and brown ink: *Del Sigr Sebastian Rizzi ma est donné par Il Sigr Ant.o Maria Zanetti qondam Gerolin . . . merquant a Venise tres fameux dilectant.*

PROVENANCE:
A. M. Zanetti □ Crozat (Mariette, no. 744?) □ C. G. Tessin (List 1739-42, p. 35 v.; Cat. 1749, livré 17, no. 132) □ Kongl. Biblioteket (Cat. 1790, no. 1330) □ Kongl. Museum (Lugt 1638).

BIBLIOGRAPHY:
A. Rizzi, *Sebastiano Ricci disegnatore*, Udine, Sala Aiace del Comune, 1975 (cat. Electra Editrice, Milano), p. 90 □ Bjurström 1979, no. 213.

EXHIBITIONS:
Stockholm 1962, no. 272 □ Venice 1974, no. 86.

After four years in England (1712-16), Sebastiano Ricci returned home via Paris, where Pierre Crozat introduced him to Antoine Watteau.[1] He was greatly impressed by the young French artist and even copied some of his drawings.[2]

This sheet reflects the influence of Watteau in style and technique, though no direct prototype has been found in the latter's work. However, the girl's costume dates from the 1620s or 1630s, and certain characteristics in the drawing remind one of Rubens (heavy accents around the mouth, tip of the nose and eyes).
The present sheet may well be a pastiche or copy by Ricci after Rubens in the spirit of Watteau. We know of several copies after Rubens in this spirit by Watteau.[3]

NOTES:
1. Rizzi, *op. cit.*, p. 26.
2. A. Blunt and E. Croft-Murray, *Venetian Drawings of the XVII & XVIII Centuries in the collection of Her Majesty the Queen at Windsor Castle*, London 1957, p. 47 and nos. 351, 352.
3. K. T. Parker and J. Mathey, *Antoine Watteau*, 1, Paris 1957, nos. 282 and 290.

30

GIOVANNI BATTISTA TIEPOLO
Venice 1696 - Madrid 1770

Reproduced in color.

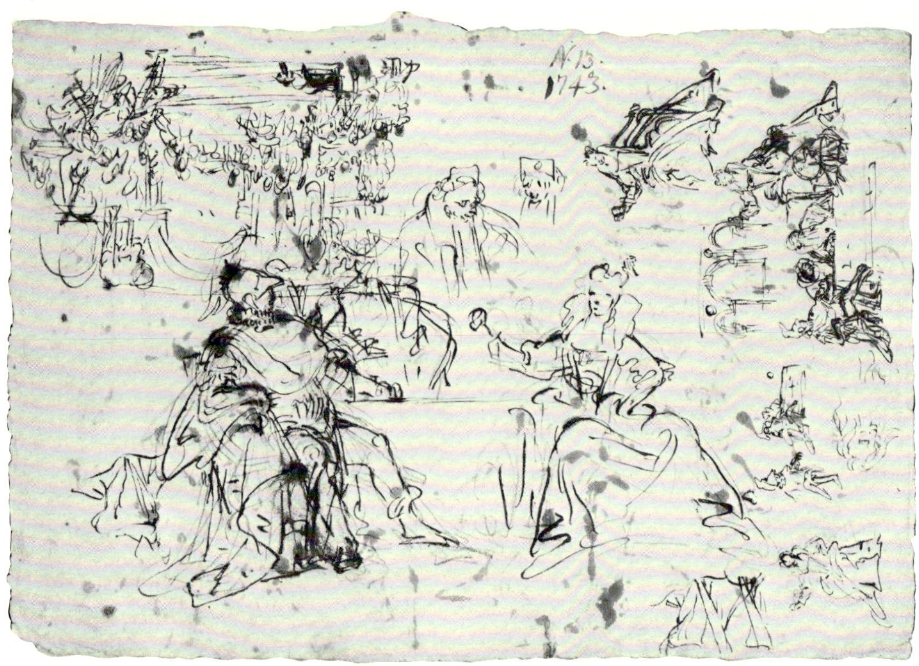

Variations on the Theme of Anthony and Cleopatra

Pen and brown ink, black chalk, on blue paper. 30.7 x 46 cm. No watermark. NM 3/1976. Dated at upper center in pen and brown ink: *N. 13 1743.*

VERSO:
Further studies for the same composition. Pen and brown ink, black chalk.

PROVENANCE:
Humphrey □ Sotheby's sale 8 December 1972, lot 60 □ Adolphe Stein.

BIBLIOGRAPHY:
G. Knox, "Giambattista Tiepolo: Variations on the Theme of Anthony and Cleopatra," *Master Drawings*, 12 (1974), pp. 378 ff. □ Bjurström 1979, no. 222.

EXHIBITIONS:
Stockholm, Nationalmuseum, *1700-tal Tanke och form i rokokon*, 1980, no. 115.

During the first half of the 1740s, Tiepolo worked on two themes, *The Meeting of Anthony and Cleopatra* and *The Banquet of Anthony and Cleopatra*, producing several variants of each.

Knox has put forward the plausible idea that *The Meeting* represents Anthony as he hands over the fruits of his victories to Cleopatra on his return from Armenia in 34 B. C., while *The Banquet* signifies Cleopatra's symbolic sacrifice of her magnificent pearl, i.e., of herself to Anthony. No literary sources have yet been found for this pair of scenes depicting princely love and munificence, although it is suspected that a search of texts produced in Vicenza around 1740 might yield results.[1]

Our drawing is probably an initial rough idea for *The Banquet*. Anthony is seated on the left, Cleopatra on the right. To their right and turned ninety degrees are further studies of the two main figures as well as suggestions of architecture, indicating a three-arched opening. Upside down above the main group is a small but very elaborate study for a vast composition for *The Banquet.*

On the verso there is a further study for Anthony and a mass of studies for écorché arms and legs, heads and feet.

Comparisons with inscriptions on other sheets lead Knox to conclude that the verso inscription "N.13.1743" is a date.[2]

Tiepolo seems to have taken Veronese's large banquet scenes as his starting point, besides playing with the compositional scheme of Raphael's *School of Athens*. Further compositional work by Tiepolo is to be found on a sheet in the Victoria and Albert Museum[3] in London; this in turn is a preliminary study for the little *modello* in the National Gallery, the latter being a reduced variant of the magnificent conception of the composition in our sheet.[4] The London sketch also served as a preliminary study for a large painting that, together with a companion piece of *The Meeting*, is now in the Archangel Museum (formerly the Yousoupoff Gallery) outside Moscow and which is dated 1747, though supposedly almost finished in 1743.[5]

Starting from the composition in our drawing, Tiepolo produced another version for Consul Smith that is now in the Musée Cognac-Jay in Paris (1743). He subsequently developed this into the large Melbourne canvas[6] of the theme as well as a variant of this in the P. Gerli collection, Milan.[7]

The banquet theme recurs for the last time in the fresco of the Ca' Labia, Venice, which Knox dates to the summer of 1744. This painting demanded some fundamental reconsideration of the compositional problems, as the main scene had to be disposed vertically rather than horizontally. A reworking of the theme for the new format is to be found in a sketch by Tiepolo belonging to Stockholm University.[8]

NOTES:

1. Knox, *op. cit.*, p. 385.
2. Knox, *op. cit.*, p. 379.
3. G. Knox, *Catalogue of the Tiepolo Drawings in the Victoria and Albert Museum*, London 1960, no. 85.
4. A. Morassi, *A Complete Catalogue of the Paintings of G. B. Tiepolo*, London 1962, p. 18; G. Piovene and A. Pallucchini, *L'opera completa di Giambattista Tiepolo*, Milan 1968, no. 177a. Formerly Coll. Alexander. No. 222 ref.
5. Morassi, *op. cit.*, p. 2; Piovene and Pallucchini, *op. cit.*, no. 177.
6. Morassi, *op. cit.*, pp. 39 and 23; Piovene and Pallucchini, *op. cit.*, nos. 155a and 155. For the Melbourne variant there are three preliminary studies in the Victoria and Albert Museum in London. See G. Knox, *Catalogue*, *op. cit.*, nos. 71-73.
7. Piovene and Pallucchini, no. 161.
8. Morassi, *op. cit.*, pp. 59 and 49; Piovene and Pallucchini, *op. cit.*, 187b and 187c.

31

GIOVANNI BATTISTA PIRANESI
Mogliano Veneto 1720 - Rome 1778

A Two-storied Interior of a Temple

Red and black chalk, pen and brown ink, gray wash. 19 x 22.2 cm. No watermark. THC 1844. Inscribed at lower right by a nineteenth-century hand in pencil: *Piranesi. . .*

VERSO:
Architectural Studies

PROVENANCE:
Kongl. Museum (Lugt 1638).

BIBLIOGRAPHY:
Bjurström 1979, no. 205.

This drawing, recently rediscovered and identified in the Museum's collections, reveals a mixture of Venetian and Roman features. Its general appearance is related to Piranesi's *Prima Parte di Architettura e Prospettiva. . .*, published in 1743. The first half of the 1740s is a probable date for the drawing, relatively soon after the artist's arrival in Rome from Venice.

The closest parallels for the work seem to be the early parts of a drawing in the J. Pierpont Morgan Library, *Central View of a Church Interior*, which was reworked later by Piranesi,[1] a drawing of *Two Courtyards*,[2] and a study for *Vestibolo d'antico Tempio*[3] in the British Museum.

The diverse *Architectural Studies* on the reverse also have clear parallels, chiefly in the studies after Fischer von Erlach, *Entwurff einer Historischen Architektur*, Vienna 1721, also in the J. Pierpont Morgan Library, New York.[4]

The style of drawing on this sheet was common at the time, e.g. the light brown contours and gray washes as well as the architectural inventions based on Palladio and seventeenth-century scenography. Piranesi's manner is evident in such elements as the staffage figures.

NOTES:

1. J. Bean and F. Stampfle, *Drawings from New York Collections III, The Eighteenth Century in Italy*, The Metropolitan Museum of Art and The J. Pierpont Morgan Library, New York 1971, no. 217.
2. H. Thomas, *The Drawings of Giovanni Battista Piranesi*, London 1954, no. 1.
3. A. Robison, "Preliminary Drawings for Piranesi's Early Architectural Fantasies," *Master Drawings*, 15 (1977), pp. 387-401, p. 396, fig. 8.
4. Bean and Stampfle, *op. cit.*, no. 216.

Reproduced in color.

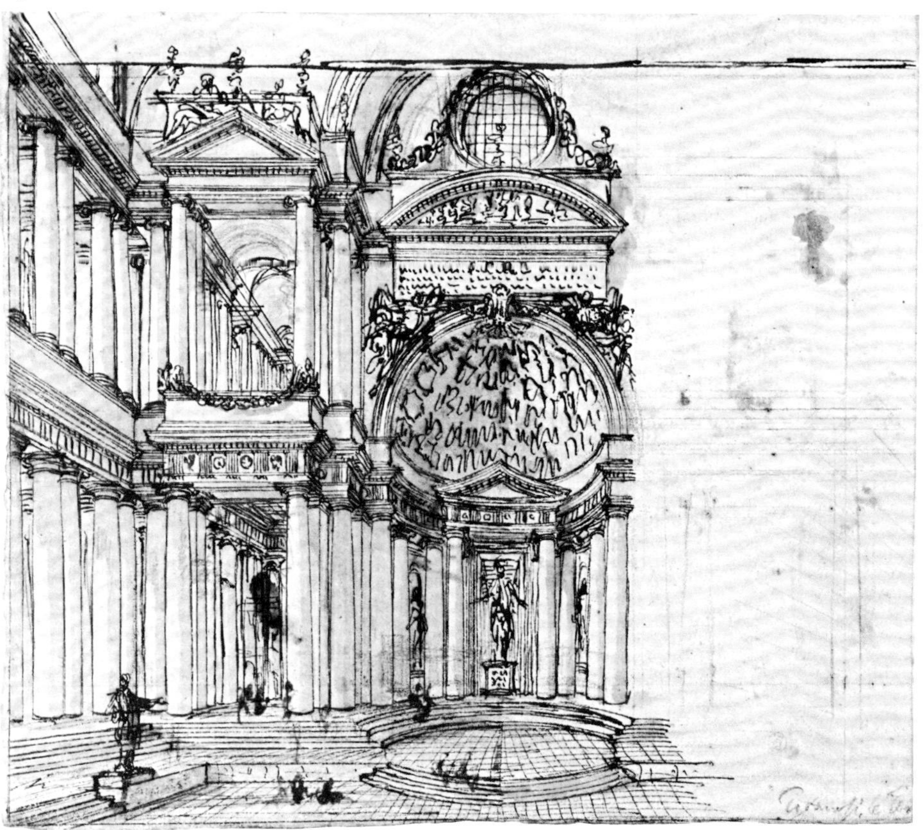

32

AMBROISE DUBOIS
Antwerp 1543 - Fontainebleau 1614

A Shoulder-length Study of a Female Head

Black chalk on brownish gray paper, pricked for transfer. 41.5 x 35 cm. Watermark: Reflected G in a laurel wreath. NM 1150/1973.

PROVENANCE:
Sotheby's sale 8 June 1972, no. 203.

BIBLIOGRAPHY:
L'École de Fontainebleau, Exh. cat., Grand Palais, Paris 1972, pp. 81 ff. □ Bjurström 1976, no. 25.

Dubois (Ambrosius Bosschaert) is known to have left his native Antwerp for France before 1570 where he joined the second school of Fontainebleau. His chief contribution to the palace was the adornment, c. 1604-05, of the Salle Ovale (Grand Cabinet du Roi) with fifteen paintings of scenes from *Aethiopica*, an account by Heliodorus, the Greek writer, c. 400 A.D., of the romance between Theagenes of Thessaly and Chariclea, an Ethiopian princess. Dubois continued Primaticcio's elegant use of line, and the clarity and harmony of his compositions presage the classicism of Poussin.

This sheet differs in scale from most other drawings by Dubois, but in this respect it has a parallel in the Louvre in a sheet with the form of a fallen figure.[1] Both sheets have been blackened on the verso for transfer to canvas or a wall. Both also exhibit the use of a characteristic line with long, parallel outlines and clear shading.

Dubois drew a highly individual female type. The face in the drawing is almost identical with that of princess Chariclea in the Fontainebleau series. It is tempting to suggest that our sheet served as a preparatory study for one of the Salle Ovale paintings.

NOTE:
1. Inv. no. 26 244.

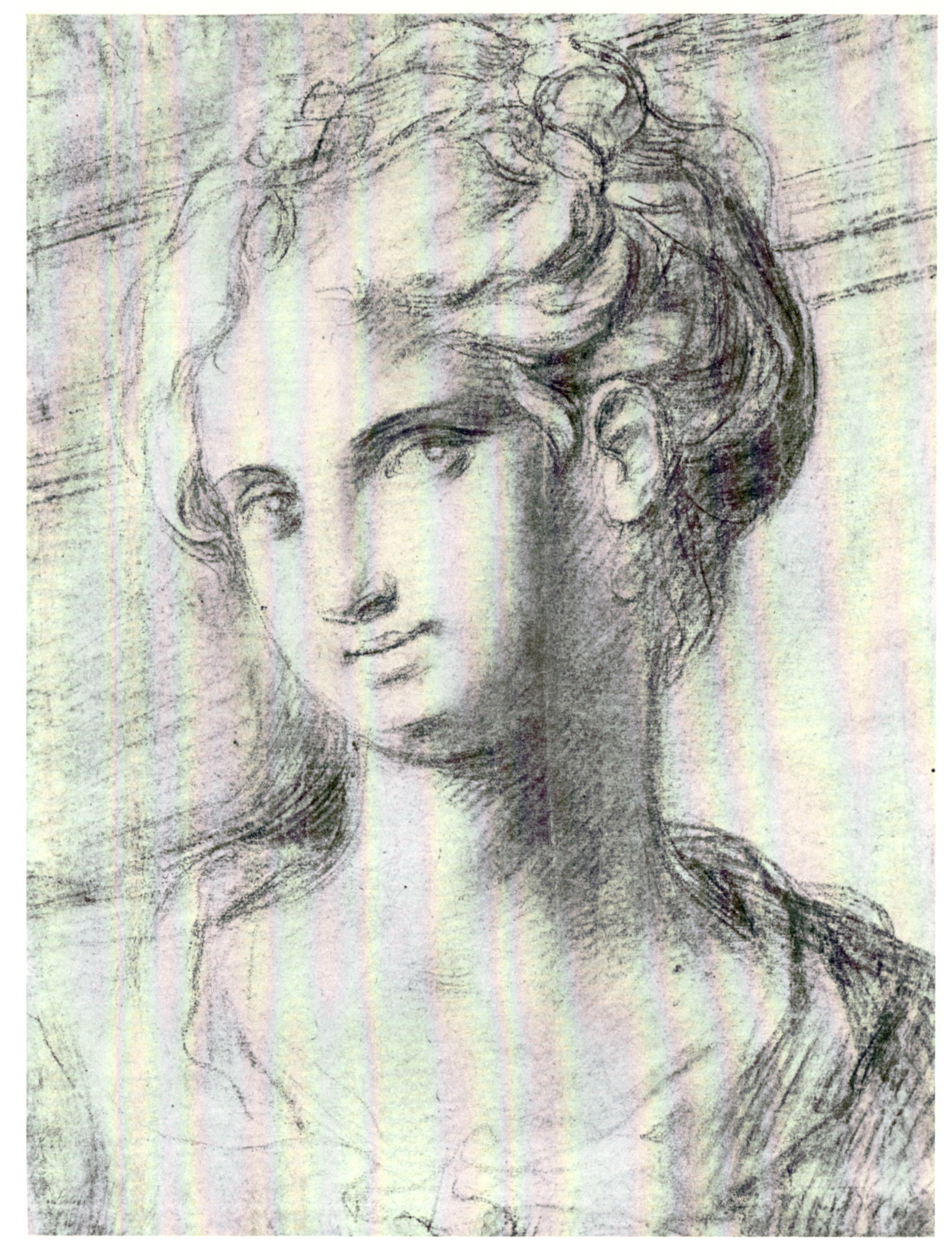

33

FRANCESCO PRIMATICCIO
Bologna 1504 - Paris 1570

Reproduced in color.

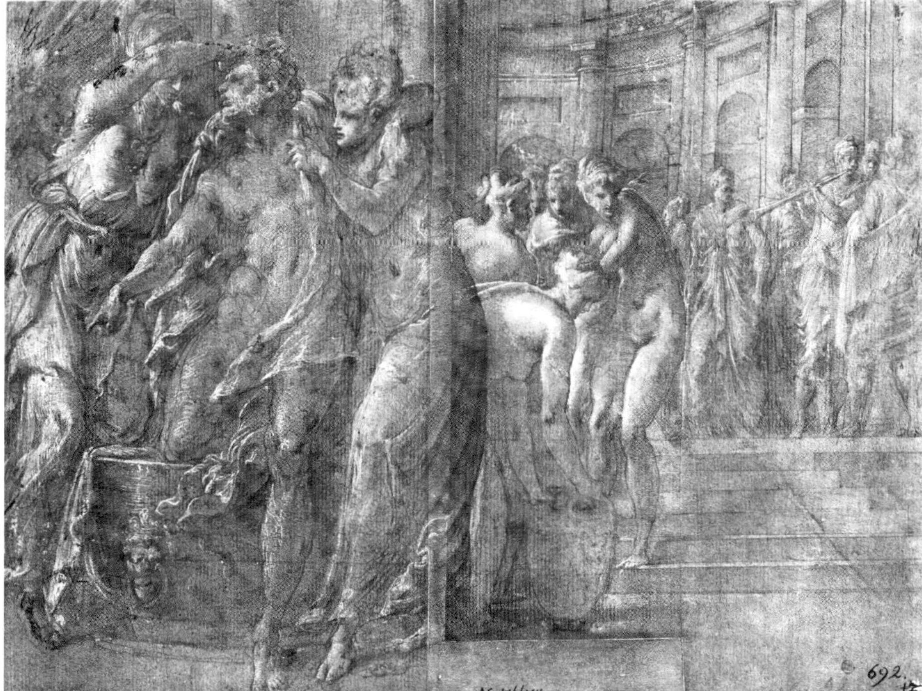

Minerva Beautifies Ulysses

Red chalk, heightened with white (partly oxidized) on paper tinted light red. 21.3 x 30.1 cm. Drawn on three pieces of paper 14, 7.5, and 8 cm broad; 0.6 cm broad strip between pieces one and two and a 1.7 cm high surface under piece two was restored long ago. Laid down. NM 834/1863. Inscribed at lower center in pen and brown ink: *45, tableau*. Numbered at lower right: *692*. (Sparre) and *17* (struck out).

PROVENANCE:
Crozat (Mariette, nos. 399, 400) □ C. G. Tessin (List 1739-42, p. 55 r.; Cat. 1749, livré 5, no. 33) □ Kongl. Biblioteket (Cat. 1790, no. 692) □ Kongl. Museum (Lugt 1638).

BIBLIOGRAPHY:
L. Dimier, *Le Primatice*, Paris 1900, no. 181 □ Sirén 1917, no. 247 □ Bjurström 1976, no. 42.

Recommended by Giulio Romano, who was his master for the work on the Palazzo del Té and the Palazzo Ducale in Mantua, Primaticcio arrived in Fontainebleau in 1532. He was responsible chiefly for the decoration of the palace after the death of Rosso Forentino in 1540. The work was collaborative, and Primaticcio's own style is chiefly discernible in his drawings.

This compositional drawing for one of the paintings in La Galerie d'Ulysse at Fontainebleau belongs to a set of nineteen similar drawings in Stockholm. The composition has been engraved by van Thulden as no. 45.

La Galerie d'Ulysse at Fontainebleau, which depicted the changing fortunes of Ulysses after leaving Troy, was executed between 1541 and 1570. The wall paintings to which this subject belongs were executed at the beginning of this period, 1541-1547.

There are other Primaticcio drawings in the Albertina, Vienna, in the Museum Boymans van Beuningen, and at Chantilly, which are related to this work.

34

FRANCESCO PRIMATICCIO

Alexander and Thalestris

Pen and brown ink, watercolors, over traces of black chalk. 25.3 x 33.9 cm. Watermark: Grapes with letters D I. NM 848/1863. Inscribed under the figures in pen and brown ink: *La Regina de le . . . alisander* (Primaticcio's hand). Numbered at lower right in pen and brown ink: *705.* (Sparre) and *21.*

PROVENANCE:
Crozat (Mariette, no. 412, as Nicolo dell'Abate) □ C. G. Tessin (List 1739-42, p. 41 v.; Cat. 1749, livré 26, no. 49) □ Kongl. Biblioteket (Cat. 1790, no. 705) □ Kongl. Museum (Lugt 1638).

BIBLIOGRAPHY:
L. Dimier, "Några minnen från den gamla Fontainebleauskolan," *Ord och bild*, Stockholm 1899, pp. 594ff. □ Idem, *Le Primatice*, Paris 1900, no. 254 □ Idem, *Le Primatice*, Paris 1928, pp. 67ff □ Sirén 1917, no. 254 □ Bjurström 1976, no. 52.

This sheet is one of the "dessins des Mascarades pour des Ballets et pour un Tournoy" (Mariette) that Tessin purchased at the Crozat auction. Tessin assumed, mistakenly, that "ils son faits pour des Fêtes données a Charles V par François lr,"[1] but the drawings are later than this. Dimier compares them with the description of François II's entry in 1560 into Chenonceau, which his mother had just acquired.

Twelve of these drawings — one of which is exhibited here — can be regarded as a relatively homogeneous group on external grounds, such as inscriptions and paper. According to McAllister Johnson and Massenet, the inscriptions indicate that the drawings were made between 1555 and 1562.[2]

The question of the occasion or occasions for which these costumes were intended is still unsettled. However, the presence of torches and other symbols suggests that several figures had to do with a wedding. In this drawing Alexander's identity is conveyed by the helmet crowned with ram's horns and the goddess of victory holding a laurel wreath and palm leaves. Thalestris, the last queen of the Amazons, is similarly identified by her helmet crowned with an Eros.

NOTES:
1. "They are made for the festivities held for Charles V by François I."
2. Paris, Grand Palais, *L'école de Fontainebleau*, 1972, no. 178.

Reproduced in color.

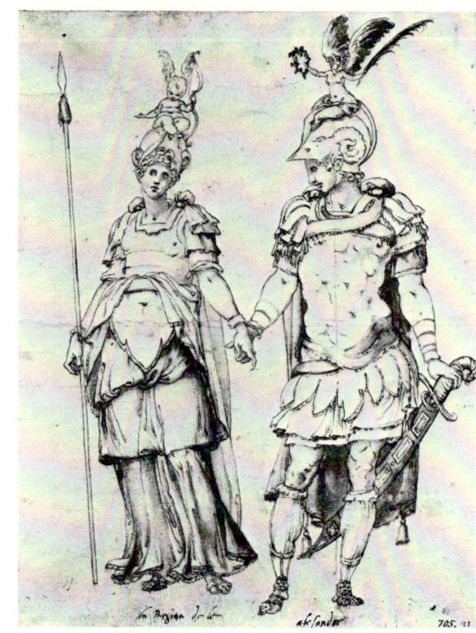

35

ETIENNE DELAUNE
Orléans c. 1518 - Strasbourg 1583

Dialectic

Pen and grey ink, gray wash on vellum. 29 x 20.5 cm. NM 155/1979.

PROVENANCE:
Private collection, Orléans □ Prouté.

BIBLIOGRAPHY:
Dessins originaux anciens et modernes exposés chez Paul Prouté S. A., Paris 1978, p. 7, no. 6 □ P. Bjurström, "Annual Report for 1979," *Nationalmuseum Bulletin*, 4 (1980): 1, pp. 4 f. □ Idem, 1983, no. 788.

This drawing belongs to a series of seven sheets representing the liberal arts. All are executed on vellum, and six of the seven are to be found in public collections in France and Germany: *Grammar* (Berlin, Kunstbibliothek), *Rhetoric* (Paris, Louvre, Collection Rothschild), *Geometry* (Chantilly, Musée Condé), *Arithmetic* (Berlin-Dahlem, Kupferstichkabinett), *Astronomy* (Paris, Louvre, Collection Rothschild), and *Music* (Paris, Louvre, Cabinet des dessins). This sheet completes the set.

As an allegory of Dialectic, the entire composition consists of pairs of opposites: Wisdom and Folly dispute on the stage, the attributes of War and Peace appear in the central cartouche above, and so on.

In the drawing of Geometry, a pillar on the right is inscribed with a list of the seven liberal arts. A frontispiece for the series, now in the Venice Accademia,[1] shows the arts, personified by seven scholars with their respective attributes, receiving laurels from a young Charles IX, whose device — PIETATE ET IVSTITIA — runs along a banderole above the composition. The king is accompanied by his mother, Catherine de' Medici, and his brothers, Henri d'Anjou (later Henry III) and Hercule, known as François, Duc d'Alençn.

Apart from the frontispiece, the drawing of Dialectic is the only one that alludes directly to Charles IX. The crowned C above a cornucopia inserted on either side of the stage seems to clinch the argument that the drawing, and thus the series, was dedicated to the young monarch. The drawing of Music bears the initial of Nicolas Houel, a famous pharmaceutical chemist of Paris, who probably originated the series. The drawing can be dated to around 1570.

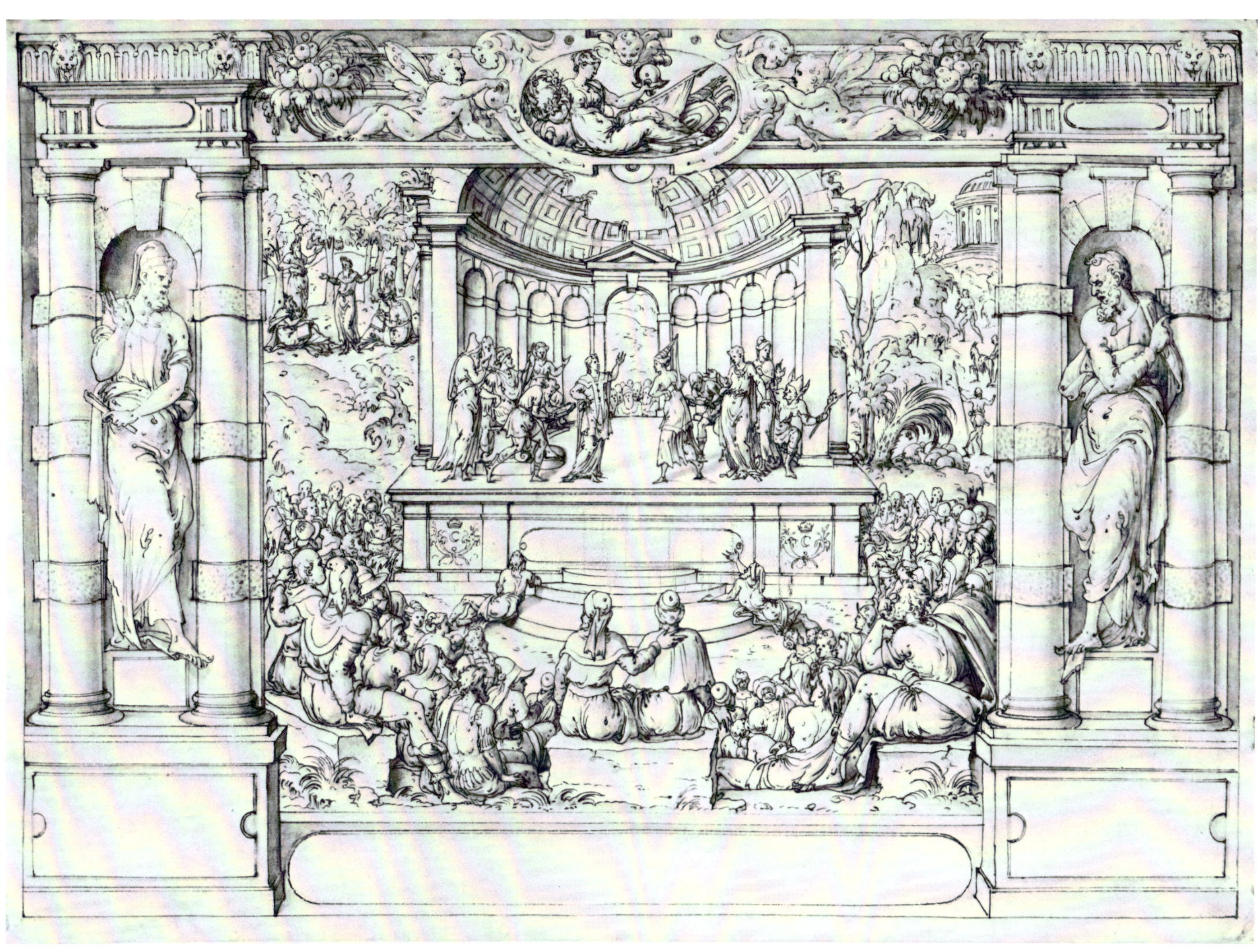

The hypothesis that the liberal arts series was done for tapestries has now been abandoned in favor of the view, put forward by Bacou and Béguin, that they were drafts for engravings.[2] An alternative suggestion by Berckenhagen is that they were sketches for work in enamel.[3]

NOTES:

1. I. Toesca, "Quelques dessins attribués à Etienne Delaune," *La Revue des arts, Musées de France*, 1969, pp. 254-59.

2. Paris, Grand Palais, *L'Ecole de Fontainebleau*, 1972, p. 73 f., no. 72.

3. E. Berckenhagen, *Die französischen Zeichnungen der Kunstbibliothek, Berlin*, Berlin 1970, p. 22, Hdz. 3419.

36

FRANÇOIS QUESNEL
Paris 1543 - Paris 1617

Reproduced in color.

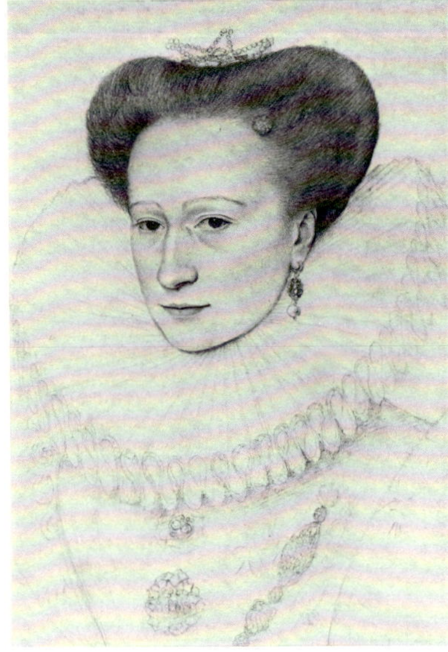

Portrait Said to Be Christine of Lorraine, Grand Duchess of Tuscany

Black and red chalk. 30 x 21 cm. No watermark. NM 117/1974. According to Dimier, inscribed on a separate piece of paper (now lost): *Duchesse de Florence fille de Carle V.*

PROVENANCE:
Henri du Bouchet de Bournonville, dit Villeflix? □ Jean-Jacques du Bouchet de Villeflix? □ Charles Wickert □ Edward M. Hodgkin □ Duveen Brothers Inc. □ Sotheby's sale 27 June 1974, no. 8.

BIBLIOGRAPHY:
L. Delteil, *Catalogue de crayons français du XVI siècle, composant la collection de M. Ch. W****, Sale Galeries Georges Petit, Paris, 3 May 1909, no. 29 □ E. Moreau-Nelaton, *Les Clouets et leurs émules*, Paris 1924, 2, pp. 99 f., 3, p. 153 □ L. Dimier, *Histoire de la peinture de portrait*, 1911, p. 227 □ Bjurström 1976, no. 78.

EXHIBITIONS:
Cincinnati, Art Museum, 1921 □ Toledo, Museum of Art, *Exhibition of French Drawings and Watercolors*, 1941, no. 4 □ Jacksonville, Cummer Gallery of Art, *French Art of the Sixteenth Century*, 1964, no. 19.

From the beginning of Henri II's reign until the middle of Henri IV's, a subtle portrait art was developed at the French court. These chalk drawings translated the subject's features, full of grace and character, with precision and finesse. This type of drawing first appeared at the court of King René in Aix-en-Provence. It was practiced chiefly by Jean Clouet, who perfected the psychological portrait, and continued by his son François, who was however less free in his technique and prone to produce a charming picture rather than a likeness.

The genre threatened to lapse with the death of François Clouet in 1572, but François Quesnel gave it a new lease of life. His experience as a painter led him to add a coloristic dimension to his portrait drawings, with a suggestion of red on cheeks and lips as well as an intimation of color in the rendering of hair.

The sheet is attributed to Quesnel by Dimier, who proposed 1582 as an approximate date. Christine of Lorraine (1565-1637), daughter of Charles II of Lorraine, was the wife of Grand Duke Ferdinand I of Tuscany who died in 1609. If she is in fact the model and Dimier's date is correct, the portrait was made when she was seventeen years of age.

37

JACQUES BELLANGE
Active c. 1600 - 1616

Soldier with a Banner

Pen and brown ink. 30.5 x 19.7 cm. Cut to the outline of the subject. Laid down. NM 81/1874:94.

PROVENANCE:
Prince Victor-Amédée de Carignan □ C. G. Tessin □ Gustaf III □ The Royal Family □ Karl XV (Rosersberg) □ Kongl. Biblioteket □ Transferred to the museum in 1874.

BIBLIOGRAPHY:
B. Dahlbäck, "De Bellange à Deruet," *Bulletin de la société de l'histoire de l'art français* (1953), p. 79 □ Bjurström 1976, no. 118.

In the early years of the seventeenth century, Nancy supplanted Paris and Fontainebleau as the artistic capital of France. The court of Lorraine had strong links with Italy in particular as well as with the Germanic and Netherlandish spheres. Jacques Bellange is an artist who unites mannerist influences from all these cultures with the new baroque taste. Life at an international court is reflected in his subjects — ladies, courtesans, warriors, and cavaliers. Charles III of Lorraine engaged him to participate in or perhaps direct the festivities that marked Margherita of Gonzaga's visit to the court in 1614.

Bellange is a mysterious figure. Details about his life are lacking, and there is even reason to suspect that he may have been burnt as a magician.

This drawing is probably a costume study for a cavalcade. Its calligraphic elegance is a hallmark of of this kind of drawing by Bellange. A similar figure occurs in the right foreground of one of his etchings with a religious subject, *Bearing the Cross.*[1]

NOTE:
1. N. Walch, *Die Radierungen des Jacques Bellange*, Munich 1971, no. 23.

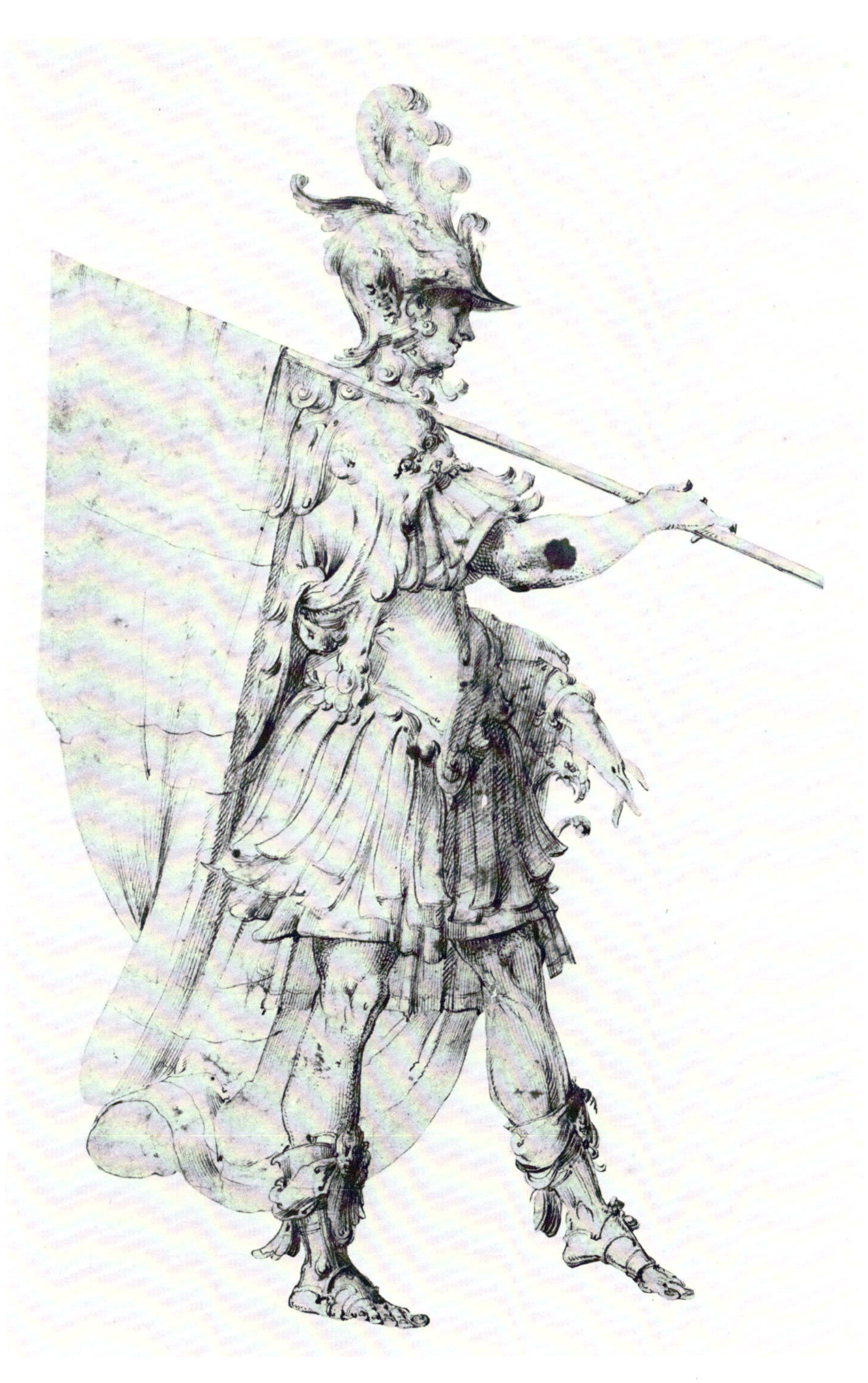

38

JACQUES CALLOT
Nancy 1592 - Nancy 1635

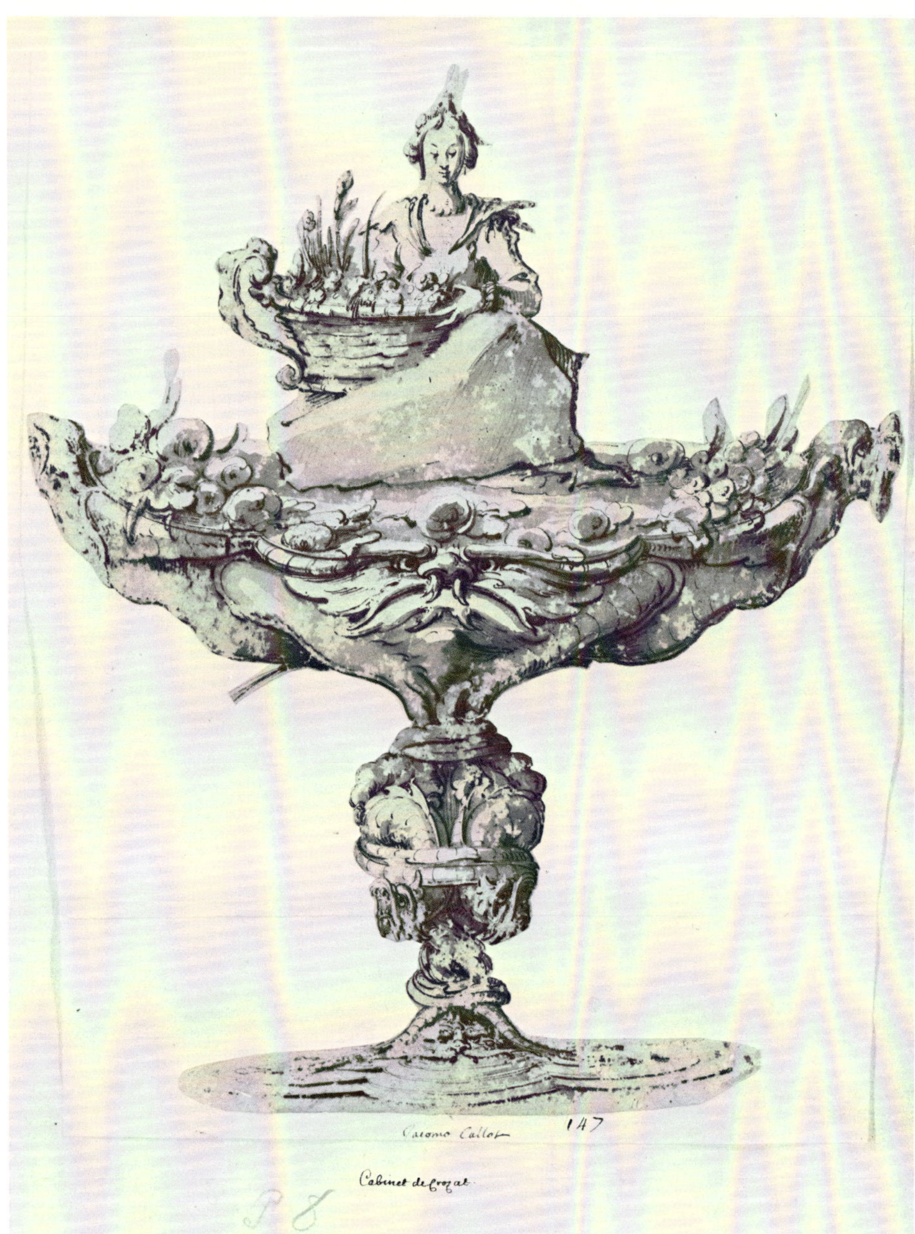

Design for a Fruit Bowl or a Fountain

Pen and brown ink, brown wash. 34.2 x 29 cm. Cut to the outline of subject. Laid down. NM THC 2082. Inscribed at the lower center in pen and brown ink: *Jacomo Callot*. Numbered *147* and inscribed on another piece of paper further below: *Cabinet de Crozat*, pen and brown ink.

PROVENANCE:
C. G. Tessin (List 1739-42, p. 62 v.) □ Kongl. Biblioteket □ Kongl. Museum (Lugt 1638).

BIBLIOGRAPHY:
G. Paulsson, "Handteckningar av Jacques Callot i Nationalmuseum," *Nationalmusei Årsbok*, 2 (1920), pp. 83 f., no. 8, fig. 22 □ D. Ternois, *L'Art de Jacques Callot*, Paris 1962, p. 138 □ Idem, *Jacques Callot, Catalogue complet de son oeuvre dessiné*, Paris 1962, no. 555 □ Th. Schröder (Intr.), *Jacques Callot, Das gesamte Werk, Handzeichnungen*, Munich and Berlin 1971, p. 555 □ Bjurström 1976, no. 181.

EXHIBITIONS:
Paris, Brussels, Amsterdam 1970-71, no. 33.

Jacques Callot, a native of Lorraine like Bellange, grew up in Nancy where his father was a heraldic painter. Accordingly Callot was familiar with arrangements for festivals and celebrations, subjects that came to be the principal motifs in his art. At the age of sixteen he left Rome and in 1611 moved to Florence, where he settled for some time.

Greatly influenced initially by Bellange, Callot developed his own personal, dynamic style in Italy. In this work the woman holding a basket of fruit harks back to drawings of his earlier mentors, while the new influences from Giulio Parigi, his Florentine master, are chiefly evident in the bowl itself.

The drawing is a replica of a sheet in the Uffizi, with which it agrees in detail.[1] The Uffizi also has a number of drawings which can be regarded as preliminary studies for this motif,[2] dated by Ternois on stylistic grounds to c. 1615.

The drawing is usually interpreted as a study for a fruit bowl, but Ternois claims that it depicts a fountain. Certain details can be said to resemble jets of water, for example, the area to the left below the bowl. Another jet, on the right, was no doubt lost when the drawing was cut out along the outline.

The drawing has not been engraved.

NOTES:
1. D. Ternois, *Jacques Callot, Catalogue complet*, no. 554.
2. Ternois, *op. cit.*, nos. 548-552.

39

JACQUES CALLOT

The Village Place

Black chalk, brown wash. 17.1 x 33.7 cm. Central vertical fold. Laid down. NM THC 3282.

PROVENANCE:
Crozat? □ C. G. Tessin? □ Kongl. Biblioteket □ Kongl. Museum (Lugt 1638).

BIBLIOGRAPHY:
G. Paulsson, "Handteckningar av Jacques Callot i Nationalmuseum," *Nationalmusei Årsbok*, 2 (1920), p. 84, no. 9, fig. 24 □ D. Ternois, *Jacques Callot, Catalogue complet de son oeuvre dessiné*, Paris 1962, no. 1338 □ J. Thuillier, "Dessins français du XVIIe siècle: Le 'vrai' Callot," *Art de France*, 3 (1963), p. 232, p. 235 □ Unsigned review of Ternois, Jacques Callot, *Sele arte*, 69 (1964), p. 53 □ Th. Schröder (Intr.), *Jacques Callot, Das gesamte Werk, Handzeichnungen*, Munich and Berlin 1971, p. 789 □ Bjurström 1976, no. 188.

EXHIBITIONS:
Stockholm 1958, no. 208 □ Paris, Brussels, Amsterdam 1970-71, no. 34 □ Washington, National Gallery, *Jacques Callot*, 1975, no. 259.

After the death of Cosimo II of Tuscany in 1621, Callot returned to Nancy, where he soon had established contact with the court of Lorraine. This drawing and two in the Teyler Museum, Haarlem,[1] are larger than Callot's other landscape drawings. The village motif is repeated in a more finished pen drawing in the Chatsworth Collection,[2] with the additions of a tree on the right and three figures in the foreground. The Chatsworth drawing was engraved by one of Callot's followers.[3]

Our sheet belongs to a group which Félibien[4] claims was made for the instruction of Gaston, Duc d'Orléans, during his stay in Lorraine from 1629 to 1631. According to Ternois, the group comprises more than forty unusually detailed pen drawings (most of them at Chatsworth) and some thirty sketches (some of them for the pen drawings) done in black chalk and wash, Callot's most usual technique at that time.

Reproduced in color.

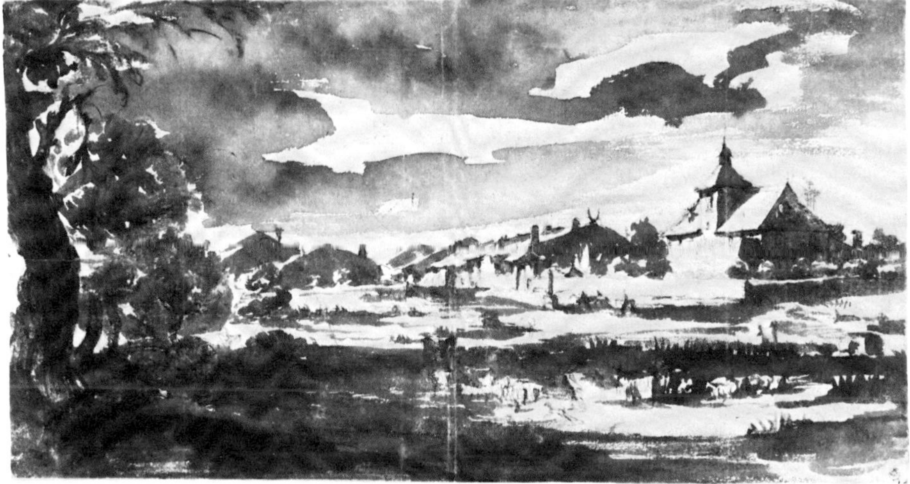

Four of the black chalk and wash sketches are now in the Nationalmuseum. Some of the drawings were later etched for the series *Livre des paysages* (etcher unknown), others were etched by unknown followers of Callot. It should be noted that Ternois' attribution of the drawings to Callot has been the subject of discussion.[5]

NOTES:
1. Ternois, *op. cit.*, nos. 1336 and 1337.
2. Ternois, *op. cit.*, no. 1295.
3. E. Meaume, *Recherches sur la vie et les ouvrages de Jacques Callot*, Nancy 1853, no. 1128.
4. A. Félibien, *Entretiens sur les vies et sur les ouvrages des plus excellens peintres anciens et modernes...*, Paris 1684, ed. Trevoux 1725, III, p. 380.
5. Vienna, Albertina, *Jacques Callot und sein Kreis*, 1968-69, no. 621.

40

CLAUDE GELLÉE, called LORRAIN
Chamagne 1600 - Rome 1682

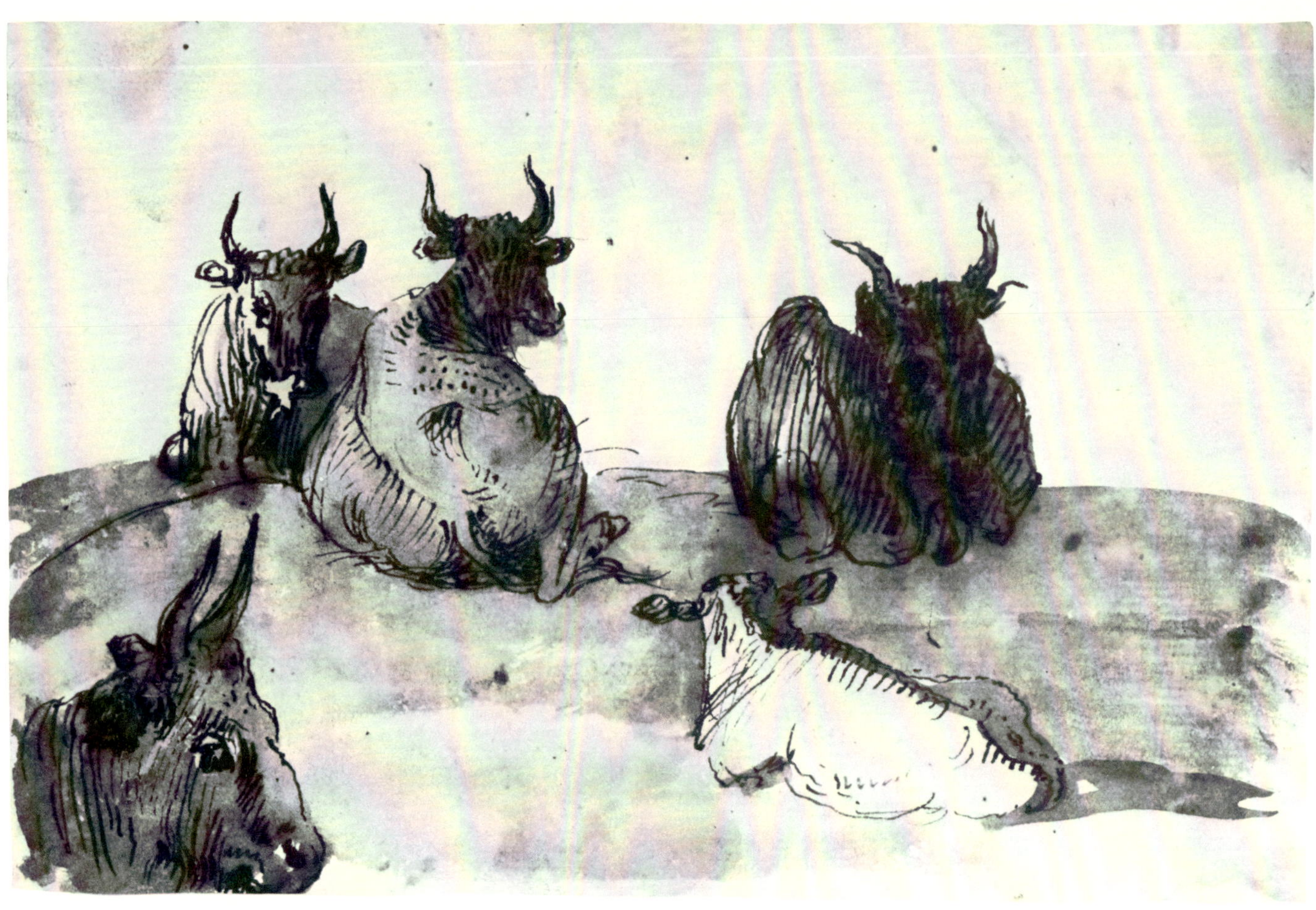

Cattle

Pen and brown ink, brown wash. 12.6 x 18.7 cm. Patches of glue at the top. Laid down. NM 99/1958.

PROVENANCE:
Queen Christina □ Decio Azzolino? □ Pompeo Azzolino? □ Livio Odescalchi and then by descent to Prince Ladislao Odescalchi □ Sotheby's sale 20 November 1957, lot 67 □ H. M. Calmann.

BIBLIOGRAPHY:
M. Röthlisberger, "Bemerkungen zum zeichnerischen Oeuvre von Claude Lorrain," *Zeitschrift für Kunstgeschichte*, 24:2 (1961), p. 165, p. 174 no. 5 □ Idem, *Claude Lorrain, The Drawings*, Berkeley and Los Angeles 1968, no. 226 □ Bjurström 1976, no. 538.

EXHIBITIONS:
Stockholm 1958, no. 201.

Claude, the third of the great artists to come from Lorraine, was only thirteen years of age when he left for Rome. Apart from a brief return to Nancy in 1626-27, he spent the rest of his life in Italy.

Claude is the illustrator par excellence of the Roman Campagna. His work includes broad landscapes as well as detailed studies of vegetation and animals. This drawing comes from an album consisting mainly of animal studies, the *Animal Album*, which had belonged to Prince Livio Odescalchi[1] and was broken up in 1957. All the animal studies from this album are small and sketch-like. Each species is portrayed separately in typical poses against a neutral ground. The studies were not used directly in Claude's paintings, with a few exceptions, and it is not possible to date them exactly. Röthlisberger suggests a date in the 1630s and 1640s. The sheets no doubt come from a number of different sketchbooks, as they differ in size, style, technique, and subject.

This study of cattle is numbered 37 in the *Animal Album*. It corresponds in size and execution to number 36,[2] which shows a similar group of animals.

NOTES:
1. Death inventory 1713-14, p. 354 r.-v.
2. Röthlisberger 1968, no. 225.

41

CLAUDE GELLÉE, called LORRAIN

Reproduced in color.

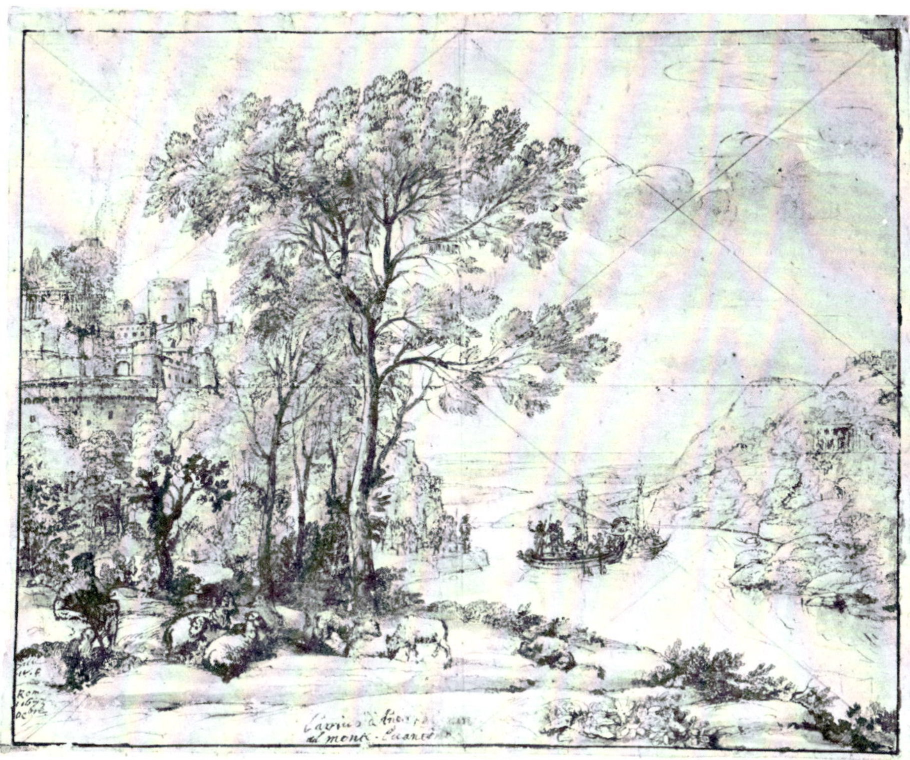

Landscape with the Landing of Aeneas in Latium

Pen and brown ink, gray wash. 26.1 x 33 cm. Laid down. NM 358/1969. Inscribed at the bottom left: *Claudio / Gille / I.V.F. / Roma / 1673 / Oc*[bre], at the bottom center: *l'arrivo d'Anea (a palante) / al monte Evantino.* Squared with diagonals in black chalk.

PROVENANCE:
Coll. Camuccini, Rome, early 19th century □ Sotheby's sale 18 October 1969, cat. no. D23.

BIBLIOGRAPHY:
M. Röthlisberger, *Claude Lorrain, The Paintings*, New Haven 1961, I, p. 437 □ Idem, *Claude Lorrain, The Drawings*, Berkeley and Los Angeles 1968, no. 1081 □ *Statens konstsamlingars tillväxt och förvaltning*, 94 (1969), p. 6, pp. 18 f. □ *Apollo*, vol. 90:2 (1969), p. 551, no. 16 □ A. Zwollo, "An Additional Study for Claude's Picture 'The Arrival of Aeneas at Pallantium,'" *Master Drawings*, 8 (1970), p. 274 □ Bjurström 1976, no. 542.

This is one of three preliminary studies in the Nationalmuseum for the painting *The Arrival of Aeneas at Pallantium* of 1675 (*Liber Veritatis* number 185) done for Prince Gaspare Altieri (today at Anglesey Abbey, National Trust). An inscription on the verso of one of the other sheets (NM 360/1969) indicates that it was the Prince who decided on the motif, which is based on the *Aeneid* VIII, 79-123. A large number of other studies for the painting exist.[1] According to A. Zwollo, the painting may have been commissioned as early as 1670.[2]

In this sheet from 1673, Virgil's text has been followed and includes the two ruined cities of Janiculum and Saturnia on the right. Moreover, the two ships have been placed deeper into the background than in the earlier version, and changes have been made to the group of trees. Röthlisberger has shown that another drawing,[3] probably from 1673, comes between those from 1672 and this one. It is an exploratory sheet; the stand of trees is still reminiscent of the earlier version, the ruined cities have been added, with inscriptions above to identify them, and various positions have been tried out for the ships. For the Aventine there is a detailed study from 1673.[4] The British Museum has another study from 1675 featuring the ships and the central group of figures.[5]

In the present drawing a shepherd and his flock have been added in the left foreground. The composition is essentially the same as the painting, although in the latter Aeneas' ship is placed in the foreground.

NOTES:
1. Röthlisberger 1968, nos. 1077-1086.
2. Zwollo, *op. cit.*, p. 247.
3. Röthlisberger 1968, no. 1079.
4. *Op. cit.*, no. 1082.
5. *Op. cit.*, no. 1083.

42

NICOLAS POUSSIN
Les Andelys 1593/94 - Rome 1665

Reproduced in color.

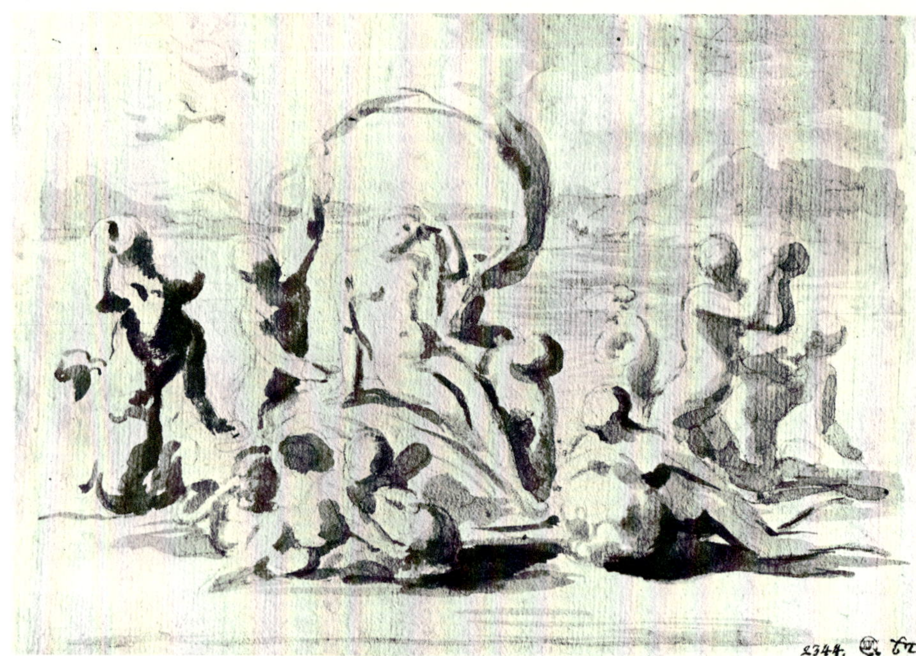

The Triumph of Galatea

Black chalk, brown wash. 15.6 x 22.9 cm. Watermark: Star and dove. NM 2445/1863. Numbered at lower right in brown ink: *2344* (Sparre) and *62* (struck out).

VERSO:
Studies of Dolphins and Venus on the Shell Attended by Mercury

PROVENANCE:
Crozat (Mariette, no. 971) □ C. G. Tessin (List 1739-42, p. 43 r.; Cat. 1749, livré 13, no. 18 or 19) □ Kongl. Biblioteket (Cat. 1790, no. 2344) □ Kongl. Museum (Lugt 1638).

BIBLIOGRAPHY:
G. Wengström, "Teckningar av Poussin i Nationalmuseum," *Nationalmusei Arsbok*, 6 (1924), pp. 140 f., p. 146, no. 14 □ Idem, *Nicolas Poussin, Dix-huit fac-similés en couleurs...* (Collection de dessins du Musée National 2), Malmö 1935, no. 14 □ W. Friedländer and A. Blunt, *The Drawings of Nicolas Poussin*, London 1953, 3, no. 217, pl. 166, no. 204, pl. 158 (verso) □ K. Badt, *Die Kunst des Nicolas Poussin*, Cologne 1969, p. 255.

EXHIBITIONS:
London, Royal Academy, *French Art 1200-1900*, 1932, no. 708 □ Stockholm 1933, no. 60 □ Paris, Gazette des Beaux-Arts, *Le dessin français dans les collections du XVIIIe siècle*, 1935, no. 75 □ Paris, *Chefs-d'oeuvre de l'art français*, 1937, no. 493 □ Stockholm 1958, no. 192 □ Paris, Musée du Louvre, *Nicolas Poussin*, 1960, no. 138 □ Leningrad, State Hermitage Museum, *Risunki XV - nacala XIX vv. iz nacional'nogo muzeja Stokgolma*, 1963 □ Paris, Brussels, Amsterdam 1970-71, no. 37 □ Bjurström 1976, no. 626.

Poussin, like Claude Lorrain, spent most of his life as an active artist in Rome, though he arrived there in 1624 at a more mature age. He returned to France in 1640-42 for a brief period of work at the French court.

The twin foundations of Poussin's artistic development were antique sculptures, primarily reliefs, which inspired his forms, and open air studies, which gave his pictures their luminosity.

This sheet exemplifies his early drawn art, where the key principle is the distribution of light and shade over the composition. The drawings tend to have the appearance of reliefs and demonstrate a fresh, spontaneous imagination.

Closely connected to this sheet is another drawing of *The Triumph of Galatea* in the Nationalmuseum. At first sight they appear to be related to *The Triumph of Amphitrite*, executed for Richelieu at the end of the 1630s and today in the Philadelphia Museum of Art. As Blunt has pointed out, the likeness can be accounted for on the basis of a common ancestry in Raphael's and Annibale Carracci's versions of the theme. There is no motif, however, that matches the drawing to the painting. The drawing may have been executed in the same period, c. 1635.

The verso displays close resemblances to a *Birth of Venus* in Chantilly. Along with Galatea and Amphitrite, this theme belongs to a group of motifs that occupied Poussin in the mid-1630s.

43

NICOLAS POUSSIN

The Finding of Queen Zenobia

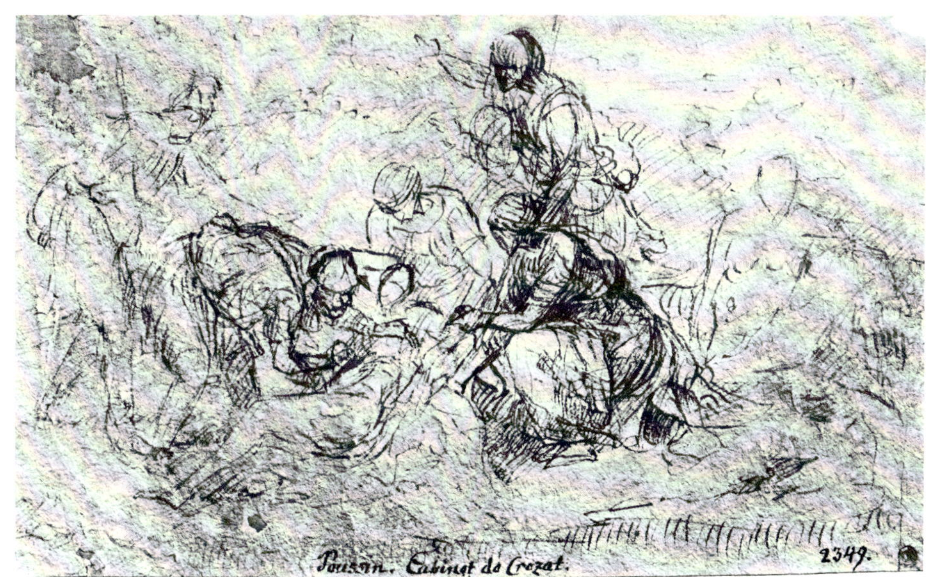

Pen and brown ink. 11.3 x 19.3 cm. Several repairs at the edges. Laid down. NM 2451/1863. Inscribed at lower center in pen and brown ink: *Poussin. Cabinet de Crozat.* Numbered at lower right in pen and brown ink: *2349* (Sparre).

PROVENANCE:
Abbé Quesnel (Cf. E. Magne, *Nicolas Poussin, premier peintre du Roi*, Paris 1914, p. 202) □ Crozat (Mariette, no. 971) □ C. G. Tessin (List 1739-42, p. 43 r.; Cat. 1749, livré 13, no. 23) □ Kongl. Biblioteket (Cat. 1790, no. 2349) □ Kongl. Museum (Lugt 1638).

BIBLIOGRAPHY:
Wengström 1924, pp. 133 f., p. 145, no. 7 □ Idem 1935, no. 7 □ W. Friedländer, *The Drawings of Nicolas Poussin*, 2, London 1949, no. 133, pl. 104 □ Bjurström 1976, no. 630.

EXHIBITIONS:
Leningrad, State Hermitage Museum, *Risunki XV - nacala XIX vv. iz nacional'nogo muzeja Stokgolma*, 1963 □ New York, Boston, Chicago 1969, no. 88.

Poussin's works from the 1640s indicate that with his advanced years he experienced physical maladies, for example, an increasing shakiness that meant his hand would no longer comply with his intentions. However, he had the power to cope by renewing his approach, simplifying forms, and concentrating on the absolute essentials.

Queen Zenobia, wife of Rhadamistus, King of Armenia, had escaped from Artaxata, the capital of Armenia, after an insurrection. Seized with the pains of childbirth during her flight, she begged her husband to kill her rather than allow her to fall into the hands of their enemies. Rhadamistus attempted to do so, and after stabbing her, threw her body into the river Araxes. But she was seen by shepherds, taken out of the water, and revived. The story, told by Tacitus (*Annales XII*, 51), is represented here.

The drawing is similar in composition to the *Finding of Moses* of 1647 and is dated by Friedländer to about the same period.[1] A painting ascribed to Dufresnoy (The Hermitage, Leningrad) follows this sketch very closely.

NOTE:
1. Friedländer, *op. cit.*, no. 133.

44

FRANÇOIS BOUCHER
Paris 1703 - Paris 1770

Reproduced in color.

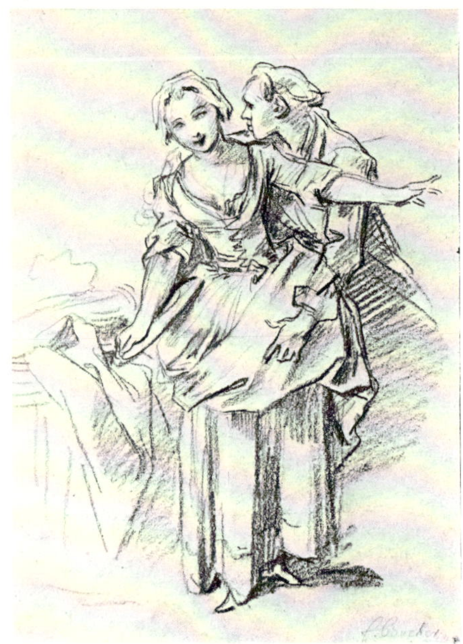

A Seduction

Red chalk, heightened with white on brownish gray paper. 34.5 x 24.8 cm. Laid down. NM 2928/1863. Signed at lower right in red chalk: *f. boucher*. Numbered in pen and brown ink on the old mount: *2821* (Sparre) and *93* (struck out).

PROVENANCE:
C. G. Tessin (Cat. 1749, livré 14, no. 93) □ Kongl. Biblioteket (Cat. 1790, no. 2821) □ Kongl. Museum (Lugt 1638).

BIBLIOGRAPHY:
Hoppe 1930, p. 16, pl. 26 □ Ananoff 1966, no. 217, fig. 38 □ Ananoff 1976, 1, pp. 178 f. □ Bjurström 1982, no. 829.

EXHIBITIONS:
Stockholm 1922, no. 59 □ London, Royal Academy, *French Art 1200-1900*, 1932, no. 783 □ Paris 1935, no. 31 □ Paris, Palais National des Arts, *Chefs-d'oeuvre de l'art français*, 1937, no. 515.

The Nationalmuseum has some forty drawings by François Boucher. Most were acquired from the artist himself by Carl Gustaf Tessin when he was Sweden's ambassador in Paris from 1739-42. The collection includes early studies belonging to the periods before and during Boucher's years in Rome (1727-31), as well as finished compositional sheets, intended to adorn the walls of private chambers. Boucher was the first to recognize that such drawings could have a commercial potential, and he exhibited them at the Salon as early as 1745.

Boucher's residence in Rome left little obvious trace in his work. Ignoring the art of antiquity and the Renaissance, he developed his own gracious style, ultimately inspired by Rubens, Tiepolo, and Watteau. This work is a preliminary study for the corresponding scene in the painting *La ferme* in the Alte Pinakothek, Munich, which Ananoff dates 1730.[1] The Nationalmuseum owns two further studies for the same painting.[2]

NOTES:
1. Ananoff 1976, I, no. 41.
2. Bjurström 1982, nos. 830, 831.

45

FRANÇOIS BOUCHER

Reproduced in color.

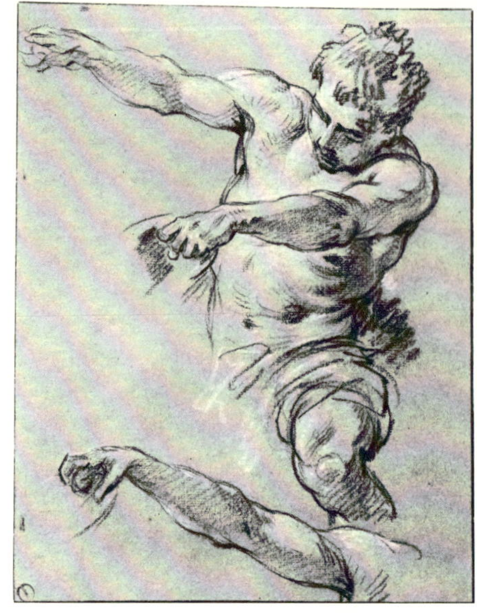

Male Nude Study

Black chalk, heightened with white on blue paper. 33.4 x 26 cm. Laid down. NM Anck. 65.

PROVENANCE:
M. G. Anckarsvärd □ A. Michelson □ K. Michelson □ Acquired by the museum in 1896.

BIBLIOGRAPHY:
Hoppe 1930, p. 16, no. 31 (repr. p. 9) □ Ananoff 1976, 1, p. 251, as no. 126/3 □ Bjurström 1982, no. 856.

Boucher developed a great capacity for the rendering of nude figures. In his figure studies his affinity with the work of Rubens is closer than that of an influence. Ananoff links this drawing with *La chasse au crocodile*, where a hunter in a similar stance is thrusting a staff between the crocodile's jaws.

This comparison is not convincing, however, as our man clearly holds a piece of cloth in both hands. In this detail and in his attitude, the figure displays a great similarity, though not complete agreement, with Boucher's Chiron, the skillful centaur, in *Allégorie sur l'éducation de Louis XV* of 1752.[1]

NOTE:
1. Ananoff 1976, 2, pp. 91 ff., no. 391.

46

JEAN-BAPTISTE-SIMÉON CHARDIN
Paris 1699 - Paris 1779

Reproduced in color.

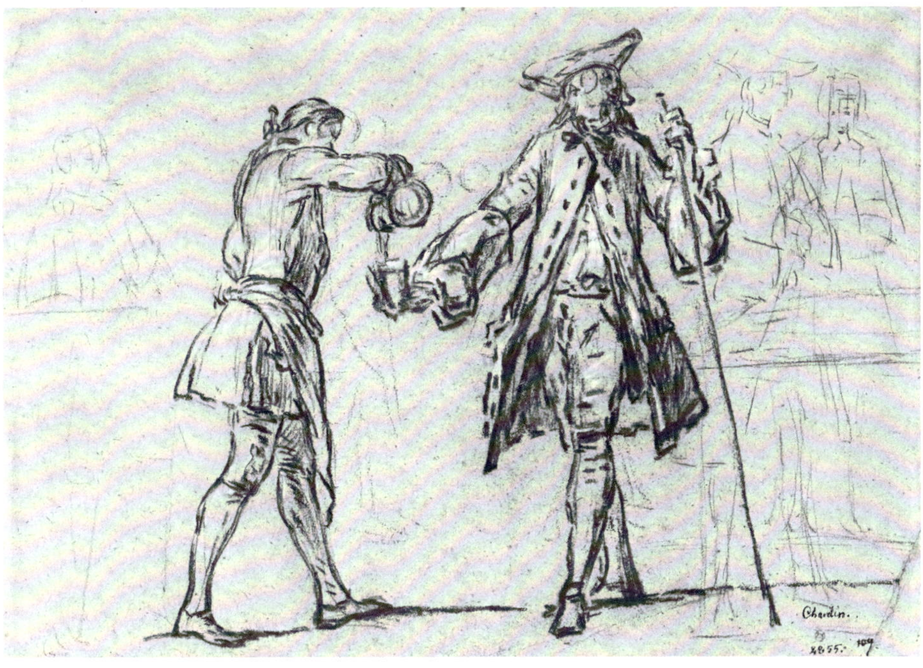

Servant Pouring a Drink for a Billiard Player

Red and black chalk, heightened with white on gray-brown paper. 24.7 x 37 cm. No watermark. NM 2962/1863. Inscribed at lower right in pen and brown ink: *Chardin* (Tessin). Numbered 2885 (Sparre) and *109* (struck out).

PROVENANCE:
C. G. Tessin (List 1739-42, p. 69 v.; Cat. 1749, livré 14, no. 107) ☐ Kongl. Biblioteket (Cat. 1790, no. 2855) ☐ Kongl. Museum (Lugt 1638).

BIBLIOGRAPHY:
E. F.-S. Dilke, "Chardin et ses oeuvres à Potsdam et à Stockholm," *Gazette des Beaux-Arts*, 3:22 (1899), p. 341 ☐ Schönbrunner and Meder, no. 1008 ☐ Guiffrey, *Catalogue de l'Oeuvre de Chardin*, Paris 1908, no. 246 ☐ A. Gauffin, *Konstverk och människor*, Stockholm 1915, p. 146 ☐ A. de Ridder, *J. B. S. Chardin*, Paris 1932, pl. 93 ☐ E. Goldschmidt, *J. B. S. Chardin*, Stockholm 1945, p. 65, pl. 15 ☐ Idem, *J. B. S. Chardin*, Copenhagen 1947, pl. 17 ☐ D. Sutton, *French Drawings of the XVIIIth Century*, London 1949, pl. 50 ☐ J. Mathey, "Les dessins de Chardin," *Albertina-Studien*, 1 and 2 (1964), pp. 17 ff., no. 3 ☐ A. Ananoff, "Chardin," *Connaissance des arts*, 153 (1967), p. 60 ☐ P. Hulton, "France in the Eighteenth Century," *Master Drawings*, 6:2 (1968), p. 163 ☐ P. Bjurström, "Letter to the Editors," *Master Drawings*, 7:1 (1969), pp. 58 ff. ☐ Wilhelm, "'La Partie de Billard,' est-elle une oeuvre de Jeunesse de Chardin, ? Nouvelle Acquisition," *Bulletin du Musée Carnavalet*, 22 (1969), pp. 7-12 ☐ P. Rosenberg, "Le XVIIIe siècle français à la Royal Academy," *Revue de l'art*, 3 (1969), p. 99 ☐ Bjurström 1982, no. 908.

EXHIBITIONS:
Stockholm 1922, no. 43 ☐ London, Royal Academy, *French Art 1200-1900*, 1932, no. 770 ☐ Stockholm 1933, no. 72 ☐ Paris 1935, no. 58 ☐ London, Royal Academy, *France in the 18th Century*, 1968, no. 146 ☐ Paris, Brussels, Amsterdam 1970-71, no. 55 ☐ Paris, Grand Palais, *Chardin 1699-1779*, 1979, no. 2.

Opinions differ about the attribution of drawings to Jean-Baptiste Chardin, and not a single sheet has been accepted unanimously. Three sheets in the Nationalmuseum, however, can be traced back to Tessin, who very probably obtained them directly from the artist.

The Stockholm drawings are all rather large and of the same size as his paintings. This raises the question if Chardin normally prepared his compositions directly on the canvas. One of the Stockholm drawings can be connected with Chardin's first known work, a sign for a surgeon, which is known only from an engraved illustration in the study of Chardin by the Goncourt brothers. Supposedly executed in the 1720s and traceable to the collection of the engraver Le Bas, the sign was acquired by a nephew of Chardin after the death of Le Bas in 1783; it then disappeared. Jules de Goncourt etched the illustration for *L'Art au dix-huitième siècle* (Paris 1880-82) after a sketch of the sign that was once in the Hôtel de Ville but was destroyed by fire in 1871.

The present drawing is clearly connected with a composition entitled *La Partie de Billard* in Musée Carnavalet, of which there is a smaller copy in the Pushkin Museum in Moscow. The Carnavalet painting was formerly regarded as either an English work, by an artist close to Gravelot, or by Étienne Jeaurat. In 1969, however, an attribution to Chardin was put forward by Jacques Wilhelm, an opinion now shared by Pierre Rosenberg.[1]

The crucial point for both authors in their attribution is the link with our drawing; both date the painting to early in Chardin's youth. It also resembles the surgeon's sign in the wealth of figures; in later works Chardin seldom includes more than three figures.

The painting in the Musée Carnavalet may have had the same function as the surgeon's sign, in which case Chardin could well have done it for his father, who manufactured billiard equipment and was succeeded in business by the artist's younger brother, Juste. The latter took over the enterprise entirely when the father died in 1731. It can be noted also that during his stay in Paris, Carl Gustav Tessin rented "a billiard" from Chardin's firm.[2]

Although differences in technique are evident between this and the other Chardin drawings, they are outweighed by the similarities: the large scale; the broad, resolute contours of the figures; and their slightly posed attitudes.

NOTES:

1. Exh. cat. Paris, Grand Palais, *Chardin 1699-1779*, pp. 105 ff.
2. According to a note in Tessin's cashbook from Paris, National Record Office (Riksarkivet), Stockholm E. 5720: "1741, nov. 13 Chardin hyra för Billarden 200" ([paid to] Chardin rent for the Billiard 200 [livres]).

47

JEAN-HONORÉ FRAGONARD
Grasse 1732 - Paris 1806

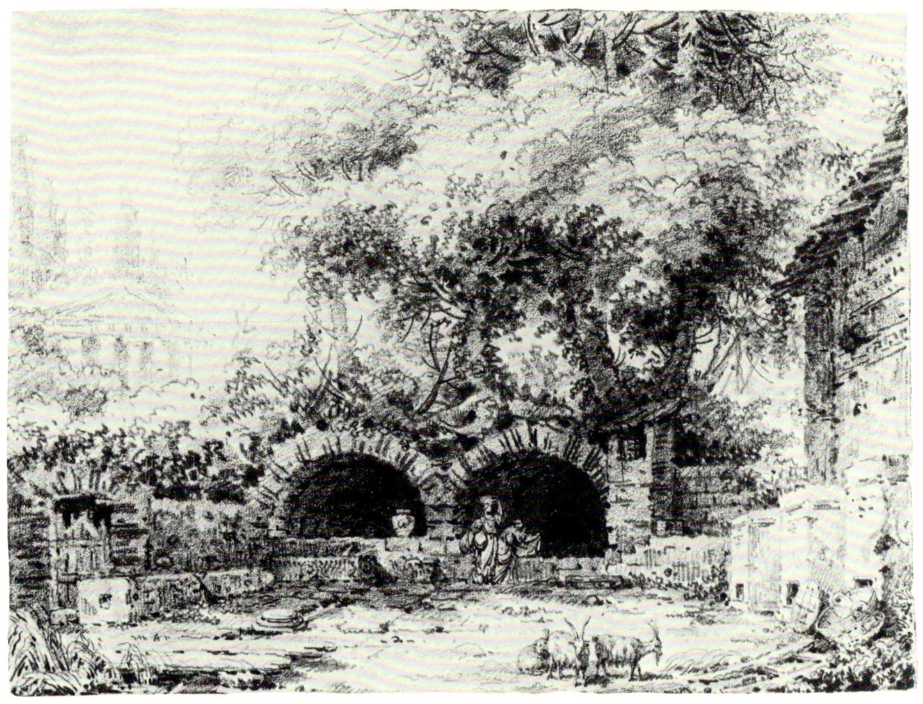

Landscape with Ruins

Red chalk. 21 x 29.3 cm. No watermark. NM Z 1/1967.

PROVENANCE:
Rosersberg □ Entered the museum in 1874.

BIBLIOGRAPHY:
A. Ananoff, *L'oeuvre dessiné de Fragonard*, 3, Paris 1968, no. 1607 □ P. Bjurström, "Drawings by Jean-Honoré Fragonard in Nationalmuseum," *Nationalmuseum Bulletin*, 2:1 (1978), pp. 39 f. □ Idem, 1982, no. 952.

EXHIBITIONS:
Stockholm 1922, no. 100 □ Bordeaux, Musée des Beaux-Arts, *La peinture française en Suède*, 1967, no. 126, pl. 61.

As one might expect of François Boucher's pupil, Jean-Honoré Fragonard greatly admired Peter Paul Rubens. Fragonard's own means of expression were first developed in his work in the parks of Rome and Tivoli.

Fragonard went to Rome in 1756 and spent four years in Italy, coming into contact with the Abbé de Saint-Non and travelling with him to Venice, Naples, and other sites. Fragonard produced numerous drawings during this period, including his famous series of ten red chalk sheets from the Villa d'Este in Tivoli, done in the spring of 1760 while the artist was staying there with Saint-Non.[1]

Although there is no direct evidence to support the tradition that Hubert Robert was also staying at the Villa d'Este at that time, he and Fragonard influenced each other to such an extent that it is very difficult to distinguish their work from each others during this period.

The present drawing can be compared with *Terrace and Garden of an Italian Villa* by Fragonard in Washington dated to 1760-61. In both drawings, the landscape with its lush vegetation appears deceptively natural in its overgrown disarray. As Williams notes,

> . . . the arrangement of the box-like space, its carefully controlled patterns of light, and its closed diagonal vistas are typical of Fragonard's theatrical sense of composition. The sharply drawn accents - small sawtooth lines and staccato dots that suggest the variety of foliage, and disconnected dashes of chalk that form dramatic, bare branches - demonstrate his expressive use of graphic conventions.[2]

NOTES:

1. L. Cornillot, *Collection Pierre-Adrien Paris Besançon*, 1 (Inventaire général des dessins des musées de province), Paris 1957, nos. 32-41.
2. E. Williams, *Drawings by Fragonard in North American Collections*, National Gallery of Art, Washington 1978, no. 8, p. 42.

48

JEAN-HONORÉ FRAGONARD

Reproduced in color.

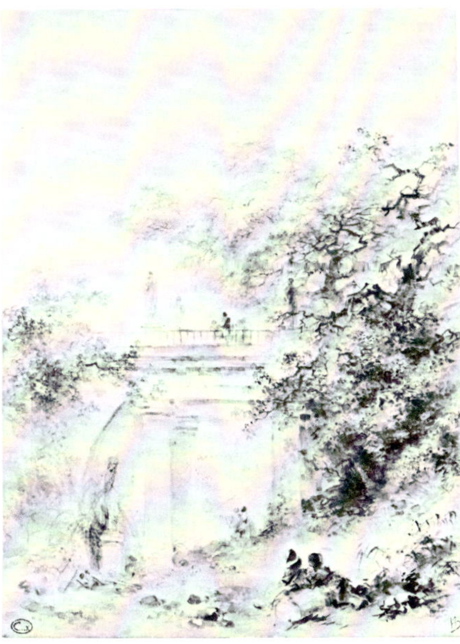

Italian Landscape

Black chalk, point of the brush and brown ink, brown wash. 23.2 x 17 cm. No watermark. NM 6/1977.

PROVENANCE:
Coll. Chabot and Duc de La Mure or Desmarets (sale 17-22 December 1787, no. 173) □ Coll. Constantin □ Coll. Marquiset (sale 27 April 1890, no. 88) □ Coll. Henri Delacroix (sale Palais Galliéra, 31 March 1962) □ Coll. Cailleux.

BIBLIOGRAPHY:
A. Ananoff, *L'oeuvre dessiné de Jean-Honoré Fragonard*, 1, Paris 1961, no. 350; 2, Paris 1963, p. 308, no. 350, fig. 366 □ P. Bjurström, "Drawings by Jean-Honoré Fragonard in Nationalmuseum," *Nationalmuseum Bulletin*, 2:1 (1978), pp. 42-45 □ Idem, 1982, no. 954.

EXHIBITIONS:
Paris, Hôtel de Sagan, *Fragonard*, 1931, no. 94 □ Paris, Musée Carnavalet, *Chefs-d'oeuvre des collections parisiennes*, 1950, no. 107.

This highly finished landscape study is a portrayal or a reminiscence of a view from the park of an Italian villa. It no doubt dates from Fragonard's second Italian journey (1773-74) which he undertook together with Bergeret de Grandcour. The motif is closely connected with two paintings from that time, now in The Metropolitan Museum of Art in New York. In one of these, *View of an Italian Villa,*[1] we recognize the colonnade and in the other, *The Shady Avenue,*[2] the dominant tree on the right takes the same position. The paintings form a pair and measure 29 x 24 cm, which is only slightly larger than our sheet.

Of course there is no means of telling to what extent these pictures represent an observed reality. But the relative freedom with which Fragonard rearranges the various elements does suggest that they were compiled from the artist's repertoire of Italian landscape motifs.

The presentation, however, has clearly been adapted to the medium. The paintings radiate a light, optimistic atmosphere, with an almost intoxicating happiness evoked by the greenery and trembling heat of summer. They are pictures of carefully tended parks, peopled by the leisured class and children at play.

The message conveyed by the drawing is more complex. A damaged statue, half overgrown, stands in the park. Nature is rampant and threatens to envelop the architectural elements. The ground is rocky and uneven, in contrast to the broad, trim walks in the paintings. The drawing hints at the passage of time, decay, and mortality.

The differences in handling and attitude between the washed drawing and the painting do not seem to be accidental. Although the instances of fragments of a particular motif being treated in different ways are rare, a general comparison of Fragonard's drawn landscapes with his paintings suggests that the drawing was conceived chiefly as an intimate work of art addressed, even though it hangs on a wall, to the individual beholder, an object for close contemplation. The paintings played a prominent part as decorative elements in a room, while the drawings were assigned to small chambers and intellectual settings. In the drawings the artist portrayed the entire register of expressions; the wash is applied in an infinite range of values, from barely discernible surfaces to the bold outlines that are most apparent in the branches of the tree and the foreground vegetation. The forms vary from delicately indicated figures to boldly shaped plants.

NOTES:
1. G. Wildenstein, *The Paintings of Fragonard*, London 1960, no. 349.
2. Wildenstein, *op. cit.*, no. 350.

49

JEAN-HONORÉ FRAGONARD

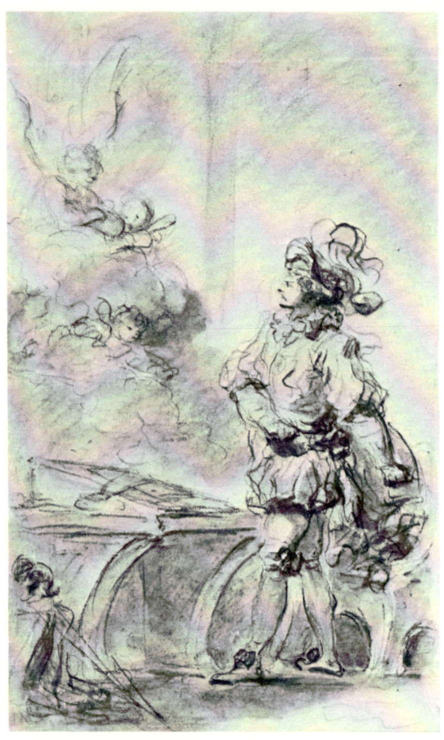

Ruggiero, Troubled in Mind, Prepares to Write to Bradamante

Black chalk, point of the brush and brown ink, brown wash. 39.8 x 24.4 cm. No watermark. NM 236/1975.

PROVENANCE:
Fragonard family ☐ Hippolyte Walferdin, Paris ☐ Louis Roederer, Reims ☐ A. S. W. Rosenbach, Philadelphia ☐ Arthur A. Houghton, Jr., New York ☐ Agnew's, London ☐ Artemis S. A. & R. M. Light Co., Boston.

BIBLIOGRAPHY:
E. Mongan, Ph. Hofer, and J. Seznec, *Fragonard Drawings for Ariosto*, New York 1945, p. 78, pl. 129 ☐ P. Bjurström, "Fragonard och Ariosto," *Kontakt med Nationalmuseum*, Stockholm 1976, pp. 15-27 ☐ Idem, "Drawings by Jean-Honoré Fragonard in Nationalmuseum," *Nationalmuseum Bulletin*, 2:1 (1978), pp. 46-48 ☐ Idem 1982, no. 9.

Nearly 160 illustrations by Fragonard for Ariosto's *Orlando Furioso* are known. They relate largely to twenty-five of the work's forty-six cantos. The distribution of illustrations among these cantos is uneven, and Fragonard presumably did not produce a complete series (this would imply the loss of a great number of drawings). The variety of watermarks among these illustrations indicates that he worked on them over a considerable period.

Besides the 137 illustrations published by Mongan, Hofer, and Seznec in 1947, Mongan knew of several others from the series, among them those in the Louvre.[1] Since then Ananoff has catalogued another twenty-three sheets with motifs from Ariosto.[2]

There are no documentary pegs on which to hang a dating of these pictures. As Elizabeth Mongan notes:

> It is extremely difficult to attempt to date this series of drawings. If some note from Didot about the edition, or some letter from Fragonard, was preserved, all would be easy. One can only hazard the guess that both stylistically, and in consideration of the events in Fragonard's life, they might have been done late in the 1780's after the La Fontaine series and before Fragonard's departure from Paris for the south.[3]

All of the Ariosto drawings are sketches rather than finished works suitable for an engraver to copy. But they differ quite considerably and are by no means a homogeneous set. Moreover, because Fragonard varied his means of expression, there are few stylistic criteria for a dating. However, the freedom of the compositions and the technical virtuosity make Mongan's dating in the 1780s, when Fragonard was at the height of his powers, the most probable.

The subject has been identified tentatively by Seznec as "Ruggiero, troubled in mind, prepares to write to Bradamante." The reference is to an episode in the twenty-fifth canto, where Ruggiero is so disappointed at not having encountered Bradamante during one of his heroic deeds that sleep evades him, and he decides to write to her about his exploits and tender feelings.

The bold warrior has set aside his sword but is not able to relinguish his magic shield. As his thoughts dwell on Bradamante, Inspiration appears before him in the guise of a winged genius assisted by a pair of putti. Ruggiero the fighter is portrayed here as a poet too, and one recognizes Ariosto's features from Fragonard's own imaginative portrait of the writer, seated at his table gazing mysteriously at a pair of small putti that symbolize love and folly.[4]

In the drawing Ruggiero has arisen and reels back from his vision, a manner of depicting the moment of inspiration that is commonly used by Fragonard. The dramatic tension is evident from the writer's face as well as his physical attitude.

Ariosto's text runs:

> . . . Intanto sopravenne e gli occhi chiuse Ai signori e ai sergenti il pigro Sonno Fuor ch'a Ruggier; chè, per tenerlo desto, Gli punge il cor sempre un pensier molesto.
>
> Poi che più cose imaginate s'ebbe, Pensa scriverle alfin quanto gli accada . . .
>
> . . . Più non s'indugia, e salta della piume: Si fa dar carta, inchiostro, penna e lume.[5]

NOTES:

1. E. Mongan et al., *op. cit.*, p. 21.
2. A. Ananoff, *L'oeuvre dessiné de Jean-Honoré Fragonard*, 1-4, Paris 1961-1971, nos. 482-485, 1133-1140, 1910-1912, 1918, 2662-2666.
3. E. Mongan et al., *op. cit.*, p. 22.
4. E. Mongan et al., *op. cit.*, opposite p. 9.
5. *Orlando Furioso* XXV, 80, 85.

50

JEAN-BAPTISTE GREUZE
Tournus 1725 - Paris 1806

Reproduced in color.

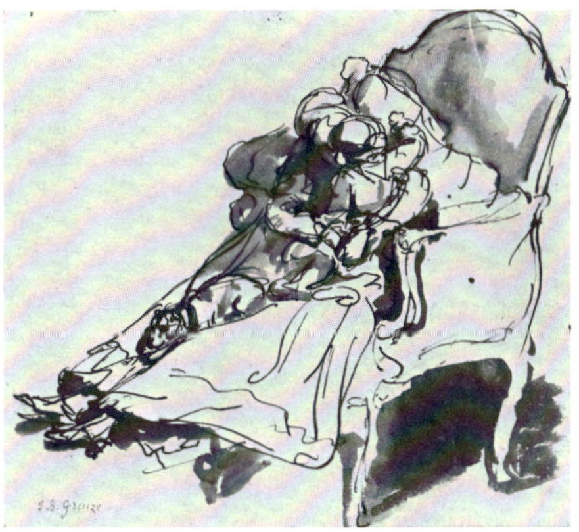

Woman with a Child and a Dog on a Chaise-longue

Pen and brown ink, gray wash. 17.1 x 19.7 cm. Laid down. NM 172/1920. Inscribed at lower right in pen and brown ink: *J. B. Greuze.*

PROVENANCE:
French art market.

BIBLIOGRAPHY:
Bjurström 1982, no. 971.

EXHIBITIONS:
Stockholm 1958, no. 244.

A reaction to the elegance of Boucher is evident in drawings by Greuze. Like Chardin, he strives for realism and turns to domestic life for unpretentious subjects. Moreover, the drawings display the reduced sentimentality that won Diderot's admiration.

This drawing is in all probability a document from Greuze's own family life depicting Mme Greuze and one of their daughters, presumably Anne-Geneviève, born in 1762, and the first of the couple's children to survive infancy. The age of the child shown here then points to a date around 1762-64 for the drawing.

Greuze met his future wife, Ann-Gabrielle Babuti, the attractive daughter of a bookseller in the Rue St. Jacques, when he returned from his Italian journey in 1757, and he married her in 1759. The drawing embodies the memories of the happy early years of the marriage. Greuze later divorced his wife when he discovered that she had been repeatedly unfaithful to him.

Another drawing of Mme Greuze on the same chaise-longue, in the Rijksprentenkabinet, Amsterdam, is inscribed by the artist: Madame Greuze dessinée par J. B. Greuze son mari.[1] That sheet likewise includes the little dog on its mistress's knee. This animal also occurs in two paintings from the mid-1760s.[2]

NOTES:

1. J. W. Niemeijer, *Franse tekenkunst van de 18de eeuw uit nederlandse verzamelingen*, Rijksprentenkabinet/Rijksmuseum, Amsterdam, 1974, no. 54.

2. Cf. "'Le chien au ruban blue', pastel in Musée Magnin, Dijon" (E. Munhall, *Jean Baptiste Greuze*, Palais des états de Bourgogne, Dijon 1977, no. 45). This drawing is a study for a pastel "La Philosophie endormi," that appeared in the Salon of 1765. The dog also occurs in the painting "Enfant jouant avec un chien," which is mentioned for the first time in 1767 (private collection, London, Munhall, *op. cit.*, cat. no. 55).

51

CHARLES-JOSEPH NATOIRE
Nimes 1700 - Castel Gandolfo 1777

Reproduced in color.

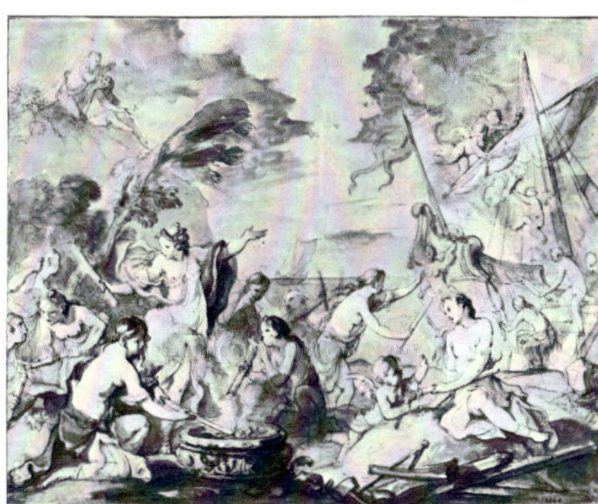

Calypso's Nymphs Set Fire to Telemachus' Ship

Black chalk, watercolor. 31.2 x 40 cm. Laid down. NM 2920/1863. Inscribed on the old mount at lower right: *Natoire*. Numbered *2813* (Sparre).

PROVENANCE:
C. G. Tessin (List 1739-42, p. 44 v.; Cat. 1749, livre 14, no. 84) ☐ Kongl. Biblioteket (Cat. 1790, no. 2813) ☐ Kongl. Museum (Lugt 1638).

BIBLIOGRAPHY:
F. Boyer, *Catalogue raisonné de l'oeuvre de Charles Natoire*, Archives de l'art français, Nouvelle periode, 21 (1946-49), no. 519 ☐ Bjurström 1982, no. 1073.

EXHIBITIONS:
Stockholm 1922, no. 50.

Charles-Joseph Natoire, like François Boucher, was a pupil of François Le Moyne. He spent the years 1721-28 in Rome, but it was chiefly the art of Venice that inspired his Italianate attitudes. At an early stage in his career he developed a gracious, elegant style in which Le Moyne's teachings are evident.

This is a study for a painting in the Hermitage, Leningrad, signed and dated 1731. The painting is one of six works based on the story of Telemachus that Philibert Orry commissioned from Natoire for the château, La Chapelle-Godefroy.[1] The series was intended to balance the six pictures illustrating the life of Clovis which the artist had already finished for Orry.

The museum in Troyes has two of the Telemachus paintings (*Telemachus Listens to the Counsel of Mentor* and *Calypso Listens to the Counsel of Cupid*); two are in Leningrad (*Telemachus and Calypso* and *Calypso's Nymphs Set Fire to Telemachus' Ship*); and one is in the Pushkin Museum in Moscow (*Venus Entrusts Cupid to Calypso*).[2]

The series is clearly inspired by *Télémaque*, the famous didactic novel, published in 1699, which Fénelon wrote for the Duke of Burgundy.

NOTES:

1. Boyer, *op. cit.*, no. 161.

2. Boyer, *op. cit.*, no. 160, exhibited at the Salon of 1739.

52

HUBERT ROBERT
Paris 1733 - Paris 1808

Reproduced in color.

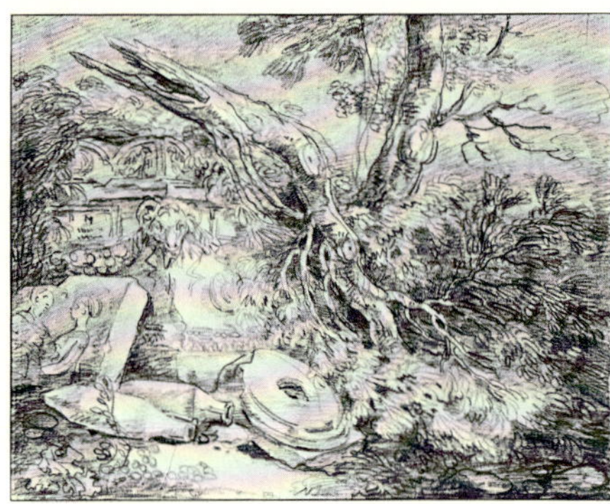

Antique Fragment in an Abandoned Garden

Red chalk. 35 x 45.5 cm. Laid down. NM 86/1980.

PROVENANCE:
L. Deglatigny (Lugt 1768a) □ Coll. Pobbé, Basle □ Acquired from Cailleux.

BIBLIOGRAPHY:
J. Cailleux, *Hubert Robert (1733-1808), Dessins et peintures*, Galerie Cailleux, Geneva, 1979, no. 7 (145) □ Bjurström 1982, no. 1143.

Although Hubert Robert arrived in Rome in 1754 to study at the French Academy, his first extant dated drawings are from 1757. Pannini was his teacher, and Fragonard and Saint-Non were his fellow students and friends. They left Rome in 1761, but Robert stayed on until 1765.

Robert produced a series of sheets showing antique remains in Roman parks in 1763-64. In this version, the scene is dominated by a tomb with the initials D. M. (Diis Manibus), a fragment of a relief, several earthenware vessels, and the base of a pillar.

The closest parallel is found in a Louvre drawing which is almost the same size, *Les dessinateurs dans le jardin Farnese.*[1] But the Louvre work, like three sheets in the Musée de Valence,[2] also incorporates human figures. In our sheet it is just the absence of figures that conveys the impression of nature as sovereign and which ultimately conceals the remains of human cultivation. Human decay is also symbolized by the branch of a tree, still in leaf, which has fallen over the tomb.

NOTES:
1. 34 x 45 cm. Dated c. 1763.
2. M. Beau, *La collection des dessins d'Hubert Robert au musée Valence*, Lyon 1968, nos. 53, 54, and 55. The Museum of Fine Arts in Boston has another drawing that belongs to this group.

53

HUBERT ROBERT

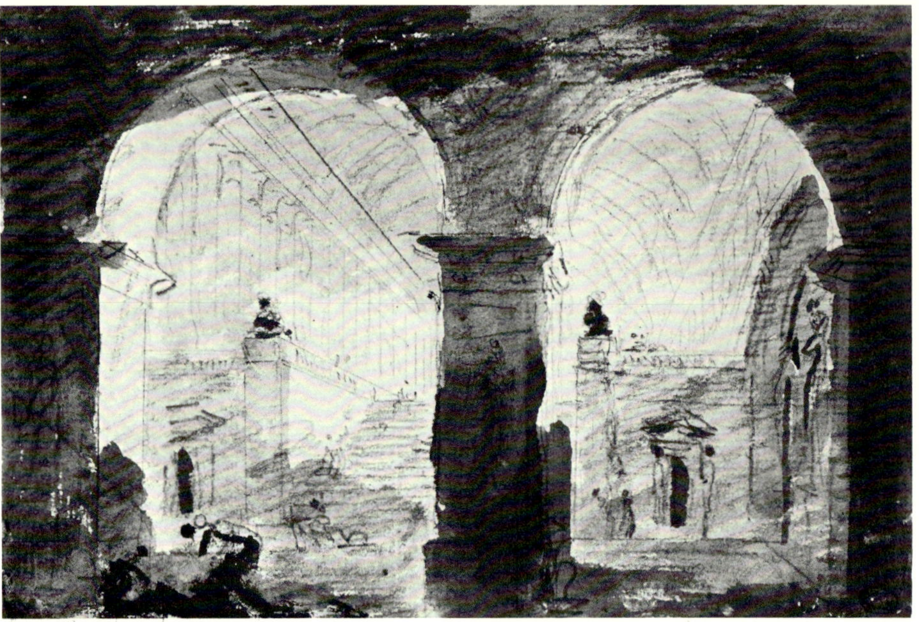

The Steps, San Martino ai Monti, Rome

Black chalk, gray wash. 10.2 x 14.2 cm. Watermark: J KOOL. NM 78/1980.

PROVENANCE:
Ernest May □ Cailleux.

BIBLIOGRAPHY:
J. Cailleux, *Un album de croquis d'Hubert Robert*, Geneva 1979, no. 53 □ Bjurström 1982, no. 1144.

This drawing repeats a composition that Robert executed in red chalk around 1758-59, now in the Bibliothèque Municipale, Besançon.[1]

It can be observed that Robert used a ruler and compass to construct the architecture and then applied the wash all the more freely. Cailleux dates the drawing around 1765.

Robert used the composition as the starting point for a painting that is a free representation of a great hall. The foreground arcade, the stairs and the deep hall are recognizable from the drawing, but the heavy pillars in the foreground are replaced in the painting by a group of four Ionic columns. Cailleux dates the painting, now in the Hermitage, Leningrad, to 1765-70.

NOTE:
1. Collection P.-A. Paris, album 451, no. 49. This drawing is considered by Victor Carlson, *Hubert Robert, Drawings and Watercolors* (Exh. cat.) National Gallery of Art, Washington 1978, p. 151, fig. 5. He includes a copy after Robert's drawing done by Jean François Thérèse Chalgrin (p. 151, fig. 4).

54

GABRIEL DE SAINT-AUBIN
Paris 1724 - Paris 1780

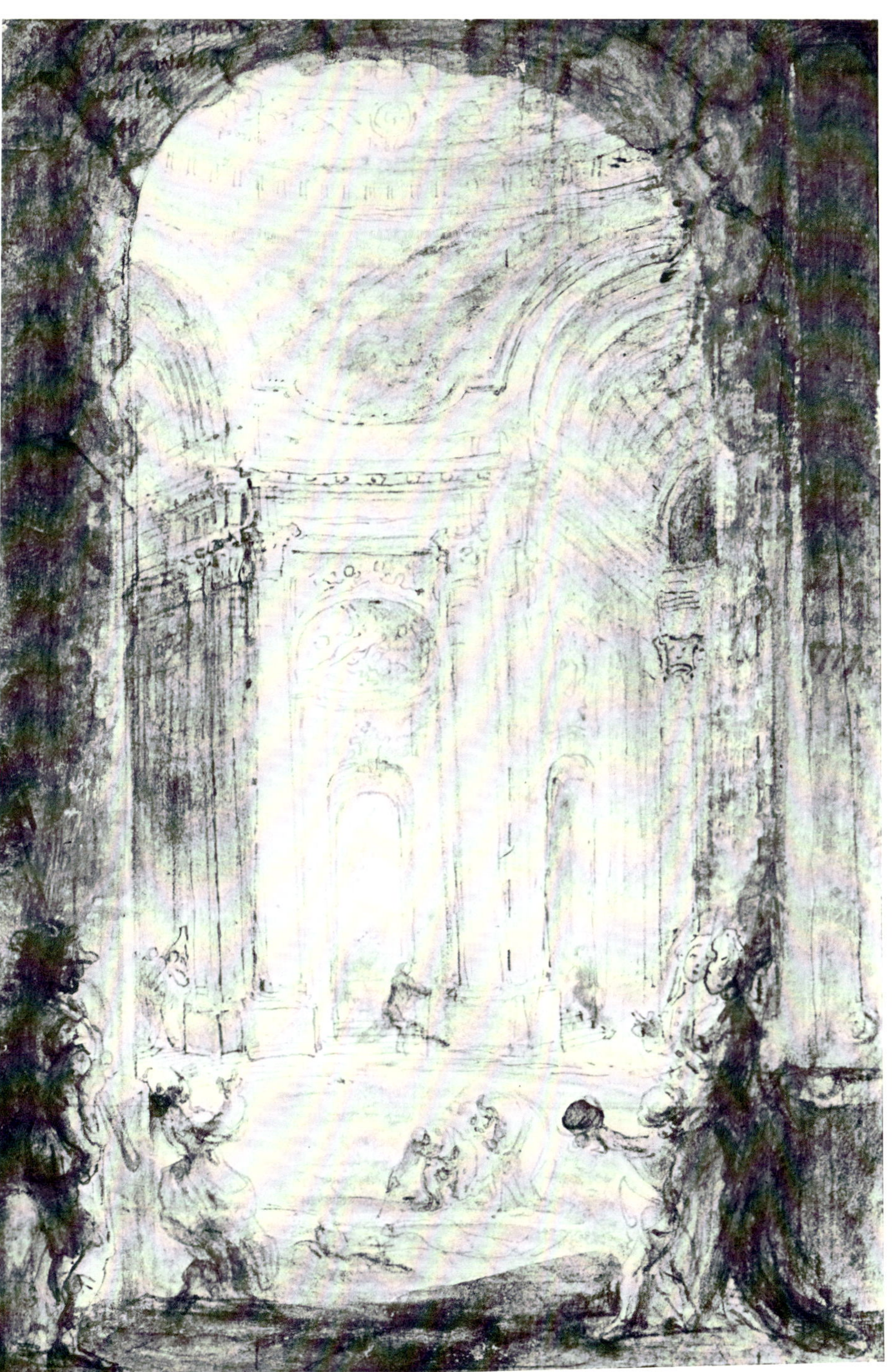

The Dôme des Invalides

Black chalk, pen, and black ink, touches of bodycolor. 18.2 x 12 cm. Laid down. NM 387/1891. Inscribed by the artist on the pillar to the right in pen and black ink: *Vue prophétique des Invalides pour l'an 2000 en l'an 1779.*

PROVENANCE:
W. Wohlfart ☐ F. W. Wohlfart.

BIBLIOGRAPHY:
A. Gauffin, "Gabriel de Saint-Aubin i Nationalmuseum," *Konsthistoriska sällskapets publikation*, Stockholm 1915, p. 28 ☐ Idem, *Konstverk och människor*, Stockholm 1915, pp. 148 ff ☐ Idem, "Gabriel de Saint-Aubin au Musée National de Stockholm," *Gazette des Beaux-Arts*, 6:3 (1930), 1, pp. 47 ff. ☐ E. Dacier, *Gabriel de Saint-Aubin*, 2, Paris 1931, p. 69, no. 433 ☐ Bjurström 1982, no. 1179.

EXHIBITIONS:
Stockholm 1922, no. 95 ☐ Stockholm 1933, no. 81 ☐ Paris 1947, no. 57 ☐ Stockholm 1958, no. 233 ☐ Munich, Haus der Kunst, *Das Aquarell 1400-1950*, 1972-73, no. 84.

The Dôme's interior is seen through a dark arch that enhances the flood of light under the cupola. Saint-Aubin shows a throng of visitors studying inscriptions on the floor or expressing their reactions to the brilliant architecture. The sense of the inscription on the pillar is obscure. The size and technique of this drawing are the same as in the following sheet. Both works are dated 1779.

Saint-Aubin's artistic production was unusual for his time: he painted very few pictures and produced only a limited number of engravings, but he made numerous drawings. He found in drawing an end in itself. With a virtuoso technique he documented with chalk and ink whatever he saw, whether at the theatre, exhibitions, festivities, or in everyday life. Saint-Aubin had few contemporary admirers, yet for us his sketchbooks and the miniature sketches in the margins of exhibition catalogues provide one of the most insightful pictorial sources for mid-eighteenth-century Paris.

The Royal Library in Stockholm has one of his sketchbooks, like this sheet dated the year before Saint-Aubin's death.

55

GABRIEL DE SAINT-AUBIN

Reproduced in color.

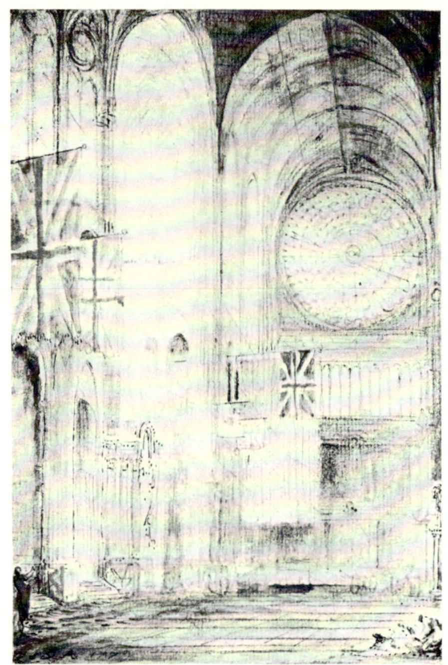

The South Transept of Notre-Dame

Black chalk and black ink, watercolor, touches of bodycolor. 18.1 x 12.2 cm. Laid down. NM 389/1891. Signed at lower left in pen and gray ink: *G.d.S.A. 1779*. Inscribed on the old mount: NOTRE DAME DE PARIS.

PROVENANCE:
W. Wohlfart □ F. W. Wohlfart.

BIBLIOGRAPHY:
M. Aubert, *Société d'iconographie parisienne*, 3 (1910), p. 11, pl. 10 □ Gauffin 1915a, p. 27 □ Idem, 1915b, pp. 148 ff. □ Idem, 1930, 1, pp. 47 ff. □ Dacier 1931, p. 63, no. 408 □ Bjurström 1982, no. 1181.

EXHIBITIONS:
Stockholm 1922, no. 93 □ London, Royal Academy, *French Art 1200-1900*, 1932, no. 836 □ Stockholm 1933, no. 83 □ Paris 1937, no. 579 □ Paris 1947, no. 571 □ Stockholm 1958, no. 231 □ Paris, Société des Amis de Nôtre Dame de Paris, Paris 1958-59.

The view shown in the drawing is from the north transept of Notre-Dame and centers on the Archbishop's door, the galleries, and the large rose window remade by Germain Boffrand in 1726. On the left, the approach to the choir as it was prior to the restoration by Viollet-le-Duc is depicted. On the right, at the base of the first pillar in the nave, the front part of an equestrian statue of Philip the Fair or Philip of Valois (destroyed in 1793) is illustrated. Standards and trophies captured from the English, presumably in the war of 1778-79, hang from the arches.

56

ANTOINE WATTEAU
Valenciennes 1684 - Nogent sur Marne 1721

Reproduced in color.

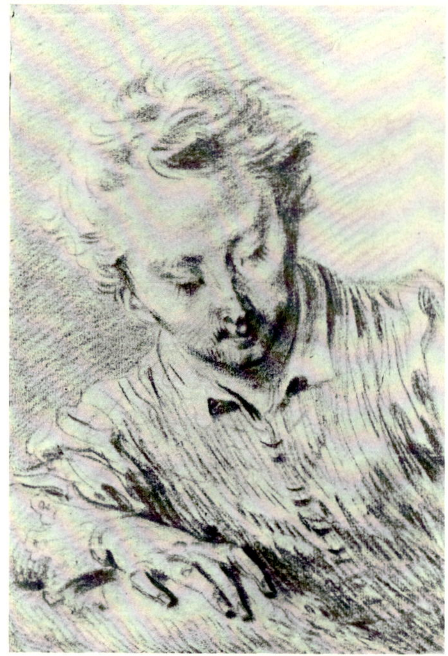

Portrait of a Young Man

Red chalk. 20 x 13.7 cm. No watermark. NM A 3/1979.

PROVENANCE:
King Oscar I (1799-1859)?

BIBLIOGRAPHY:
P. Bjurström, "Two more drawings by Watteau," *Nationalmuseum Bulletin*, 3 (1979): 3, pp. 141-148 □ Bjurström 1982, no. 1267.

EXHIBITIONS:
Watteau i Nationalmuseum, Stockholm 1984, p. 15 □ Paris 1984, no. 136.

This portrait of a young man is so like another version of the same motif[1] that one of them must be a copy after the other. It is difficult to discern which is the original, but our sheet does display a spontaneous line and an assurance, particularly in the rendering of the hand and face, which make a copyist seem improbable.

We have asserted elsewhere that this man's features resemble pictures of Watteau so closely that the drawing might be an early self-portrait. However, Margaret Morgan Grasselli convincingly argues that this work stems from the artist's mature period, 1716-18, and points to a number of stylistic features—the delicate outline of the face and the rendering of the eyes, mouth, and hand—that are absent from Watteau's earlier work. She considers, as do Parker and Mathey, that the sixteenth-century look of the clothing makes it probable that the drawing is a copy after an older master.

NOTE:
1. Parker and Mathey 1957, 1, no. 34.

57

ANTOINE WATTEAU

Singerie

Red chalk, pencil; left half partly counterproof. 69.7 x 49.5 cm. Watermark: IHS. NM CC II: 163.

PROVENANCE:
Claude Audran III □ C. J. Cronstedt and descendants □ E. Langenskiöld □ Gift to the museum in 1941.

BIBLIOGRAPHY:
C. Nordenfalk, Kärlekslektionen av Watteau, *Antoine Watteau och andra franska sjuttonhundratalsmästare i Nationalmuseum*, Stockholm 1953, p. 125, fig. 39 □ Parker and Mathey 1957, 1, no. 183 □ Bjurström 1982, no. 1252.

EXHIBITIONS:
Stockholm 1942, no. 145 □ Paris, Bibliothèque Nationale, *Dessins du Nationalmuseum de Stockholm, Collections Tessin & Cronstedt*, 1950, no. 79 □ London, Royal Academy, *European Masters of the Eighteenth Century*, 1954-55, no. 607 □ Stockholm, *Watteau i Nationalmuseum*, 1984, p. 17.

Reproduced in color.

This is a sketch for a wall painting at Marly for which Watteau's master Claude III Audran was paid in 1709.[1] Audran's own version of the same composition also belongs to the Nationalmuseum.[2] One can therefore assume that Watteau did this drawing while he was with Audran, that is, not later than 1709.

The different styles of the two sheets prompted Parker and Mathey to regard our drawing as Watteau's work since the artist was assisting Audran at the time. However, the attribution to Watteau has been rejected by Margaret Morgan Grasselli on the grounds that Audran would hardly have entrusted the planning of the royal project for a painting at Marly to an assistant and that the drawing has a dry facture and lacks every stylistic characteristic that would warrant such an identification.[3]

These arguments are not convincing. As the style is evidently not Audran's, the hand must surely be that of an assistant. The reason for suggesting Watteau is primarily the correspondence in the decorative details with arabesques in Watteau's graphic work, a characteristic combination of spiraling vegetation and rhombic moulding. The decorative nature of the project calls for a certain precision—and therefore dryness—in the representation. It is, moreover, difficult to propose an alternative hand for the deft rendering of the monkeys.

NOTES:
1. "A Claude Audran . . ., pour un tableau représentant un berceau où des singes sont à table, posé à Marly en 1709," *Comptes des bâtiments*, ed. J.-J. Guiffrey, 5, col. 340.
2. CC IV: 133. This drawing inspired by an engraving after Jean I Bérain (Bibliothèque Nationale, Ed. 65, fol. p. 88).
3. *Watteau 1684-1721*, exh. cat. Washington, Paris, Berlin 1984-85, French version p. 56.

58

ANTOINE WATTEAU

Reproduced in color.

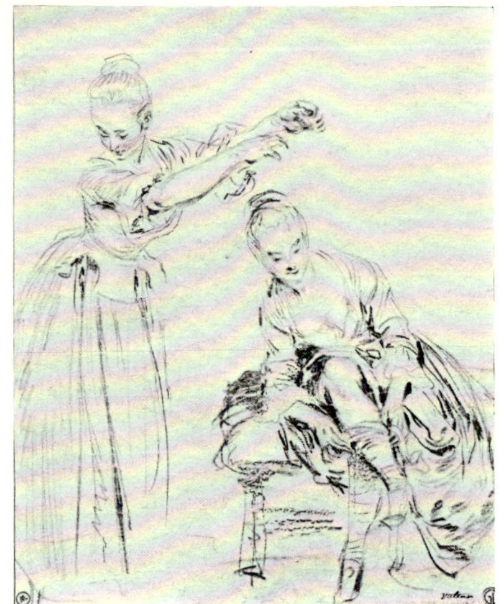

Two Studies of a Young Woman

Black, white, and red chalk. 26 x 20.5 cm. Laid down. NM 280/1980. Inscribed at lower right in pen and brown ink: *Vateau*.

PROVENANCE:
Villenave (Lugt 2598; sale 1842, no. 611) ☐ Watson (Lugt 2599)? ☐ James (sale 1891, no. 307) ☐ Josse (sale 1894, no. 473) ☐ Crosnier (sale 1905, no. 47) ☐ Dormeuil (Lugt 1146 a; sale 13 June 1978, no. 9) ☐ A. Stein.

BIBLIOGRAPHY:
Société de reproduction, 3e année, no. 29 ☐ K. T. Parker, *The Drawings of Antoine Watteau*, London 1931, no. 58 ☐ R. Huyghe, "L'univers de Watteau," in H. Adhémar, *Watteau, sa vie—son oeuvre*, Paris 1950, p. 31 ☐ C. Nordenfalk, "Kärlekslektionen av Watteau," *Antoine Watteau och andra franska sjuttonhundratalsmästare i Nationalmuseum*, Stockholm 1953, pp. 88-89 ☐ Parker and Mathey 1957, 2, no. 632 ☐ C. Nordenfalk, "The Stockholm Watteaus and Their Secret," *Nationalmuseum Bulletin*, 3 (1979): 3, p. 111 ☐ Bjurström 1982, no. 1303.

EXHIBITIONS:
London, Royal Academy, *Exhibition of French Art*, 1932, no. 727 ☐ Copenhagen, Charlottenburg, *L'art français du XVIIIe siècle*, 1935, no. 547 ☐ Paris, Gallerie Cailleux, *Les dessins français de Watteau à Prudhon*, 1950, no. 154 ☐ Stockholm, *Watteau i Nationalmuseum*, 1984, p. 44.

The two studies of a model who has been called Watteau's servant are done from life and involve commonplace occupations. According to René Huyghe, the left figure is hanging up washing, the right is dressing.

The drawings belong to the category of studies after models which Watteau assembled in his sketchbooks and later used for his compositions.

The figure on the left occurs in *Leçon d'amour*, Nationalmuseum, Stockholm, a painting which Nordenfalk dates to around 1716, thereby providing a *terminus ante quem*. In that composition the woman is picking roses in the background; the gesture is the same, yet its implications are different.

The theme of the right-hand study, on the other hand, is alien to Watteau's paintings and has more in common with his few extant nude studies. Caylus gives two reasons for their rarity: one, that Watteau seldom worked in this way and the other that, shortly before his death, Watteau destroyed a number of sheets which he considered to be excessively free.[1]

NOTE:
1. Parker, *op. cit.*, p. 22.

59

ANTOINE WATTEAU

Three Studies of a Woman, Seated in One, Standing in Two, Study of a Hand

Red chalk. 16.5 x 24.8 cm. Laid down. NM 2824/1863. Numbered at lower right in pen and brown ink: *2710* (Sparre) and *31* (struck out).

PROVENANCE:
C. G. Tessin (List 1739-42, p. 43 v.; Cat. 1749, livré 14, no. 31) ☐ Kongl. Biblioteket (Cat. 1790, no. 2710) ☐ Kongl. Museum (Lugt 1638).

BIBLIOGRAPHY:
Engwall 1935, no. 24 ☐ Parker and Mathey 1957, 2, no. 637 ☐ Bjurström 1982, no. 1304.

EXHIBITIONS:
Stockholm 1922, no. 20 ☐ Stockholm 1958, no. 224 ☐ Leningrad 1963 ☐ Paris, Brussels, Amsterdam 1970-71, no. 52 ☐ Stockholm, *Watteau i Nationalmuseum*, 1984, p. 29.

These studies were produced during the artist's mature period, c. 1716. The sheet was used for at least four paintings: for the figures in the left foreground and right background in *Rendez-vouz de Chasse* (Wallace Collection),[1] for the figures on the right in *Le bosquet de Bacchus*,[2] for the central figure in *Les deux cousines* (Marquis H. de Ganay),[3] and in *Entretiens amoreux*.[4]

NOTES:
1. Dacier and Vuaflart 1921-29, 3 and 4, no. 213.
2. Dacier and Vuaflart 1921-29, 3 and 4, no. 265.
3. Dacier and Vuaflart 1921-29, 3 and 4, no. 146.
4. Dacier and Vuaflart 1921-29, 3 and 4, no. 124.

60

ANTOINE WATTEAU

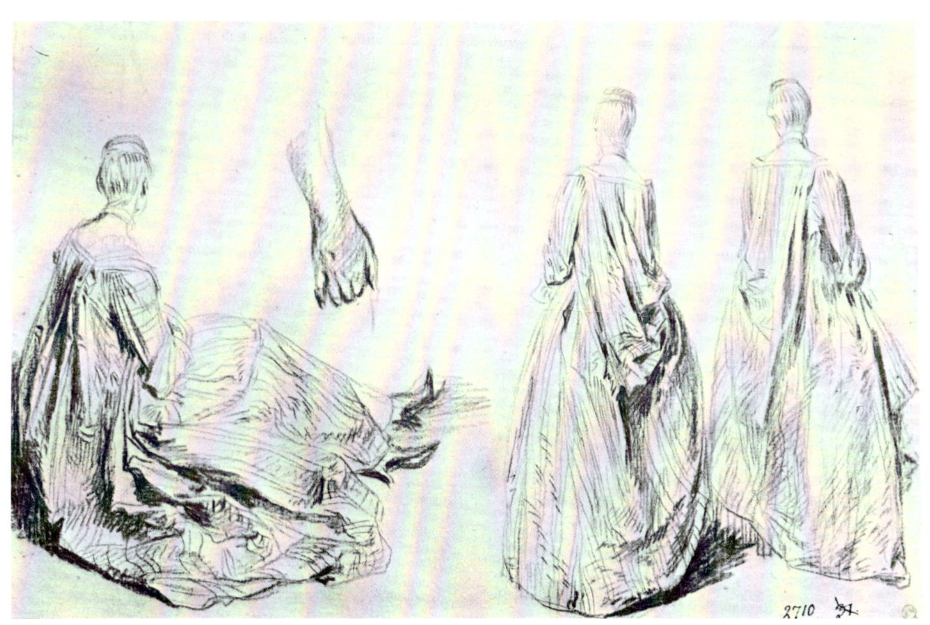

Reproduced in color.

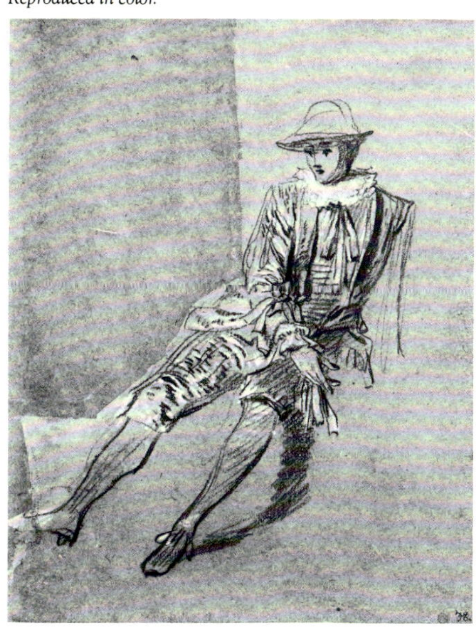

Man Seated Facing Left

Red and white chalk on brownish paper. 24.7 x 19.4 cm. A 9.6 cm wide and 16.5 cm high section cut away at the upper left part of the paper. Laid down. NM 2819/1863. Numbered at lower right in pen and brown ink: *38* (struck out).

PROVENANCE:
C. G. Tessin (List 1739-42, p. 43 v.; Cat. 1749, livré 14, no. 38) □ Kongl. Biblioteket (Cat. 1790, no. 2705) □ Kongl. Museum (Lugt 1638).

BIBLIOGRAPHY:
Parker and Mathey 1957, 2, no. 663 □ Bjurström 1982, no. 1305.

EXHIBITIONS:
Paris 1935, no. 63 (as Lancret) □ Stockholm, *Watteau i Nationalmuseum*, 1984, p. 36.

Although in the 1920s and 1930s this sheet was seen as a work by Lancret, Tessin and successive catalogues have attributed it to Watteau. The figure was used in *La Troupe italienne en vacances*,[1] and the same pose occurs in one of the figures in *Rêve de l'artiste*, in the former David-Weill collection.[2]

NOTES:
1. Dacier and Vuaflart 1921-29, 3 and 4, no. 309.
2. G. Henriot, *Collection David Weill* (catalogue), Paris 1927-28, 2, p. 385, repr.

61

JACQUES LOUIS DAVID
Paris 1748 - Brussels 1825

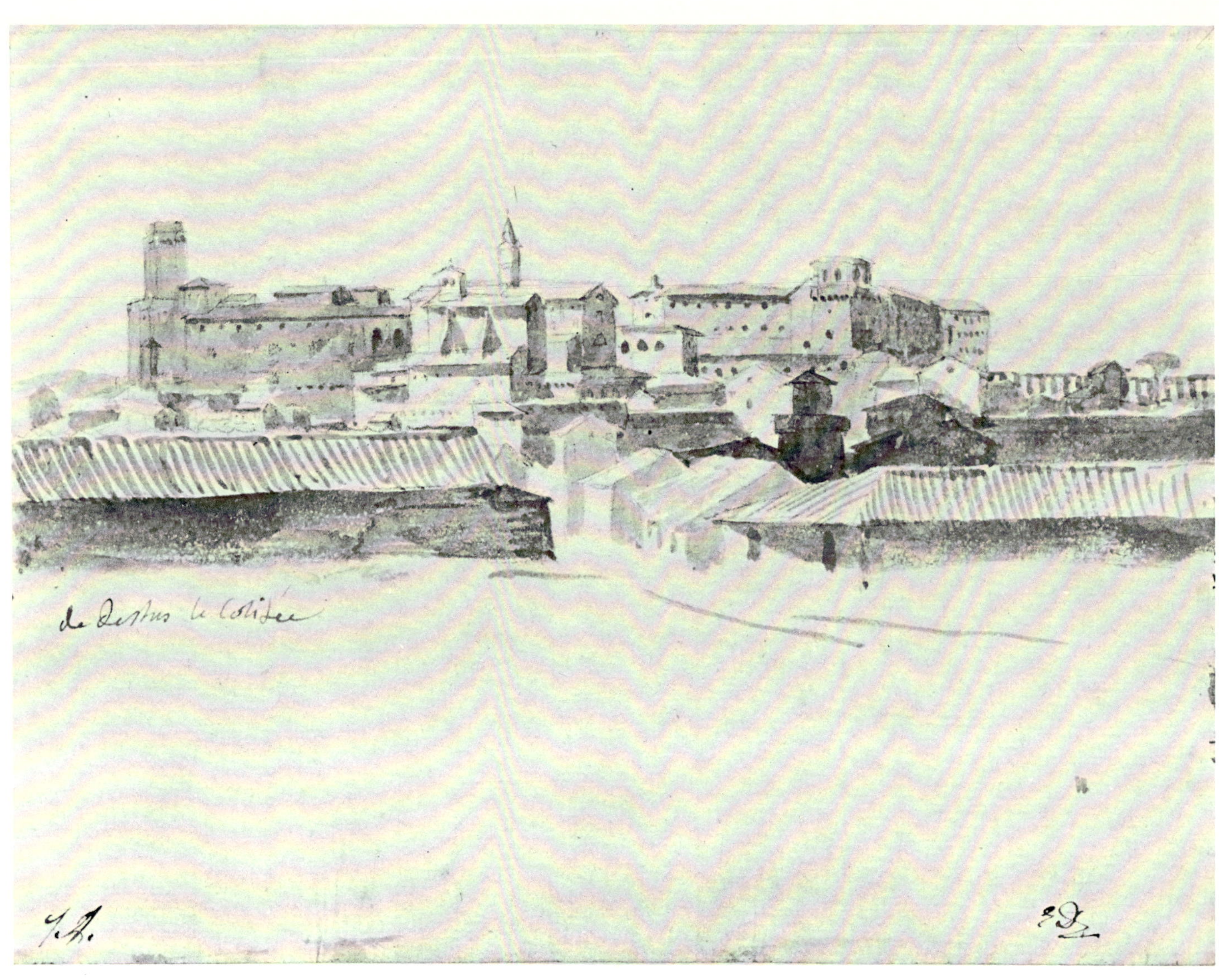

View over Rome from the Coliseum

Point of brush, gray ink. 15.5 x 21.1 cm. Watermark: Bird (fragment; close to Heawood 166). NM 82/1969. Inscribed *J.D.* (Jules David) and *E.D.* (Eugène David) and at lower left in pen and gray ink: *de dessus le Colisée.*

PROVENANCE:
David sale (17 April 1826, lot 66; 11 March 1835, lot 16) ☐ La Marquise de Ludre (Galerie Charpentier sale, Paris, 15 March 1956, lot 11) ☐ Germain Seligman, New York.

BIBLIOGRAPHY:
P. Bjurström, En skissbok av David, *Kontakt med Nationalmuseum*, Stockholm 1969, p. 17 ☐ *David et Rome* Exh. cat., Académie de France à Rome, Rome 1981-82, p. 57, fig. 23 ☐ Bjurström 1985, no. 1449.

During the five years that David spent in Italy as a student at the French Academy, he did many drawings after classical subjects, from nature, and as preparatory work for his compositions. He assembled a large part of this material in a dozen big albums, of which two are now in the Louvre, one is in the Fogg Art Museum, Cambridge, and one in Stockholm. This and the two landscapes that follow come from the latter album.

David has attracted very little attention for his drawings of landscapes, yet these studies are a fresh and stimulating feature of his art. Their clear disposition of light and shade, together with their harmonious composition, earn David a place in the series of eminent French landscapists in Rome. Like Claude and Poussin, as well as Ingres, David stresses the horizontals in the landscape, thereby differentiating his work from that of the preceding generation, whose choice of landscapes reveals a penchant for the picturesque.

62

JACQUES LOUIS DAVID

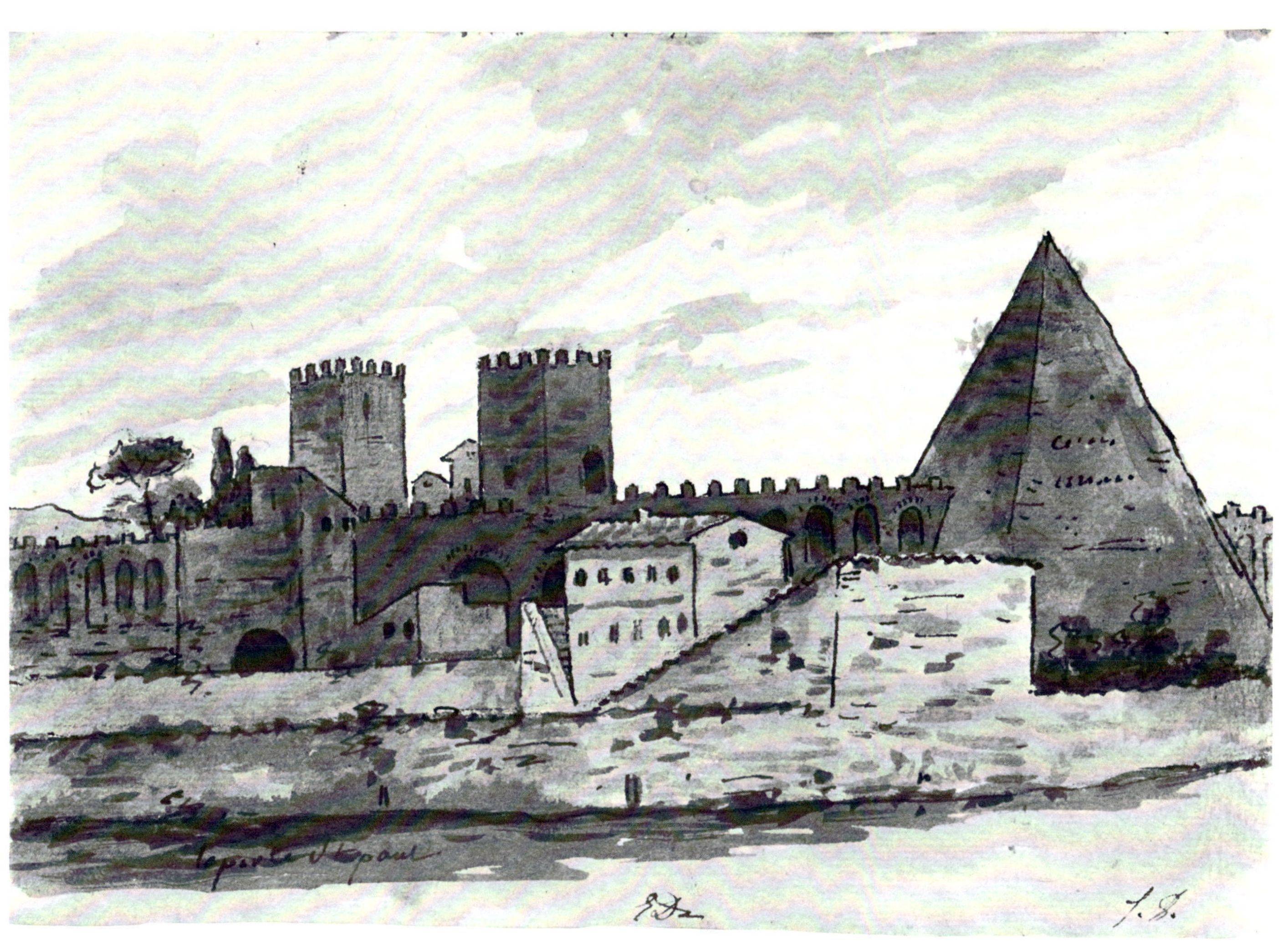

Porta San Paolo and the Pyramid of Cestius

Point of the brush, gray ink. 12.4 x 21 cm. No watermark. NM 87/1969. Inscribed *J.D.* (Jules David) and *E.D.* (Eugène David) and at lower left in gray ink: *porte St. paul.*

PROVENANCE:
David sale (17 April 1826, lot 66; 11 March 1835, lot 16) □ La Marquise de Ludre (Galerie Charpentier sale, Paris, 15 March 1956, lot 11) □ Germain Seligman, New York.

BIBLIOGRAPHY:
□ Bjurström 1985, no. 1454.

63

JACQUES LOUIS DAVID

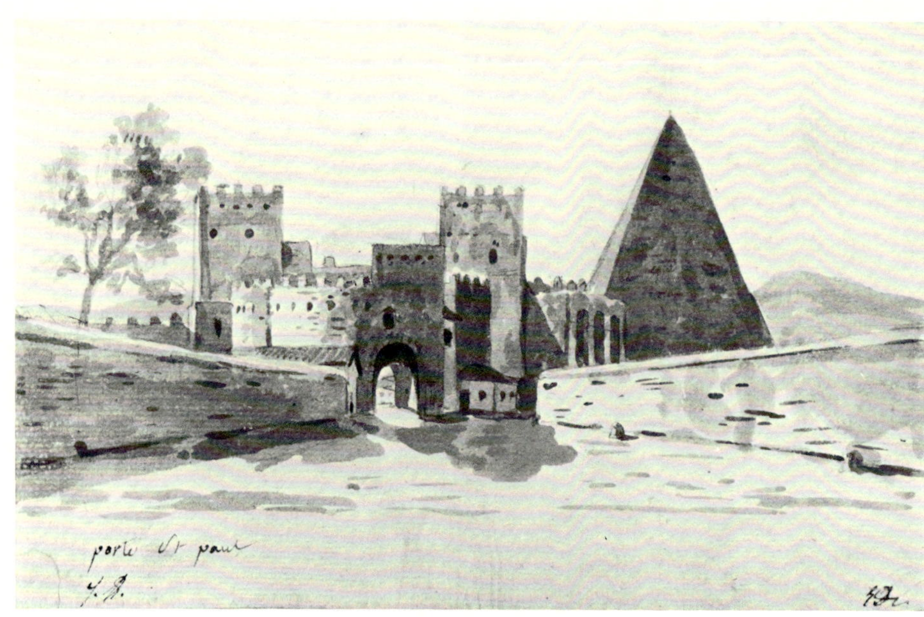

Porta San Paolo and the Pyramid of Cestius

Pen and gray ink, gray wash. 13.3 x 19.4 cm. No watermark. NM 88/1969. Inscribed *E.D.* (Eugène David) and *J.D.* (Jules David).

PROVENANCE:
David sale (17 April 1826, lot 66; 11 March 1935, lot 16) ☐ La Marquise de Ludre (Galerie Charpentier sale, Paris, 15 March 1956, lot 11) ☐ Germain Seligman, New York.

BIBLIOGRAPHY:
☐ Bjurström 1985, no. 1455.

64

PIERRE-PAUL PRUD'HON
Cluny 1758 - Cluny 1823

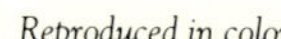

Reproduced in color.

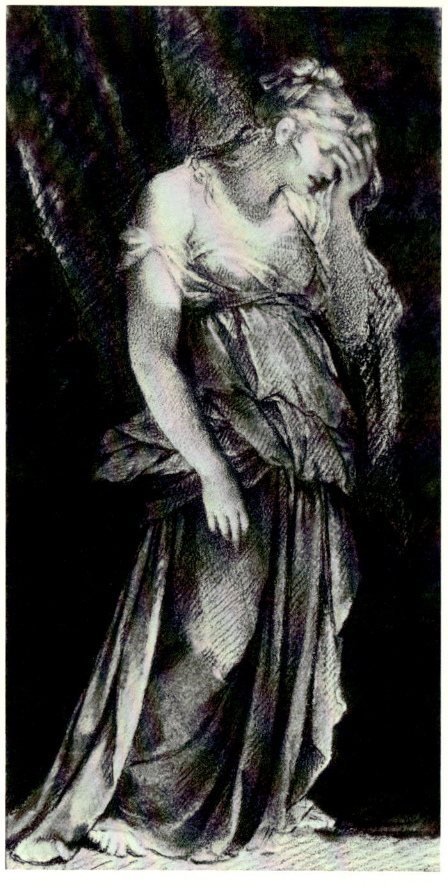

Repentance

Black chalk, heightened with white. 32 x 16 cm. No watermark. NM 274/1972.

PROVENANCE:
Jules Renouard (sale 19 May 1855, no. 25) ☐ Martial François Marcille ☐ Camille Marcille (Lugt 605a; sale 6 March 1876, no. 112) ☐ Bournet-Veron ☐ Labouchère (Hôtel Drouot sale, 13 February 1939, no. 63) ☐ Lionel Cabany (Hôtel Drouot sale, 23 February 1959, no. 140 D) ☐ Slatkin (Sotheby's sale, 26 June 1969, no. 50).

BIBLIOGRAPHY:
E. de Goncourt, *Catalogue raisonné de l'oeuvre... de P. P. Prud'hon*, Paris 1876, no. 60, pp. 141 and 144 ☐ Ch. Clément, *Prud'hon*, Paris 1880, p. 410, note ☐ J. Guiffrey, "L'oeuvre de Pierre Paul Prud'hon," *Archives de l'art français*, 13 (Collection de la société de l'art français), Paris 1924, no. 16 ☐ Bjurström 1985, no. 1664.

EXHIBITIONS:
Chartres, *Exposition archéologique*, March 1858, no. 99 ☐ Chartres, *Exposition départementale*, 1869, no. 41 ☐ Paris, École des Beaux-Arts, *Exposition des oeuvres de Prud'hon*, May 1874, no. 224 ☐ Santa Barbara, Museum of Art, *European Drawings*, 1964, no. 95.

Unlike David, who was his senior by a decade, Pierre-Paul Prud'hon retained much of the eighteenth century in his drawn oeuvre. He witnessed the careers of Greuze and Fragonard, avoided the heroic themes of the Revolution and the Empire, and preferred subjects charged with emotion rather than action. Instead of the clear light of day, he worked with an insubstantial moonlight. His forms are dissolved by soft shading, obtained through the use of the chalk stump.

This representation of *Repentance* (*Le Repentir*) is part of a larger composition, *L'Amour séduit l'Innocence, le Plaisir l'entraine, le Repentir suit*, that Prud'hon executed in 1810.[1] He had handled the subject twenty years earlier, although all the figures were shown half-length.[2]

The drawing is done after the finished painting, in connection with an engraving of the composition by B. Roger. The latter worked from two drawings, in pen and ink and in black and white chalk, respectively. Prud'hon then provided him with two more drawings, one of *Amour and Innocence* and this one of *Repentance*.[3]

A drawing of the whole composition is now in the Fogg Art Museum, Cambridge, and the drawing of *Amour and Innocence* is in the Louvre.

Our drawing has been reproduced, slightly enlarged, in a lithograph by Jules Boilly.

NOTES:
1. Guiffrey, *op. cit.*, p. 3, no. 5.
2. Guiffrey, *op. cit.*, p. 2.
3. Guiffrey, *op. cit.*, pp. 4-5.

65

JEAN AUGUSTE DOMINIQUE INGRES
Montauban 1780 - Paris 1867

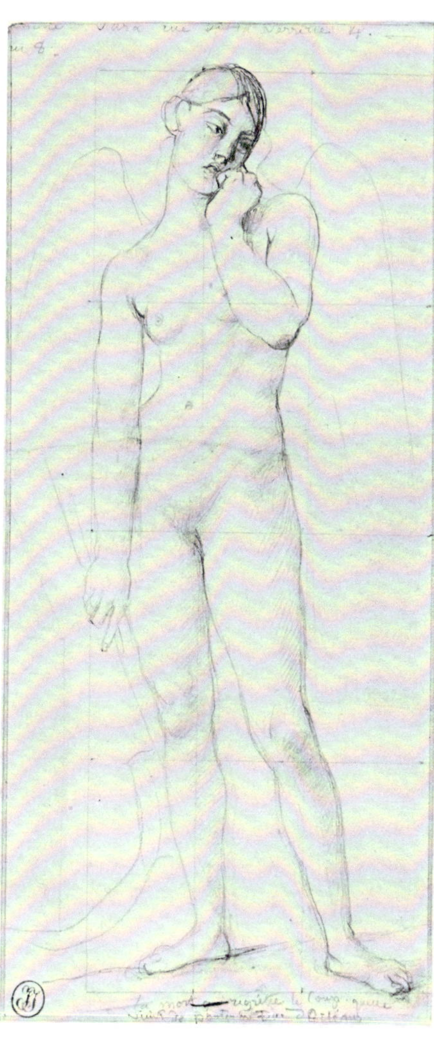

Angel of Death

Pencil. 30.4 x 15.1 cm. Irregular sheet, with one strip 15.5 x c. 2 cm added at the lower right corner and another, 8 x c. 4 cm, midway along the right-hand side. The sheet has been torn in two, almost 13 cm from the upper edge. Laid down. NM 131/1959. Inscription in pencil (fragmentary) along upper edge: *ara rue de la verrerie 4. u 8*; and along lower edge: *la mort regrette le Coup quelle vient de porter . . . le Duc d'Orléans.*

PROVENANCE:
Ingres (Lugt 1477), probably sale of 6-7 May 1867, Wildenstein.

BIBLIOGRAPHY:
Caracas, *Exposition de dibujos del renacimiento al siglio XX*, 24 May - 9 June 1957, no. 40 □ Bjurström 1985, no. 1616.

This pencil drawing is a study for an allegory, planned but never carried out, of Louis Philippe's eldest son, Ferdinand-Philippe, Duc d'Orléans (1810-1842). The drawing no doubt dates from the year of the Duke's death, 1842.

The Musée Ingres, Montauban, has three studies for the same composition.[1]

NOTE:
1. Cat. Momméja, *Inventaire des richesses d'art de la France*, 1905 no. 3778, pen and ink. 23.1 x 35, Ange, derrière lequel sont plusieurs autres figures no. 3779, pen and ink. 17.1 x 21.9, Croquis vague de figures éplorées autour du corps du duc no. 3780, pen and ink. 17.2 x 21.8, Croquis vague de figures éplorées.

66

THÉODORE GÉRICAULT
Rouen 1791 - Paris 1824

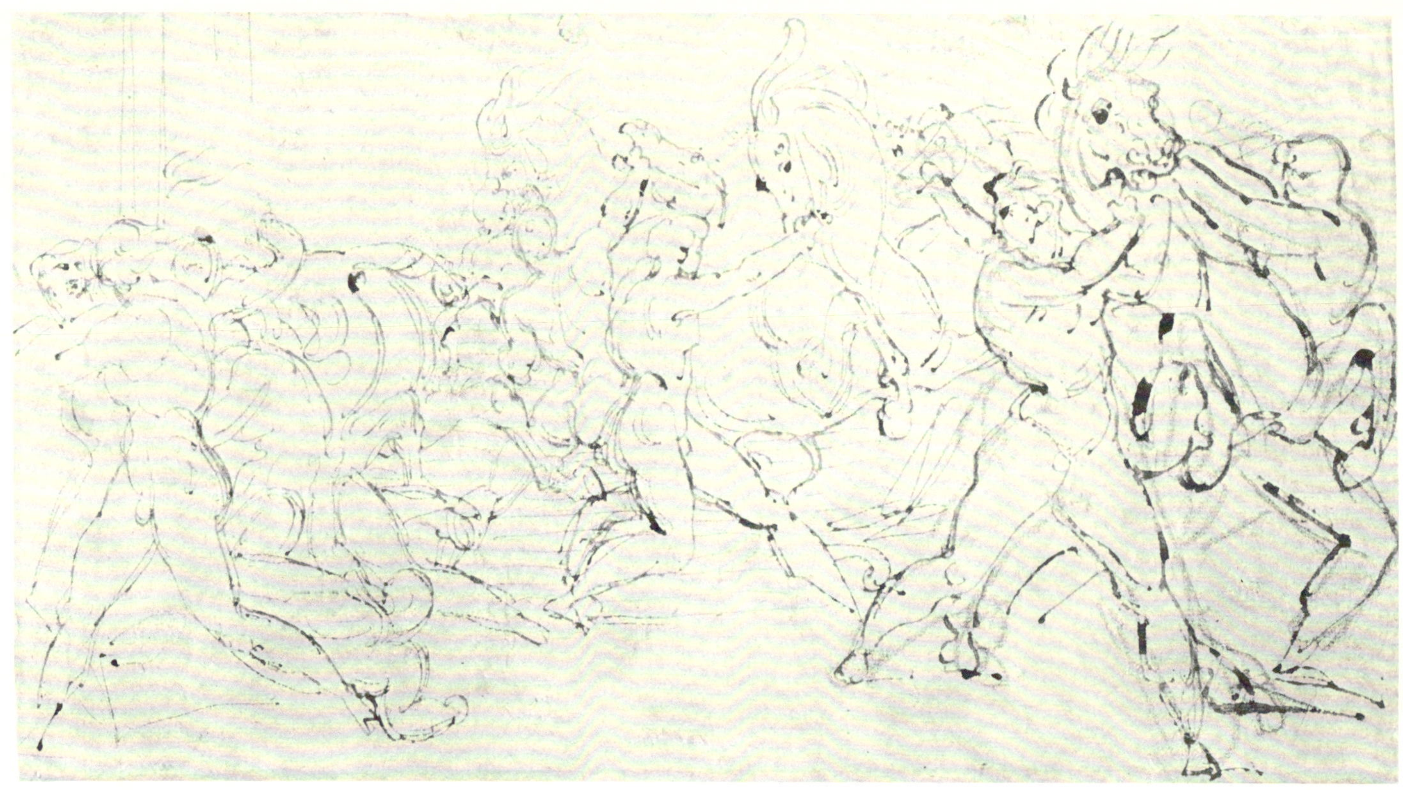

Sketch for the Race of the Barbieri Horses

Pen and brown ink over pencil. 14.2 x 27.3 cm. No watermark. NM 37/1981.

PROVENANCE:
Camille Marcille □ Duc de Trévise □ Hazlitt, Gooden and Fox.

BIBLIOGRAPHY:
M. Delacre and P. Lavallée, *Dessins de maîtres anciens*, Paris and Brussels 1927, pl. 46 □ J. Thuillier and Ph. Grunchec, *L'opera completa di Géricault*, Milan 1978, mentioned under no. 107 (ill. pl. 107) □ Rome, Villa Medici, *Géricault*, November 1979-January 1980 (exh. cat. by P. Grunchec), mentioned under no. 15 (ill. p. 208, fig. A) □ Hazlitt, Gooden, and Fox, *Nineteenth Century French Drawings*, London 1980, no. 13 □ Bjurström 1985, no. 1561.

EXHIBITIONS:
Paris, Hôtel Jean Charpentier, *Exposition Géricault*, April-May 1924, no. 110 (the exhibition was also shown at the Musée des Beaux-Arts, Rouen) □ Paris, Galerie Bernheim-Jeune, *Exposition Géricault*, May 1937, no. 111.

Most of Théodore Géricault's drawings are connected to large compositions which he tried to bring to fruition. The drawings serve to clarify the composition, to bring order into not only the forms and the disposition of light and masses but also to tighten the psychological interplay and the representation of action. Herein lies the dramatic vitality characteristic of this and other sheets.

The races of riderless horses (known as the *Barbieri*) down the corso, the traditional climax of the Roman Carnival, was a subject that occupied Géricault during his stay in Rome. Although his plans for a very large painting on the theme were never realized (he had barely begun work on the full-scale canvas when he abruptly departed for France in the autumn of 1817), the existence of numerous preparatory drawings and oil sketches demonstrates that this project was unquestionably the major preoccupation of his year in Italy.

While working towards his final expression of the climactic scene, Géricault produced studies of various episodes in the race. His ultimate choice seems to be the start from the Piazza del Popolo, though he converted this moment into an ordered, classical frieze. A sketch in the Louvre gives an impression of the composition.[1]

This drawing showing the recapture of the horses by their grooms at the finish of the race, is closely related to an oil sketch in the Musée des Beaux-Arts in Lille,[2] in which the figures are depicted in classical nudity. There is also a similar drawing in the Royal Institution of Cornwall, Truro.[3]

NOTES:
1. Ch. Clément, *Géricault. Etude biographique et critique*, Paris 1879, no. 85; Thuillier and Grunchec 1978, no. 115; R. F. 2042.

2. J. Thuillier and Ph. Grunchec, *op. cit.*, no. 107.

3. L. Eitner, *Géricault*, Exh. cat. Los Angeles County Museum, The Detroit Institute of Arts, and Philadelphia Museum of Art 1971-72, no. 39.

67

THÉODORE GÉRICAULT

Reproduced in color.

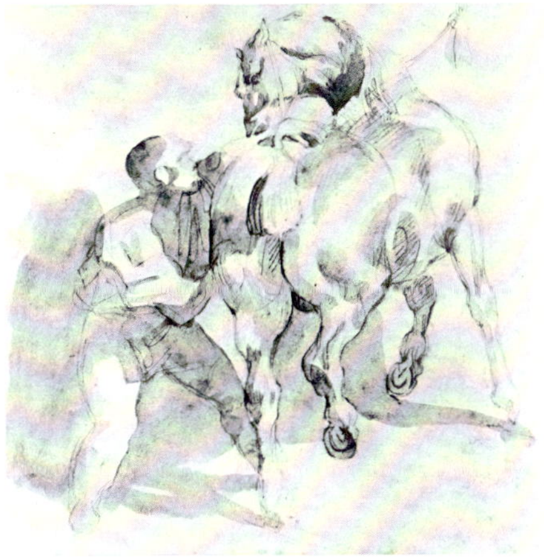

Stableboy Grooming a Horse

Pencil brown wash. 18.9 x 18.5 cm. NM 216/1982.

PROVENANCE:
Binder □ P. O. Dubaut (Lugt 2103b).

BIBLIOGRAPHY:
Bjurström 1985, no. 1565.

EXHIBITIONS:
Paris, Hotel Charpentier, *Exposition Géricault*, April-May 1924, no. 220 (the exhibition was also shown at the Musée des Beaux-Arts, Rouen).

Géricault joins the company of Delacroix as the outstanding Romantic draftsmen. It is noteworthy that Géricault's magnificent effects are achieved with the aid of studies of classical forms. Even with a theme so charged with action as the scene depicted in this drawing, his representation has the monumentality of a classical statue.

This subject of stableboys at work occurs in Géricault's early production, around 1814, as well as during his stay in England, when he did a number of lithographs of men shoeing horses. The style of our sheet, which dates around 1818-20, presages the latter.

An initial sketch for our drawing is now in a French private collection. A version that is practically identical, though preceding our sheet in date, is in the sketchbook in Chicago.[1]

NOTE:
1. L. Eitner, *Géricault. An Album of Drawings in the Art Institute of Chicago*, Chicago 1960, folio 27.

68

EUGÈNE DELACROIX
Charenton-Saint-Maurice 1798 - Paris 1863

Reproduced in color.

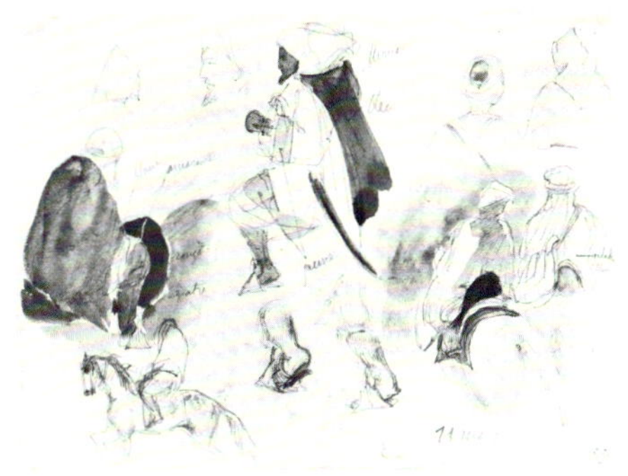

Studies of Arabs on Horseback

Pencil with touches of watercolor. 15.5 x 21.6 cm. Laid down. NM 66/1949. Inscriptions in the artist's hand at left: *blanc, amarante, rouge vif, rougeâtre*; at center: *burnous, bleu, jaune*; at right: *gelabia bleue*,[1] at lower right: *11 mars.*

PROVENANCE:
Delacroix sale (Lugt S. 838 a-b), 22-27 February 1864, perhaps part of no. 571 or 572 □ Robaut □ Marcel Guyot.

BIBLIOGRAPHY:
M. Sérullaz, "Unpublished Drawings by Eugène Delacroix at the Nationalmuseum, Stockholm," *Master Drawings*, 5 (1967): 4, p. 405, no. 5, pl. 42 b □ Bjurström 1985, no. 1503.

EXHIBITIONS:
Stockholm, Nationalmuseum, *Delacroix'lejonjakter*, 1981, no. 2.

This study was executed on Sunday, 11 March 1832, a day when Delacroix was near the river Sebou at the ford of El-Aïtem, Morocco. He noted in his sketchbook (Louvre album RF 1712 bis, folios 12 verso and 13 recto):

> A la rivière Sébou, au passage de El-Aïtem. Depuis trois jours nous sommes suivis par un shérif de Fez, ami de Bias, qui veut absolument avoir un cadeau.
>
> Quand les Maures veulent obtenir quelque chose, comme une grâce, de manière à n'être pas refusés, ils vont porter près de votre tente un mouton, même un boeuf comme présent, et l'égorgent en manière de sacrifice, et pour constater l'offrande.
>
> On est lié très fort par l'espèce d'obligation que cette action impose.
>
> Le jour que nous avons campé à Alcassar, on est venu tuer trois moutons, l'un à la tente de Bias, le second à celle du caïd, le troisième à la nôtre, pour obtenir la grâce d'un homme accusé d'assassinat. Bias s'intéresse à l'affaire. Le pacha et son frère avaient toujours un homme de chaque côté du cheval, marchant à côté et qui prennent le fusil quand ils viennent de courir.
>
> Je n'ai pas parlé à Alcassar de la visite au pacha dans sa tente. La selle à sa droite, son sabre sur son matelas blanc, couvertures; un homme à ses pieds dormant enveloppé dans un burnous noué par derrière.
>
> Presque toujours le derrière de la selle est dans l'ombre à cause des vêtements.
>
> Le second du pacha n'ayant pas de bottes avait mis à une de ses jambes le fourreau de son fusil, un mouchoir à l'autre; ils ont presque tous la jambe blessée par l'étrier.[2]

NOTES:
1. Delacroix wrote on Friday, 4 February 1832: "La *gélabia* costume du peuple, des marchands, des enfants. Je me rappel cette gélabia, costume exactement antique, dans une petite figure du Musée: capuchon, etc. Le bonnet est le bonnet phrygien." *Journal*, 1, pp. 125-26.
2. *Journal*, 1, pp. 135-36:

> At the river Sebou, at the passage of El-Aitem. For three days we were followed by a sheriff of Fez, a friend of Bias, who wanted absolutely to have a gift.
>
> When the Moors want to obtain something, as a special favor, in a manner not to be refused, they bring sheep close to one's tent, even an ox as now, and strangle it in the manner of a sacrifice and to confirm the offering.
>
> One is strongly bound by the type of obligation that this action imposes.
>
> The day we camped at Alcassar, three sheep were killed, one at the tent of Bias, the second at that of the caid, the third at ours, to obtain pardon for a man accused of a killing. Bias was interested in the affair.
>
> The pascha and his brother always had a man walking on either side of their horse and taking a gun after they have just run.
>
> I did not talk at Alcassar of the visit to the pascha in his tent. The saddle at his right, his sabre on his white mattress, the covers; a man at his feet sleeps wrapped in a burnous tied from behind.
>
> Almost always the back of the saddle is in the shade because of clothing.
>
> The second to the pascha, not having any boots, had put the case of his gun on one of his legs and a handkerchief on the other; they almost all have legs hurt by stirrups.

69

EUGÈNE DELACROIX

Quentin Durward Overhears the Plot of Hayraddin and Lanzknecht Heinrich

Pen and brown ink, gray wash. 27 x 21 cm. No watermark. NM 60/1920.

PROVENANCE:
Delacroix sale (Lugt S. 838 a-b), 22-27 February 1864 ☐ Jean Gigou (Lugt 1164) ☐ Erik Rusén.

BIBLIOGRAPHY:
A. Robaut (and E. Chesneau), *L'Oeuvre complet de Eugène Delacroix*, Paris 1885, no. 1545 ("sujet inconnu," 1828) ☐ L. Johnson, "A Delacroix Recovered: Quentin Durward and Le Balafré," *Burlington Magazine*, 108 (1966), p. 569, no. 10, fig. 36 ☐ M. Sérullaz, "Unpublished Drawings by Eugène Delacroix at the Nationalmuseum, Stockholm," *Master Drawings*, 5 (1967): 4, p. 405, no. 2, pl. 40 ☐ Bjurström 1985, no. 1500.

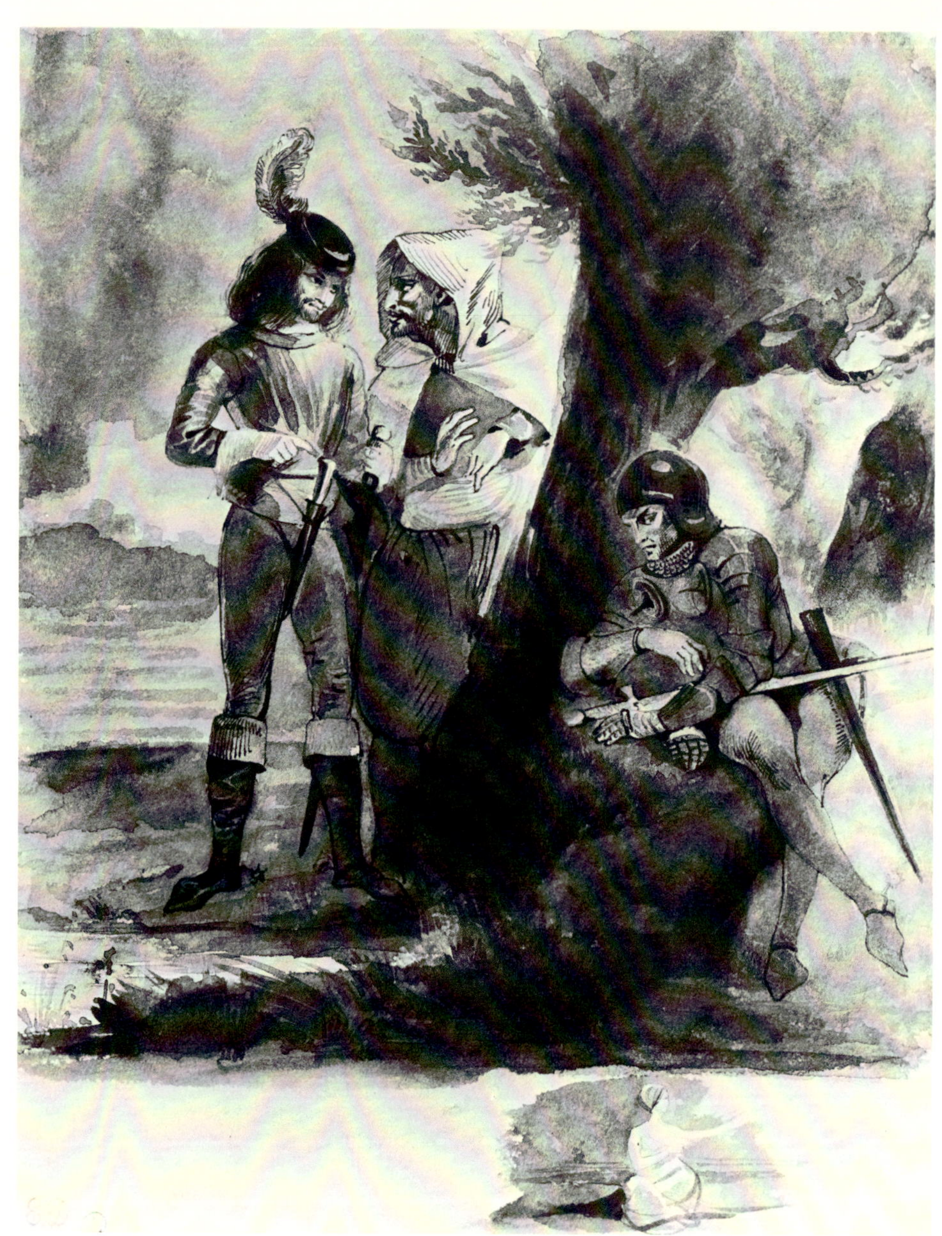

The subject of this drawing was identified by L. Johnson as inspired by Chapter XVII of *Quentin Durward* by Sir Walter Scott. In this scene Quentin Durward overhears a conversation between the Moor Hayraddin and the German Heinrich, who sit beside a stream. They plot to ambush Isabelle de Croye and her aunt Hameline, whom Quentin Durward is accompanying on their voyage from the French court to Liège, in order to take them to Guillaume de la Marche.

Sérullaz discovered that in the annotated edition of *L'oeuvre complet*, Robaut writes that this drawing, of a "sujet inconnu," figured in the Delacroix exhibition of the École des Beaux-Arts in 1885, but that it had been included too late to appear in the catalogue.[1] Having identified the subject, Sérullaz is tempted to connect it with a list of paintings and sketches drawn up by Delacroix,[2] in which he included the title "Quentin Durward and the Sarrazin by the Fountain." It is possible that the subject, which was not used in a painting, can be connected with our drawing.

Johnson compares the style of this drawing with that of a study dated 1826 for the *Execution of the Doge Marino Faliero*.[3] He suggests the same year for this drawing, which Sérullaz finds reasonable.

NOTES:

1. Bibliothèque National, Cabinet des Estampes, (Y6[3] 753, Réserves).
2. *Journal*, III, p. 372.
3. M. Sérullaz, *Mémorial de l'exposition E. Delacroix*, Paris 1963, no. 95, repr.; Johnson, *op. cit.*, p. 569 ff.

70

EUGÈNE DELACROIX

Reproduced in color.

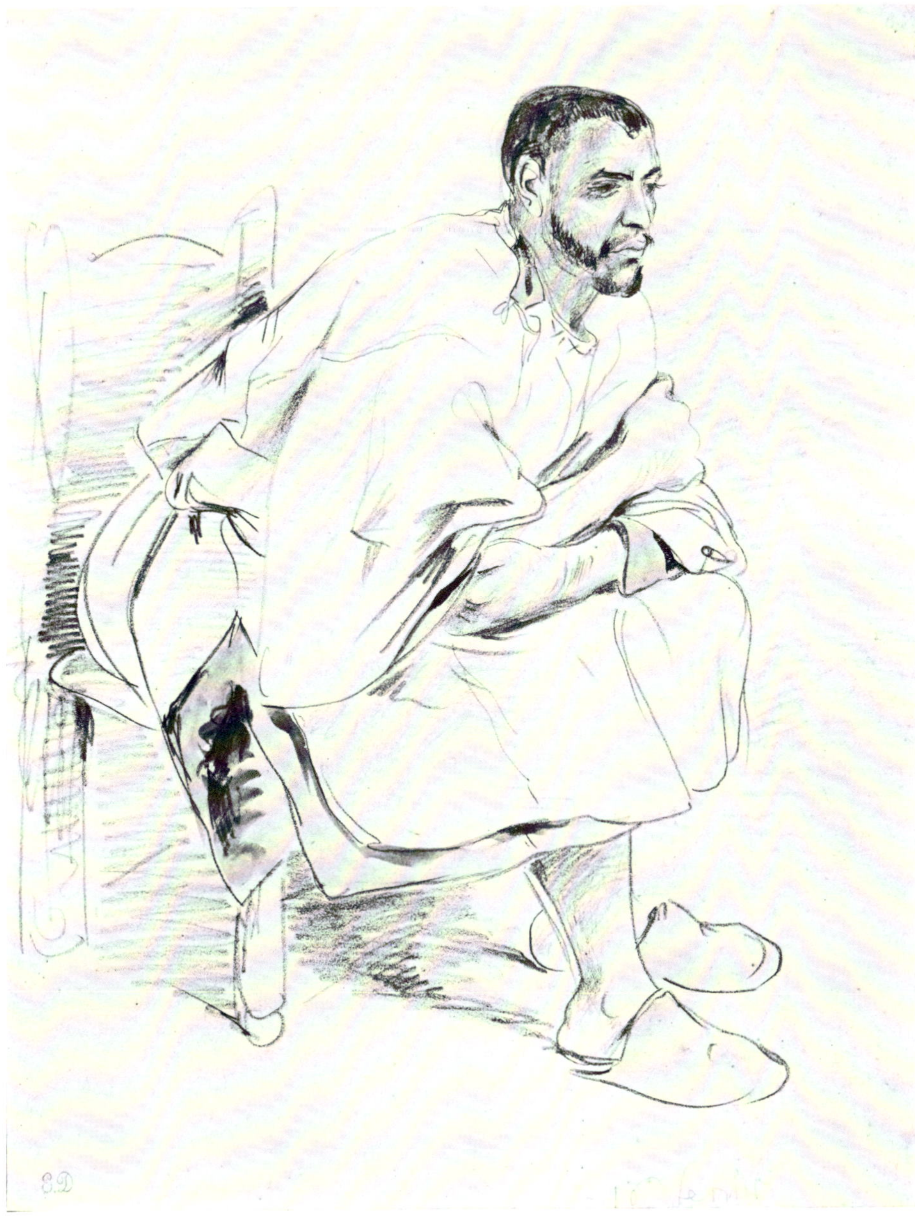

A Seated Moor

Black and red chalk with touches of watercolor. 36.5 x 30 cm. Laid down. NM 71/1915. Notations at lower right in the artist's hand: *16 février.*

PROVENANCE:
Delacroix sale (Lugt S. 838 a-b), 22-27 February 1864, no. 529 □ M. Planté □ A. Robaut □ Winkler and Magnusson.

BIBLIOGRAPHY:
A. Robaut (and E. Chesneau) 1885, no. 1589 □ M. Sérullaz 1967, 4, p. 405, no. 3, pl. 41 □ Bjurström 1985, no. 1501.

EXHIBITIONS:
Paris, École des Beaux-Arts, *Eugène Delacroix*, 1885, no. 390(?) □ Stockholm, Nationalmuseum, *Delacroix' lejonjakter*, 1981, no. 4.

This drawing was executed on 16 February 1832, during Delacroix's first visit to Tangiers (January 25-March 6). Two preliminary studies for the drawing are in the Louvre.[1] The same figure is depicted on a sheet in the collection of Edward M. M. Warburg in New York, where the Moor is standing.[2]

NOTES:
1. A. and M. Sérullaz, *Dessins d'Eugène Delacroix 1798-1863* (Inventaire géneral des dessins école français), 2, Paris 1984, nos. 1734 and 1735.
2. M. Sérullaz, *Mémorial de l'exposition Eugène Delacroix, organisée au Musée du Louvre à l'occasion du centenaire de la mort de l'artiste*, Paris 1963, no. 171.

71

FRANCISCO GOYA
Fuendetodos 1746 - Bordeaux 1828

Reproduced in color.

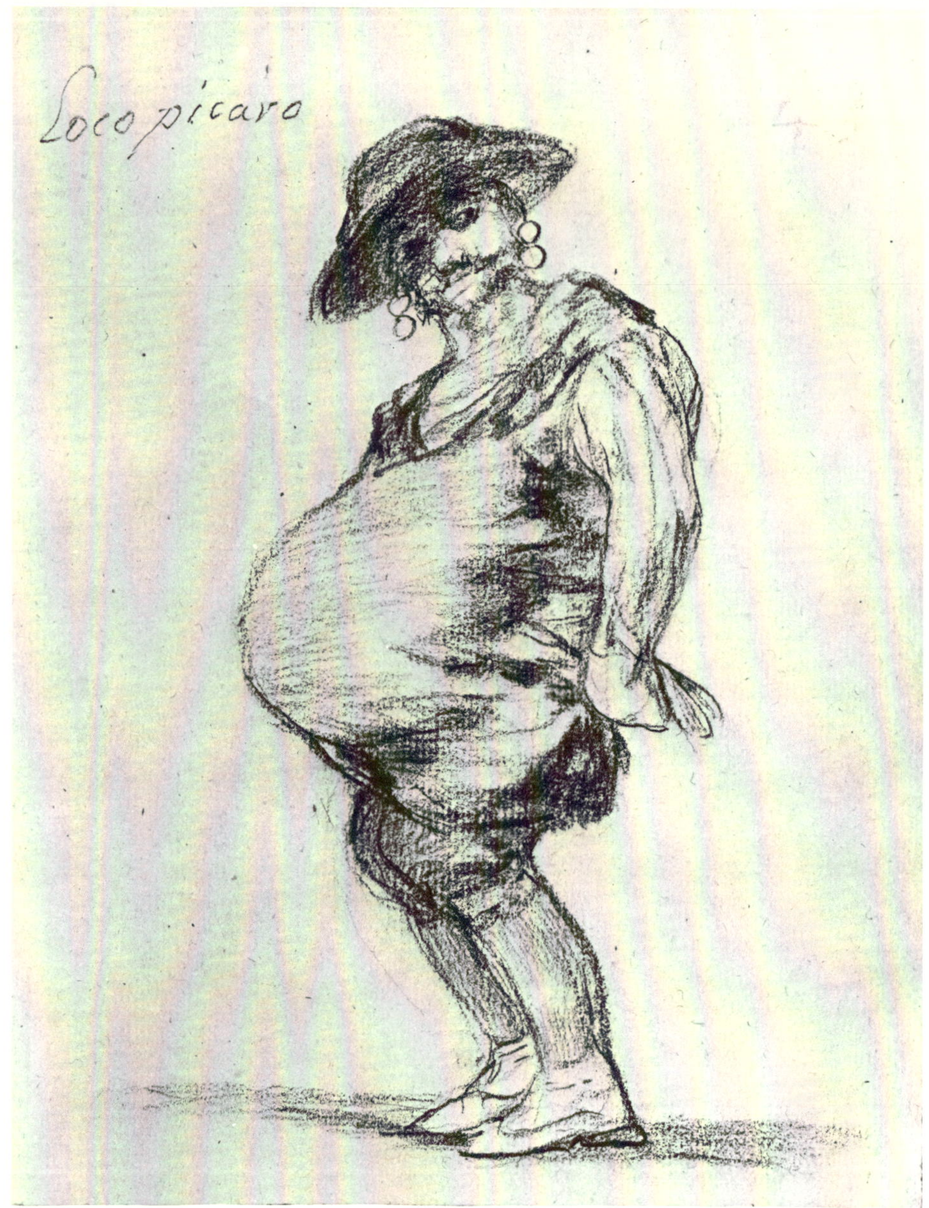

Loco Picaro

Black chalk. 19.2 x 15 cm. NM 274/1968. Inscribed twice, at upper left and at the bottom: *Loco picaro*. Numbered at upper right: 43.

PROVENANCE:
Stroelin, Lausanne ☐ H. M. Calmann, London.

BIBLIOGRAPHY:
A. L. Mayer, "Dibujos desconocidos de Goya," *Revista Espanol de Arte*, 9 (1923), v. p. 381 ☐ P. Bjurström, *Stateas konstsamlingars tillväxt och förvaltning 1968*, Stockholm 1969, pp. 17, 19 ☐ P. Gassier and J. Wilson, *Francisco Goya*, Fribourg 1970, p. 339, no. 1748.

EXHIBITIONS:
Frankfurt am Main, Städtische Galerie im Städelschen Kunstinstitut, M. Stuffman, *Francisco Goya, Zeichnungen und Druckgrafik*, 1981, no. L 84.

A fresh wave of reaction after the restoration of Ferdinand VII prompted Francisco Goya to leave Spain in January 1824. Having spent July and August of that year in Paris, he settled in voluntary exile in Bordeaux where he died in 1828. During his years in Bordeaux he visited Madrid several times.

Our sheet comes from one of the two albums that Goya produced during his residence in Bordeaux. He had then abandoned the brush for the lithographer's chalk, sometimes combined with black chalk. The two albums are technically similar in other respects as well, having the same paper and the same format. Album G, from which our drawing comes, contained at least 60 sheets, of which 54 can still be traced, including 13 in the Prado and 16 in the Gerstenberg (formerly Beruete) collection, Berlin. Most of the sheets from Album H are likewise now in the Prado or the Gerstenberg collection.

The interpretation of this drawing is problematical, as always with Goya. Rather than being deranged in the usual sense, this 'loco' seems to be a vehicle for Goya's criticism and irony. With the hat, the earrings, and the cushion on his belly, the man attempts to transform himself into a pregnant woman in an ostentatious posture.

72

LUCAS VAN LEYDEN
Leiden 1494 - Leiden 1533

Reproduced in color.

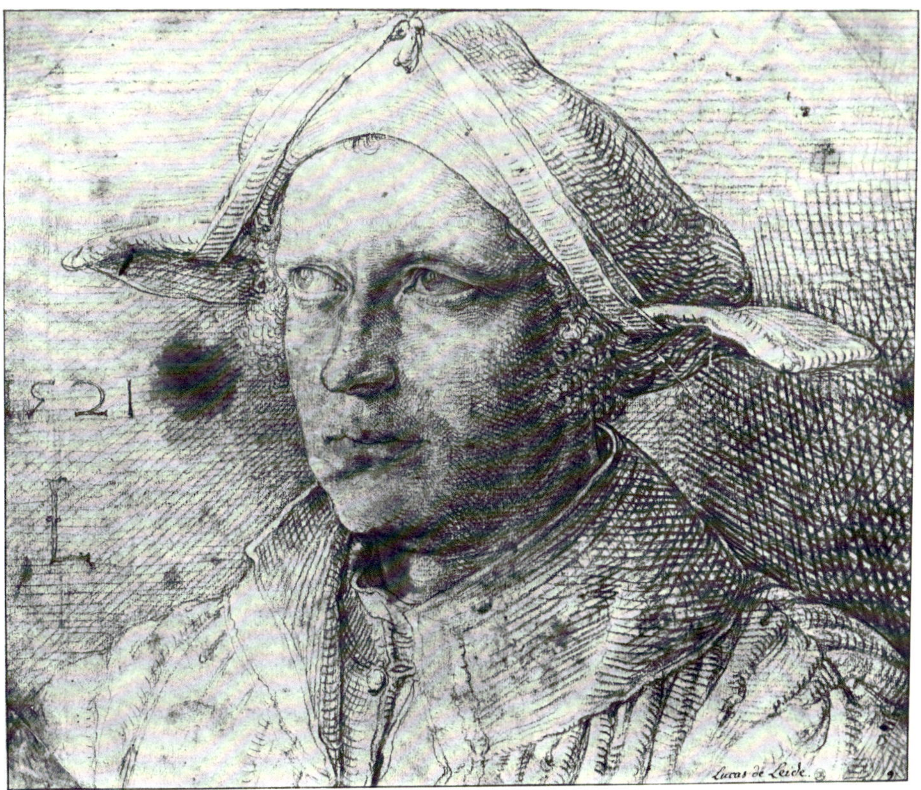

Portrait of a Young Man

Black chalk. 26.2 x 32.3 cm. All four corners cut off and restored. Horizontal tear near the center of the right hand side. No watermark. NM 1858/1863. Signed with monogram and dated in black chalk *1521 L.* Inscribed in the lower right corner in pen and brown ink: *Lucas de Leide* (Tessin).

PROVENANCE:
Crozat ☐ C. G. Tessin (List 1739-42, p. 35v; Cat. 1749, livré 17, no 137) ☐ Kongl. Biblioteket (Cat. 1790, no. 1668) ☐ Kongl. Museum (Lugt 1638).

BIBLIOGRAPHY:
Schönbrunner and Meder, no. 869 ☐ F. Dülberg, "Lucas van Leyden," *Onze Kunst* (1909), p. 10 ☐ N. Beets, *Lucas van Leyden*, Berlin 1913, p. 77 ☐ F. Dülberg, *Elzevier's Maandschrift*, 2 (1933), p. 10 ☐ M. Friedländer, *Die altniederländische Malerei*, Berlin 1932, 10, p. 102 ☐ L. Baldass, "Die Bildnisse des Lucas van Leyden," *Pantheon*, 20 (1937), pp. 205 ff. ☐ C. G. Hoogewerff, *De Noord-Nederlandsche Schilderkunst*, The Hague 1939, 3, p. 273 ☐ M. Friedländer and F. Winkler, *Lucas van Leyden*, Berlin 1963, no. 17 ☐ F. Lugt, *Musée du Louvre, Inv. gén. Maitres des anciens Pays-Bas nés avant 1550*, Paris 1968, p. 31 ☐ W. Kloek, "The Drawings of Lucas van Leyden," *Nederlands Kunsthistorisch Jaarboek*, 29 (1978), no. 14.

EXHIBITIONS:
Stockholm 1933, no. 43 ☐ Rotterdam, Museum Boymans, *Jeroen Bosch. Noord-Nederlandsche Primitieven*, 1939, no. 52 ☐ Stockholm 1953, no. 8 ☐ Amsterdam, Rijksmuseum, *Middeleuwse kunst der noordelijke Nederlanden*, 1958, no. 203 ☐ New York, Boston, Chicago 1969, no. 43 ☐ Brussels, Palais des Beaux-Arts, *Albert Dürer aux Pays-Bas*, 1977, no. 381.

This drawing belongs to a group of black chalk portrait subjects, all presumably done in 1521: a man in the Stadelijk Museum, Leiden; a woman in the Schlossmuseum, Weimar; and two of men and one of a woman in the Louvre, Paris. The Louvre also has a copy of the portrait in Stockholm. There are several indications that the group was not split up for quite some time. Two of the Paris drawings are numbered in the same hand as the Stockholm sheet, and as the latter was definitely acquired at the Crozat auction in 1741, this trio may be the "trois beaux portraits" which were sold on that occasion.

The function of the drawings is obscure. No connection has been found with the artist's engraved oeuvre. And as they were kept as a group they can hardly have been commissioned by the sitters or done as gifts. We know, however, that Lucas van Leyden met Dürer in Antwerp in 1521, and the latter relates in his diary that they drew each other's portrait. There is a Dürer drawing in the Musée Wicar, Lille, that is thought to resemble Lucas (the model happens to have the same headgear as the model in the Stockholm portrait). Dürer did a great many portraits during his journey in the Netherlands, and one is tempted to suppose that it was the encounter of the two artists which stimulated the young Lucas to try his hand in this genre.

73

LAMBERT VAN NOORT
Amersfoort ca. 1520 - Antwerp 1571

Studies of an Elephant

Red chalk, on the separate study of an eye also black chalk. 40.3 x 28.1 cm. No watermark. NM Z 384/1953. Measurements in red chalk. Inscribed in the lower right corner in red chalk: *in anversa. / Lamberto van Noort / apres del vivo Ao 1563 / primo di(e) de october*. Numbered in the lower right corner in pen and brown in ink: 8. Inscribed on the verso in pen and brown ink: *N:o 52 / Battistino simo(?) leo Veronese*. This is a repetition of an inscription in red chalk, barely readable, at the top of the verso.

PROVENANCE:
Crozat ☐ C. G. Tessin (Cat. 1749, livré 20, no. 119) ☐ Kongl. Museum (Lugt 1638).

BIBLIOGRAPHY:
J. Reznicek, *Die Zeichnungen von Hendrick Goltzius*, The Hague 1961, I, p. 208 ☐ M. Winner, "Raffael malt einen Elefanten," *Mitteilungen des Kunsthistorischen Institutes in Florenz*, 11 (1963-65), p. 76.

EXHIBITIONS:
Stockholm 1953, no. 25 ☐ Stockholm 1984-85, no. 266.

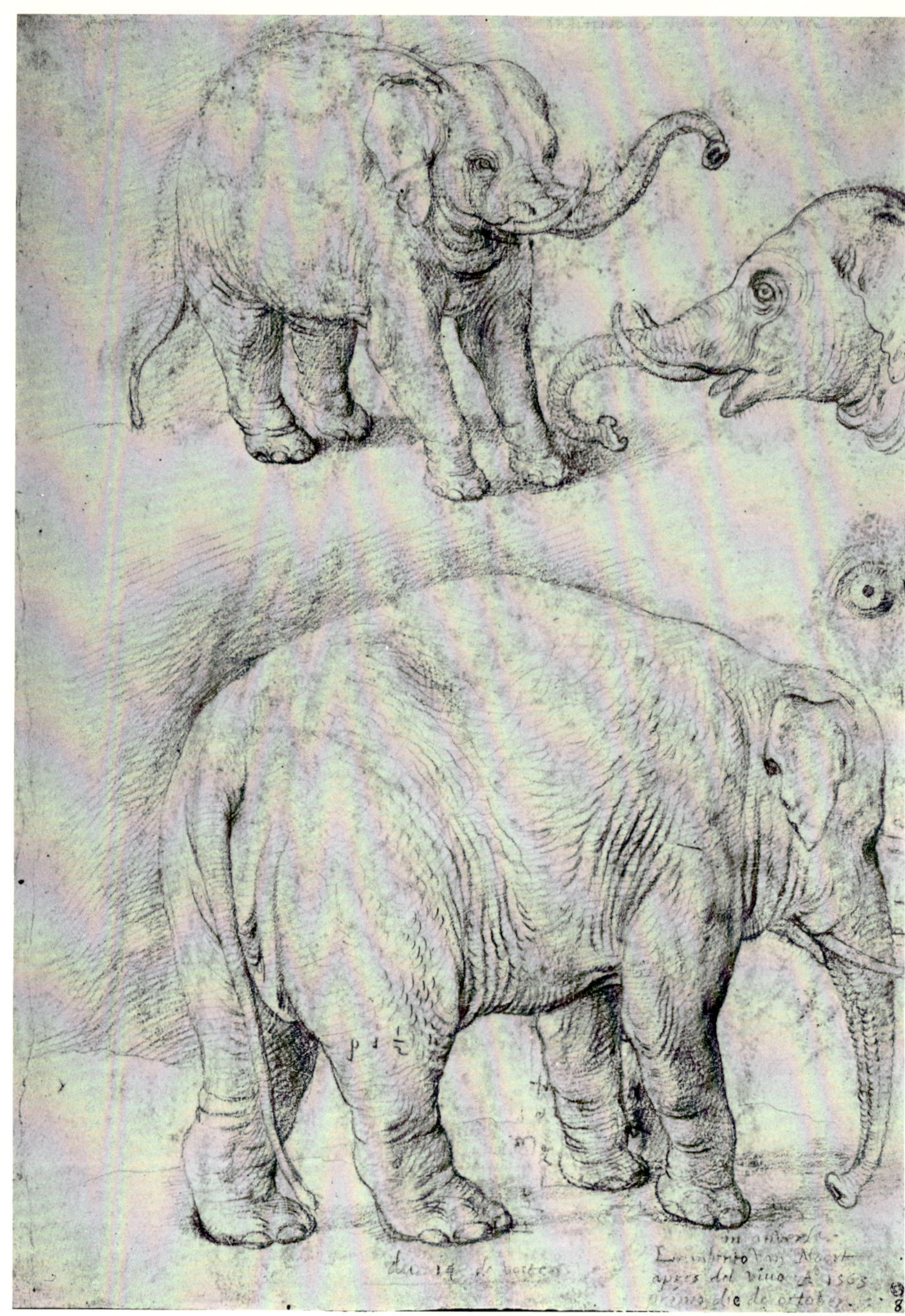

These studies were done, as the inscription tells us, after a live elephant in Amsterdam on 1 October 1563. The animal, a gift from the king of Portugal to Maximilian of Bavaria, had arrived in the city two days earlier.

This was not the only elephant, shipped from their new colonies overseas, that the Portuguese used as presents. The best known was Hanno, given to Leo X in 1514 and portrayed by Raphael. Another was transported from Portugal via Genoa and Milan to the court in Vienna and was pictured, fairly accurately, in a German flysheet dated 1552.

Lambert could well have seen reproductions of elephants before he met this one in the flesh. The animal occurs in compositions by a number of Raphael's pupils, works that may have been known to the Italian artists' colony in Antwerp. The Elephant Well in the Villa Madama, Rome, associated with Giovanni da Udine, has a notably realistic three-dimensional rendering of an elephant's head after which Maerten van Heemskerck did a study in the 1530s.

Nor was Lambert the only person to draw the Antwerp elephant. A contemporary anonymous woodcut bears witness to the excitement caused by the remarkable animal. There is an engraving from 1563 by Gerhard Groening (Paludanus) showing the elephant in eight positions, dominated by a side view in a larger scale in the middle, in the same way as in Lambert's drawing. A number of sheets by Bernaert de Rijkere (Maître B) in the Louvre, signed and dated 1563, present the animal from various aspects and include a keeper.[1]

NOTE:
1. K. G. Boon, "De Antwerpse schilder Bernaert de Rijkene en zijn tekeningen oeuvre," *Oud Holland*, 91 (1971), pp. 116 ff.

74

ROELANDT SAVERY
Courtrai 1576 - Utrecht 1639

Reproduced in color.

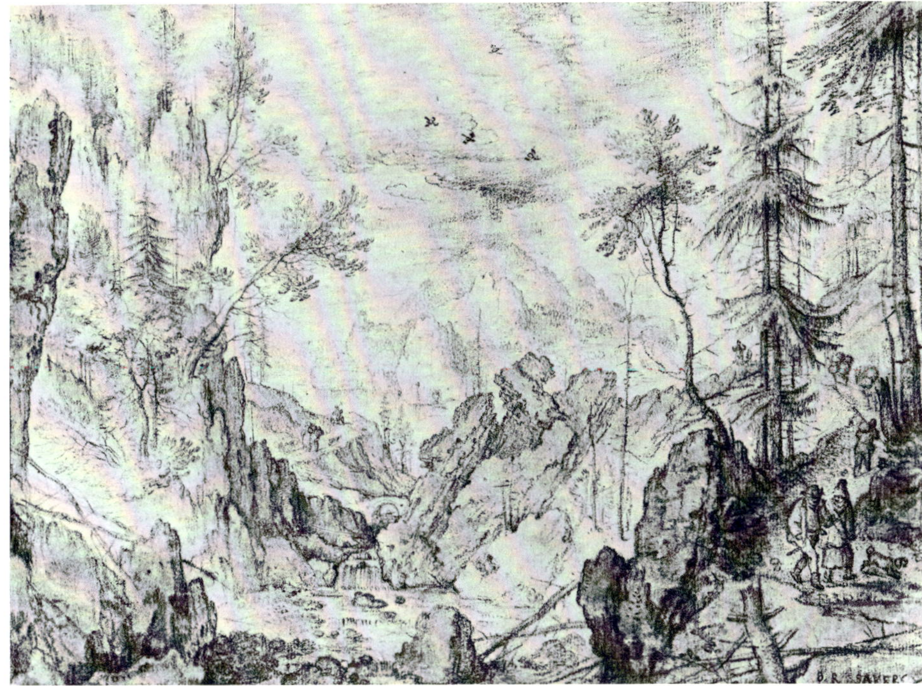

Mountain Landscape with Travellers

Black and red chalk, blue wash. Some additions in pen and brown ink in the upper left corner. 18.9 x 26.4 cm. Partly traced for transfer, verso rubbed red. No watermark. NM THC 3246. Inscribed in the lower right corner in black chalk: *R Savery*.

PROVENANCE:
N. Tessin Jr.? □ Kongl. Museum (Lugt 1638).

BIBLIOGRAPHY:
W. Bernt, *Die Niederländischen Zeichner des 17 Jahrhunderts*, Munich 1958, II, no. 530 □ J. Spicer-Durham, *The Drawings of Roelandt Savery*, New Haven 1979, I, pp. 72 f.; II, p. 440.

EXHIBITIONS:
Stockholm 1953, no. 93 □ Stockholm 1984-85, no. 314.

Roelandt Savery executed this landscape in Prague during his most creative period, 1604-11. Besides acting as a center for international late mannerism, the imperial court of Rudolf II encouraged studies of nature. The Netherlandish landscape artists assembled there made important contributions to the evolution of realism in landscape art. One of the pioneers was Paulus van Vianen, a silversmith by profession, who was remarkably free from the clichés of the landscape genre.

Opinions differ as to whether this mountain landscape is the product of the Tyrolean journey that Savery is said to have undertaken at the behest of the emperor or whether its inspiration is to be found in the Tyrolean sketches of van Vianen. Whatever the case, the result is a composed landscape where impressions of nature are combined with clear evidence of the tradition of landscape depiction from Pieter Bruegel the Elder.

This sheet, together with other drawings in the same technique and of much the same size, served as a basis for two etchings in a series of landscape etchings by Aegidius Sadeler in Prague. Two of these etchings carry the date 1609. Our picture is the only one in the series to show a truly forbidding rocky landscape, although in the etching the blue mountains in the distance have been replaced by a view of a harbor. A painting of the same subject, in a Berlin collection, is signed and dated 1607.

75

ROELANDT SAVERY

76

HENDRICK GOLTZIUS
Venlo 1558 - Haarlem 1616

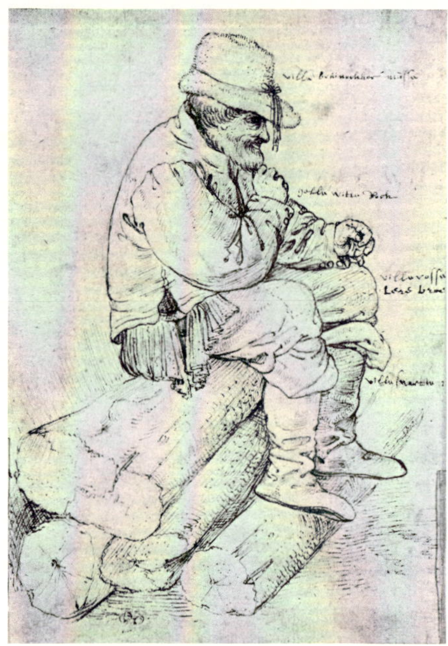

Peasant Seated on a Woodpile

Black chalk, pen and brown ink. 16.2 x 11.4 cm. No watermark. Kulturhistoriska museet, Lund. XXXIX: 5. Deposited in Nationalmuseum. Inscribed with color notes in pen and brown ink over almost erased notes in black chalk: *wille bruinockker musse / gelle witte Rock / wille rosse / Lere bra(?) / wille swartte.*

VERSO:
Seated Man with a Rod. Red chalk, color notes in red chalk: *swart / brin ler / ler / swart.* Inscribed on the mount in pen and brown ink: *Zes stucks No* 96, and in pencil: *Stomme.*

PROVENANCE:
G. Tamm □ C. Grill, purchased 1925 □ Kulturhistoriska museet as a gift 1939.

BIBLIOGRAPHY:
P. Bjurström, "Three Unpublished Drawings by Pieter Bruegel the Elder," *Master Drawings*, 3 (1965), pp. 48 f., pl. 43 □ J. Spicer, "The 'naer het leven' drawings of Pieter Bruegel or Roelandt Savery?," *Master Drawings*, 8 (1970), pp. 11, 20 □ J. Spicer-Durham 1979, II, p. 590.

EXHIBITIONS:
Stockholm 1984-85, no. 313.

We know of about a hundred figure studies of this kind, annotated with the colors of the clothing and inscribed *naer het leven* ("done from life"). The great majority were executed with chalk in the streets and markets of Prague and subsequently gone over with the pen. They constituted a repertoire of figures for the artist's paintings.

Here, as in his landscapes, Savery is reminiscent of Pieter Bruegel the Elder, to whom these drawings were assigned until as recently as the early 1970s. A younger generation of Netherlandish artists was influenced by them in turn. A copy of this sheet belongs to a series of copies by the painter Pieter Quast (1606-1647, Hermitage, Leningrad).

Three Fantastic Figures

Pen and brown ink, heightened with white, on green, prepared paper. 34.5 x 25.4 cm. No watermark. NM 1871/1863.

PROVENANCE:
Crozat (Mariette, no. 808) □ C. G. Tessin (List 1739-42, p. 36; Cat. 1749, livré 17, no. 171) □ Kongl. Biblioteket (Cat. 1790, no. 1700) □ Kongl. Museum (Lugt 1638).

BIBLIOGRAPHY:
E. K. J. Reznicek, *Hendrick Goltzius. Zeichnungen*, Utrecht 1961, no. 160.

EXHIBITIONS:
Stockholm 1953, no. 60 □ Rotterdam and Haarlem, *Hendrick Goltzius als tekenaar*, 1959, no. 103 □ Stockholm 1967, no. 203 □ Paris, Brussels, Amsterdam 1970-71, no. 70 □ Stockholm 1984-85, no. 252.

The three heads placed close together in the foreground dominate this composition. The one on the left is cut by the edge of the sheet; this is not a later cut, but an intentionally bold, mannerist conception.

The meaning of the work, presumably a learned allegory, is still obscure. The man in the middle is reading a book, and on the wall behind the man on the right are cabalistic symbols. The two figures debating on the background terrace, one pointing up to the sky, suggest the possibility of a reference to astronomy or astrology.

The slightly grotesque heads recall a group of phantasy portraits, done by Goltzius around 1600, of figures in clothes from the early sixteenth century. His manner there is closely linked to his two great predecessors, Albrecht Dürer and Lucas van Leyden. The same technical virtuosity and desire to match these masters with their own means of expression are to be found in some of the engravings by Goltzius from this period.

The drawing includes the artist's monogram and the year 1598.

77

PETER PAUL RUBENS
Siegen 1577 - Antwerp 1640

Reproduced in color.

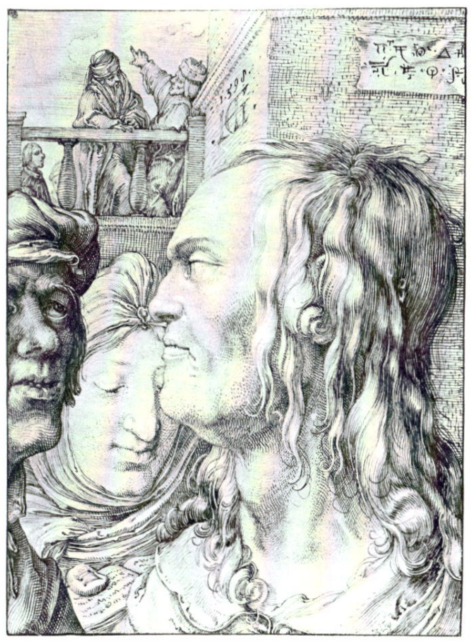

Reproduced in color.

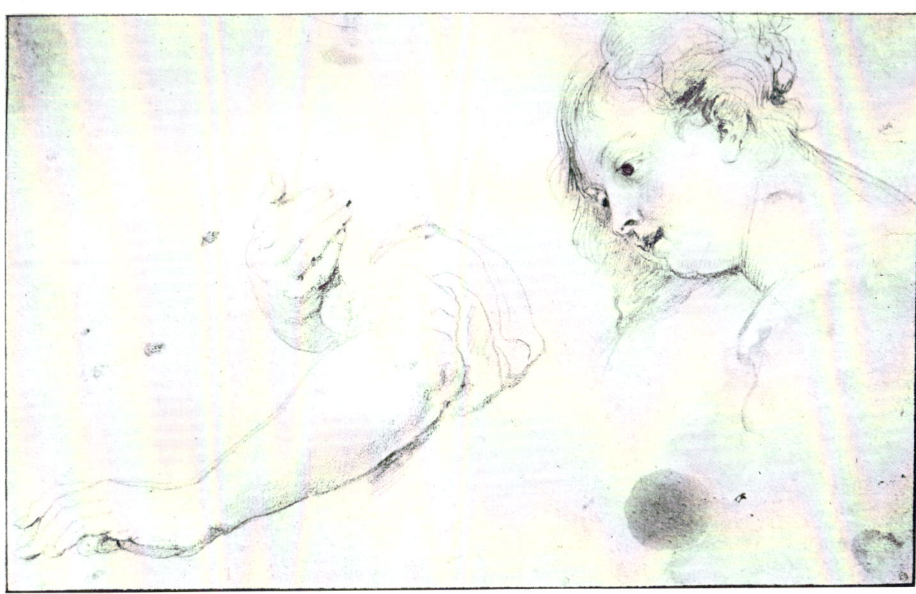

Head, Left Arm, and Right Hand of a Woman

Black, white, and red chalk on gray paper, brown wash around the woman's ear. 24.4 x 39.3 cm. Watermark: Elephant. NM 1982/1863.

PROVENANCE:
Crozat □ C. G. Tessin (List 1739-42, p. 69 v.; Cat. 1749, livré 18, no. 47) □ Kongl. Biblioteket (Cat. 1790, no. 1789 as van Dyck) □ Kongl. Museum (Lugt 1638).

BIBLIOGRAPHY:
G. Glück and J. H. Haberdietzl, *Die Handzeichnungen von P. P. Rubens*, Berlin 1928, no. 206 □ L. Burchard and R.-A. d'Hulst, *Rubens Drawings*, Brussels 1963, no. 186 □ J. Müller-Hofstede, Review of Burchard-d'Hulst in *Master Drawings*, 4 (1966), p. 453 □ J. I. Kuznetsov, *Risunki Rubensa*, Moscow 1974, no. 124.

EXHIBITIONS:
Brussels, Palais des Beaux-Arts, *Dessins de Rubens*, 1938-39 □ Helsinki, Ateneum, *P. P. Rubens*, 1952-53, no. 33 □ Stockholm 1953, no. 103 □ Stockholm, *Rubens i Sverige*, 1977, no. 31.

These studies were drawn for the figure of the kneeling Catherine in the painting *The Mystic Marriage of St. Catherine* of 1633 (Toledo Museum of Art) and show details done after a model while the painting itself was in progress. Heads and hands often feature in such studies, as they are particularly important for the expression of feelings. Such sheets were also retained for subsequent use in other compositions. Rubens likewise also used studies done for the roughly contemporary painting *The Garden of Love* (Waddeston Manor, England) in the Toledo painting.

78

PETER PAUL RUBENS

Reproduced in color.

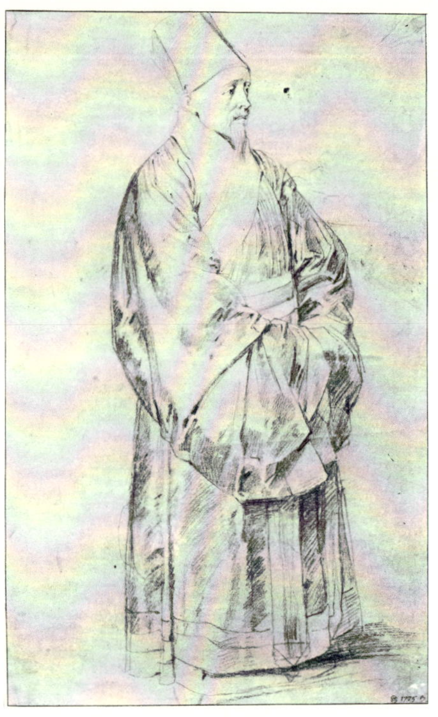

A Jesuit in a Chinese Dress

Black chalk on gray paper, touches of red and yellow chalk in the face, and light green chalk on the collar 41 x 25.4 cm. NM 1968/1863. Numbered in the lower right corner in pen and brown ink: *1775* (Sparre) and *3*.

PROVENANCE:
Crozat □ C. G. Tessin (List 1739-42, p. 36; Cat. 1749, livré 17, no. 149) □ Kongl. Biblioteket (Cat. 1790, no. 1775) □ Kongl. Museum (Lugt 1638).

BIBLIOGRAPHY:
C. S. Wortley, "Rubens' Drawings of Chinese Costume," *Old Master Drawings*, 9 (1934-35), no. 3, pl. 43 □ J. S. Held, *Rubens. Selected Drawings*, London 1959, p. 127 □ Burchard and d'Hulst 1963, pp. 231 f. □ E. Haverkamp-Begeman and A. M. Logan, "Dessins de Rubens," *La Revue de l'Art*, 42 (1978), p. 97 □ New York, J. Pierpont Morgan Library, *Rubens and Rembrandt in their Century* (by F. Stampfle), 1979, pp. 52 f.

EXHIBITIONS:
Rotterdam, Museum Boymans, *Van Eyck tot Rubens. Tekeningen*, 1948-49, no. 125 □ Paris, Bibliothèque Nationale, *De van Dyck à Rubens*, 1949, no. 93 □ Stockholm 1953, no. 101 □ Stockholm, *Rubens i Sverige*, 1977, no. 30.

This is one of four studies of Europeans in Chinese clothing published by Wortley in 1934 as by Rubens. Previously they had been attributed to van Dyck. The other three studies are in Wolfgang Burchard's collection, London, the J. Pierpont Morgan Library, New York, and Robert Smith's collection, Washington. The clothing is the same in all four drawings, and the model seems to be the same in three, the exception being the sheet in New York. The drawing owned by Robert Smith is actually a more carefully executed version of the sheet exhibited here. Besides a number of changes, the latter has some loose chalk strokes that are difficult to interpret. As Rubens did not normally repeat himself in this way, Haverkamp-Begeman and Logan have suggested that Smith's sheet is a copy by van Dyck after Rubens.

An inscription in Rubens' hand on Smith's sheet refers to the use of Chinese dress by Jesuit missionaries and accordingly explains the models:

> Note that the dark color is not peculiar to Chinese scholars but to the Fathers of the Society of Jesus, except for the blue facings which are common to all. The Chinese, furthermore, do not use one color only in their clothing, but any color they like, except yellow, which is reserved for the King.

Rubens was a lay brother of the Society of Jesus and worked from 1615 on the decoration of the new Jesuit church in Antwerp, besides producing book illustrations for the Society. He may have seen Jesuits in Chinese clothing in Antwerp in 1622 as participants in a great parade to mark the canonization of François Xavier and Ignatius Loyola. But there were other opportunities, for example, the two propaganda tours of Europe that Nicolas Trigault, a renowned Jesuit missionary, made in 1615 and 1616-17.

It can be assumed that Rubens intended to use these studies in his painting. There is a man in Korean dress, likewise the subject of a drawn study, in one of the altarpieces that were painted around 1617 for the Jesuit church in Antwerp.

The Chinese costume occurs in a sketch in oils in the Musée Bonnat, Bayonne. The motif has not been identified but may be a religious allegory. Various dates have been proposed for the drawing, but the most recent suggestion, by Julius Held, places it before 1620.

79

PETER PAUL RUBENS

Studies of a Male Nude

Black and white chalk on grayish paper. 57 x 44.4 cm. Two pieces of paper added along the right border. Watermark: Fleur-de-lis. NM 1926/1863. Inscribed at the bottom center in pen and brown ink: *Rubens* and *Cabinet de Crozat* (Tessin). Numbered in the lower right corner in pen and brown ink: *1735* (Sparre) and *41*, (struck out).

PROVENANCE:
Crozat (Mariette, no. 836?) □ C. G. Tessin (List 1739-42, p. 42; Cat. 1749, livré 19, no. 62) □ Kongl. Biblioteket (Cat. 1790, no. 1735) □ Kongl. Museum (Lugt 1638).

BIBLIOGRAPHY:
Glück and Haberditzl 1928, no. 88 □ Held 1959, no. 80, pl. 91 □ Burchard and d'Hulst 1963, no. 72 □ Müller-Hofstede 1966, pp. 447 and 450 □ Kuznetsov 1974, no. 41 □ M. Bernhard, *Rubens. Handzeichnungen*, Munich 1977, p. 217.

EXHIBITIONS:
Helsinki, Ateneum, *P. P. Rubens*, 1952, no. 34 □ Stockholm 1953, no. 97 □ Antwerp, Rubenshuis, *Tekeningen van Peter Paul Rubens*, 1956, no. 44 □ Paris, Brussels, Amsterdam 1970-71, no. 73 □ Antwerp, Musée Royaux des Beaux-Arts, *P. P. Rubens*, 1977, no. 134 □ Stockholm, *Rubens i Sverige*, 1977, no. 26.

This sheet containes studies for the figure of Job in *Job Tortured by Devils and Abused by His Wife*, the left wing of a triptych in St. Nicholas, Brussels, painted in 1612. Although destroyed in 1695, the painting's composition is preserved in a drawing by van Dyck (Louvre, Paris) and was also engraved by Lucas Vorsterman. The position of the figure's trunk and legs, the arrangement of the loincloth, and the facial expression all tally with the engraving. The position of the arms in our drawing, however, shows several alternatives.

The drawing is seen by Burchard-d'Hulst as a study for the contemporary *Martyrdom of St. Lawrence* and was used subsequently for the figure of Job. The drawing is so close to the latter and differs so much from the former that this seems unlikely. The Nationalmuseum, Stockholm, has a large sheet with figure studies for the *Lawrence* in which the plastic form of the figures is stressed with the aid of systematic crosshatchings. In this drawing, in contrast, the broad manner accentuates the play of the light over the forms.

80

ANTONIS VAN DYCK
Antwerp 1599 - London 1641

Reproduced in color.

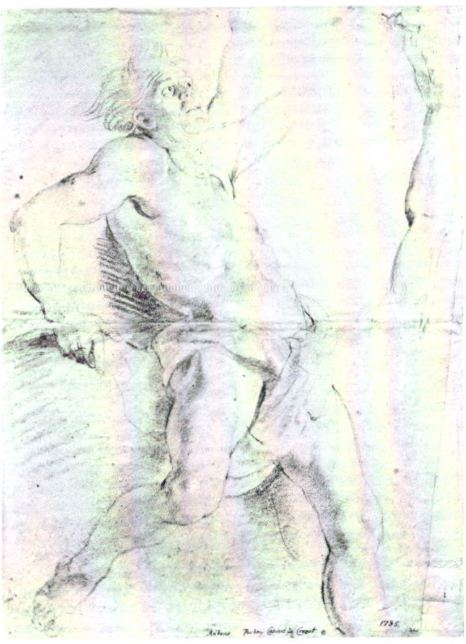

Portrait of Cornelius van der Geest

Black chalk. 25.5 x 18.4 cm. Small brown stains all over the paper. Watermark: Coat of arms and the number 4. NM 1973/1863. Inscribed in pen and brown ink in the lower right corner: *CORNELIVS VAN DER GEEST* and numbered *1780* (Sparre).

PROVENANCE:
Crozat (Mariette, no. 848) ☐ C. G. Tessin (List 1739-42, p. 36; Cat. 1749, livré 17, no. 158) ☐ Kongl. Biblioteket (Cat. 1790, no. 1780) ☐ Kongl. Museum (Lugt 1638).

BIBLIOGRAPHY:
P. J. Mariette, *Abécédario*. Archives de l'Art Français, IV (ed. P. de Chennevières and A. de Montaiglon), Paris 1853-62, II, p. 202 ☐ Schönbrunner and Meder, no. 1028 ☐ M. Rooses, "De tekeningen de Vlaamsche Meestere," *Onze Kunst*, II (1903), p. 138 ☐ T. W. Muchall-Viebrook, *Flemish Drawings of the Seventeenth Century*, London 1926, no. 42 ☐ M. Delacre, "Recherches sur le role du dessin dans l'iconographie de van Dyck," *Mémoires*, 2nd series, Academie Royale de Belgique, Brussels (1932), II and IV, p. 95 ☐ A. J. J. Delen, "Cornelius van der Geest," *Antwerpen*, V (1959), pp. 51-71 ☐ H. Vey, *Die Zeichnungen Anton van Dycks*, Brussels 1962, no. 262.

EXHIBITIONS:
Stockholm 1933, no. 42 ☐ Stockholm 1953, no. 152 ☐ Antwerp, Rubenshuis - Rotterdam, Museum Boymans-van Beuningen, *Antoon van Dyck. Tekeningen en olieverfschetzen*, 1960, no. 84 ☐ New York, Boston, Chicago 1969, no. 61.

Cornelius van der Geest was prominent in Antwerp as a merchant and art collector. The drawing was used by Paulus Pontius for his engraving for the "Iconography," van Dyck's collection of portraits of his contemporaries.[1] The drawing was probably done on one of the artist's two stays in Antwerp between the autumn of 1627 and the end of 1634.

NOTE:
1. M. Mauquoy-Hendrickx, *L'iconographie d'Antoine van Dyck*, Brussels 1956, no. 48.

Reproduced in color.

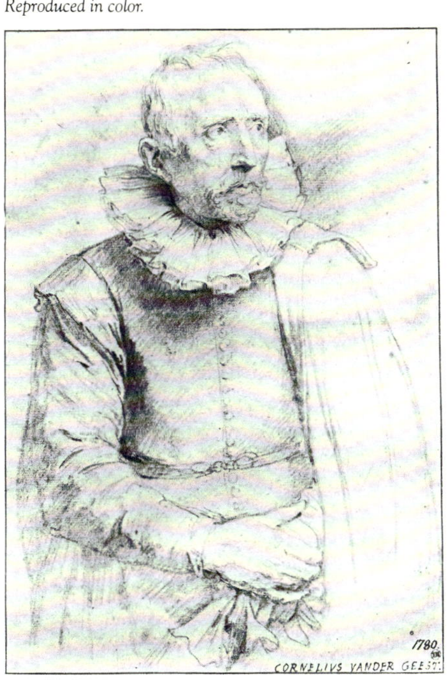

81

ANTONIS VAN DYCK

82

JACOB JORDAENS
Antwerp 1593 - Antwerp 1678

Reproduced in color.

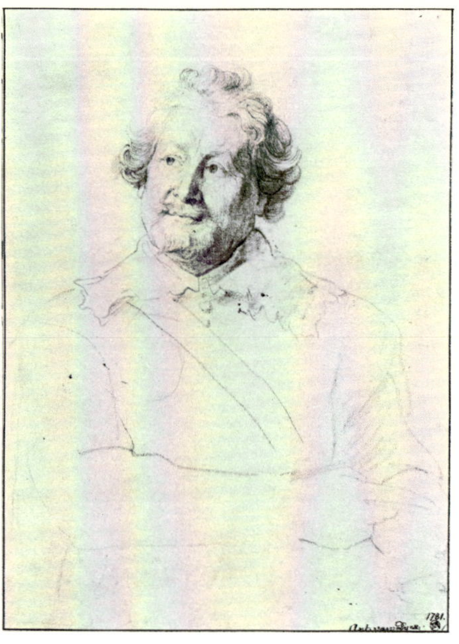

Portrait of a Middle-Aged Man

Black chalk. 25.1 x 18.1 cm. Watermark: Letter A V in a rectangle. NM 1974/1863. Inscribed in the lower right corner in pen and rown ink: *Ant. van Dyck* and numbered *1781* (Sparre).

PROVENANCE:
Crozat (Mariette, no. 848?) □ C. G. Tessin (List 1739-42, p. 36; Cat. 1749, livré 17, no. 159) □ Kongl. Biblioteket (Cat. 1790, no. 1781) □ Kongl. Museum (Lugt 1638).

EXHIBITIONS:
Stockholm 1953, no. 154 □ Paris, Brussels, Amsterdam 1970-71, no. 77.

The model in this drawing has not been identified. Meticulous characterization of the features, combined with just a suggestion of the body, is common in several of van Dyck's portrait drawings for the "Iconography."

Reproduced in color.

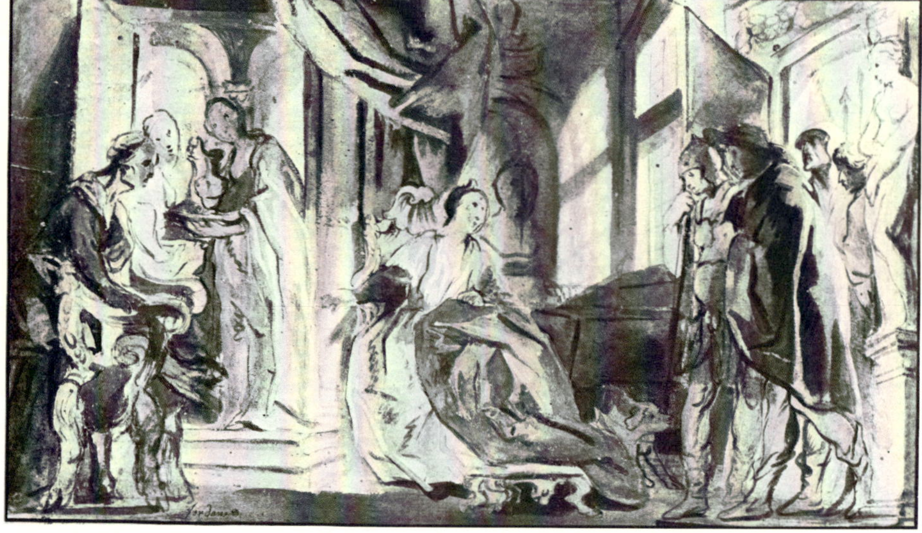

Telemachus Brings Theoclymenus Before his Mother Penelope

Black chalk, point of brush and brown wash, watercolor, and gouache. 28.3 x 50.7 cm. No watermark. NM 1954/1863. Inscribed in the lower left corner in pen and brown ink: *Jordans*

PROVENANCE:
Crozat (Mariette, no. 856) □ C. G. Tessin (List 1739-42, p. 60; Cat. 1749, livré 16, no. 84) □ Kongl. Biblioteket (Cat. 1790, no. 1761) □ Kongl. Museum (Lugt 1638).

BIBLIOGRAPHY:
L. van Puyvelde, *Jordaens*, Paris and Brussels 1953, p. 200 □ R.-A. d'Hulst, "De tekeningen van Jacob Jordaens in het Museum Boymans," *Bulletin Museum Boymans*, 4:2 (1953), p. 49 □ Idem, "Jordaens and His Early Activities in the Field of Tapestry," *Art Quarterly* (1956), p. 240, fig. 4 □ Idem, *De tekeningen van Jacob Jordaens*, Brussels 1956, no. 39, pp. 161, 335, fig. 97 □ Idem, *Jordaens Drawings*, Brussels 1974, no. A 81 □ Idem, *Jacob Jordaens*, London 1982, pp. 297, 312, fig. 111.

EXHIBITIONS:
Stockholm 1933, no. 38 □ Stockholm 1953, no. 129 □ Antwerp, Rubenshuis, Rotterdam, Museum Boymans-van Beuningen, *Tekeningen van Jacob Jordaens*, 1966-67, no. 37 □ New York, M. Knoedler & Co., *Masters of the Loaded Brush: Oil Sketches from Rubens to Tiepolo*, 1967, no. 52 □ Ottawa, The National Gallery of Canada, *Jacob Jordaens 1593-1678*, 1968-69, no. 180 □ Paris, Brussels, Amsterdam 1970-71, no. 85.

This is a preliminary study for a tapestry in a series featuring the *Odyssey*. The Musée Granet, Aix-en-Provence, has a large oil painting that may have served as a model for the weavers. The total number of scenes in the series is not known, but a dozen or so drawings and paintings are extant. The series was woven several times, although only parts have been preserved. The most complete set was produced in 1665-66 for Duke Charles Emanuel of Savoy: the extant scenes include our composition, but it is divided into two parts. The section on the far left with Penelope's three female attendants has been woven as a rather narrow unit to hang between windows (Museo Civico, Turin), while the main body of the composition has wider dimensions (Quirinal Palace, Rome).

The cartoons for the *Odyssey* series were executed around 1630-35. One source of inspiration may have been Primaticcio's cycle in the Ulysses gallery at Fontainebleau (see no. 33 above). This was a topical theme, made popular by drawings by Rubens and engravings by van Thulden, which were published in 1633.

83

LUCAS VAN UDEN
Antwerp 1595 - Antwerp 1672

Reproduced in color.

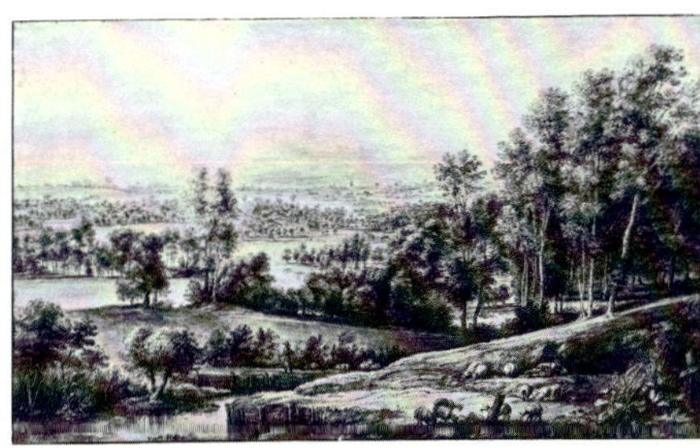

Landscape with a Setting Sun

Pen and brown ink, watercolors, and gouache. 20.1 x 34.2 cm. No watermark. NM Z 390/1957. Inscribed in the lower left corner in pen and brown ink: *van Uden* (C. G. Tessin)

PROVENANCE:
C. G. Tessin □ Kongl. Museum (Luft 1638).

EXHIBITIONS:
Stockholm 1953, no. 139.

This artist continued the specifically Flemish tradition of composed landscapes, strongly influenced by Rubens. Small watercolored pen drawings like this one were his foremost means of expression.

84

CORNELIS VROOM
Haarlem 1591 - Haarlem 1661

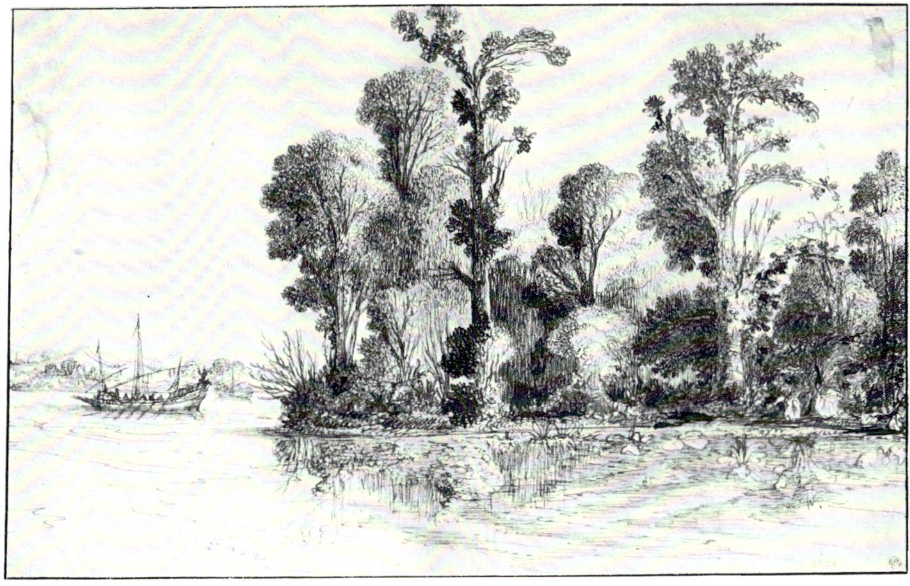

Riverview with Galleys

Pen and brown ink, brown wash. 18.7 x 31.2 cm. Old repairs along the left border and in the upper right corner. Watermark: Undecipherable. NM THC 3238.

PROVENANCE:
Kongl. Museum (Lugt 1638).

BIBLIOGRAPHY:
C. Müller and J. Q. van Regteren Altena, "Der Maler Jacob van Geel," *Jahrbuch der Preuszischen Kunstsammlungen*, 52 (1931), pp. 182 ff. (as Jacob Pynas) □ K. Bauch, "Beiträge zum Werk der Vorläufer Rembrandts: IV. Handzeichnungen von Jacob Pynas," *Oud Holland*, 54 (1937), pp. 241 ff. (as Jacob Pynas) □ W. Bernt, *Die Niederländischen Zeichner des 17. Jahrhunderts*, Munich 1957, II, no. 482 (as Jacob Pynas) □ G. Keyes, *Cornelis Vroom: Marine and Landscape Artist*, Alphen 1975, I, pp. 56-58; II, no. D33, fig. 27.

EXHIBITIONS:
Stockholm 1953, no. 120.

The current attribution to Cornelis Vroom, replacing an earlier ascription to Jacob Pynas, was made by Keyes in 1975. Cornelis Vroom began his artistic career as a marine painter but soon changed to landscapes. He was influenced by the group of Haarlem artists — Hercules Seghers, Willem Buytewech and Esaias and Jan van de Velde — who helped create realistic representations of the Dutch landscape at the beginning of the seventeenth century.

This drawing, datable c. 1620, testifies to the impact of the Haarlem artists' pioneering landscape etchings. But the galleys and the hills in the background introduce an evocative element which is not to be found in the genre of commonplace landscapes. The drawing represents an important link between Vroom's early marine paintings and his later landscape art.

85

PHILIPS KONINCK
Amsterdam 1619 - Amsterdam 1688

Reproduced in color.

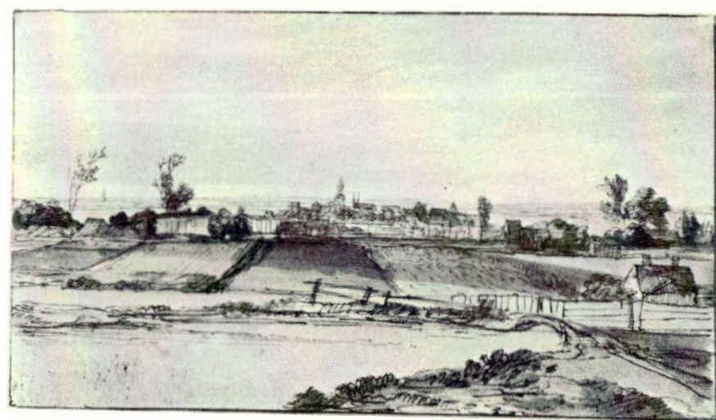

Landscape with a Canal and a Town

Pen and brown ink, gray wash, watercolors. 13 x 24 cm. No watermark. NM Z 378/1957.

PROVENANCE:
King Karl XV, Rosersberg Castle.

BIBLIOGRAPHY:
H. Gerson, *Philips Koninck*, Berlin 1936, pp. 60, 146, no. Z77.

EXHIBITION:
Stockholm 1953, no. 210.

Philips Koninck is one of the many Dutch artists whose work reflects the influence of Rembrandt. His landscapes, however, illustrate the structure of the Dutch countryside in a more down-to-earth manner in which the local colors offset atmospheric effects and reflecting water.

Koninck arrived in Amsterdam in 1641. This is a fairly early drawing, probably from the end of that decade. The city in the background is said to be Arnhem.

86

REMBRANDT VAN RIJN
Leiden 1606 - Amsterdam 1669

Reproduced in color.

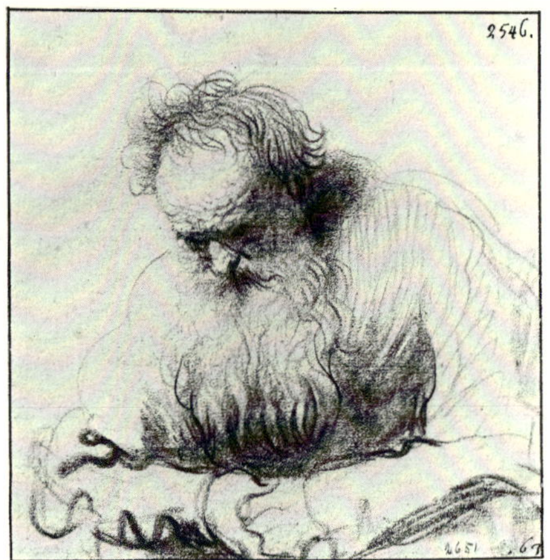

Seated Old Man

Red chalk. 14.4 x 14.6 cm. No watermark. NM 2651/1863. Numbered in pen and brown ink in the upper right corner: *2546* (Sparre), and in the lower right corner: *63*.

PROVENANCE:
Crozat ☐ C. G. Tessin (List 1739-42, p. 38 as Mellan; Cat. 1749, livré 17, no. 243) ☐ Kongl. Biblioteket (Cat. 1790, no. 2645) ☐ Kongl. Museum (Lugt 1638).

BIBLIOGRAPHY:
O. Benesch, "Rembrandt - Relicta aus der Münchener Graphischen Sammlung," *Mitteilungen der Geschuhle für vervielfältigende Kunst: Beilage der Graphische Künste*, Vienna 1925, nos. 2-3, pp. 26, 29 ☐ K. Bauch, *Die Kunst des jungen Rembrandts*, Heidelberg 1933, p. 202, fig. 137 ☐ O. Benesch, *Werk und Forschung. Rembrandt*, Vienna 1935, p. 10 ☐ Idem, *Rembrandt. Selected Drawings*, London 1947, no. 16 ☐ Idem, *The Drawings of Rembrandt*, London 1954-57, I, no. 38 ☐ Idem, *Collected Writings I. Rembrandt*, New York 1970, pp. 57, 87, 249 ☐ Idem, *The Drawings of Rembrandt* (ed. E. Benesch), London 1973, no. 38 ☐ P. Schatborn, *The Figurstudies. Nederlands tekeningen uit de 17de eeuw*, The Hague 1981, p. 50, fig. 2.

EXHIBITIONS:
Stockholm, *Rembrandt*, 1956, no. 64 ☐ Rotterdam and Amsterdam, *Rembrandt*, 1956, no. 15 ☐ Vienna, *Rembrandt*, 1956, no. 5 ☐ Stockholm, *Holländska mästare i svensk ägo*, 1967, no. 266.

Around 1630, Rembrandt did a number of studies of old men and used them for paintings of saints and prophets. This drawing also served as a draft for a small etching, dated 1630 (B. 325). Facial studies like this are particularly common in Rembrandt's early work.

87

REMBRANDT VAN RIJN

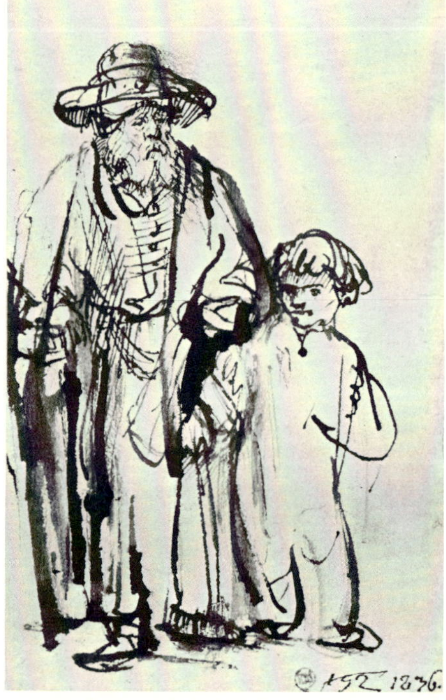

Old Man Guided by a Little Boy

Pen and brown ink, brown wash. 13 x 8.4 cm. No watermark. NM 2035/1863. Numbered in pen and brown ink in the lower right corner: *192* (struck out) and *1836* (Sparre).

PROVENANCE:
Crozat ☐ C. G. Tessin (List 1739-42, p. 46v.; Cat. 1749, livré 15, no. 44) ☐ Kongl. Biblioteket (Cat. 1790, no. 1836) ☐ Kongl. Museum (Lugt 1638).

BIBLIOGRAPHY:
C. H. de Groot, *Die Handzeichnungen Rembrandts*, Haarlem 1906, no. 1601 ☐ J. Kruse and C. Neumann, *Die Zeichnungen Rembrandts und seiner Schule im Nationalmuseum zu Stockholm*, The Hague 1920, no. IV:24 ☐ A. Romdahl, "Rembrandts teckningar," *Nationalmusei Årsbok* (1921), pp. 106f. ☐ Benesch 1935, pp. 38, 41 ☐ Idem, 1947, no. 107 ☐ Idem, 1954-57, no. 189 ☐ Idem, 1973, no. 189 ☐ D. Vogel-Köhn, *Rembrandts Kinderzeichnungen*, Cologne 1981 (Diss. 1977), no. 56.

EXHIBITIONS:
Amsterdam, *Rembrandt Tentoonstelling*, 1935, no. 53 ☐ Stockholm, *Rembrandt*, 1956, no. 113 ☐ Rotterdam and Amsterdam, *Rembrandt*, 1956, no. 93 ☐ Vienna, *Rembrandt*, 1956, no. 45.

88

REMBRANDT VAN RIJN

There is an almost identical rendering of the old man in one of the many black chalk drawings by Rembrandt from the early 1640s (Ben. 665b. Coll. Ch. A. Duit, London). In the present sheet a few strokes have transformed the tall hat into a turban-like headdress; this is how the figure recurs in a drawing in Dr. Rudolf's collection, London (Ben. 190). There the man and youth are accompanied by another figure, probably a woman, while the man's shrunken posture and introverted gaze convey a more concentrated expression.

The drawing has proved difficult to interpret. Several researchers compare it with the *Visitation* from 1640 (Detroit Institute of Arts) and see the man as Zacharias, who is sometimes represented as supported by a youth. The pair also bring to mind Abraham taking Isaac to be sacrificed at God's bidding, a recurrent theme in Rembrandt's drawn and engraved work in the 1640s. The introduction of a female figure in the London sheet suggests yet another subject, Abraham's dismissal of Hagar and Ishmael, to which Rembrandt devoted a series of drawings in the early 1640s (one is in the National Gallery, Washington; Ben. 499). Benesch has objected that if the figure really is female and Hagar, she is not grieving. But Rembrandt and his contemporaries varied her expression from sorrow to resignation or even fatalistic determination.

A conception that seems to have started as a study from life proves to possess a number of artistic possibilities, and perhaps one will never be able to separate the themes which simultaneously occupied the artist's imagination.

Reproduced in color.

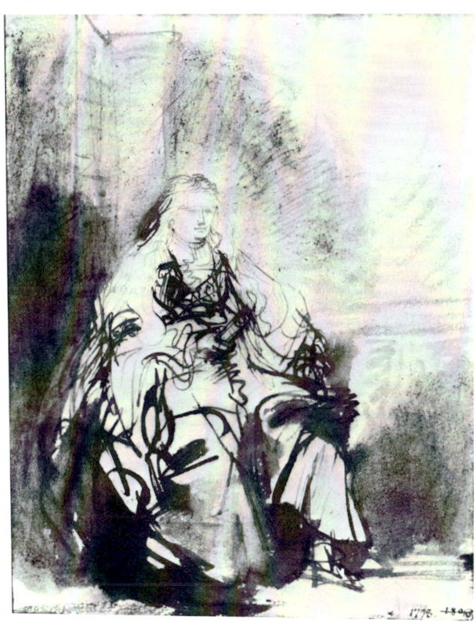

Esther

Pen and brown ink, brown wash. 21.1 x 19.1 cm. No watermark. NM 1992/1863. Numbered in the lower right corner in pen and brown ink: *1798* (Sparre) and *180* (struck out).

PROVENANCE:
Crozat □ C. G. Tessin (List 1739-42, p. 46 v.; Cat. 1749, livré 15, no. 5) □ Kongl. Biblioteket (Cat. 1790, no. 1798) □ Kongl. Museum (Lugt 1638).

BIBLIOGRAPHY:
E. Michel, *Rembrandt*, Paris 1893, p. 221 □ F. Lippman, *Zeichnungen von Rembrandt*, Berlin 1900-01, II: 18 □ C. H. de Groot, *Die Handzeichnungen Rembrandts*, Haarlem 1906, no. 1596 □ F. Saxl, "Zu einigen Handzeichnungen Rembrandts," *Repertorium für Kunstwissenschaft*, 31 (1908), p. 336 □ C. Neumann, *Aus der Werkstatt Rembrandts*, Heidelberg 1918, p. 122 □ J. Kruse and C. Neumann, *Die Zeichnungen Rembrandts und seiner Schule im Nationalmuseum zu Stockholm*, The Hague 1920, no. IV:15 □ W. von Seidlitz, *Die Radierungen Rembrandts*, Leipzig 1922, p. 239 □ A. M. Hind, *A Catalogue of Rembrandt Etchings*, London 1923, p. 75 □ W. R. Valentiner, *Rembrandt, des Meisters Handzeichnungen*, Berlin and Leipzig 1925-34, no. 572 □ Idem, Komödiantendarstellungen Rembrandts, *Zeitschrift für Bildende Kunst* (1925-26), p. 270 □ W. Weisbach, *Rembrandt*, Berlin 1926, p. 233 □ Benesch 1935, p. 23 □ Idem 1947, no. 50 □ L. Münz, *A Critical Catalogue of Rembrandt's Etchings*, London 1952, p. 239 □ Benesch 1954-57, no. 292 □ Idem 1960, no. 16 □ S. Slive, *Drawings by Rembrandt*, New York 1965, no. 235 □ P. Desargues, *Rembrandt et Saskia a Amsterdam*, Lausanne 1965, p. 110 □ M. Kahr, "Rembrandt's Esther. A Painting and an Etching Newly Interpreted and Dated," *Oud Holland*, 81 (1966), p. 242 □ Benesch 1973, no. 292.

EXHIBITIONS:
Amsterdam, *Rembrandt Tentoonstelling*, 1935, no. 35 □ Stockholm, *Rembrandt*, 1956, no. 74 □ Rotterdam and Amsterdam, *Rembrandt*, 1956, no. 32.

This is a preliminary study for the etching *The Great Jewish Bride*, the date of which is difficult to decipher; the year 1635 is the usual reading but another possibility is 1637.

The etching was titled in the eighteenth century, although everything points instead to a representation of the Old Testament heroine Esther who used her influence over Ahasuerus of Persia to prevent a pogrom of the Jews during their captivity. Having fasted and prayed for three days, she dons her queenly apparel before interceding on behalf of her people. In the painting *Esther Prepares to Intercede with Ahasuerus* of 1633 (National Gallery, Ottawa), she is already magnificently attired and a servant is combing her hair.

The drawing shows a monumental seated female figure whose air of determination is accentuated by forceful features as well as by the brown wash. She is holding her husband's royal decree which would destroy the Jews. In the final etching the three-quarter figure of Esther makes a more intimate impression. This is reinforced by her features which are those of the less stern Saskia and her sense of apprehension about the imminent encounter which is conveyed.

89

REMBRANDT VAN RIJN

Reproduced in color.

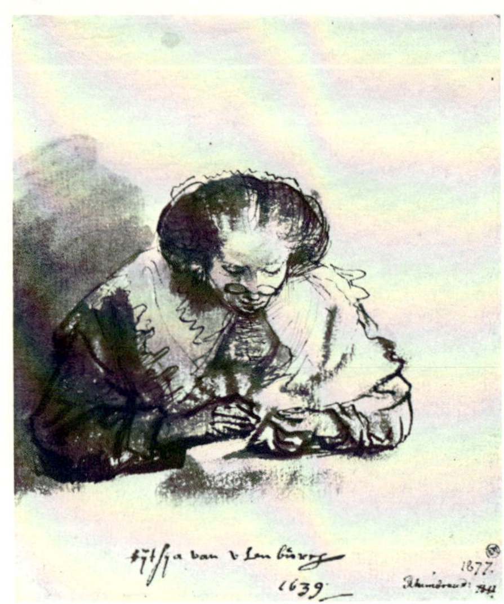

Portrait of Titia van Uylenburch

Pen and brown ink, brown wash. 17.6 x 14.6 cm. No watermark. NM 2978/1863. Inscribed and dated in the artist's hand: *Tijthija van Ulenburch / 1639*, pen and brown ink. Inscribed in pen and brown ink in the lower right corner: *Rhimbrand* (Tessin) and numbered *1877* (Sparre) and 44 (struck out).

PROVENANCE:
Crozat ☐ C. G. Tessin (List 1739-42, p. 46 v.?; Cat. 1749, livré 18, no. 44) ☐ Kongl. Biblioteket (Cat. 1790, no. 1877) ☐ Kongl. Museum (Lugt 1638).

BIBLIOGRAPHY:
G. Upmark, *Stockholmer Handzeichnungen*, Stockholm 1893, no. 15 ☐ Michel 1893, p. 260 ☐ Lippman 1900-01, no. II:15 ☐ H. de Groot 1906, no. 1567 ☐ Idem, *Die Urkunden über Rembrandt*, The Hague 1906, p. 66, no. 63 ☐ R. Graul, *Rembrandt*, Leipzig 1906, no. 12 ☐ J. Kruse, *Rembrandt*, Stockholm 1907, p. 117 ☐ W. Weisbach, *Impressionismus, ein Problem der Malerei in der Antike und Neuzeit*, Berlin 1910, I, p. 168 ☐ F. Schmidt-Degener, "Portretten door Rembrandt, I. Titia van Uylenburch en François Coopal," *Onze Kunst* (1913), pp. 2 f. ☐ C. Neumann, *Rembrandt Handzeichnungen*, Heidelberg 1918, no. 35 ☐ Kruse and Neumann 1920, no. III:1 ☐ Neumann, *Rembrandt*, Munich 1922, I, p. 258 ☐ Valentiner 1924-34, no. 703 ☐ J. van Rijkevorsel, *Rembrandt en de traditie*, Rotterdam 1932, p. 156 ☐ Benesch 1935, p. 28 ☐ Idem, 1947, no. 99; J. Rosenberg, *Rembrandt*, Cambridge, Mass. 1948, I, p. 248, II, pl. 205 ☐ Benesch 1954-57, no. 441 ☐ Slive 1965, no. 232 ☐ Benesch 1970, p. 253 ☐ Idem, 1973, no. 441.

EXHIBITIONS:
Amsterdam, *Rembrandt*, 1935, no. 45 ☐ Stockholm, *Rembrandt*, 1956, no. 95 ☐ Rotterdam and Amsterdam, *Rembrandt*, 1956, no. 92 ☐ Vienna, *Rembrandt*, 1956, no. 44.

The inscription in Rembrandt's hand states that this portrait of Titia, his sister-in-law, was done in 1639. Besides being a portrait, this is a penetrating depiction of a woman sewing.

90

REMBRANDT VAN RIJN

Reproduced in color.

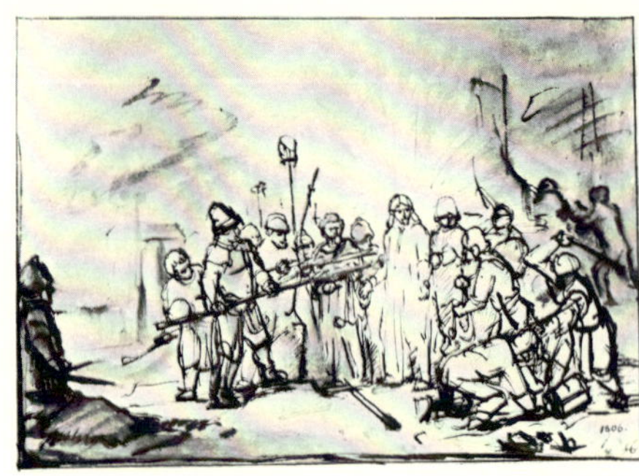

The Arrest of Christ

Pen and brown ink, brown and gray wash, touches of white body color. 20.5 x 29.8 cm. No watermark. NM 2002/1863. Numbered in the lower right corner in pen and brown ink: *1806* (Sparre) and 56 (struck out).

PROVENANCE:
Crozat (Mariette, no. 869 or 873) ☐ C. G. Tessin (List 1739-42, p. 46 v.; Cat. 1749, livré 15, no. 73) ☐ Kongl. Biblioteket (Cat. 1790, no. 1806) ☐ Kongl. Museum (Lugt 1638).

BIBLIOGRAPHY:
Lippman 1900-01, II:13 ☐ H. de Groot 1906, no. 1556 ☐ Saxl 1908, p. 336 ☐ H. de Groot, *Rembrandtbibel*, 2, Amsterdam 1912, no. 25 ☐ Neumann 1918, p. 123 ☐ Kruse and Neumann 1920, no. II:1 ☐ Valentiner 1925-34, no. 456 ☐ H. Hell, Die späten Handzeichnungen Rembrandts, *Repertorium für Kunstwissenschaft*, 1930, p. 32 ☐ Benesch 1935, p. 63 ☐ Idem, 1947, no. 273 ☐ Idem, 1954-57, Vol. V, no. 1044 ☐ Idem, 1960, p. 98 ☐ Slive 1965, no. 230 ☐ Benesch 1970, p. 98 ☐ Idem, 1973, no. 1044.

EXHIBITIONS:
Amsterdam, *Rembrandt*, 1935, no. 84 ☐ Stockholm, *Rembrandt*, 1956, no. 161 ☐ Rotterdam and Amsterdam, *Rembrandt*, 1956, no. 203 ☐ Vienna, *Rembrandt*, 1956, no. 138 ☐ Stockholm, *Holländska mästare i svensk ägo*, 1967, no. 297 ☐ Paris, Brussels, Amsterdam 1970-71, no. 83.

91

REMBRANDT VAN RIJN

Three Rembrandt drawings with this theme are known, but no accompanying painting. They are relatively late works, produced in the course of a decade, and show a gradual change in the motif and a refinement in meaning.

The earliest drawing (Berlin, Print Room, Ben. 882, around 1651-52) presents the actual betrayal, Judas kissing Christ, in accordance with the first two gospels. The foreground is occupied by the soldier whose ear was cut off by one of Christ's followers. A later drawing (Count Antoine Seilern, London, Ben. 1022, around 1656-57) follows John 18:6 in showing how those who are to apprehend Christ fell to the ground when he declared himself. His divinity is manifested here by the light radiating from him, a means that Rembrandt frequently uses to indicate the godhead revealed; Christ is also drawn larger than those around him. An episode from Mark 14:51-52 has also been added in the foreground, the young man who was laid hold of but escaped naked.

In the Nationalmuseum drawing the emphasis has shifted again. The outward conflicts have been played down, and the figures are arranged as in a frieze with Christ as the dominant central figure. He has been apprehended but ignores the soldiers and is turned to the foreground, where the scene with the soldier whose ear is cut off has been restored. This episode is included in different versions in all four gospels at the point where Christ is arrested. The arrangement stresses that apprehension is part of the divine plan, in keeping with the words of Christ in John 18:11, "Put up thy sword into the sheath: the cup which my Father hath given me, shall I not drink it?" The angular, rough-hewn forms indicate a late work, the usual assumption being a date around 1659-60.

Woman Suckling a Child

Pen and brown ink. 8.5 x 6.8 cm. No watermark. NM 2055/1863. Numbered in pen and brown in in the lower right corner: *1855* (Sparre) and *84* (struck out).

PROVENANCE:
Jan van de Capelle? □ Crozat □ C. G. Tessin (List 1739-42, p. 46 v.; Cat. 1749, livré 15, no. 24) □ Kongl. Biblioteket (Cat. 1790, no. 1855) □ Kongl. Museum (Lugt 1638).

BIBLIOGRAPHY:
Hofstede de Groot 1906, no. 1594 □ Kruse and Neumann 1920, no. IV:11 □ Benesch 1935, p. 49 □ Idem, 1954-57, no. 1073 □ Idem, 1970, p. 258 □ Idem, 1973, no. 1073 □ D. Vogel-Köhn, *Rembrandts Kinderzeichnungen*, Cologne 1981 (Diss. 1977), no. 91.

EXHIBITIONS:
Stockholm, *Rembrandt*, 1956, no. 151 □ Rotterdam and Amsterdam, *Rembrandt*, 1956, no. 95 □ Vienna, *Rembrandt*, 1956, no. 29 □ Stockholm, *Holländska mästare i svensk ägo*, 1967, no. 272.

Of the many drawings of women and children which Rembrandt produced, the Nationalmuseum has seven of the hundred-odd extant. Rembrandt arranged his drawings in folders according to their subject. One such folder, originally containing 135 drawings of women and children, was owned by the painter Jan van de Capelle (1624-1679) and seems to have been auctioned in 1707.

Rembrandt often used a sheet for more than one sketch, and it was not uncommon for collectors to cut out individual items, which was clearly the fate of the present small drawing.

Most of Rembrandt's studies of children were done in the late 1630s but this one, which catches the subject with just a few simple strokes, has been dated on stylistic grounds to the first half of the 1650s.

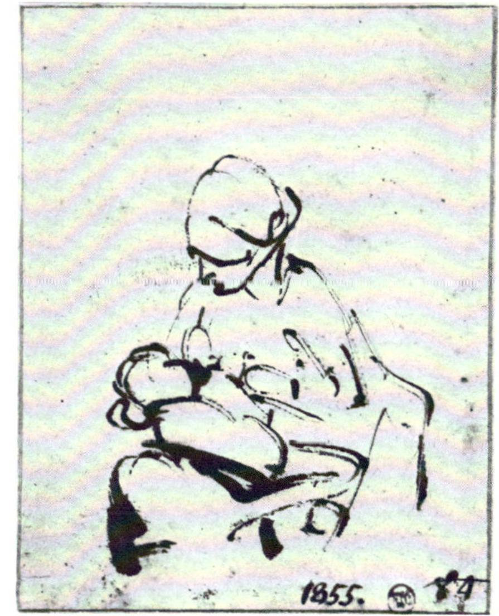

92

REMBRANDT VAN RIJN

An Eye Operation

Pen and brown ink, brown wash, white body color. 24.3 x 18.8 cm. Watermark: Fleur-de-lis. NM 2046/1863. Inscribed in pen and brown ink in the lower left corner: *R*, and numbered in pen and brown ink in the lower right corner: *1846* (Sparre) and *76* (struck out).

PROVENANCE:
Crozat ☐ C. G. Tessin (List 1739-42, p. 46 v.; Cat. 1749, livré 15, no. 29) ☐ Kongl. Biblioteket (Cat. 1790, no. 1846) ☐ Kongl. Museum (Lugt 1638).

BIBLIOGRAPHY:
Michel 1893, p. 524 ☐ Lippman 1900-01, I:129 ☐ H. de Groot 1906, no. 1602 ☐ R. Greef, *Rembrandts Darstellungen der Tobiasheilung*, Stuttgart 1907, pp. 60 f. ☐ Saxl 1908, p. 234 ☐ Kruse and Neumann 1920, no. IV:16 ☐ A. Romdahl, "Rembrandts teckningar," *Nationalmusei Arsbok* (1921), p. 102 ☐ Valentiner 1925-34, no. 254 ☐ H. Kauffmann, "Zur Kritik der Rembrandt-zeichnungen," *Repertorium für Kunstwissenschaft*, 47 (1926-27), p. 159 ☐ Benesch 1935, p. 51 ☐ Idem, 1954-57, no. 1154 ☐ Slive 1965, no. 133 ☐ "S.J.", Rembrandt's "Eye Operation," *Bulletin of the New York Academy of Medicine*, Vol. 45, no. 12 (December 1969), pp. 1396-98 ☐ Benesch 1973, no. 1154.

EXHIBITIONS:
Amsterdam, *Rembrandt Tentoonstelling*, 1935, no. 50 ☐ Stockholm, *Rembrandt*, 1956, no. 159 ☐ Rotterdam and Amsterdam, *Rembrandt*, 1956, no. 200 ☐ Vienna, *Rembrandt*, 1956, no. 92 ☐ Jerusalem 1965, no. 43.

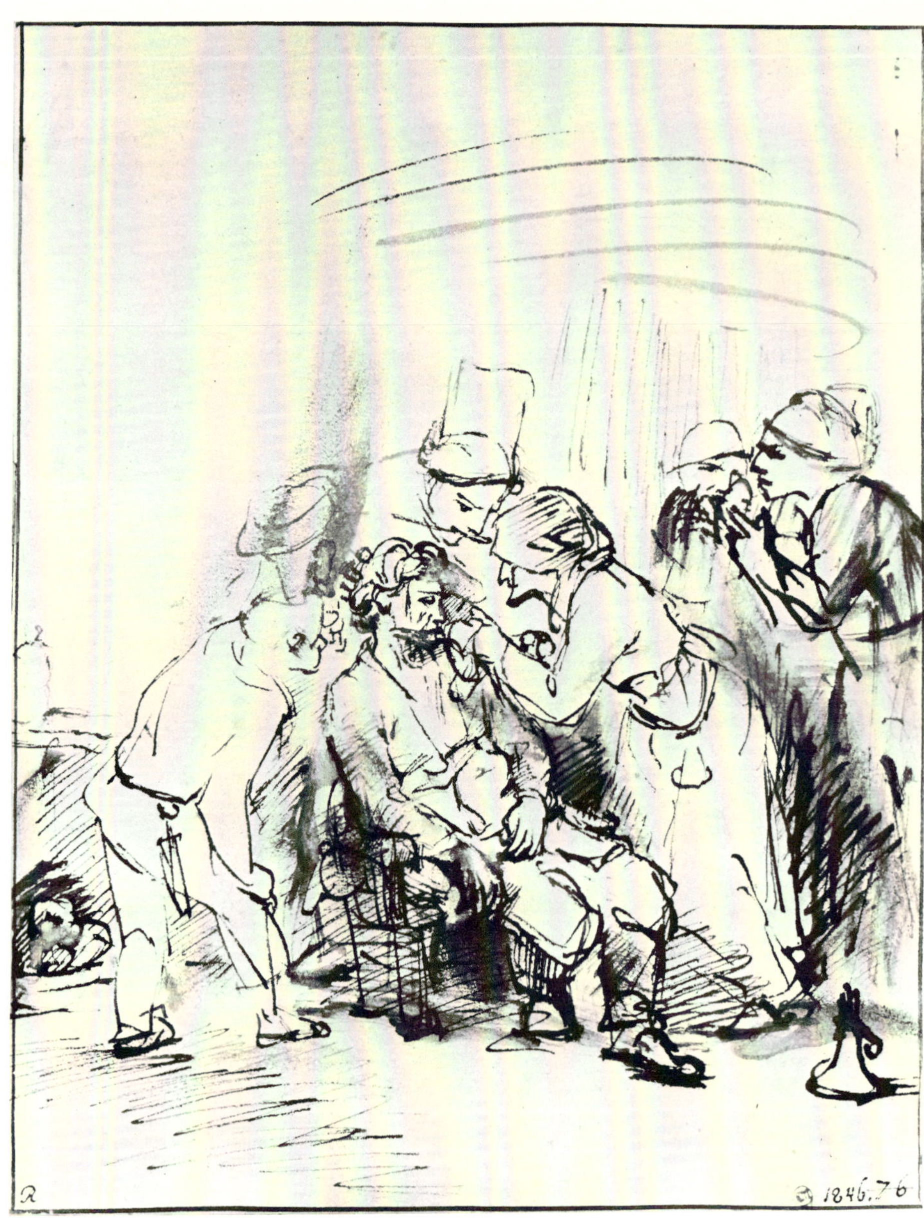

The apocryphal story of Tobias was used by Rembrandt in a great many works, including a series of drawings concerning Tobias' cure of his father Tobit's blindness. In the series he performs the operation with a pointed instrument which he holds behind his father; he is assisted by his mother who evidently has the fish liver that works the cure. The whole procedure is supervised by an angel.

Our drawing agrees in essentials with this series, but it seems to illustrate an ordinary eye operation. The surgeon behind the chair is holding a cataract knife between his teeth and the woman seems to be applying a swab to the surgical field. The patient's dress is in disarray, unlike the imposing bearded and manteled elder in the series. None of the other figures in the drawing has angel's wings.

One is tempted to assume that an eye operation provided Rembrandt with the starting point for his Tobias series, perhaps recorded in this drawing. The representation of the cure as an operation is the artist's invention and is independent of the contemporary Dutch text.[1]

If our drawing does initiate the Tobias series, however, it must be dated around 1641-42, which is about a decade earlier than has been generally supposed. This date may be defensible on stylistic grounds.

NOTE:
1. J. S. Held, "Rembrandt and the Book of Tobit," *Rembrandt's Aristotle and Other Rembrandt Studies*, Princeton 1969, p. 114.

93

REMBRANDT VAN RIJN

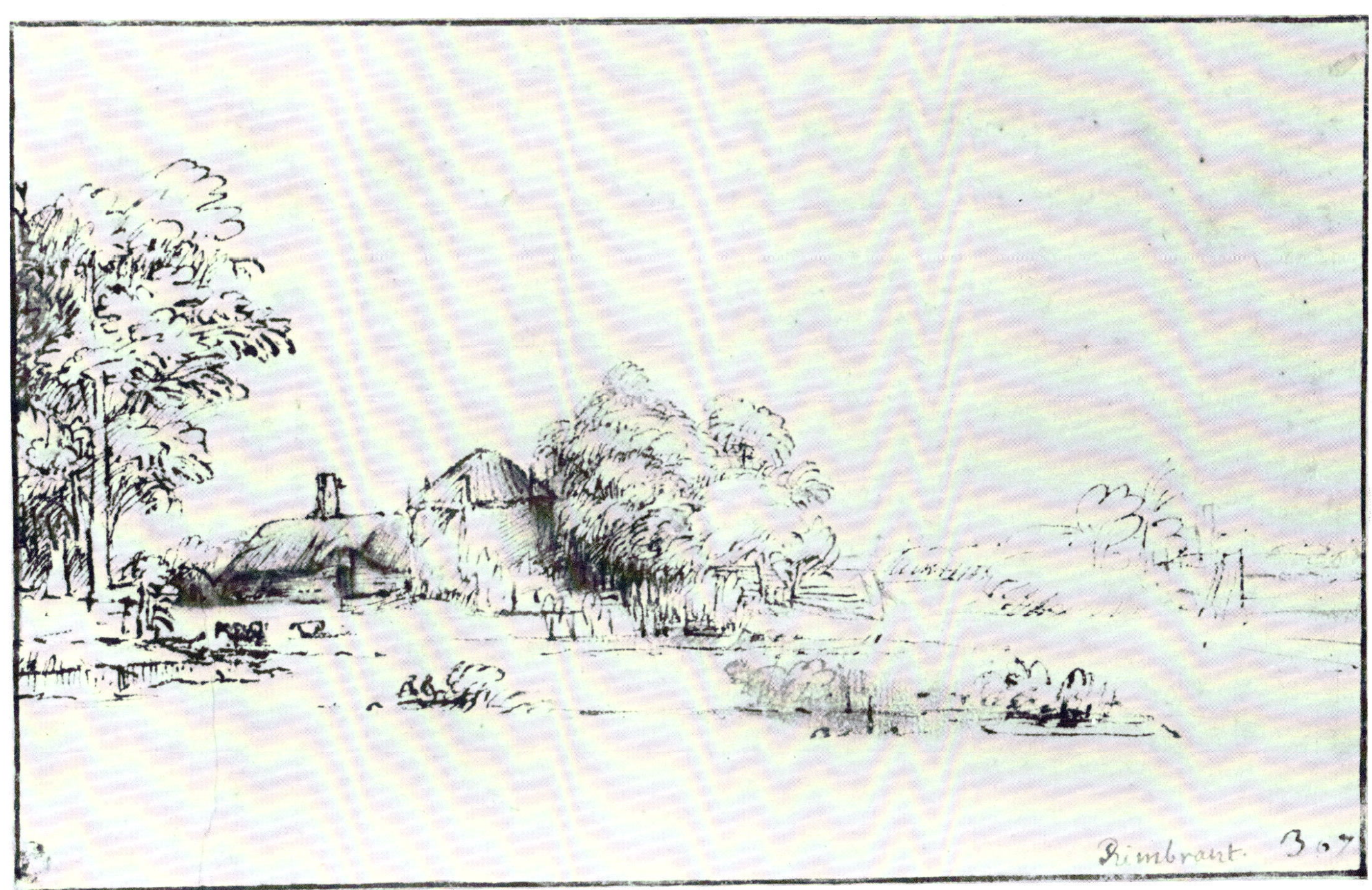

Landscape with a Farm House and High Trees

Pen and brown ink, brown wash. 10.7 x 17.7 cm. Watermark: Coat of arms (fragment). NM Anck. 374. Inscribed in the lower right corner in pen and brown ink: *Rimbrant* (Tessin), and numbered *307.*

PROVENANCE:
C. G. Tessin (List 1739-42, p. 31?; Cat. 1785, no. 223) □ M. G. Anckarsvärd □ Acquired by the museum 1896.

BIBLIOGRAPHY:
H. de Groot 1906, no. 1613 □ Kruse and Neumann 1920, no. VII:3 □ G. Wengström, "Rembrandts landskapsskisser i Nationalmuseum," *Festskrift vid Föreningen Nationalmusei Vänners tioarsjubileum*, Stockholm 1921, p. 120 □ Benesch 1935, p. 57 □ Idem, 1947, no. 214 □ Idem, 1954-57, no. 1292 □ Idem, 1973, no. 1292 □ P. Schatborn, "Van Rembrandt tot Crozat," *Nederlands Kunsthistorisch Jaarboek*, 32 (1981), pp. 44 f.

EXHIBITIONS:
Amsterdam, *Rembrandt Tentoonstelling*, 1935, no. 67 □ Stockholm, *Rembrandt*, 1956, no. 131 □ Rotterdam and Amsterdam, *Rembrandt*, 1956, no. 171.

In the eighteenth century, connoisseurs of Rembrandt drawings were particularly impressed by his landscapes. Tessin acquired a large group in 1741, and the present drawing is one of those he retained even when financial hardship obliged him to transfer the bulk of his collection to the royal family. This explains why the sheet came to the Nationalmuseum at a later date than the other Tessin drawings and via other channels.

The small-scale landscape displays the artist's ability to convey salient features and to suggest space and movement with great economy. Details are finely delineated. Here, as elsewhere, he uses a fairly dry pen to reinforce the atmospheric effect. A few accents in wash give the composition depth and life.

The style points to a date at the beginning of the 1650s, but Rembrandt was already drawing and etching landscapes of much the same type a decade earlier.

94

MASTER OF THE COBURG ROUNDELS
Late 15th Century

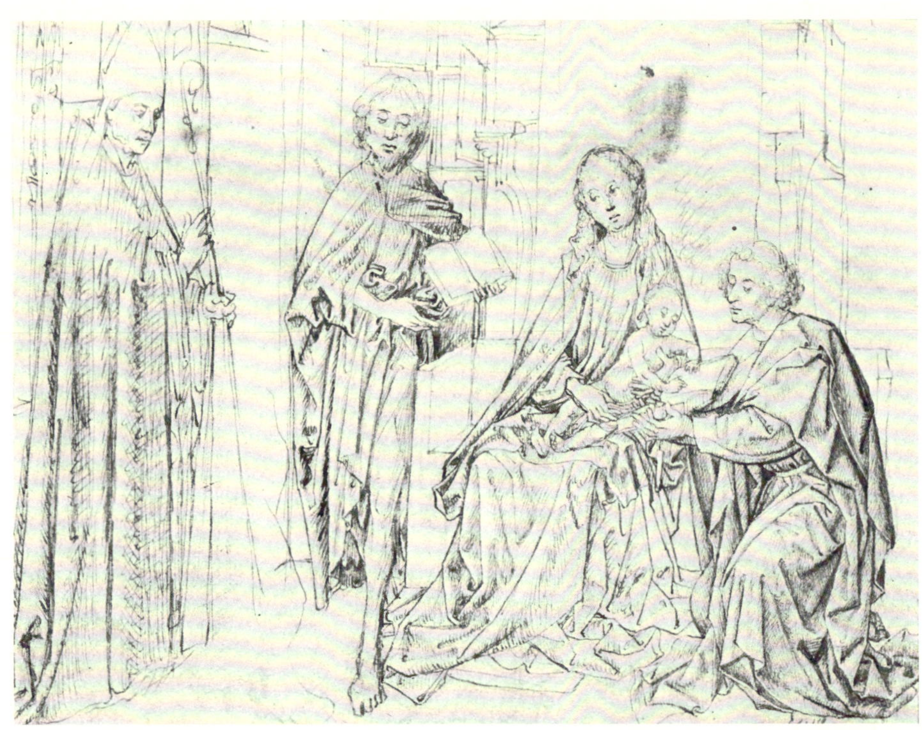

A Bishop, St. John the Baptist, the Madonna, and St. John the Evangelist

Pen and brown ink. 16.6 x 23 cm. No watermark. NM 148/1918.

VERSO:
Madonna with Child. Pen and brown ink.

PROVENANCE:
Sergel? □ Unknown owner, Berlin c. 1916 □ Christian Langaard.

BIBLIOGRAPHY:
F. Winkler, "Skizzenbücher eines unbekannten rheinischen Meisters um 1500," *Wallraf-Richartz Jahrbuch*, N.F. 1 (1930), pp. 234, 152, fig. 130 □ M. Davies, "Rogier van der Weyden's Magdalen Reading," *Miscellanea Prof. Dr. D. Roggen*, Antwerp 1957, pp. 79-89, fig. 4 □ Director's report January 1955-June 1956, 4. The Conservation Department, "The Magdalen Reading by van der Weyden," *The National Gallery, January 1955-June 1956*, London 1956, p. 34 □ K. G. Boon, Boekbespreking, Erwin Panofsky's "Early Netherlandish Painting," *Oud-Holland*, 72 (1957), p. 186 (ill.) □ F. Winkler, "Grenzen der Stilkritik," *Eberhard Hanfstaengl zum 75. Geburtstag*, Munich 1961, p. 199 □ M. S(onkes), *L'Oeuvre de Roger de le Pasture--van der Weyden*, (Brussels 1964), p. 32 □ M. J. Friedländer, *Early Netherlandish Painting, 2, Rogier van der Weyden and the Master of Flémalle*, Leiden-Brussels 1967, pl. 21 □ M. Davies, *National Gallery Catalogues, Early Netherlandish School*, 3 ed., London 1968, pp. 169-70 □ M. Sonkes, *Dessins du XVe siècle: Groupe van der Weyden* (Les primitifs flamands, 3, Contribution à l'étude des primitifs flamands, 5), Brussels 1969, pp. 104-06, no. C9, pls. xxiii a and xxiv b □ J. L. Ward, "A Proposed Reconstruction of an Altarpiece by Rogier van der Weyden," *Art Bulletin*, 53 (1971), pp. 27-35 □ Bjurström 1972, no. 2 □ A. J. Klant-Vlielander Hein, "Rogiers 'Lezende Magdalena' geconfronteerd med de Heiliga Catharina," *Miscellanea J. Q. van Regteren Altena*, Amsterdam 1969, pp. 20, 251, fig. 1.

EXHIBITIONS:
Brussels, Musée Communal, *Rogier van der Weyden/Rogier de la pasture*, 1979, p. 162, no. 26.

The drawing was attributed by Winkler in 1930 to the Master of the Coburg Roundels, but Boon in 1957 refrained from making an attribution, referring to the artist simply as "unknown, second half of the 15th century." Sonkes explicitly states that it cannot be by the Master of the Coburg Roundels.

The group of the Madonna, John the Baptist, and John the Evangelist can be traced back to a composition by Rogier van der Weyden, only fragments of which have been preserved. The right hand part of John the Evangelist's mantel also occurs to the left in *The Magdalen Reading*, now in the National Gallery, London. Two other fragments of the painting are in the Calouste Gulbenkian Collection in Lisbon.

The drawing is likely a direct, though fragmentary, copy of the original. A standing figure, probably Joseph, positioned behind and to the right of the Magdalen, is preserved in one of the fragments in Lisbon. The other fragment is thought to depict St. Catherine, who should appear to the left of John the Baptist. The Bishop on the left in our drawing is unconnected with the central composition; his gesture of blessing cannot be associated with the Madonna but it is possible that he figured on an altar wing. This figure also deviates stylistically from the rest of the work, being drawn in a more schematic manner with long, unbroken lines.

The Madonna on the *verso* is rendered in a heavier style. On the mount of the drawing Winzinger has made the highly plausible reflection that the drawing was made from a sculpture.

Verso

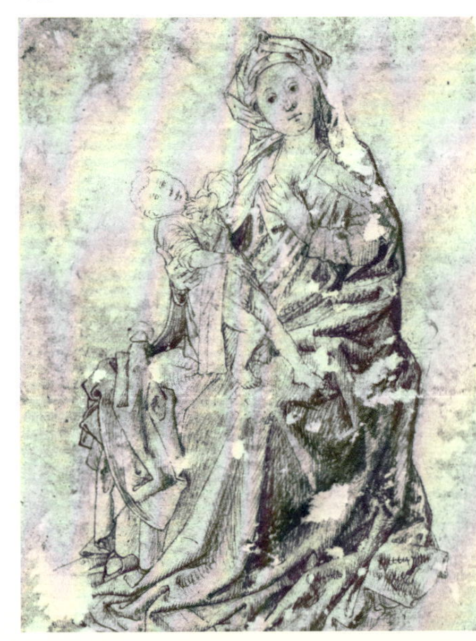

95

HANS BALDUNG GRIEN
Schwäbisch Gmünd 1484/5 - Strasbourg 1545

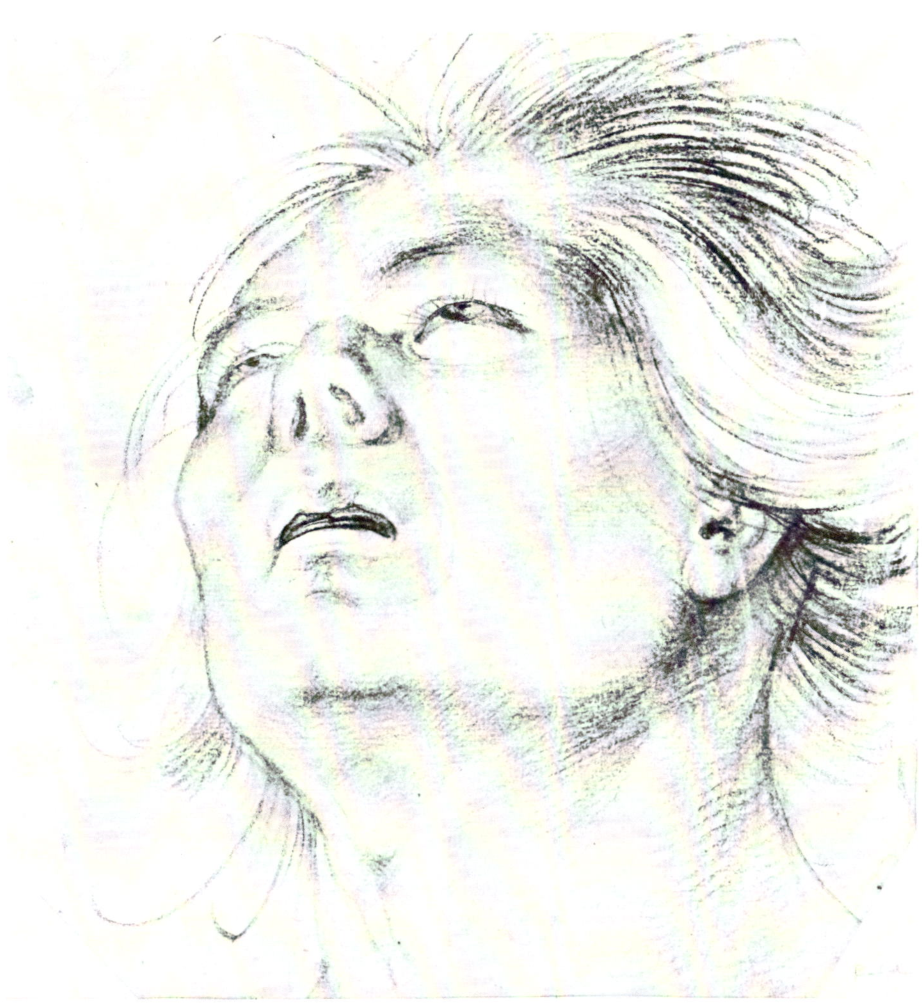

Head of a Young Man, Seen from Below

Black chalk. 20.5 x 20 cm. All four corners cut diagonally. Laid down. NM 35/1918.

PROVENANCE:
J. T. Sergel? □ Unknown owner, Berlin c. 1916 □ Christian Langaard.

BIBLIOGRAPHY:
K. T. Parker, "Quelques dessins de l'école Alsacienne du XVe et du XVIe siècle," *Archives Alsaciennes d'histoire de l'art*, 2 (Strasbourg 1923), pp. 67ff., fig. 27 □ Idem, *Elsässische Handzeichnungen des XV. und XVI. Jahrhunders*, Freiburg 1928, no. 35 □ C. Koch, *Die Zeichnungen Hans Baldung Griens*, Berlin 1941, p. 28, no. 47 □ H. Möhle, review of C. Koch, "Die Zeichnungen Hans Baldung Griens," *Zeitschrift für Kunstgeschichte*, 10 (1941-42), p. 219 □ Idem, "Hans Baldung Grien zur Karlsruher Baldung-Ausstellung Sommer 1959," *Zeitschrift für Kunstgeschichte*, 22 (1959), p. 129 □ Bjurström 1972, no. 9.

EXHIBITIONS:
Karlsruhe, Staatliche Kunsthalle, *Hans Baldung Grien*, 1959, no. 152.

Identified by Parker in 1923 as the work of Baldung Grien on the basis of a closely related drawing in Basel (Koch 46), the drawing was subsequently included in Koch's monograph on Baldung's drawings. In 1928, Parker pointed out the connection with *The Flood* from 1516 in Bamberg, to which Koch also referred. On the strength of this relation, Parker dated the drawing to the late 1510s, whereas Koch placed it in the same period as *The Flood* in Freiburg of 1516. Reviewing Koch's book in 1941, Möhle argued that the early 1530s would be more plausible in view of the picturesque qualities of the drawing, but having seen the original at an exhibition in 1959 he too came round to suggest a date of about 1516.

96

JÖRG BREU THE ELDER
C. 1475 - Augsburg 1537

Design for an Epitaph. The Fourteen Auxiliary Saints

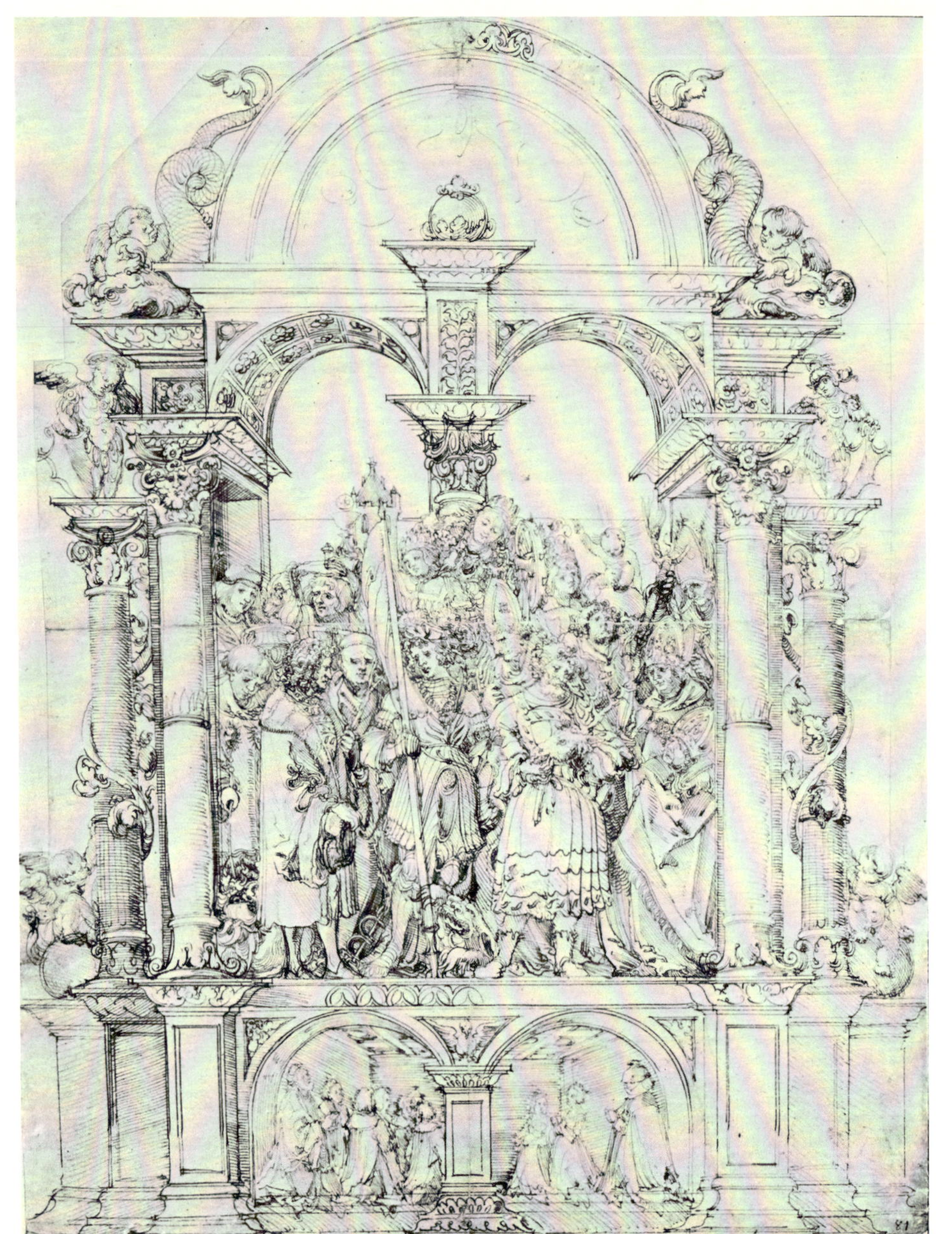

Pen and dark brown ink. 41.4 x 31 cm. Vertical and horizontal fold. Upper part of the paper cut close to the composition and lined to a paper of similar color. NM 1712/1875. Numbered at lowr right: *81*.

PROVENANCE:
J. T. Sergel (Lugt 2339 b).

BIBLIOGRAPHY:
C. Dodgson, "Jörg Breu the Elder, Design for an Altar," *Old Master Drawings*, 2 (1927-28), pp. 44f., pl. 49 ☐ E. Buchner, "Der ältere Breu als Maler," in E. Buchner and K. Feuchtmayr, ed., *Beiträge zur Geschichte der Deutschen Kunst*, 2, Augsburg 1928, pp. 362ff., fig. 270 ☐ Bjurström 1972, no. 18.

EXHIBITIONS:
Augsburg, Schaezler-Haus, *Augsburger Renaissance*, 1955, no. 68.

The drawing was first recognized as a work by Jörg Breu the Elder by Dodgson, who compares the architecture with Augsburg altars from about 1515-20 and woodcuts by Hans Weiditz. He further identifies the saints, known as *Die Vierzehn Nothelfer*, as follows: front row, from left to right: St. Acacius, with a thorny branch; St. George, with the dragon; St. Eustace, with a stag's head and antlers; St. Dionysius, holding his head which rests on a book. A little further back: St. Cyriac, a deacon, holding a demon by a cord; St. Leonard, a Benedictine monk, with chain and fetters; St. Erasmus, a bishop, with his entrails wound about a windlass; St. Christopher, bearing the Holy Child seated on a globe, and grasping a staff. Back row: St. Vitus, a youth with a cock; St. Pantaleon, whose hands are nailed to his head; St. Barbara, with chalice and tower; St. Margaret, with a dragon; St. Catherine, with a wheel; and St. Blasius with a twisted taper.

Dodgson presupposes that the saints were intended to be carved, presumably in wood, and that the predella with the donors was to be painted.

Buchner relates the drawing stylistically with the paintings on the organ shutters of St. Anna in Augsburg from 1522 and with the *Ursula Altar* of Dresden from the mid-1520s. He wrongly identifies the drawing with one sold by Gilhofer and Rauschberg, Vienna, 11/5, 1917, no. 198 as *Augsburger Meister*. In the Augsburg exhibition catalogue of 1955, the drawing is listed as attributed to Jörg Breu the Elder.

97

HANS BURGKMAIR THE ELDER
Augsburg 1473 - Augsburg 1531

Reproduced in color.

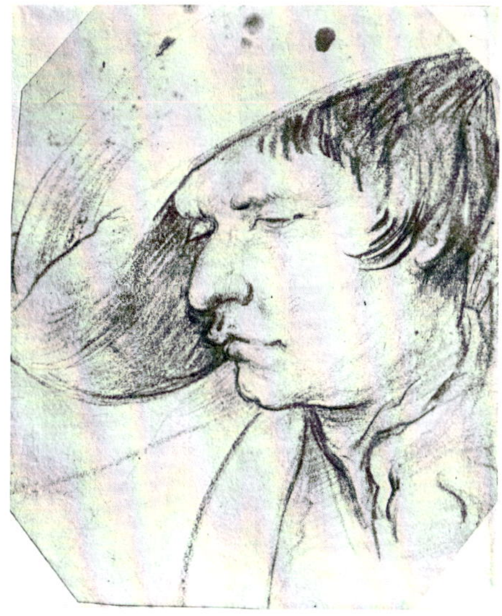

Young Man with a Large Cap

Charcoal. 24.5 x 20.2 cm. All four corners cut diagonally. Watermark: Star (Part of "Ochsenkopf"?). NM 36/1918.

PROVENANCE:
J. T. Sergel? □ Unknown owner, Berlin c. 1916 □ Christian Langaard.

BIBLIOGRAPHY:
K. Th. Parker, "Weiteres über Hans Burgkmair als Zeichner," in E. Buchner and K. Feuchtmayr, ed., *Beiträge zur Geschichte der Deutschen Kunst*, 2, Augsburg 1928, p. 218, no. 41, pl. 160 □ E. Schilling, "Zu den Zeichnungen Hans Burgkmairs d.ä.," *Wallraf-Richartz Jahrbuch*, N.F., Doppelband 2-3 (1933-34), p. 261 □ A. Burkhard, *Hans Burgkmair d.ä.*, Leipzig s.a. (1934), pp. 136, 140f. □ P. Halm, "Hans Burgkmair als Zeichner," *Münchner Jahrbuch der bildenden Kunst*, 3. Folge, 13 (1962), p. 75 □ Bjurström 1972, no. 26.

EXHIBITIONS:
Munich and Augsburg, *Burgkmair-Ausstellung*, 1931, no. 49 □ Augsburg, Schaezler-Haus, *Augsburger Renaissance*, 1955, no. 123.

The drawing was first recognized by Parker, who compared it with a pair of drawings formerly in Dresden: *Portrait of the Artist's Father*, dated 1520 and a *Portrait of a Young Woman*.[1] The latter is, however, no longer accepted as a work by Burgkmair. This drawing belongs to a group of portraits executed from 1515 to the early 1520s with further examples in Oxford, Hamburg, Chatsworth, Berlin, and London, all demonstrating Burgkmair's interest at this time in capturing the individuality of his models. All the portraits display a monumental simplification and a concentration on the important features of the subject.

NOTE:
1. Parker, *op. cit.*, nos. 13 and 14.

98

HANS BURGKMAIR THE ELDER

Reproduced in color.

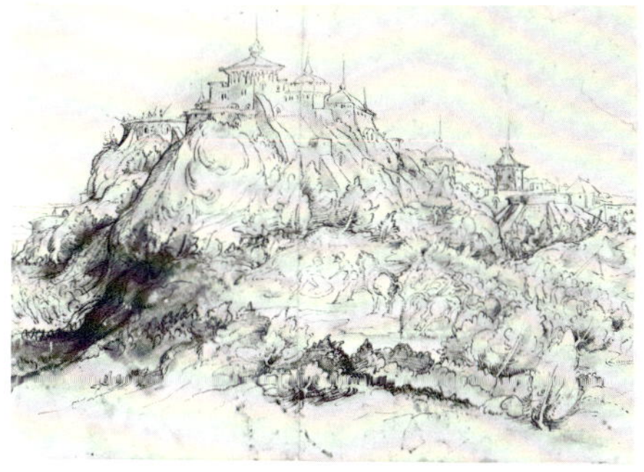

Study of the Landscape for The Battle of Cannae

Pen and black ink. Watercolor. 21.7 x 31.6 cm. Vertical fold at center. Stains of black color and oil. Laid down. NM 130/1918.

PROVENANCE:
J. T. Sergel? □ Unknown owner, Berlin, c. 1916 □ Christian Langaard.

BIBLIOGRAPHY:
Schilling 1933-34, p. 262, pl. 212, p. 272, no. 1 □ Burkhard 1934, pp. 178, 198, no. 5 □ Halm 1962, p. 100, pl. 25, p. 162 □ Bjurström 1972, n. 30.

EXHIBITIONS:
Stockholm 1933, no. 25.

In 1933, the drawing was identified by Edmund Schilling as a study for *The Battle of Cannae* of 1523, now in the Schleissheim Gallery. It is the only colored landscape study by Burgkmair known today. Schilling notes that the drawing does not seem to be a study from nature but rather an imaginative view with Renaissance, Gothic, and Oriental elements appearing in the architecture. He compares it further to a study of a stronghold on a rock in the Albertina, Vienna. This work shows the same characteristic combination of architecture and nature as well as the same treatment of the rock with its rounded forms.

The drawing is significant as a datable example of Burgkmair's late style in which his earlier technique with its strong accentuation of the contours has been replaced by a fast script with short, nervous strokes and hooks.

99

ALBRECHT DÜRER
Nuremberg 1471 - Nuremberg 1528

Reproduced in color.

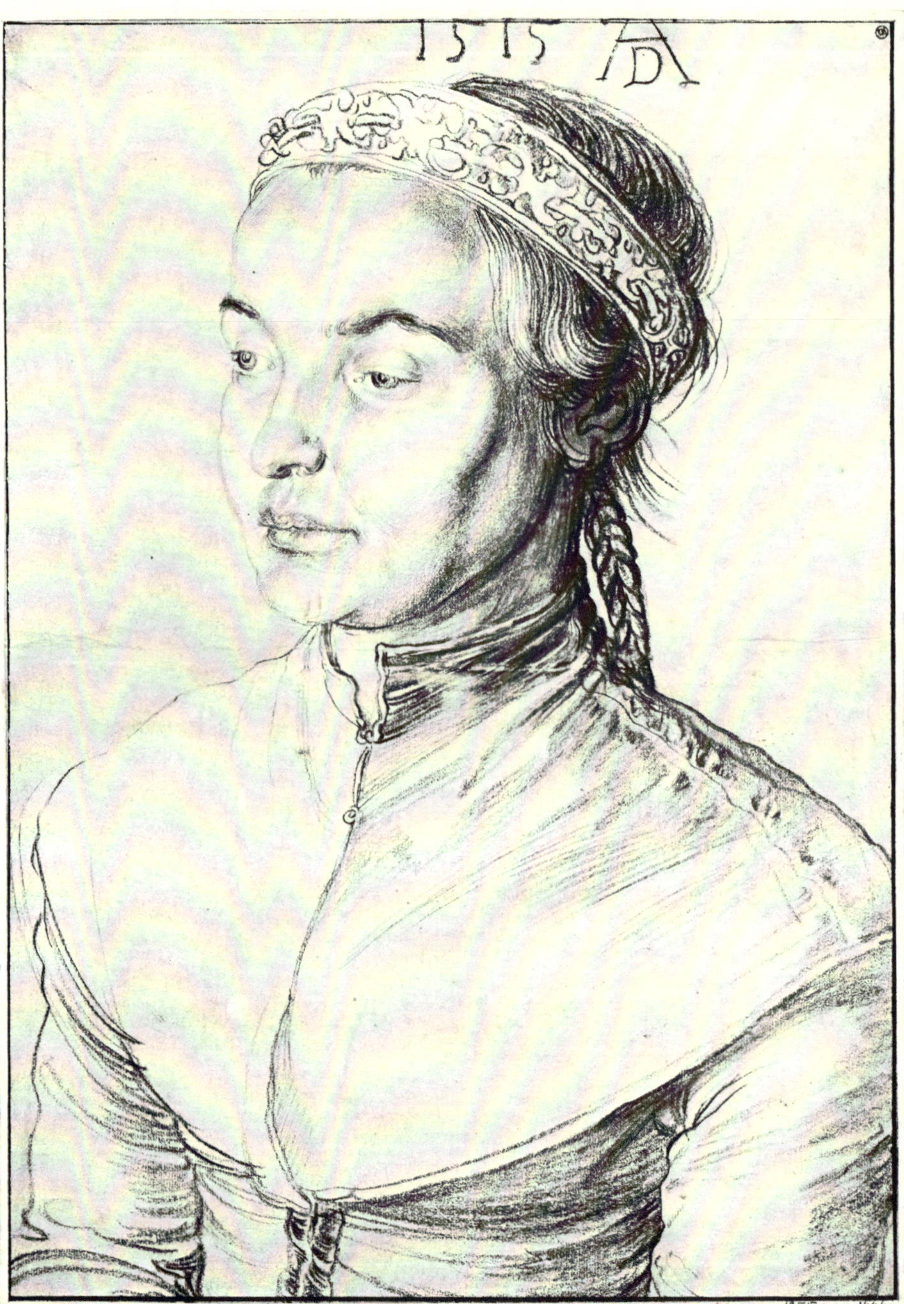

Portrait of a Girl

Black chalk and a faint brownish watercolor in the background. 42.3 x 29.4 cm. Laid down. NM 1855/1863. Dated *1515* and signed with monogram *AD* at upper center in charcoal. Numbered in pen and black ink at lower left: *1666* (Sparre), in pencil *40* and *1855* (Nationalmuseum).

PROVENANCE:
C. G. Tessin (List 1739-41, p. 67 v.; Cat. 1749, livré 18, no. 40) □ Kongl. Biblioteket (Cat. 1790, no. 1666) □ Kongl. Museum (Lugt 1638).

BIBLIOGRAPHY:
F. Lippman (and F. Winkler), *Zeichnungen von Albrecht Dürer in Nachbildungen herausgegeben*, Berlin 1883-1929, no. 811 □ H. Tietze and E. Tietze-Conrat, *Kritisches Verzeichnis der Werke Albrecht Dürers*, 2:1, Basel and Leipzig 1937, no. 643 and pp. 116, 138, 141, fig. 275 □ E. Flechsig, *Albrecht Dürer, Sein Leben und seine künstlerische Entwicklung*, 2, Berlin 1931, pp. 462-63 □ F. Winkler, *Die Zeichnungen Albrecht Dürers*, 3, Berlin 1938, no. 561 □ E. Panofsky, *The Life and Art of Albrecht Dürer*, Princeton 1945, no. 1110 □ F. Winkler, *Albrecht Dürer, Leben und Werk*, Berlin 1957, p. 267 □ R. Hänsler and J. E. Schuler, *Meisterzeichnungen von der Welt bewundert*, Stuttgart 1962, p. 68 □ L. Grote, "Albrecht Dürers Anna Selbdritt, Ein Auftrag von Linhart Tucher," *Anzeiger des Germanischen Nationalmuseums*, 1969, p. 84 □ W. Hütt, *Albrecht Dürer 1471 bis 1528, Das gesamte graphische Werk, 1, Handzeichnungen*, Munich, 1970, no. 632 □ P. Reuterswärd, "Felicitas," *Svenska Dagbladet* 16/9 1971, p. 5 □ Bjurström 1972, no. 39.

EXHIBITIONS:
Nürnberg, Germanisches Nationalmuseum, *Albrecht Dürer*, 1971, no. 535.

Albrecht Dürer's moving portrait of his mother (Winkler no. 559) of 1514 introduced a new monumental style to portraiture. Another portrait, also the same size, of a young girl (Winkler 561, now in Berlin) is considered, like the present drawing, to represent a relative of the artist. The two girls are very alike in appearance, and Lippman, Tietze, and Winkler all accept the possibility that they were sisters.

Dürer used this portrait for the head of Mary in the painting of the *Madonna and Child with St. Anne* (dated 1519, now in the Metropolitan Museum, New York). The model has been identified tentatively by Patric Reuterswärd as Felicitas Pirkheimer at the age of eighteen or nineteen, when she was engaged to be married, which would explain the gorgeous hair ribbon.

100

MATHIS GOTHART NITHART,
called GRÜNEWALD
Würzburg ca. 1475/80 - Halle A.D. Saale 1528

Reproduced in color.

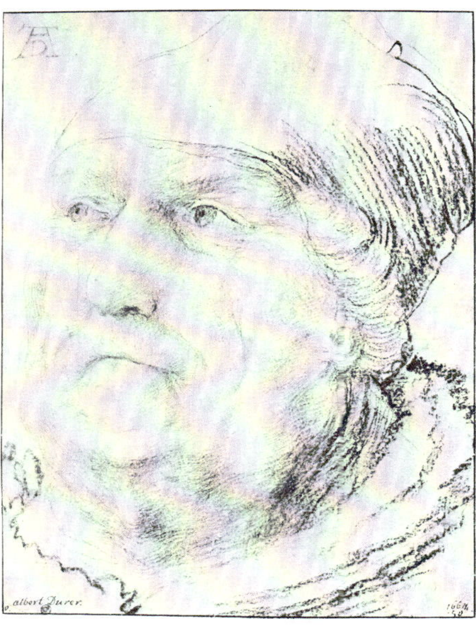

Head of a Beardless Old Man

Black chalk on yellow-brown paper. 25.2 x 19 cm. No watermark. NM 1853/1863. Inscribed at upper left *AD* (monogram) in black ink, at lower left *Albert Durer*, in pen and brown ink. Numbered at lower right in pen and brown ink: *1664* (Sparre) and *30*.

PROVENANCE:
Crozat (Mariette, no. 785 "et un Portrait")? ☐ C. G. Tessin (List 1739-41, p. 35 v.; Cat. 1749, livré 17, no. 134) ☐ Kongl. Biblioteket (Cat. 1790, no. 1664) ☐ Kongl. Museum (Lugt 1638).

BIBLIOGRAPHY:
M. J. Friedländer, "Zwei Grünewaldzeichnungen," *Jahrbuch der königlich preussischen Kunstsammlungen*, 39 (1918), pp. 201ff. (fig.) ☐ L. Reau, *Matthias Grünewald et le retable de Colmar*, Strasbourg 1920, p. 298 ☐ M. J. Friedländer, *Die Zeichnungen von Matthias Grünewald*, Berlin 1927, pl. 33 ☐ H. Feuerstein, *Matthias Grünewald*, Bonn 1930, p. 144 ☐ E. Buchner, "Die Bildnisse der Thomas und Johan von Rieneck von Matthias Grünewald," *Wallraf-Richartz Jahrbuch*, 6 (1930), p. 170 ☐ R. Graul, *Grünewaldzeichnungen*, Leipzig 1935, no. 16 ☐ A. Burkhard, *Mathias Grünewald, Personality and Accomplishment*, Cambridge, Mass. 1936, pp. 64, 71, fig. 99 ☐ W. Fraenger, *Matthias Grünewald, ein physiognomischer Versuch*, Berlin 1936, p. 69 ☐ W. K. Zülch, *Der historische Grünewald, Mathis Gothart Neithardt*, Munich 1938, pp. 338, 406, pl. 202 ☐ O. H. Förster, "Der historische Grünewald. Mathis Gothart Neithardt," *Pantheon*, 23 (1939), pp. 119ff. ☐ W. K. Zülch, *Grünewald, Mathis Neithart, genannt Gothart*, Leipzig 1954, fig. 35 ☐ G. Schoenberger, *The Drawings of Mathis Gothart Nithart, called Grünewald*, New York 1948, no. 36 ☐ A. Weixlgärtner, *Dürer und Grünewald*, Göteborg 1948-49, no. 35 ☐ L. Behling, *Die Handzeichnungen des Mathis Gothart Nithart genannt Grünewald*, Weimar 1955, no. 35 ☐ G. Jacobi, *Kritische Studien zu den Handzeichnungen von Matthias Grünewald* (Diss.), Cologne 1956, p. 112 ☐ M. Meier, *Grünewald*, Zürich and Freiburg im Br. 1957, l. 37 ☐ N. Pevsner and M. Meier, *Grünewald*, New York 1958, no. 37 ☐ I. Moskowitz, ed., *Great Drawings of All Time*, New York 1962, no. 409 ☐ A. Weixlgärtner, *Grünewald*, Vienna and Munich 1962, p. 122, no. 35 ☐ W. Hütt, *Mathis Gothardt Neithardt, genannt "Grünewald,"* Leipzig 1968, p. 150, no. 101 ☐ E. Ruhmer, *Grünewald Drawing Complete Edition*, London 1970, no. 37 ☐ L. Oehler, "Das Dürermonogramm auf Werken der Dürerzeit," *Städel Jahrbuch*, N.F.3 (1971), pp. 85 f., fig. 2 (as Burgkmair?) ☐ M. Lanckorońska, "Eine Bildniszeichnung Rudolf von Scherenbergs im stockholmer Nationalmuseum," *Konsthistorisk tidskrift*, 41 (1972), pp. 1-7 cf. also E. Panofsky, *Albrecht Dürer*, Princeton 1945, p. 147, fig. 200 ☐ Bjurström 1972, no. 46 ☐ F. Baumgart, *Grünewald, tutti i disegni*, Florence 1974, no. xxix.

EXHIBITIONS:
Delft, Stedelijk Museum, Het Prinsenhof, 1949, no. 132 a.

This sheet, on which the monogram AD is a later addition, was acquired by Tessin as a work of Dürer. Friedländer was the first to recognize it as a work of Mathis Grünewald, an attribution that has gained general acceptance.

The cap with a button on top was a type worn by canons. Several attempts have been made to identify the model: Burkhard suggested Johann Pals,[1] the provost of the Neue Stiftskirche at Halle, who stands behind St. Erasmus in the painting in Munich (1044) from c. 1522-24; Zülch[2] in turn proposed Johannes de Indagine, comparing the drawing with the portrait of Indagine by Hans Baldung Grien which appears as a woodcut on the title page of his book on physiognomy from 1522. It has been pointed out by Schoenberger, however, that the drawing, which should be roughly contemporary with Baldung Grien's portrait, represents a considerably older man. Lanckorońska, at last, identified the model as Rudolf von Scherenberg.

The work is generally held to be one of Grünewald's most important drawings. It is regarded as a late work because of its tendency, as Ruhmer writes, "to a heaviness of form coupled with the half gloomy, half calm expression which registers inward rather than outward emotion."[3] He further compares the technical bravura to that in the *Screaming Head* in Berlin, datable about 1520.

NOTES:
1. Burhard, *op. cit.*, p. 64.
2. Zülch, *op. cit.*, p. 406.
3. Ruhmer, *op. cit.*, p. 96.

101

WOLF HUBER
Feldkirch im Voralberg c. 1485 - Passau 1553

The Decapitation of St. John the Baptist

Pen and brown ink, gray wash. 17.3 x 17.3 cm. Laid down. NM 97/1918.

PROVENANCE:
J. T. Sergel? □ Unknown owner, Berlin c. 1916 □ Christian Langaard.

BIBLIOGRAPHY:
K. Schwarz, *Augustin Hirschvogel*, Berlin 1917, p. 182, no. 71 and plate □ Bjurström 1972, no. 51 □ F. Winzinger, *Wolf Huber, Das Gesamtwerk*, Munich 1979, no. 199 (as copy).

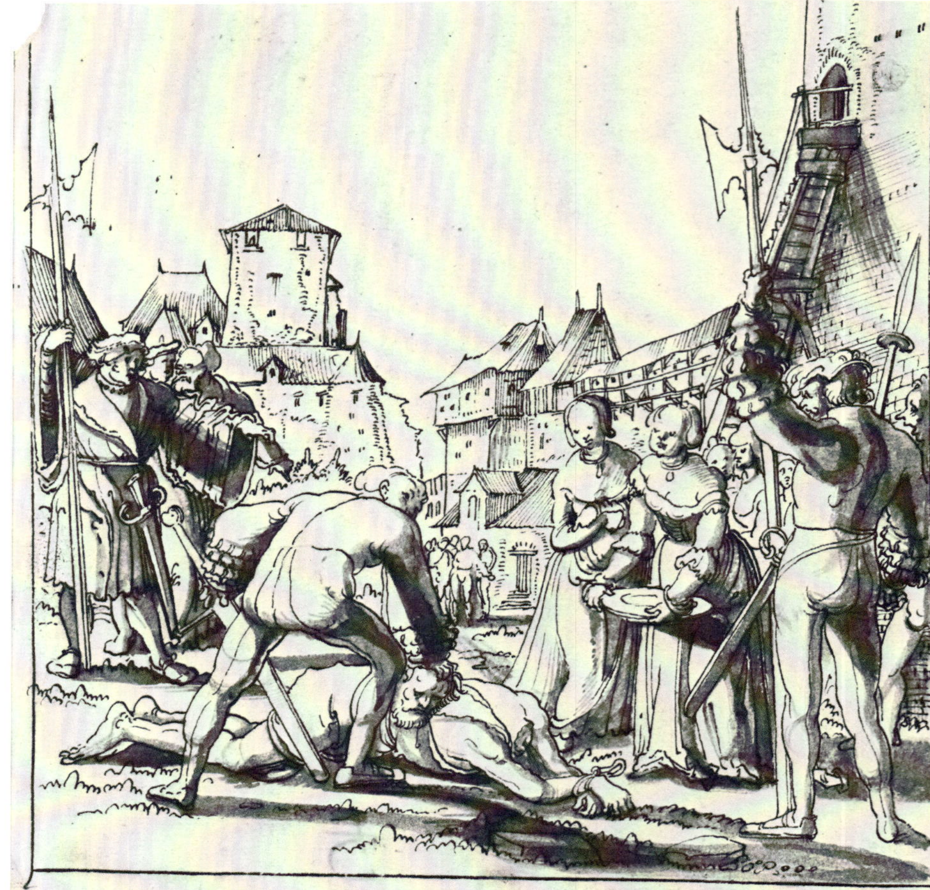

In this rendering of John the Baptist's execution, Wolf Huber combines the group of figures with a castle in the background. The architecture serves to enclose the participants, while the perspective is greatly accentuated by the low viewpoint. These compositional characteristics are also found in the composition studies in the Stenman Collection which Peter Halm acquired for Munich in 1965, all of which are dated to the 1520s. The present drawing, which Halm has said is probably an original, displays a framing line along the sides and bottom that may indicate it is a copy, though the sheets in Munich have similar lines.

The drawing gives the impression of being a completed work, with a finished wash. The castle environs in the background are also found in a sheet in Budapest (P. 33-14c), which is connected in turn with Augustin Hirschvogel's etching (Bartsch 71), dated 1546. Part of the architecture can further be recognized in Huber's painting of *Joachim and Anna under the Golden Gate* (Kloster Riedenberg, Bregenz).

102

MELCHIOR LORCK
Flensburg 1526/27 - The Gold Coast? after 1583

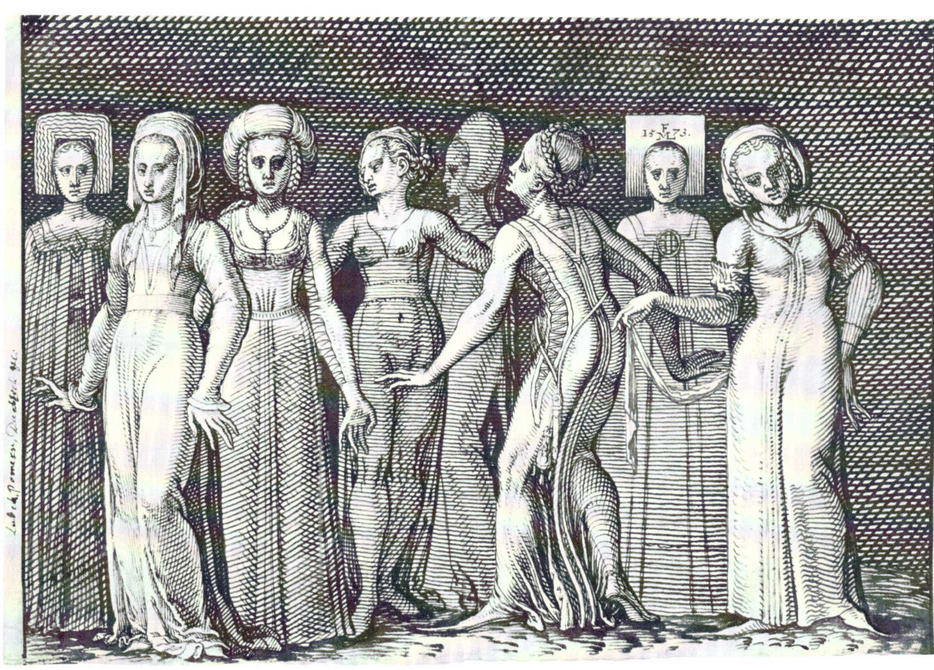

Eight Women of Lübeck, Pomerania, and Danzig

Pen and brown ink. 21.7 x 31.9 cm. Indistinct watermark. NM 272/1968. Signed and dated *1573 MLF* (monogram). Inscribed in the margin to the left: *Lübeck, Pomern, Dantzich etc.*

PROVENANCE:
Evelyn coll. (probably acquired by John Evelyn on a visit to the Netherlands in 1641) □ Sotheby's sale 15 March 1966, no. 12 □ H. M. Calmann.

BIBLIOGRAPHY:
P. Ward-Jackson, "Some Rare Drawings by Melchior Lorck," *Connoisseur*, 135 (1955), pp. 83-93, no. 44 (pl. 15) □ E. Fischer, *Melchior Lorck* (exh. cat. Statens Museum for Kunst), Copenhagen 1962, p. 63, no. 74 (reprod.) □ P. Bjurström, "Avdelningen för teckning och grafik," *Statens konstsamlingars tillväxt och förvaltning*, 1968, pp. 17f.

EXHIBITIONS:
Copenhagen 1962, no. 74 (cf. above).

Melchior Lorck was a poet, explorer, ethnographic writer, cartographer, painter, draughtsman, engraver, designer of woodcuts, architect, and goldsmith. There are comparatively few known drawings by his hand: some twenty-five in the Kobberstiksamlingen, Copenhagen; a collection of copies and about twenty originals formerly in the Evelyn collection; and single sheets in Berlin, Erlangen, Paris, London, Moscow, Leningrad, and Leiden.

German *kleinmeister* were a strong influence in his youth, and after Lorck moved to Vienna at the beginning of the 1550s he came into touch with a number of Netherlandish and Italian masters. Of particular importance were such artists as Heemskerck, Marcantonio Raimondi, Martino Rota, and the Venetian wood engravers who followed Titian. From Vienna he made a number of expeditions to Turkey, the first in 1555, and spent a total of four and a half years in that country, to some extent on commissions for the emperor. Later he returned to northern Europe.

During his trips to Turkey, Lorck made costume studies for subsequent "translation" into woodcuts.[1] This also seems to have been his intention with the group of fifteen drawings, mostly of women's costumes from northern Germany, which he made in 1567-73, although it seems that these were never cut in wood.

Our drawing is one of the most magnificent in this group and in many ways the most interesting. The technique adheres strictly to the requirements for a woodcut, while the proportions and attitudes of the figures express a strong feeling for mannerist devices.

The end of Lorck's life is obscure. In 1583, he drew a woman of Gambia and a Nigerian woman. Perhaps his love of adventure was unquenched and carried him to his death on an expedition in distant Africa.

NOTE:
1. Cf. Fischer, *op. cit.*, p. 40.

103

JOHANN HEINRICH FÜSSLI (FUSELI)

Zurich 1741 - Putney Hill, London 1825

Reproduced in color.

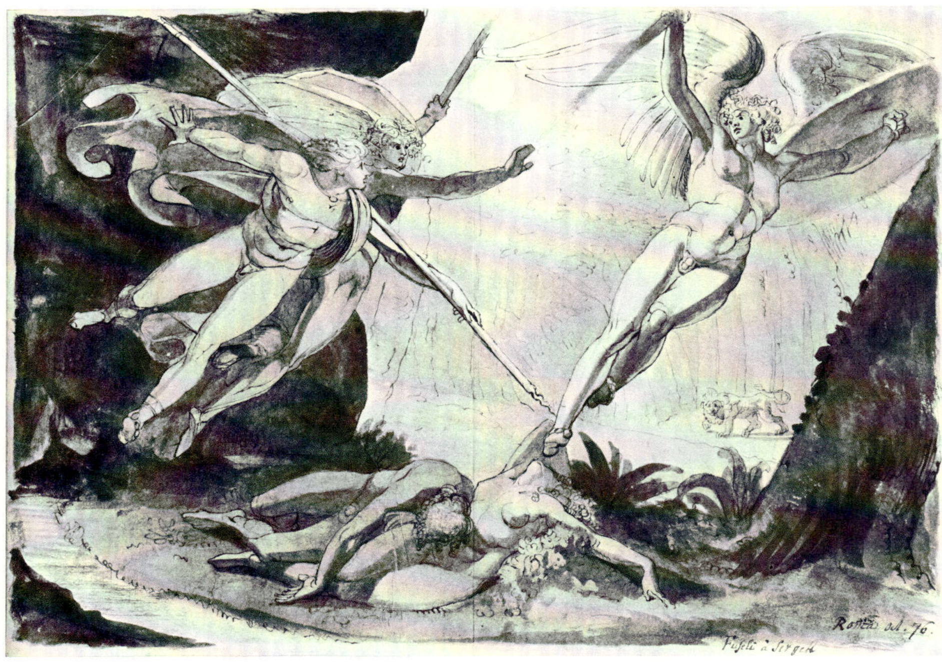

Satan Flies at the Touch of Ithuriel's Spear

Pencil, pen and brown ink; gray, brown, and reddish-brown wash. 27.1 x 39.3 cm. Watermark: Bird on three hills and the name VITTORI as countermark. NM 1685/1875. Inscribed in brown ink, lower right: *Roma Oct. 76*. Annotated by Sergel in brown ink, lower right: *Fuseli a Sergell.*

PROVENANCE:
J. T. Sergel and descendants ☐ Nationalmuseum 1875 by purchase.

BIBLIOGRAPHY:
G. Schiff, *J. H. Füsslis Milton-Galerie*, Zurich and Stuttgart 1963, p. 64, fig. 27 ☐ Bjurström 1972, no. 520 ☐ G. Schiff, *Johann Heinrich Füssli 1741-1825*, Zurich and Munich 1973, no. 482.

EXHIBITIONS:
Zurich 1926, no. 482 ☐ New Haven 1979, no. 41.

In October 1776, Fuseli was busy in Rome with illustrations for some scenes from Milton's *Paradise Lost*, a task that subsequently developed into the greatest project of his career, *The Milton Gallery*. *Satan, Sin, and Death* was one of the scenes and another was the present subject, known from three drawings that are more or less identical: one in the Cleveland Museum of Art (Schiff 483a), another in the artist's Roman album (British Museum, Bl. 13V, no. 15, Inv. no. 1885-3-14-215 Schiff 483), and our sheet, dedicated by the artist to Sergel. All three are executed in the same reddish-brown wash. The Stockholm drawing differs from the other two, however, in having a less finished background and no hatching.

The scene is described by Milton in Book IV, v. 810-22. The archangels Ithuriel and Zephon are watching over the sleeping Adam and Eve when Satan himself approaches but is driven away by Ithuriel's spear.

Classical reliefs and a Raphael fresco contributed, as pointed out by Schiff, to Fuseli's conception of the figures. The recumbent Eve with outstretched arms is based on the dead Clytemnestra on the Vatican's *Tomb of Orestes* and the two archangels are patterned on the genii in Raphael's *Expulsion of Heliodorus*, also in the Vatican. Satan, displaying wounded pride, has certain features in common with the demurring Amor in Sergel's group *Amor and Psyche*, as noted indirectly by N. Pressly in the 1979 New Haven catalogue (*The Fuseli Circle in Rome*). The latter was being executed at the time of Fuseli's drawing (see no. 105).

The subject also occurs in paintings by Fuseli. One example, now lost, was among the artist's first exhibits at the Royal Academy in 1780 after his return from Rome. A second version (Schiff 85) was included in his presentation of *The Milton Gallery* in London in 1799 and 1800.

104

JOHANN HEINRICH FÜSSLI
(FUSELI)

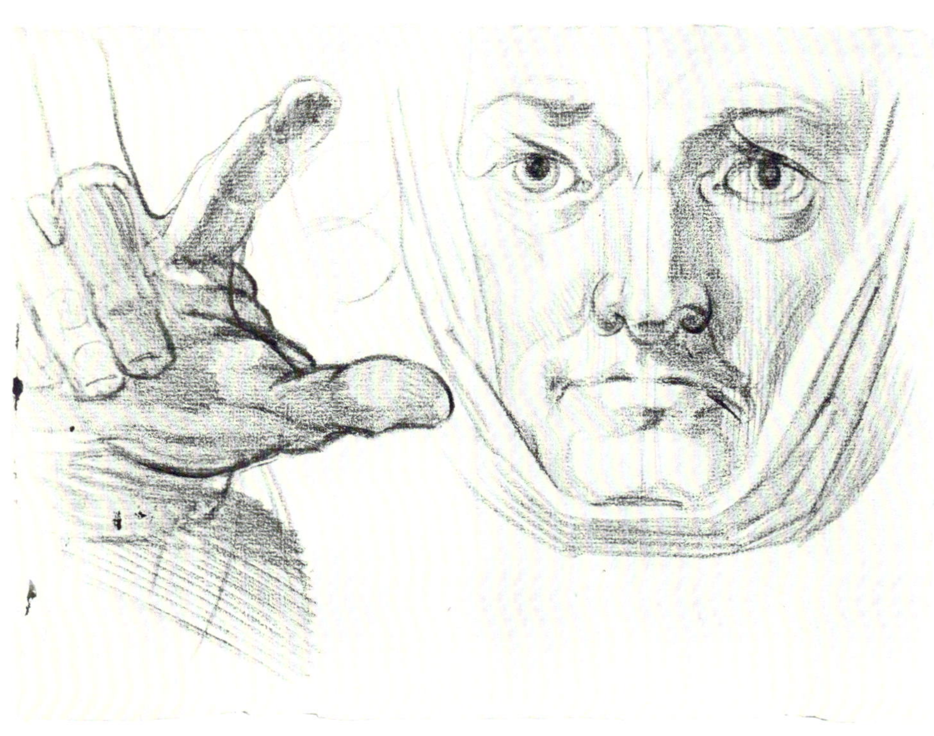

Face of Humanist or Philosopher, The Right Hand Raised in a Gesture of Invitation

Black chalk. 22.8 x 29.9 cm. Watermark: AUVERGNE 1742 (close to Heawood 3389, Paris 1773). NM Z 73/1954.

VERSO:
Copy of a detail in Michelangelo's *Brazen Serpent.* Black chalk.

PROVENANCE:
J. T. Sergel and descendants ☐ Nationalmuseum 1875 by purchase.

BIBLIOGRAPHY:
Bjurström 1972, no. 522 ☐ G. Schiff 1973, no. 504.

This geometric and highly expressive rendering of a humanist's features in broad black chalk is dated by Schiff 1770-78 and connected with the artist's illustration of a scene in Dante's *Inferno*, "Four Heads in Purgatory," for the French edition of J. G. Lavater's *Physiognomischen Fragmenten* (*Essai sur la Physiognomie*, 2, The Haag 1783, p. 230).

The verso study is a detail from the lower right corner of Michelangelo's fresco *Brazen Serpent* in an angle of the ceiling of the Sistine Chapel. The theme recurs in another drawing, which Fuseli gave to Sergel (NM Z 64/1954).

Verso

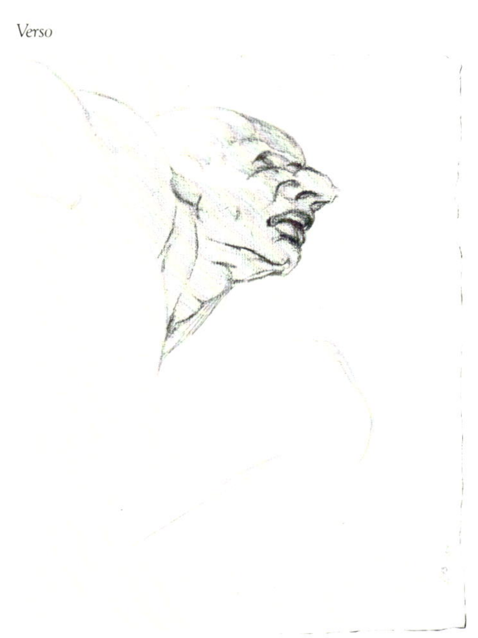

105

JOHANN HEINRICH FÜSSLI
(FUSELI)

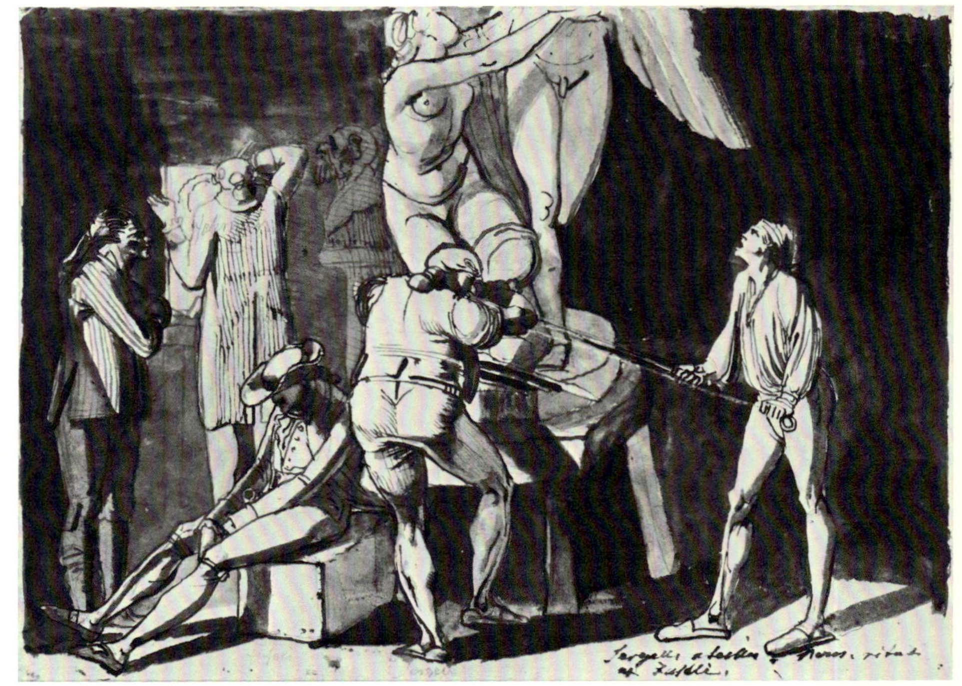

Sergel, the Swedish Sculptor, at Work in His Studio in Rome

Pen and brown ink, brown wash. 19.9 x 27.1 cm. Watermark: the name VITTORI. NM 1761/1875. Inscribed by Sergel in pen and brown ink: *Sergells atellier i Rom. ritat af Fusseli.* On the back of the standing figure seen from behind at left in pencil: *fehrman.* Below the figure sitting on a block of stone in pencil: *fuseli.* Below the standing figure seen from behind in the middle in pencil: *Sergell.*

PROVENANCE:
J. T. Sergel and descendants ☐ Nationalmuseum 1875 by purchase.

BIBLIOGRAPHY:
A. Federmann, *J. H. Füssli*, Zurich and Leipzig 1927, pl. 63 ☐ O. Antonsson, *Sergels ungdom och Romtid*, Stockholm 1942, p. 202 ☐ F. Antal, *Fuseli-Studies*, London 1956, p. 43, pl. 20 ☐ ☐ Bjurström 1972, no. 530 ☐ G. Schiff 1973, no. 566.

EXHIBITIONS:
Zurich 1926, no. 359 ☐ New Haven 1979, no. 40 ☐ Rome 1980, no. 109A.

In the first half of the 1770s, Sergel obtained a notable commission from Louis XV of France, a large-scale marble version of the *Amor and Psyche* for the royal mistress Madame Du Barry. A scale model had been completed and the marble procured when the king's sudden death led to the cancellation of the contract.

For Sergel this was a severe blow, but in the spring of 1776 the commission was revived on behalf of the King of Sweden. After a hectic year, interrupted by a period of depression, Sergel had progressed so far on the sculpture that it could be shipped to Sweden in June 1777.

In this drawing Fuseli shows Sergel in his studio in Rome at work on the group. The background figure who models something on an easel is identified in Sergel's handwriting as Carl Gustaf Fehrman (1746-1798), a medal engraver who later became Sergel's relative by marriage. He had started to work in Sergel's studio in May 1776 and reported that Fuseli, who has drawn himself passively sitting with his back to the sculpture, called almost daily during this busy year.

The other figures are Sergel himself, working on the sculpture with a drill, an assistant holding the drilling mechanism and, at the far left, Marianno, another assistant who had rough hewn the marble.

SWEDISH EIGHTEENTH-CENTURY ARTISTS

On the ruins of Stockholm's ancient royal castle, ravaged by fire in 1697, a new palace was gradually erected. Designed by the Tessins, this palace marks a crucial artistic transition from Germanic Renaissance and baroque to French and Roman classicism. As native talent was lacking for the decorative work, French artists were brought in to carry out the projects in a manner that suited Swedish funds and taste. Almost all of these artists had to be sent home, however, when Charles XII's costly wars emptied the public purse early in the new century. But at the moment construction was resumed on a larger scale in the 1730s, the time had come to recruit a new generation of talent from France. French artists continued to come until the middle of the century and while many of them, finding the climate too severe, left Sweden before their contract had expired, others decided to settle in Stockholm.

The French artists arranged informal meetings for self-improvement, spending the long winter evenings in drawing practice. The court painter, Guillaume Taraval (b. 1701), who had been part of the first newly recruited contingent in 1732, provided the instruction up to his death in 1750. In time Swedish assistants were admitted to the gatherings; the guild regulations stipulated that foreign masters were to train Swedish students. The teaching aids were rudimentary, engraved pattern sheets and models of architectural ornaments imported from Paris. Funds for hiring a male model were not provided until 1735.

The first step towards a Swedish Academy of Fine Arts was taken when Taraval's drawing school received official support. It was raised to the dignity of a Royal Drawing Academy, entitled to the use of a room in the top storey of the palace. The provision of adequate training for Swedish artists had been a vision dear to the heart of the palace architect, Nicodemus Tessin the Younger (1654-1728).

The unpaid endeavours of Taraval, followed by those of Jacques-Philippe Bouchardon (1711-1753), to instill new artistic principles into a corps of Swedish apprentices, had a lasting effect. The ideals and educational principles of the French rococo, adapted to the smaller scale of things in Sweden, left their mark on Swedish art until well into the 1770s. As the brush increasingly replaced the pen in order to provide drawings with volume and form, it introduced a lighter, more atmospheric tone. Motifs acquired a playful touch.

The teaching at the Royal Drawing Academy attracted a growing number of pupils around the middle of the century. They represented the various branches of artistic endeavour for which drawing is a prerequisite: painting, sculpture, engraving, architecture, pattern drawing, and the study of antiquities.

The eighteenth century was also a period when Swedes travelled abroad in earnest. Besides an increasing thirst for the personal experience of all that the continent of Europe had to offer, there was the more prosaic inducement of better roads and less uncomfortable coaches. Like their European counterparts, more and more young Swedish noblemen set out in continental fashion to educate themselves by touring the great monuments.

For artists the resumption of work on the Stockholm palace afforded opportunities for studying abroad. It became the custom for the artistic director to send his intended successor on a lengthy continental journey, often accompanied by one or several assistants from the palace project. In addition to educating themselves, the travellers were to search for artistic and practical solutions that could be viable in Sweden. In other words, it was a combination of study trip and industrial espionage.

Carl Hårleman (1700-1753) was the first to go abroad in 1721, sent by Nicodemus Tessin the Younger. His trip to the Lowlands, France, and Italy set the pattern for other Swedish artists until well into the second half of the century. Itineraries and objects of study crystallized into a compulsory course for later directors-to-be. It established the supremacy of French influence on artistic activities in Sweden for much of the century.

In Sweden the final transition from French rococo to neoclassicism and romanticism occured only after the second generation of artists trained at the Academy of Fine Arts returned from their studies abroad. Charged with new artistic impressions and experiences, Johan Tobias Sergel returned to Sweden in 1779 after a dozen years in Rome, followed in 1780 by Elias Martin after as long a stay in England, in 1782 by Carl August Ehrensvärd from Italy, and two years later by the King himself - Gustavus III - after an Italian journey that nourished his dreams of infusing Swedish art and public buildings with the classical ideals. The monarch drew up romantic visions of a capital city embellished with columns and other adornments, to the glory of his own era and Sweden's "magnificent" history. But when a bullet at a masked ball on 16 March 1792 cut short the King's life, it also ended the projects for transforming Stockholm and the rest of the realm. The arts in Sweden were condemned to a shadowy existence for many years to come.

CARL GUSTAF PILO

Göksäter, Södermanland 1711(?) - Stockholm 1793

Painter, draftsman, and sculptor. Member of the Russian Art Academy in St. Petersburg (1770). Director of the Danish Art Academy, Copenhagen (1771). Director of the Swedish Art Academy, Stockholm (1777).

As a personality Carl Gustaf Pilo was complex and contradictory, fluctuating between generosity and meanness. As a painter he was one of the foremost colorists in eighteenth-century Sweden. His drawing ability has generally been denied, on the basis of supposed anatomical errors and clumsy outlines. To this criticism it can be noted that most of the forty-six extant drawings were made when he had grown old and rheumatic. A close look reveals an individual poetic glimmer in the light scale of the washes and pulsating transitions between brown and gray.

Art attracted Pilo at an early age despite determined opposition from his father, himself a painter from Poland and well acquainted with the vicissitudes of an artistic profession. Pilo persisted, however, and when his school days in Nyköping were over he was apprenticed to Christman in Stockholm, receiving his diploma in 1731.

It is not clear how he spent the next few years, though there is reason to suppose that he attended the new Royal Drawing Academy under Taraval. In 1737, it is presumed that he began an itinerant existence as a portrait painter to the landed nobility in the south of Sweden. A major patron was the Ramel family at Övedskloster. It is known that in 1738 Pilo became engaged to the daughter of a churchwarden in Hofterup; when she became pregnant, Pilo fled to Denmark.

Charlotte Desmarées, a Danish governess in the Ramel household, had recommended Pilo to her brother-in-law, a language teacher at the college for sea cadets in Copenhagen, and he saw to it that the Swede obtained a vacant post as a drawing instructor there. Pilo held this post for four years while he established himself as a portrait painter to the Danish nobility. In 1745, he was appointed court painter; in 1748, he obtained a professorship at the Academy in Copenhagen; and in 1759, he was made drawing teacher to Crown Prince Christian (VII).

Some fifteen drawings are extant from the three decades and more Pilo spent in Denmark. The National Art Museum in Copenhagen has eight brush drawings on blue paper, heightened with white, which are the preliminary studies for one of the many portraits that Pilo painted in the 1750s of the Lord Chamberlain Adam Gottlob Moltke. There is also an exquisite portrait drawing of Frederik V in armor with all the insignia of his rank and office. This is penned in quick, fragmentary jottings, with patches of diluted ink and opaque white that cause the whole picture to shimmer in an ethereal Venetian light.

At the height of his career Pilo fell victim to court intrigues and in 1772 had to relinguish all his posts and leave Denmark. The official charge against him was treason; a high Swedish award, the Vasa Order, had gone to Pilo in connection with the accession and coup d'état of Gustavus III in Stockholm, and when the artist received the award in Copenhagen he had inevitably sworn the knight's oath to the Swedish monarch. In the frosty diplomatic mood existing between the two countries, this was sufficient cause for his immediate dismissal.

Pilo, now in his sixties, returned to Sweden to compete with younger talents. Commissions were hard to come by, even though he was made an honorary member of the Swedish Art Academy in August 1773. His financial position was such that in 1775 he chose to withdraw to the town of his youth, Nyköping, where he lived as a pensioner. Two years later came the long-awaited recognition — appointment as director of the Academy. Pending new premises, including a representative residence for the director, Pilo remained in Nyköping until 1780.

Meanwhile he depicted a devout celebration in honor of Gustavus III as the patron of the fine arts, as well as four ambitious but lifeless scenes of the monarch's spectacular inauguration of a new Court of Appeal at Åbo on 28 June 1776. The latter was probably a speculative venture, the aim being to have the drawings engraved in copper, but this was never done. Still the drawings from the inauguration in Åbo helped Pilo, quite unexpectedly, to win the greatest commission of his life, the huge painting, almost three by five-and-a-half meters, of the coronation of Gustavus III in 1772.

The drawings of the Åbo Court of Appeal attracted the King's attention when he visited Nyköping during an inspection of military installations in 1778. He immediately commissioned the artist to prepare a large painting of the subject and accompanied this with a request for a draft for a corresponding painting of his coronation, the idea being to obtain a pair to complete the painting by Ehrenstrahl at Drottningholm, featuring the accession of Charles XI. When the latter proposal was submitted to the King he decided that it should have priority over the Åbo painting.

Having moved back to Stockholm and settled into his directorship, Pilo was able to start his coronation painting in earnest. His studio, however, was too small for the huge canvas and he had to work on one section at a time. Together with his time-consuming technique, this resulted in the painting being unfinished when Pilo died on 2 March 1793.

As a painter Pilo worked with an unmistakable color range in dark shades of green. As a draftsman he had an individual technique, almost embroidering his pictures with a dense application of short, fine brushstrokes, alternated with light hatching in brown and gray. The result is reminiscent of a textile pattern woven with a fine warp.

106

CARL GUSTAF PILO

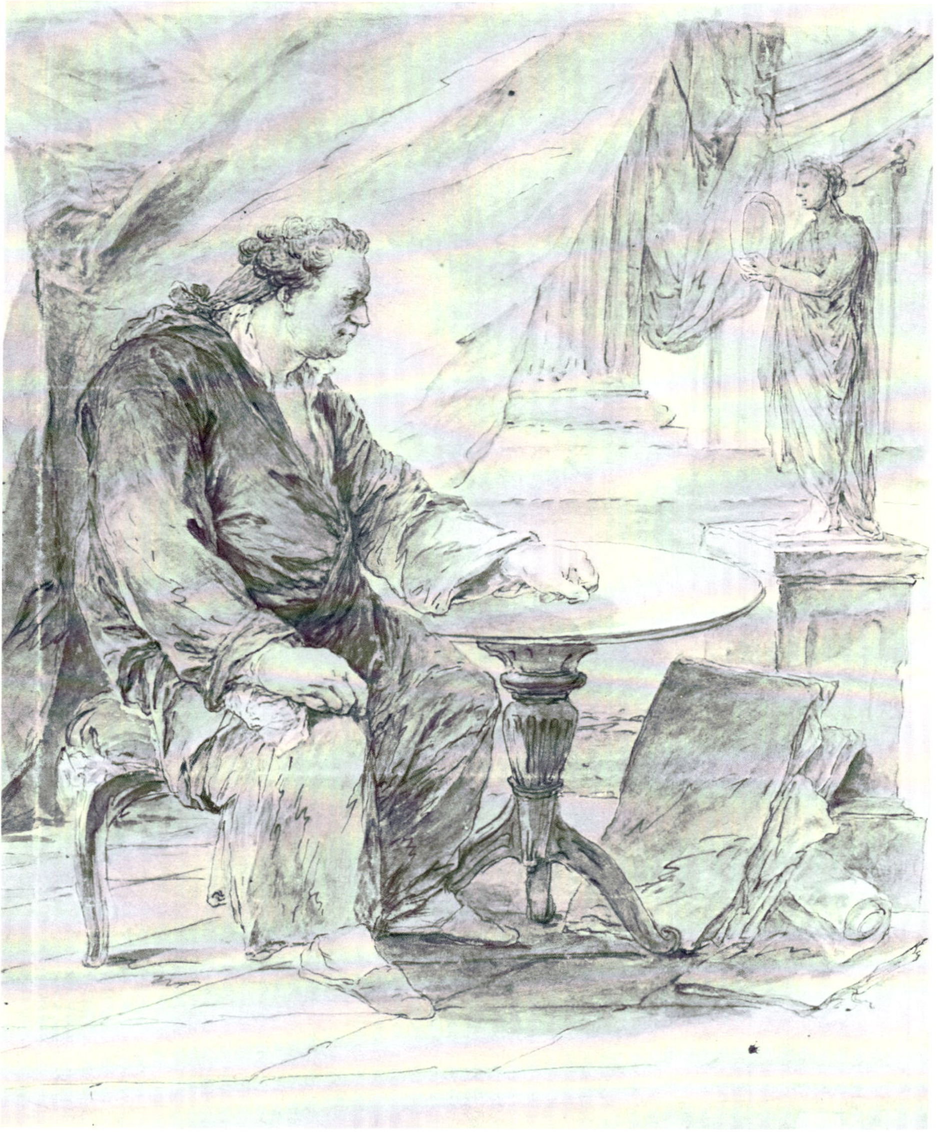

Portrait of the Aged Artist

Pencil, pen and brown ink, gray and brown wash. 33.5 x 26.0 cm. Watermark: Fleur-de-lis and the name J Kool (near Heawood 1841). NM 6/1869.

PROVENANCE:
County Adolf Lewenhaupt ☐ Nationalmuseum 1869 by purchase.

BIBLIOGRAPHY:
O. Sirén, *Carl Gustaf Pilo och hans förhållande till den samtida porträttkonsten i Sverige*, Stockholm 1902, no. 111 ☐ L. Swane, "Pilo," *Svensk sjuttonhundratalskonst*, Stockholm 1923, no. 41 ☐ G. Jungmarker, *Carl Gustaf Pilo som tecknare*, Nationalmusei skriftserie 17, Stockholm 1973, p. 72, fig. 43 ☐ U. Cederlöf, *Svenska teckningar 1700-talet*, Årsbok för Statens konstmuseer, 29 (Stockholm 1982), p. 101, fig. 88.

EXHIBITIONS:
Stockholm 1933, no. 87 ☐ Stockholm 1943, no. 41 ☐ Stockholm 1982, no. 49.

This late self-portrait presumably dates from the period after 1775 when Pilo withdrew to Nyköping after failing to obtain commissions in Stockholm. His tired expression conveys a strong air of the resignation which he must have felt in his enforced idleness. He is seated in a creased dressing gown, contemplating a classical statuette with one of his big, swollen hands resting on a round table and the other on a thigh. Below him on the floor are untouched portfolios of drawings. The background is filled with the type of palace interior that appears in so many of his portraits of the Danish nobility. There is no means of telling whether this is an ironical reference to his former status as a court painter, simply a decorative element, or an actual painting that he placed there to serve as a background. No other painting by Pilo on this scale exists today.

The drawing is meticulous in every detail. Over a faint underdrawing in pencil Pilo continues with pen and brown ink. The outlines are slightly shaky, with continual corrections in brief strokes. The wash is added in tones of brown and gray. With the finest graduated hatching from the brush the artist conjures forth his own features, neck, and the exposed part of the chest. He then proceeds to accentuate certain folds in the clothing and the background draperies, applying the gray wash more forcefully to obtain the effect of fabric. The nose, the mouth, and some curls in the wig get a final touch with pen and black ink.

ELIAS MARTIN

Stockholm 1739 - Stockholm 1818

Son of Olof Martin, alderman of the carpenters' guild in Stockholm. Painter and graphic artist. Associate member of the Royal Academy, London (1769). Member of the Swedish Academy of Art (1781). Teacher in landscape painting at the Swedish Academy (1784).

Elias Martin was apprenticed to his father at an early age, and his first drawings are copies after furniture patterns in the family collection. He soon abandoned carpentry for painting, receiving his first instruction from a friend of the family, Friedrich Schultz, a guild painter. There is no evidence that Martin attended the Academy in Stockholm. A series of red chalk studies of costumes and portraits in the Nationalmuseum point to his efforts at self-improvement.

The tasks of an artisan painter included interior decorations for the homes of the wealthy. Wall panels and lintel pieces were usually filled with views of landscapes. This was presumably how Martin started on the type of motif at which he excelled.

In the spring of 1763, F. H. Chapman, master shipbuilder and agent of the fortifications constructor Augustin Ehrensvärd, engaged Martin to draw ornaments for Sveaborg, the great naval base that was being set up at the mouth of the Gulf of Finland.

Martin spent two years at the fortress, dividing his time between ornaments for the new coastal fleet and drawing lessons for the officers of the garrison. In his free time he documented, rather like a touring photographer, everything he encountered on the barren islands and skerries. The sharp contrast between the social niceties of garrison life and the harsh toil of taming the hard rocks captivated his attention and left its mark in his representations. The evening diversions are recorded with a light hand and a light wash, while a considerably coarser pen and dark shading are used for the hard labor by day.

While Martin was at Sveaborg his father died, leaving him in a position to study abroad. He left for Paris in the summer of 1766. A recommendation from his successful fellow countryman, Alexander Roslin, opened the doors of the French Academy, where Joseph Vernet was his teacher. Martin quickly learned to apply a codified composition to the painting of town views. The sky is kept high, the foreground wide with plenty of staffage, while a building placed diagonally carries the eye beyond to open water, and city architecture is piled up in the background.

But France was not congenial to a potential painter of landscapes. With the domination of the rococo, such painting was transformed into a genre. In England, on the other hand, a landscape art more concerned with the representation of nature and reality had taken root with the aid of impulses from Venice. So by 1768 Martin was in London.

In England he found a new set of motifs in the landscape park, with its carefully arranged vistas and wide horizon. Martin places his main subject so far back that even the immediate surroundings are drawn into the picture. He is interested in atmospheric phenomena and tries to convey the effect of air shimmering over extensive fields. His palette becomes freer and clearer; the shadows take on the colors around them.

Martin was also greatly moved by the distress and poverty which prevailed in pre-industrial London. His indignation over the deep social divisions in English society is expressed by his pen. Some works have associations with the figures typified by Hogarth and even Rowlandson — puffed-up lawyers, snobbish dandies, and misguided menials. But most of all he is a sympathetic observer of the misery of the English working class. His pictures of waifs and strays reveal a perception of reality without the satire and morality of Hogarth's series.

After twelve years in England, with works accepted for the Academy Exhibition almost every year, Martin offered his services in January 1780 to his own king in Sweden. He proposed an ambitious program for travelling throughout the country in order to illustrate every place of topographical or historical interest, as well as local customs and occupations. Gustavus III granted Martin a small annual sum for the project. That autumn Martin returned home, accompanied by his brother Johan Fredrik, an engraver, to put his plan into practice. Apart from a few years in England between 1788 and 1791, he lived in Sweden for the rest of his life.

Martin continued to work with the motifs and methods he had developed during his sojourn in England. He is important for his role in introducing the romantic perception of landscape into Sweden. There are innumerable watercolors and drawings by his hand featuring picturesque views of Stockholm and its environs, rural scenes on Swedish estates, and the peaceful life of country towns.

107

ELIAS MARTIN

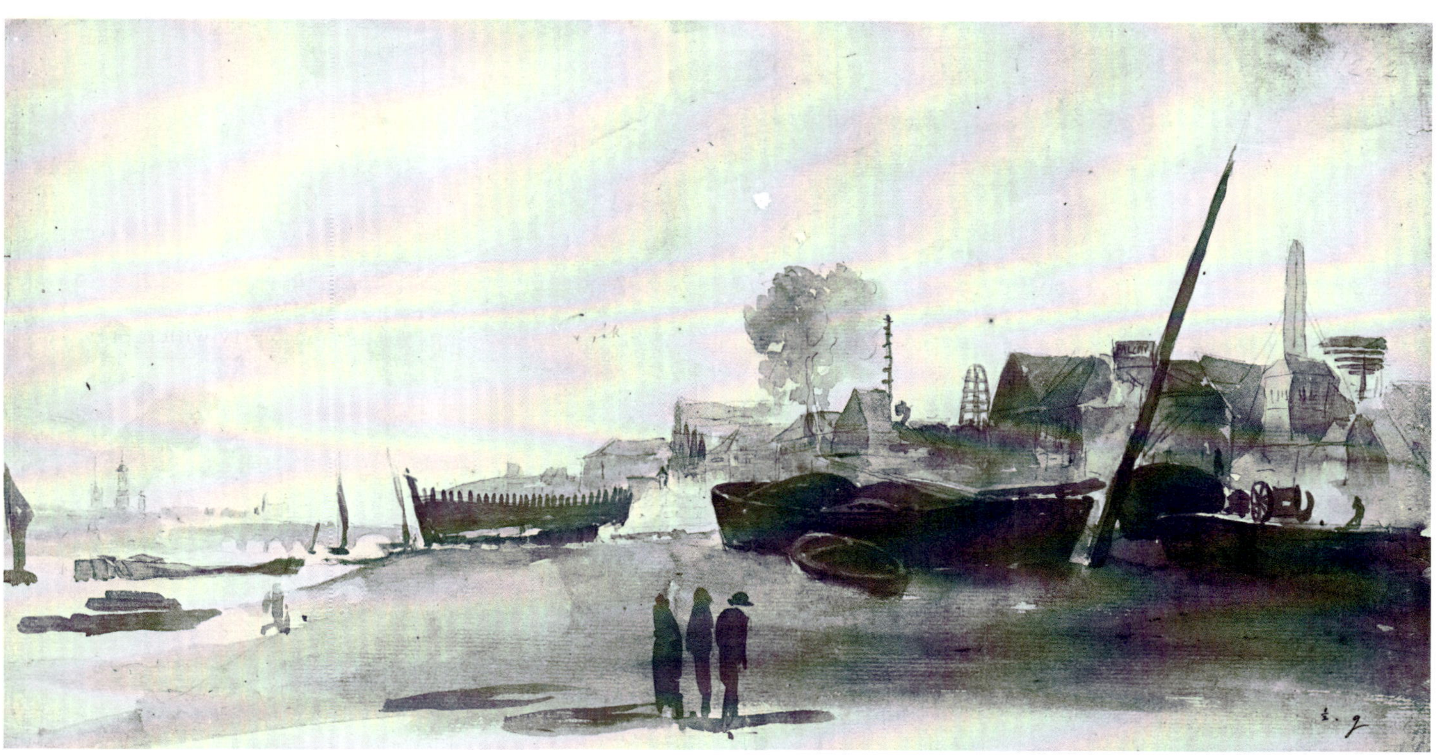

On the Bank of the Thames, London

Pencil, brush and gray wash. 23.5 x 45.0 cm. Watermark: Fleur-de-lis and below the letters LVG (close to Heawood 1843, London 1775). NM 82/1912. Inscribed in pencil, in the middle: *rök* (smoke), with pen and brown ink, lower right: *½ . g.*

PROVENANCE:
Chr. Eichorn (G. Upmark, *Chr. Eichorns samlingar af handteckningar, arkitektur- och ornamentritningar*, Stockholm 1890, no. 1262) □ AB Bukowski Auktioner, Stockholm (R. Gagge collection) □ Nationalmuseum 1912 by purchase.

BIBLIOGRAPHY:
N. Lindhagen, "Elias Martin," *Svenska Mästartecknare: Sergel/ Martin/ Ehrensvärd.* Årsbok för Svenska statens konstsamlingar 3. Stockholm 1955, p. 70, fig. 8.

EXHIBITIONS:
Stockholm 1950, no. 250.

In this view London is seen from the south bank, marked by huddled tenements and piles of coal. On the right is the ancient Falcon Inn with its sign. Some barges and rivercraft lie on the muddy flats, waiting for the tide in order to float free. On the left, the eye is carried to London Bridge, from which the superstructure of houses had been removed a decade earlier, and from there to the north bank with the Tower of London and that of St. Magnus the Martyr, discernible in the distance.

There is an early morning air about the scene as the sun's slanting rays throw long shadows. The panorama is enveloped in a diffuse direct light, resembling waves of raw, damp mist from the river.

108

ELIAS MARTIN

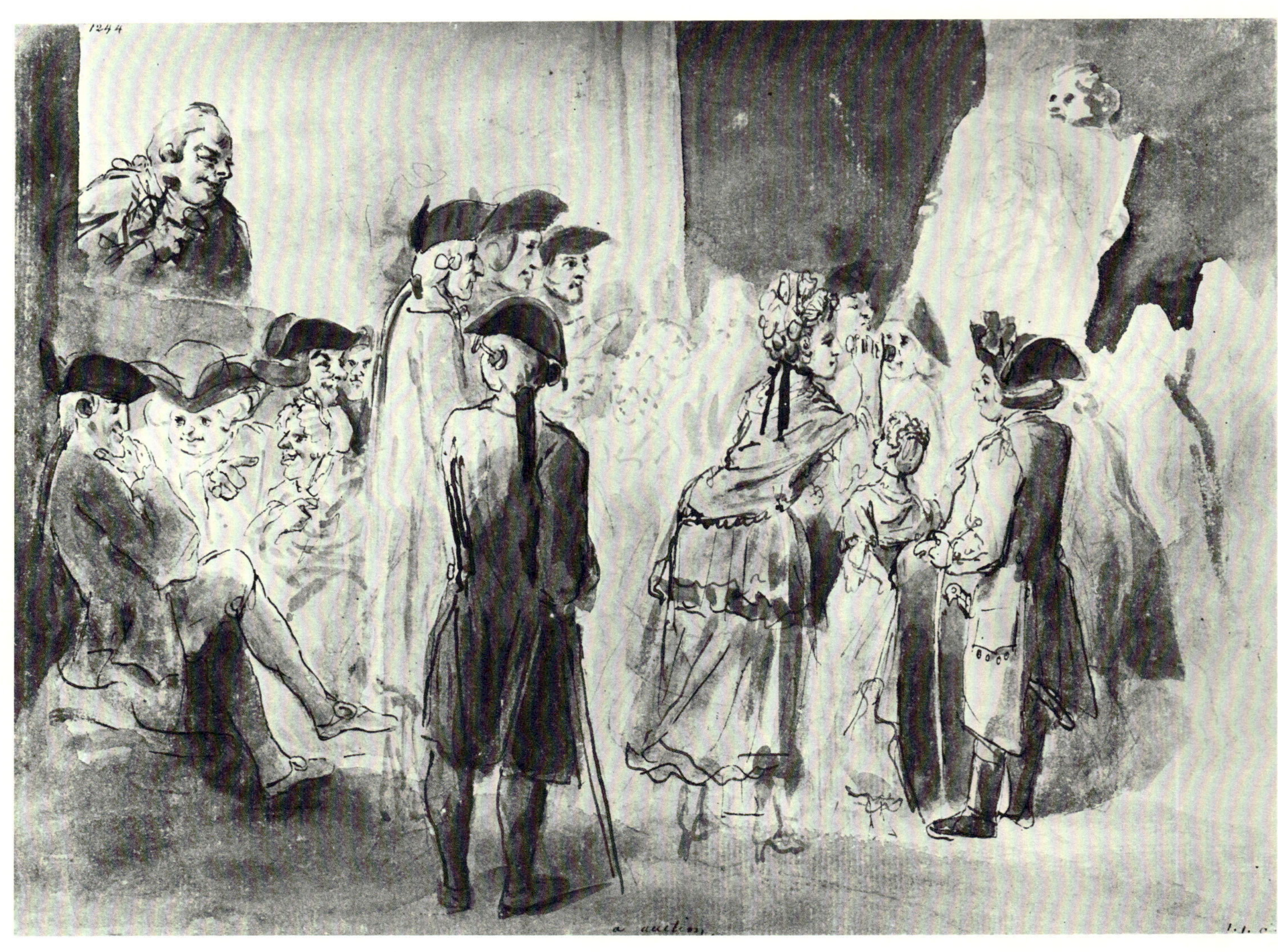

An Art Auction in London

Pencil, pen and black ink, gray wash, watercolor. 19.0 x 25.8 cm. Watermark: Britannia. NM 261/1924. Inscribed in brown ink, lower margin: *a auction*. With brown ink, lower right: *1. 1. 0*. With brown ink, upper left: *1244*.

PROVENANCE:
AB Bukowski Auktioner, Stockholm ☐ Nationalmuseum 1924 by purchase.

BIBLIOGRAPHY:
R. Hoppe, *Målaren Elias Martin*, Stockholm 1933, p. 200, fig. p. 199 ☐ R. Hoppe and G. Jungmarker, *Akvareller och teckningar av Elias Martin*, Ur Nationalmusei handtecknings-samling III, Malmö 1943, p. 20, fig. no. II ☐ U. Cederlöf, *Svenska teckningar 1700-talet*, Årsbok för statens konstmuseer 29, Stockholm 1982, p. 166, pl. IV.

EXHIBITIONS:
Stockholm 1950, no. 211 ☐ Stockholm 1982, no. 69.

The social criticism of Hogarth seems to have influenced Martin in England. The constant hardships suffered by the lower classes are the subject of many of his watercolors and drawings. But there is also the occasional sheet illustrating the life and customs of the more prosperous classes.

This is a scene from auction rooms in the 1770s — possibly one of the premises used by Christie's, which was founded in 1766. A well-to-do family is considering the painting being shown to the public; the wife has her telescope out to take a closer look, the daughter is pointing enthusiastically, and the husband is waiting for his spouse's judgement. At the other end of the room three persons are talking about the interest which the painting has aroused. One of them is thoughtfully feeling his chin; perhaps he is the owner, hoping for a good price, or a potential bidder. From the platform behind a railing the auctioneer surveys the public with a twisted smile, sensing that the bidding will be strong.

109

ELIAS MARTIN

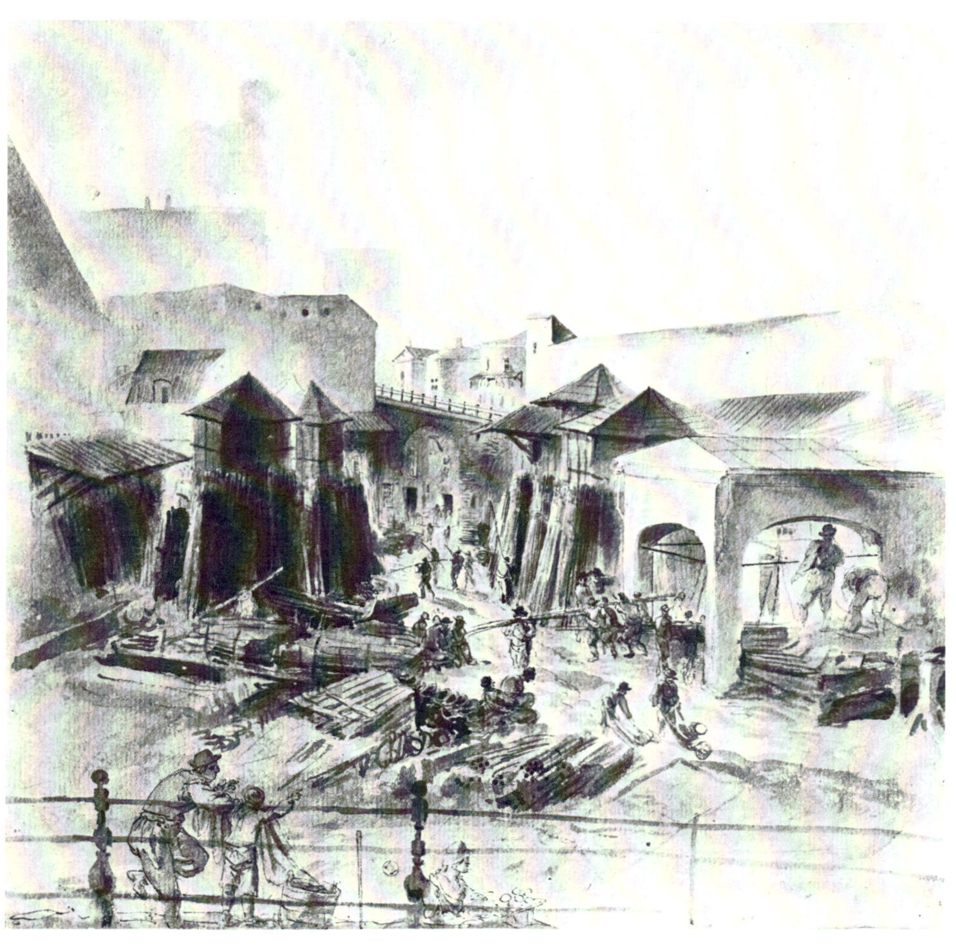

Scene from the Iron Trade in Stockholm

Pencil, pen and black ink, gray wash, watercolor. 27.0 x 26.7 cm. Laid down. NM Anckarswärd 195 b/1863.

PROVENANCE:
M. G. Anckarswärd ☐ Kongl. Museum (Lugt 1638) 1860 by gift.

BIBLIOGRAPHY:
Hoppe and Jungmarker 1943, p. 23, fig. no. XII.

EXHIBITIONS:
Stockholm 1950, no. 605.

Transport in eighteenth-century Sweden was by water. The long iron bars, into which the ore had been processed at the ironworks of the Bergslagen and Mälar regions, were taken by boat to Stockholm where they were weighed before being shipped abroad. The work of testing, weighing, and grading was undertaken at a place called Järngraven ('iron trench') where Lake Mälar runs into the Baltic.

The open, vaulted weighhouse is depicted in the watercolor. Workers are heaving and carrying the heavy bars to and from the weighing machine, which is opereated by two inspectors. A man accompanied by a child has stopped at the railing of the nearby bridge to watch the whole procedure.

This watercolor was used as a draft for an etching by Martin's pupil Mårten Rudolf Heland.[1]

NOTE:
1. H. Frölich, *Bröderna Elias och Johan Fredrik Martins gravyrer*, Stockholm 1939, p. 276, no. 31.

110

ELIAS MARTIN

Reproduced in color.

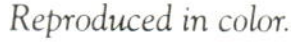

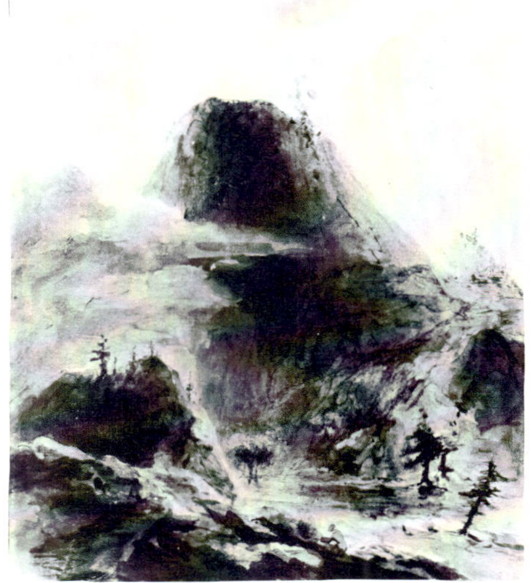

Romantic Mountain Landscape

Pencil, watercolor and gray wash. 31.4 x 26.2 cm. Laid down. NM A 85/1970.

PROVENANCE:
M. G. Anckarswärd (?).

BIBLIOGRAPHY:
Hoppe 1933, fig. p. 269 ☐ Hoppe and Jungmarker 1943, p. 24, fig. no. XVI ☐ Lindhagen 1955, p. 82, fig. p. 73 ☐ Cederlöf 1982, p. 200, fig. 166.

EXHIBITIONS:
Stockholm 1950, no. 738.

A severe illness at the end of the 1790s aroused Martin's religious convictions. His experience of nature was in future colored by moving visions of the continual presence of God in all creation. The sparsely populated Swedish countryside, with vast forests, rushing rivers, and austere granite, must have come close to his conception of the primal landscape — wild, untamable nature, aloof and untouched by the human hand.

In this watercolor his observations during constant journeys through Sweden are distilled into a cosmic landscape, a craggy, wild Arcadia. There is a sublime undertone to this idyll: titanic mountains spitting fire, solitary majestic pines, the sunlight breaking through low clouds, and clear water running deep in cleft valleys. Diminutive man takes second place to nature.

JOHAN TOBIAS SERGEL
Stockholm 1740 - Stockholm 1814

Son of a court embroiderer who had emigrated from Germany. Sculptor and graphic artist. Professor at the Swedish Art Academy (1780). Court Surveyor (1803). Ennobled (1808). Director of the Academy (1810)

Sergel learned drawing in the 1750s from Jean Eric Rehn (1717-1793), court surveyor, interior decorator, and the foremost representative of the Swedish rococo. His first insights into modelling and sculpture were obtained in 1756 from Adrien Masreliez (1717-1806), who came from France and was court sculptor. In the same year he was apprenticed to Pierre Hubert L'Archevêque (1721-1778), the premier sculptcr in Sweden who had recently arrived from France. The Frenchman's decorative, rococo art shows the strong influence of Bernini. Besides making numerous copies of his master's fountain projects, the young Sergel ventured his own variations. In 1758, he accompanied L'Archevêque on a seven-month study trip to Paris and attended the French Academy for almost half the time. He also came into contact with the two chief protagonists of the French classical tradition: Count de Caylus (Anne Claude Philippe de Tubières), a devotée of antiquity, and Edme Bouchardon, the court sculptor who Caylus admired so much and who once had been the teacher of L'Archevêque. Sergel acquired red chalk drawings by the French sculptor as well as engravings by Caylus after drafts by Bouchardon of classical subjects, chiefly scenes of sacrifice.

Back in Sweden, Sergel mastered Bouchardon's drawing style with red chalk in an apparently effortless, sweeping technique. He took his subjects from the classical and biblical motifs which Caylus had assembled with commentaries in two volumes, *Tableaux tirés d'Homère et de Virgile* and *Histoire de Joseph*, both published in Paris in 1757. Some of the scenes were also converted into etchings, a technique that Sergel learned when Per Gustaf Floding (1731-1791) returned from abroad and was appointed to teach engraving at the Academy.

At the age of twenty-seven, Sergel reached Rome in the late summer of 1767. Adelcrantz, the Academy director, had personally intervened to obtain funds for him as the most promising talent in Sweden.

Technically it was not difficult for Sergel to exchange his training in Stockholm for the status of a visiting pupil at the French Academy in Rome; he was familiar with the language as well as the teaching methods. But whereas his French colleagues saw their stay in Rome as a natural step in their education, Sergel felt he had to justify his backers in Sweden. And while the French cultural heritage was in the mainstream of European art, the Swede's contact to this heritage had largely been confined to engravings after the great masters. Rome in all its glory was therefore something of a cultural shock. A paralyzing feeling that all his acquired knowledge meant nothing forced Sergel to start drawing again from scratch. He writes in his recollections that it was a matter of pursuing two routes: antiquity and life. His days were spent copying classical artifacts in the galleries and museums of Rome, the evenings studying models at the Academy.

By about 1770, his diligence gave him sufficient command of the new formal means of expression to feel able to start sculpting. Most of what he produced in Rome was achieved in the first half of the new decade: depictions of two heroes, *Tobias with the Fish* and *Diomedes*, and three mythological couples, all illustrating female beauty distracting and seducing male strengh, *Jupiter and Juno*, *Hercules and Omphale*, and *Venus and Anchises*. He also illustrated episodes from the Iliad, *Mars and Venus*, and the story of Psyche, *Mercury and Psyche*. Finally his Roman masterpiece, *The Faun*, is an incarnation of sensual delight, showing the figure semi-recumbent, intoxicated by wine and pleasure.

On the whole, however, Rome did more for Sergel's drawing than his sculpting. It was there that he learned to specify, accentuate, or reduce his conceptions to obtain the desired impression. His penwork became increasingly skillful, creating forms in a broad plastic style reminiscent of reliefs. He sometimes started with chalk but only to make a faint underdrawing with a few summary strokes. Ink, which immediately leaves an indelible mark on the paper, was his primary medium, supported with some brushstrokes of dark wash at just those places that give the figures their greatest volume. His subjects vary but tend to be highly sensual, amusingly burlesque, or unmistakably heroic.

Sergel was not a learned artist. The theoretical idealism which served as a superstructure for neoclassicism did not attract him. While sharing the contemporary view of antiquity as the ultimate norm, he did not hesitate to add his own vigorous realism. For his *Diomedes*, the study of suitable classical figural prototypes was combined with direct observation in Rome's fencing schools.

His energetic perserverance, combined with an open, generous nature, made Sergel respected and liked by his colleagues. He was acquainted with most the French colony and many Englishmen and Germans; he shared his time and thoughts above all with the Dane Abildgaard and the Swiss Fuseli.

In 1778, on the verge of international recognition, Sergel was recalled by Gustavus III. He took his time, returning by road via France. In Montpellier he called on his aged teacher L'Archevêque to discuss the completion of commissions that ill health had forced the Frenchman to leave unfinished in Stockholm. He then spent the winter of 1778-79 in Paris, modelling an admission piece for the French Academy. The scene he chose was *Othryades*, the mortally wounded Spartan hero, erecting a memorial to the gods for the victory of his people. After a brief visit to England, Sergel was back in Sweden by the early summer of 1779.

111

JOHAN TOBIAS SERGEL

The intention had been to use Sergel's know-how for monumental tasks. The King was, however, capricious and invested Sergel's talents in secondary commissions. In his last thirty-five years Sergel executed less than half a dozen works of importance, all of them in Stockholm: *The Descartes Monument* (cast in lead, 1781), and the *Ascension* altar (plaster model completed in 1785) in Adolf Fredrik Church, the group with *Axel Oxenstierna and Clio* (model ready in 1786 for the base of L'Archevêque's equestrian Gustavus Adolphus), the *Gustavus III* statue on Skeppsbron (model ready in 1791), and a *Mars and Venus* (done in clay in Rome, sculpted in marble shortly before 1804). Otherwise he was obliged to portray the leading Swedes of his day in busts and medallions.

The richest expression of Sergel's art after his stay in Rome is to be found in his drawings. His reputation enabled him to move freely in every social stratum. An outstanding form of reportage, full of warmth and humor, his pen and brush capture the hectic social life of the Gustavian era. His discerning eye catches everything, from royal banquets with nobles and diplomats to the informal gatherings of artists in humble taverns. Then there are the tender records from his family life — his beloved Anna Elisabeth (Rella) Hellström swinging their son Gustaf on her foot or tip-toeing to his bed when he wakens in the night.

A number of personal tragedies darkened Sergel's closing years. Anna Rella, his common-law wife of thirteen years, died suddenly in January 1795, followed five years later by his much admired friend Carl August Ehrensvärd. Lonely, gout-ridden, and plagued by the lack of important commissions for sculptures, Sergel himself died on 26 February 1814.

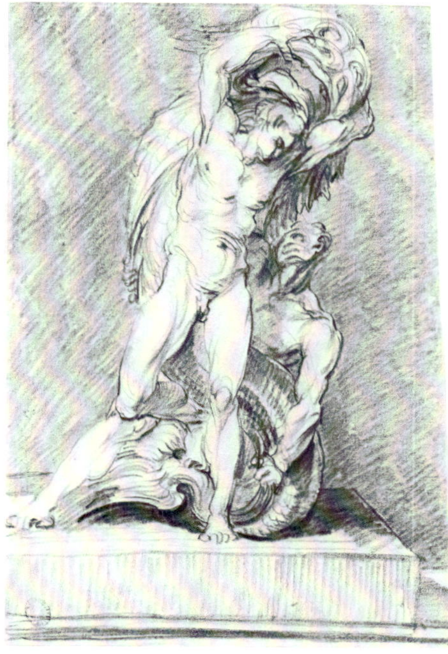

Tobias with the Fish and the Demon Asmodeus

Red chalk. 35.2 x 23.6 cm. No watermark, just lines. Italian chalked paper. NM 927/1875.

PROVENANCE:
J. T. Sergel and descendants □ Nationalmuseum 1875 by purchase.

BIBLIOGRAPHY:
O. Antonsson and G. Jungmarker, *Teckningar av Johan Tobias Sergel*, Ur Nationalmusei handteckningssamling IV, Malmö 1947, p. 31, fig. no. XXI □ R. Josephson, *Sergels fantasi*, I, Stockholm 1956, pp. 145 f., fig. 190 □ P. Bjurström, *Drawings of Johan Tobias Sergel*, Chicago 1979, p. 17, cat. no. 1D3 □ U. Cederlöf, *Svenska teckningar 1700-talet*, Arsbok för Statens konstmuseer 29, Stockholm 1982, pp. 119 f., fig. 98.

EXHIBITIONS:
Hamburg 1975, no. 53 □ Copenhagen 1976, no. 68 □ Stockholm 1976, no. 49 □ Rome 1980, no. 110 □ New York 1981, no. 43 □ Stockholm 1982, no. 55.

Perhaps it is not just a coincidence that when Sergel started to execute sculptures in Rome in 1769, one of the first subjects he chose was an episode from his apocryphal namesake's story in the *Book of Tobit*. We are told that when Tobias in his wanderings reached the river Tigris and wanted to refresh himself, a great fish leapt out of the water and threatened to swallow him. His mentor, the angel Gabriel, advised him to land the monster by holding on to its gills and extract its guts. Soon after this encounter, Tobias celebrated his marriage and placed the heart and liver of the fish on the burning incense, thereby driving off the evil spirit Asmodeus, who had strangled his wife's seven previous husbands on their wedding night.

Sergel's first conception, in the spirit of Bernini, had been a fountain group, seen in the round, with the hero forcing open the monster's mouth from behind. This he rejected for a more complex vertical group where the leviathan, already vanquished, is being held aloft by the hero, its helpless, writhing body against his back. This powerful red chalk drawing shows how much Sergel had already learned, after only a few years in Rome, about the volume and anatomy of the male body. He absorbed a good deal from his studies after Annibale Carracci's ceiling frescoes of naked youths, *ignudi*, in the Galleria of the Palazzo Farnese. In the terra-cotta version from the same year the demon at the feet of Tobias has been excluded and the hero has been transformed from a beardless youth into a mature man, akin to the forceful classical sculpture of the *Farnese Hercules*.

112

JOHAN TOBIAS SERGEL

Johann Heinrich Füssli / Henry Fuseli

Black chalk, pen and brown ink, brownish gray and gray wash. 26.8 x 19.4 cm. Watermark: Circle with bird on three hills, surrounded by the letters E S. NM 645/1875. Inscribed in brown ink, upper right: *Fuseli peintre suiss a Rome.*

PROVENANCE:
J. T. Sergel and descendants ☐ Nationalmuseum 1875 by purchase.

BIBLIOGRAPHY:
O. Antonsson, *Sergels ungdom och Romtid*, Stockholm 1942, p. 234, fig. p. 235.

Besides his more official drawings, Sergel did a number of informal portraits of friends, giving the pen free play without regard for convention. Although these sheets have been termed caricatures, they are of considerable artistic interest. The record of individual features is combined with an attempt to catch the typical element in gestures and disposition. The technique varies from calligraphic profiles in energetic short, broad strokes which alternate with hairline touches of the quill pen, to outline figures in red or black chalk, to meticulous character studies executed in pen and brush.

The subject, the Swiss painter Fuseli, arrived in Rome three years after Sergel and left, with him, in 1778. They certainly knew each other by 1772, possibly from the beginning of Fuseli's stay. Their relationship was particularly close in 1776, the year that Fuseli gave a number of his drawings to the Swede.

This is one of five portraits of Fuseli by Sergel, all highlighting the painter's demonic air. At first Sergel had been critical of his friend's highly emotional paintings illustrating subjects from Norse sagas and romantic poetry, represented in dramatic scenes whose forms tended to be taken from Michelangelo. As time passed, however, the theatrical tone made itself felt in Sergel's own work. Attacks of gout were a heavy burden and made him more susceptible to such overtures. Under Fuseli's influence, Sergel explored a more serious range of motifs, a more expressive style with the pen, and a deeper tone in the wash. On his part the Swiss acquired from Sergel a more confident plasticity in the figures and a more balanced rhythm in their interaction.

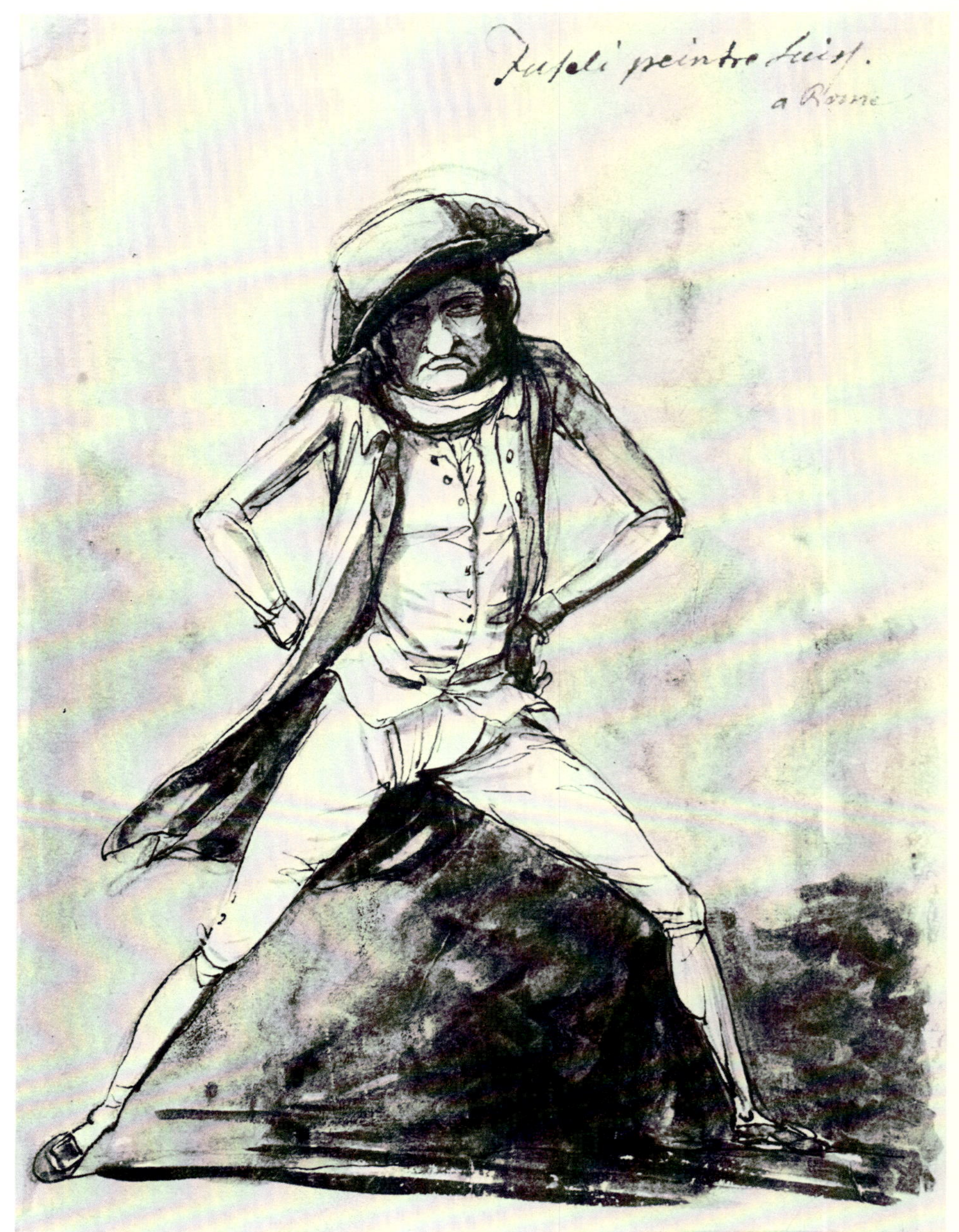

113

JOHAN TOBIAS SERGEL

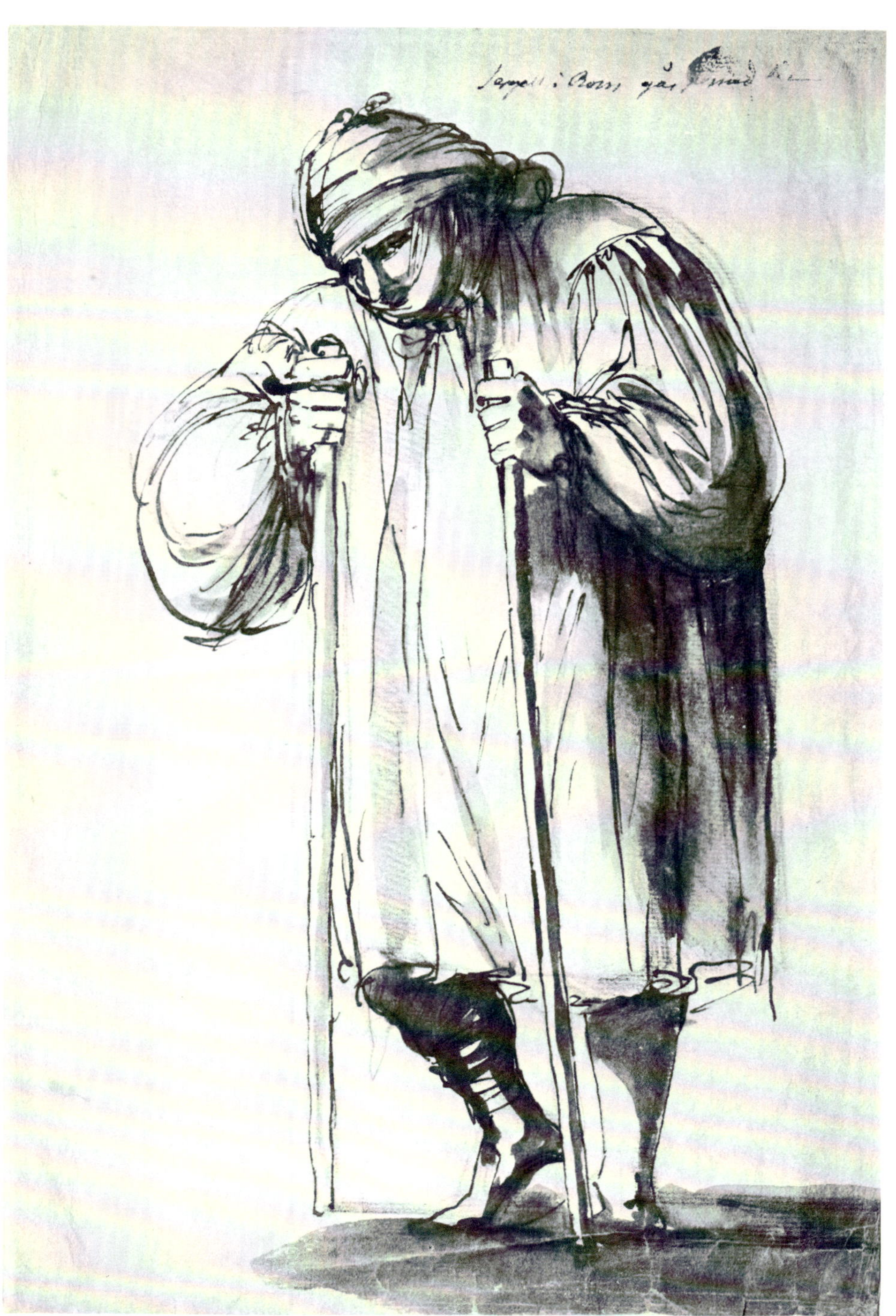

Sergel with Two Walking Sticks in Rome

Black chalk, pen and brown ink, brown and gray wash. 37.2 x 24.2 cm. Watermark: Grapes and unreadable name below. Verso: *Standing Male Nude Seen from Behind* (black chalk). NM 584/1875. Inscribed in brown ink, upper right: *Sergell i Rom går med k(äppar).*

PROVENANCE:
J. T. Sergel and descendants ☐ Nationalmuseum 1875 by purchase.

BIBLIOGRAPHY:
L. Looström, *Johan Tobias Sergel. En gustaviansk tidsbild,* Stockholm 1914, p. 15, fig. 9 ☐ Antonsson 1942, fig. p. 227 ☐ Antonsson and Jungmarker 1947, p. 26, fig. no. I ☐ P. Bjurström, "Johan Tobias Sergel," *Svenska Mästartecknare: Sergel/ Martin/ Ehrensvärd.* Årsbok för Svenska statens konstsamlingar III, Stockholm 1955, fig. 13 ☐ R. Josephson 1956, pp. 218 f., fig. 305 ☐ G. Briganti, *I Pittor dell'Immaginario Arte e Rivoluzione psicologica,* Milan 1977, fig. 111 ☐ P. Bjurström, *Drawings of Johan Tobias Sergel,* Chicago 1979, p. 6, cat. no. 1A5 ☐ Cederlöf 1982, p. 132, fig. 114.

EXHIBITIONS:
New York, Boston, Chicago 1969, no. 123 ☐ Hamburg 1975, no. 13 ☐ Copenhagen 1976, no. 17 ☐ Stockholm 1976, no. 8 ☐ New Haven 1979, no. 28 ☐ Rome 1980, no. 98.

The bantering tone in the demonic portrait of Fuseli can be compared with this forthright account of Sergel's own frailty when striken by gout in Rome. His letters home reveal that Sergel had attacks almost every summer, largely as a consequence of his unrestrained eating habits. At first he put up with the pain, joking about it with sharp irony in his drawings, but here the situation is more serious. Heavy and distressed, he leans on his sticks, his head wreathed in bandages to protect it from the glare of the sun. His gaze is lowered and hidden in the deep shadow. The drawing presumably dates from the spring of 1777, when his illness plunged Sergel into the deepest crisis of his years in Rome.

The drawing is unique among portraits by Sergel for the sculptural force with which he represents his subject.

114

JOHAN TOBIAS SERGEL

Reproduced in color.

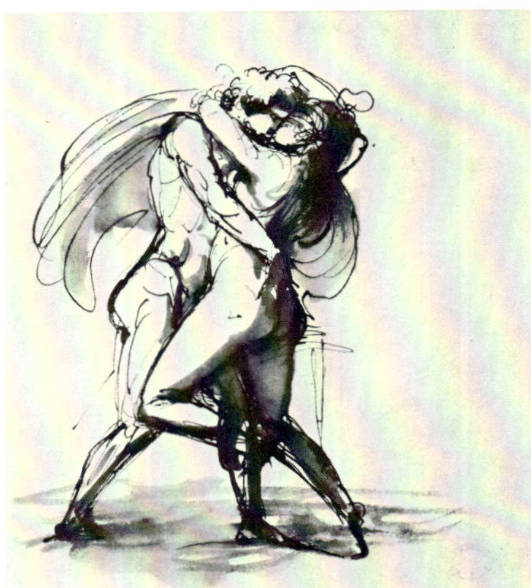

Passionate Lovers

Pen and brown ink, brown wash. 21.1 x 17.7 cm. Watermark: Unreadable name. Italian chalked paper. NM A45/1970.

PROVENANCE:
Unknown, presumably part of the Sergel family's bequest of 1875.

BIBLIOGRAPHY:
Antonsson and Jungmarker 1947, p. 26, fig. no. IV □ Bjurström 1955, fig. 4 □ H. Honour, *Neo-classicism*, London 1968, p. 101, fig. 46 □ K. Clark, *The Romantic Rebellion*, London 1973, p. 58, fig. 35 □ P. Bjurström, *Drawings of Johan Tobias Sergel*, Chicago 1979, p. 18, cat. no. 1D8 □ Cederlöf 1982, pp. 128 f., fig. 109.

EXHIBITIONS:
New York, Boston, Chicago 1969, no. 121 □ Hamburg 1975, no. 59 □ Copenhagen 1976, no. 74 □ Stockholm 1976, no. 54 □ New Haven 1979, no. 20 □ Rome 1980, no. 114.

Among the Roman drawings by Sergel, this composition has attracted the most attention in recent years, though it is not considered in either Josephson's or Antonsson's main accounts of the artist's work.

The subject follows naturally from Sergel's preoccupation in his earliest sculptures in Rome, physical love between man and woman in a mythological guise. The theme recurs again and again, but here it is entirely divorced from sculptural requirements and seems more attuned to the needs of a painting. Sergel does not make his drawing out of free imagination. He relies upon an existing model, but this he manages to transform into something personally and deeply felt.

While copying ceiling frescoes in the Palazzo Farnese, Sergel undoubtedly noticed, in the left-hand vault, Carracci's version of the secondary episode from Ovid's *Metamorphoses*, the encounter of the nymph Salmacis and the lovely son of Hermes and Aphrodite. Shortly before he left Rome, Sergel returned to the theme and produced this free rendering of the Bolognese version.

The passage in the *Metamorphoses* (iv, 276-389) relates that the fair, fifteen-year old son of the gods was wandering in the country of Carien when he came upon a crystal clear lake set among pleasant meadows. This was the home of the nymph Salmacis, who was picking flowers when she caught sight of the lovely boy and fell passionately in love with him. All her ruses and speeches failed to seduce him and when he threatened to leave if she persisted, Salmacis resorted to deception, pretending to withdraw so that he could cool himself in the inviting water. After some tentative steps on the shore, the youth undid his mantel and stepped naked into deeper water. From her hiding place in the thicket the spying nymph crept towards him through the grass, cheeks aflame and pulse racing. Embracing the loved one's body, she called upon the gods to ensure that they would never be parted. Her prayers were heard: the two bodies fused into one, both male and female, a hermaphrodite.

In Carracci's version the nymph is clinging to the youth, half-seated on his left knee. With minor alterations Sergel has created a group that is considerably more stable and powerful. The right leg of the nymph runs backwards from the youth's knee to the bed of the lake, providing a better point of balance for the fierce embrace. The water is simply suggested with rapid sweeps of the brush.

115

JOHAN TOBIAS SERGEL

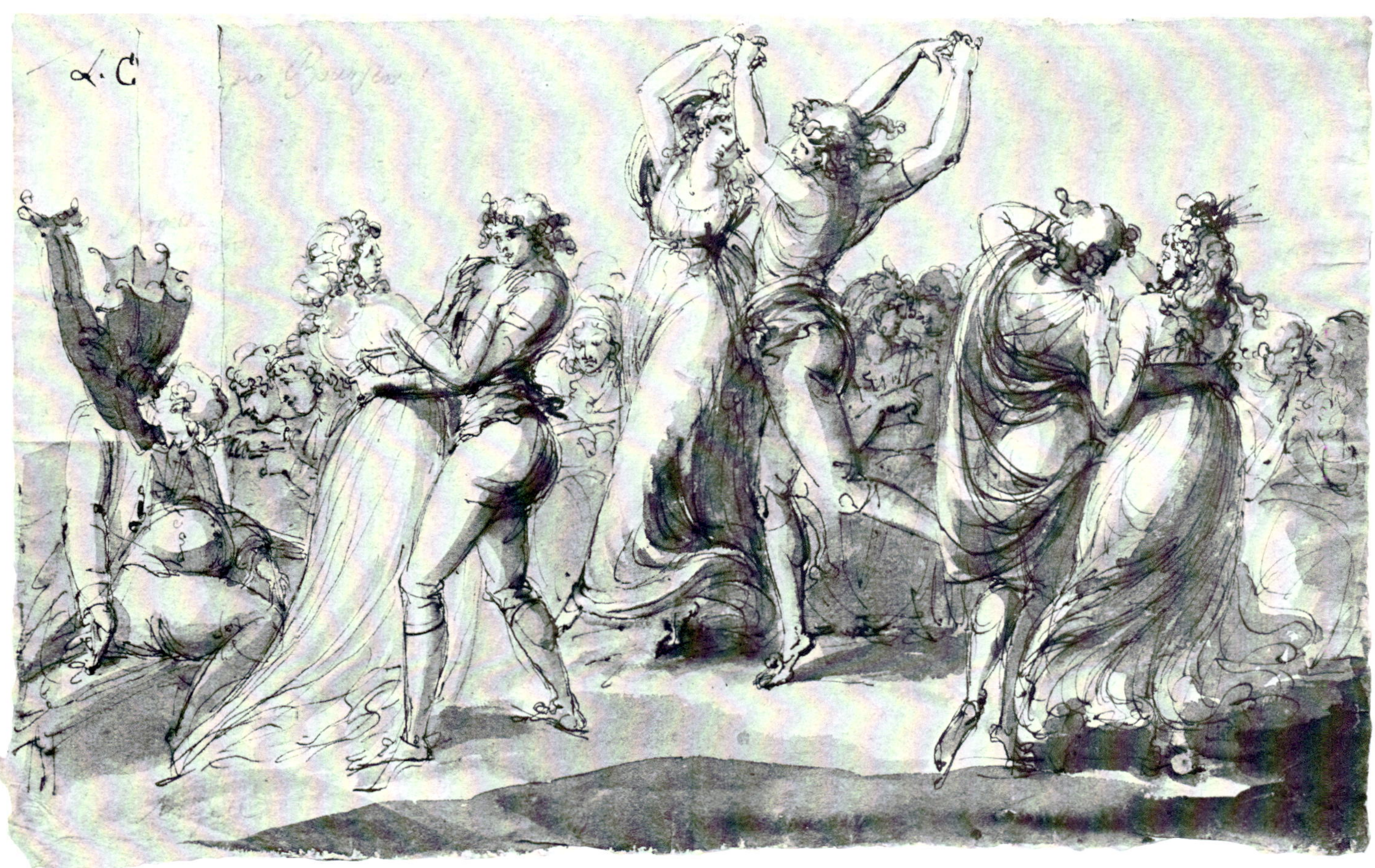

A Ball at the Stock Exchange

Pen and black ink, gray wash on bluish paper 21.0 x 33.3 cm. Watermark Three letters J C T. NM 649/1875. Signed in pencil, lower left: *Sergell*. Inscribed in ink and pencil, upper left and above the figure to the left: *L. C. på Beursen, Sergell snarkar* (Sergel snores).

PROVENANCE:
J. T. Sergel and descendants □ Nationalmuseum 1875 by purchase.

BIBLIOGRAPHY:
R. Josephson, *Sergels fantasi*, I, Stockholm 1956, pp. 582 f., fig. 759 □ P. Bjurström, *Drawings of Johan Tobias Sergel*, Chicago 1979, p. 7, cat. no. 1B2.

EXHIBITIONS:
Hamburg 1975, no. 27 □ Copenhagen 1976, no. 36 □ Stockholm 1976, n. 16.

This is an event depicted from one of many public balls arranged at The Stock Exchange in Stockholm's Old Town.

The fashion of the ball gowns, with their high waistline, indicates a date in the late 1790s. The three young couples in the center, demonstrating the different steps in the actual dance, are skillfully combined into a group that gives the picture depth. Two young bloods in the background are engrossed in flirtation with their female companions. The artist himself is seen on the far left, asleep on a sofa and snoring heavily. His head has fallen, and his arms and hands hang heavily or rest on a knee. But two young girls tickling his nose will soon waken him from his refreshing slumber. What this implies is indicated by the winged creature diving down towards him — the demon of gout with its claws ready.

The drawing seems to have been intended to accompany a letter as it has been folded twice to fit into an envelope. Whether the drawing was ever dispatched or to whom is unknown. From the provenance it seems to have been in Sergel's possession when he died.

CARL AUGUST EHRENSVÄRD
Stockholm 1745 - Örebro 1800

Son of Field Marshal Augustin Ehrensvärd, constructor of Sveaborg. Count, military officer, art philosopher, draftsman, caricaturist, and all-round talent. Commander of the Fleet of War (1784-90). Admiral of the Fleet (1792-94).

On bare rocks in the sea approach to Helsinki an imposing fortress, Sveaborg, was constructed in the middle of the eighteenth century to defend Sweden's eastern frontier. The project was directed by the artillery major, Augustin Ehrensvärd. His son, Carl August grew up in what had quickly been converted into a model society attuned to the precepts of the age of enlightenment. Locke's thesis that knowledge is best acquired from practical experience had made a deep impression on his father who established a drawing school at the fortress and brought in Elias Martin as its instructor. The elder Ehrensvärd believed that when the hand is trained to reproduce what the eye observes, the senses are made more receptive, perception is heightened, and analytical appraisal is promoted.

For two years, beginning in 1763, Carl August Ehrensvärd and Martin shared a room at Sveaborg, eating and drawing together every day. The restless, eager Ehrensvärd seized upon subject after subject until, tiring, he turned the sheet and amused himself by drawing whole galleries of grotesque types on the reverse. The burlesque and bizarre elements are also evident in the drawings that he made of social life at the fortress. Ehrensvärd seldom misses an anecdotal point, yet it is not always apparent where reality gives way to fantasy.

Martin left Sveaborg in 1765 as did Ehrensvärd who moved in the spring of that year to Stockholm and studied at the Academy, where he got to know Sergel. By the following spring the time was ripe for the young Ehrensvärd to make the customary journey south, to improve himself in Holland and France. Naval technology was his intended subject, but all the new impressions prompted a cascade of drawings. It is as though everything had to be jotted down, from sights in the streets to copies after the masters, such as Rembrandt, Rubens, and Teniers the Younger, whose works were accessible for viewing in public collections.

Ehrensvärd's technique and style are adapted according to the subject: a few scratchy strokes to catch a fleeting impression, a line that is constantly reinterpreting to produce more imaginative scenes, and washes to record impressions of light. The winter he spent in Amsterdam in 1767 resulted in excellent examples of drawings from life. These are rapid, immediate accounts of dustmen at work, outcasts in the back streets, interiors of taverns, warehouses, and a shipping agent's office, and impressions of a visit to a Dutch shipyard.

By the late summer of 1767, Ehrensvärd was back in Finland, where he stayed for a time on the family estate, Saaris, producing in October some drawings that can be described as his epilogue to his journey to Holland: stormy coasts and seascapes rendered with a bold conciseness in the use of line and a free, painterly treatment in the wash.

Soon afterward Ehrensvärd was called to active duty and for more than a decade he concentrated on his military career, which left him little time for drawing. But in December 1779, while on official business in Stockholm, he had a chance encounter with Sergel, his friend from the Academy days who was just back from eleven years in Rome, heralded by a growing reputation. This left Ehrensvärd burning with enthusiasm to experience all that Sergel had to relate. On the advice of his friend he decided to leave for the south immediately. He did so at his own expense, despite the great risk of being passed over for military promotion.

In the company of a relative he left Stockholm on 7 June 1780 and reached Rome in September. Like any tourist he was astonished by the scale of St. Peters, which he describes as a vast square topped by a roof. But it was with mixed reactions that he encountered the unseemly surroundings and the oppressive climate of the Italian capital. Having been brought up on the engraving's illusion of space and light around palaces and churches, he was unprepared for the reality of crowded streets and alleys. After a time, however, his fellow countryman, the painter Louis Masreliez, guided him among the classical ruins, the museums, and collections. Antiquity captivated Ehrensvärd, though at first mainly in its historical aspect.

Leaving Masreliez in Rome in March 1781, Ehrensvärd continued to Naples, Sicily, and Malta, which was further south than any other Swedish eighteenth-century artist had travelled up to that time. He found the journey exhilarating as the heavy baroque accents of mighty Rome gave way to a smiling landscape with comely, suitably dressed people and subtly simple, functional buildings.

As he moved south his conception of antiquity became increasingly uncompromising, until finally he rejected Roman ideals for Greek. The buildings of Rome could not match the truth and beauty to be found in the Doric colonnades of the Temple at Agrigento. Neither could the decorative art of later ages vie with even the second-best ware of the Greek potters. Ehrensvärd became convinced he had come to the primal source of art. He saw suitability as the equivalent of beauty and truth.

Returning to the Italian mainland he heard that there were plans afoot for him to succeed Adelcrantz as director and president of Sweden's Academy of Art. While wintering in Naples 1781-82, he went over the drawings he had made and edited them to some extent. His compositions related less to the motif than to his ideas about reality. Figures and staffage are sometimes inserted with the symmetry of a theatre set in order to obtain a perfectly balanced picture.

The journey back through Italy to Sweden simply confirmed his earlier observations. Outside Greece, the home of the arts was in southern Italy, primarily in Sicily, and to some extent in the district around Naples. Here were to be found the best looking people, the true descendants of antiquity. As the distance grew from these ideal places on earth, so Ehrensvärd found a proportional uglification of people, art, and nature. For him the Alps marked a clear boundary between beautiful and ugly — everything to the north was disorder.

Instead of the directorship of the Swedish Academy, Ehrensvärd was put in command of the fleet in 1783. Three years later he published the impressions from his Italian journey (*Resa til Italien 1780, 1781, 1782*). It is markedly different from most other writings in this genre in its epigrammatical, concise statements and opinions. At the same time his philosophy of the liberal arts also appeared (*De fria konsters philosophi*), an aesthetic program in the form of a catechism about what is lovely and of good report in life. Thus were the ideas of neoclassicism introduced in Sweden.

116

CARL AUGUST EHRENSVÄRD

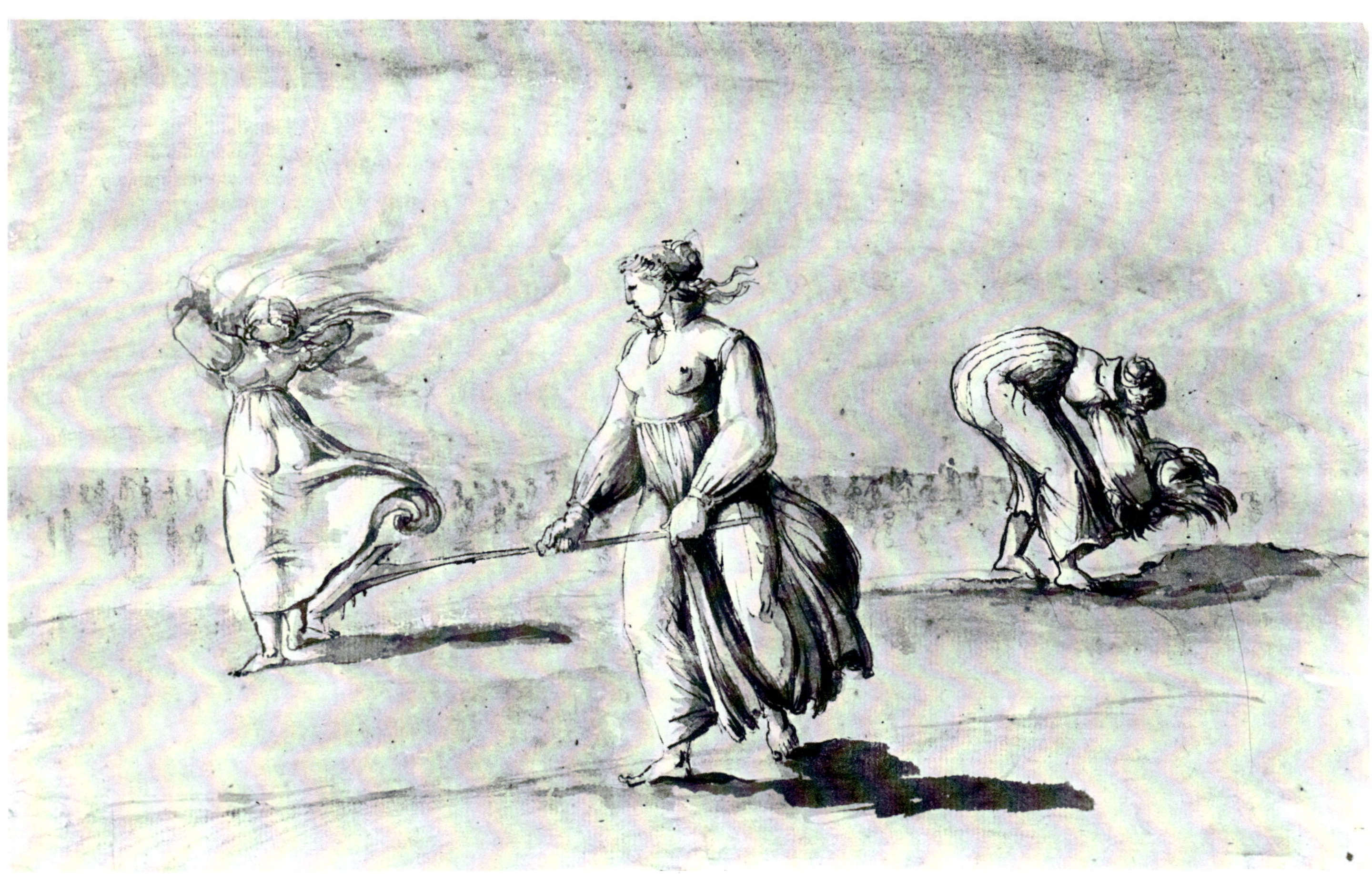

View from the Southeast of Scania

Pencil, pen and gray ink, gray wash, watercolor. 20.3 x 32.5 cm. Watermark: the name I:B Davyds. NM 164/1866. Inscribed in gray ink, lower left: *Skåne närmast ... kring Tostarp.*

PROVENANCE:
Kongl. Biblioteket □ Nationalmuseum 1866 by exchange.

BIBLIOGRAPHY:
R. Josephson, *Carl August Ehrensvärd*, Stockholm 1963, p. 295, fig. between pp. 296-97 □ S. Å. Nilsson, *Carl August Ehrensvärds resa i Skåne*, Lund 1982, p. 72, fig. pp. 72-73 □ U. Cederlöf, *Svenska teckningar 1700-talet*, Årsbok för Statens konstmuseer 29, Stockholm 1982, p. 212, fig. 179.

EXHIBITIONS:
Stockholm 1926-27, no. 157 □ London 1959, no. 676 □ New York, Boston, Chicago 1969, no. 134 □ Stockholm 1982, no. 89.

In the winter of 1794, political intrigues had for the second time obliged Ehrensvärd to relinquish his command of the Swedish warships. In the spring of the following year, he left Stockholm for Tosterup, his mother-in-law's estate in the south of Sweden. This was to be his residence while he decided what to do next. The journey reminded him of his grand expedition to Italy fifteen years before. Arriving at Tosterup, he immediately set out on a five-day trip through the province of Scania to see whether his earlier observations were applicable on a smaller scale in Sweden: whether nature, people, and how they dressed and held themselves became gradually more attractive as one moved south.

On the northern border of the province Ehrensvärd registered the pine forests, shifting sand, and granite with distaste. But he expressed enthusiasm as the dense conifers gave way to broadleaf trees and the pallid skin of the forest folk was replaced by a healthy red as the fertile, arable land took over. Similarly, striped skirts and grey jackets, signs to him of uncleanliness and confused taste, were gradually superceded by monochrome and black clothing as the fields opened out.

From this observation he concluded that the biggest and best of worldly things were to be found in the southeast corner of the province, in the heart of the area where his mother-in-law had her estate. The gently rolling Scanian plain, which reminded him of Italy, rekindled his artistic urge. A series of watercolor pen drawings picture the big house, the surrounding countryside, and neighboring villages with their crooked, half-timbered houses. People are shown working in the field (see cat. no. 117) or going home at dusk after their labor. The low hills are compressed into steep curves, the horizon line is often carried out to sea. The colors are bold, almost glaring, with red, blue, green, and yellow as the main tones.

117

CARL AUGUST EHRENSVÄRD

Reproduced in color.

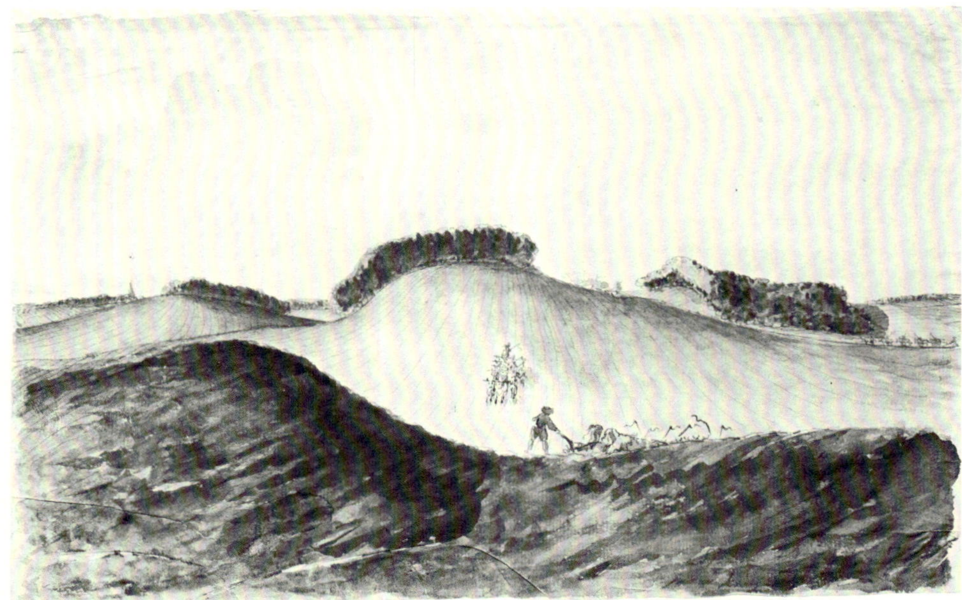

Scanian Peasant Girls

Pencil, pen and black ink, gray wash, watercolor. 18.8 x 30.1 cm. Watermark: the name I:B Davyds. NM 166/1866.

PROVENANCE:
Kongl. Biblioteket ☐ Nationalmuseum 1866 by exchange.

BIBLIOGRAPHY:
R. Josephson 1963, p. 298, fig. between pp. 296-97 ☐ S. Å. Nilsson 1982, p. 71, fig. p. 71.

The sight of Scanian farm girls working in the fields inspired Ehrensvärd to poetry. Their fresh color and healthy appearance earned them the epithet "daughters of strength." They stood in clean linen as if they were dots between hosts of redfaced men. His vision was also recorded in this drawing.

It is late summer and the grain is ripe. The setting sun has reddened the sky. In the center a girl is raking, and diagonally behind her are symmetrical illustrations of other tasks: one girl gathers the crop into suitable bundles, another ties them into sheaves. The "red-faced men" have been relegated, as a series of pencil strokes, to the background. It is the young, genuine Scanian woman whom Ehrensvärd wishes to idealize as the descendant of Ceres. Figures, movements, and clothing are all observed with realism but stripped of incidentals, in the true classical spirit. As Josephson remarked, this is "an apotheosis of life on the land, a devotional picture of the harvest."[1]

NOTE:
1. Josephson, *op. cit.*, p. 298.

118

CARL AUGUST EHRENSVÄRD

Ehrensvärd and His Wife Mourning Sergel's Departure for Denmark

Pencil, pen and black ink, gray and yellow wash on bluish paper. 19.0 x 25.0 cm. Watermark: Standing lion. NM 171/1882. Inscribed in black ink, upper margin: *Men du deltager ej endå i mitt qval. N°- 5.*

PROVENANCE:
Jean Jacques De Geer, Finspong (gift from Ehrensvärd 1797) ☐ Kongl. Biblioteket ☐ Nationalmuseum 1882 by exchange.

BIBLIOGRAPHY:
H. Frykenstedt, C. A. *Ehrensvärds lavyrer i Kobberstiksamlingen och hans förbindelser med Nicolai Abildgaard och Danmark*, Årskrift för Statens Museum for Kunst, Copenhagen 1974, pp. 1 f., fig. p. 3.

EXHIBITIONS:
Copenhagen 1982, without no.

During a journey to Denmark in 1796-97, Sergel and his companion Baron Jean Jacques De Geer (owner of the Finspong Estate in Östergötland) called several times on Ehrensvärd at the latter's estate of Dömestorp in southern Holland. The first visit had been in November 1796, before the pair moved on to meet the painter Abildgaard in Copenhagen. Sergel then returned to Ehrensvärd on 23 January 1797 and stayed with him for the whole month of February. The two men were wont to draw together until well into the night and also maintained a lively correspondence with De Geer in Copenhagen.

When Sergel returned on 1 March to Abildgaard he took with him a series of eleven drawings, dedicated to De Geer, produced by a desolate Ehrensvärd. The sheets are the artist's comments on how Abildgaard and De Geer had amused themselves while Sergel was absent, the events connected with Sergel's departure from Dömestorp, and speculations over what the three friends would get up to when they were reunited in Copenhagen. The drawings have a bantering tone. Clear jokes are imperceptibly blended with a serious note.

The present sheet, No. 5, concerns Sergel's sudden departure from Dömestorp. The sculptor is caricatured as a huge bird of passage, already winging his way over the sound. A stylized rendition of Kronborg Castle on the Danish shore beckons in the background. On his head is the sunshade he acquired because strong light was bad for his gout. His magnificent nose projects like an enormous beak.

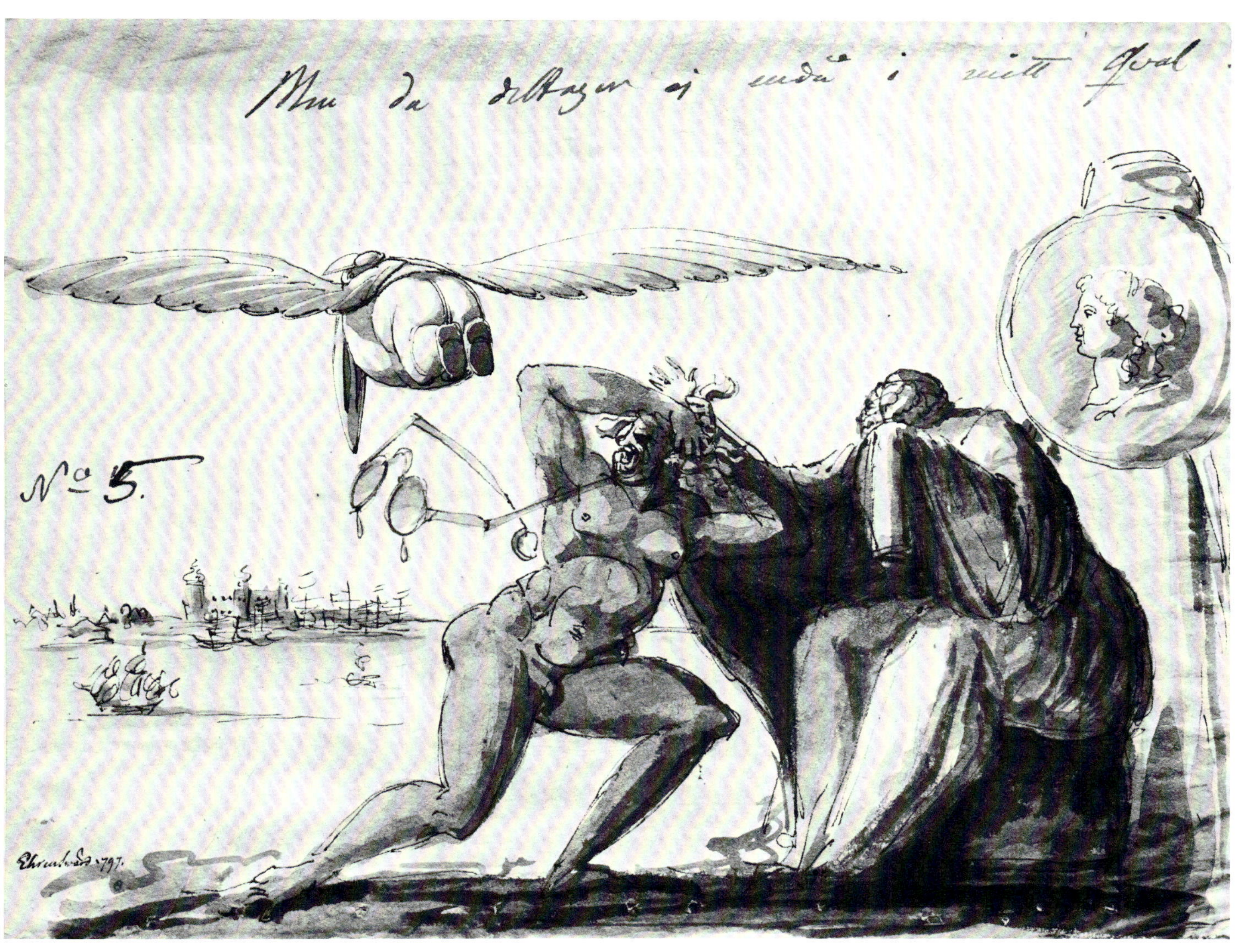

Left on the Swedish shore, a despairing Ehrensvärd is tearing his hair. Great tears run down his spectacles, which are almost falling off in the agony of parting from his friend. His wife is grieving, too, bowing her head and crying into a fold of her mantel. In the background on an easel is the medallion of her that Sergel had modelled during his stay, a reassurance that although he was leaving, his spirit would always be present at Dömestorp.

BIBLIOGRAPHIC REFERENCES AND ABBREVIATIONS

References Cited in Abbreviated Form

Ananoff 1966	A. Ananoff, *L'oeuvre dessiné de François Boucher.* Vol. 1. (Paris 1966).
Ananoff 1976 1 & 2	A. Ananoff, *François Boucher, peintures* (Lausanne and Paris 1976), 1-2.
Bartsch	A. Bartsch, *Le peintre graveur*, 21 vols. (Vienna 1803-21).
Bjurström 1972	P. Bjurström, *German Drawings*, Drawings in Swedish Public Collections 1 (Stockholm 1972).
Bjurström 1976	P. Bjurström, *French Drawings, Sixteenth and Seventeenth Centuries*, Drawings in Swedish Public Collections 2 (Stockholm 1976).
Bjurström 1979	P. Bjurström, *Italian Drawings, Venice, Brescia, Parma, Milan, Genoa*, Drawings in Swedish Public Collections 3 (Stockholm 1979).
Bjurström 1982	P. Bjurström, *French Drawings, Eighteenth Century*, Drawings in Swedish Public Collection 4 (Stockholm 1982).
Bjurström 1985	P. Bjurström, *French Drawings, Nineteenth Century*, Drawings in Swedish Public Collections 5 (In press).
Briquet	C. M. Briquet, *Les Filigranes. Dictionnaire historique des marques du papier*, 4 vols. (Geneva 1907).
Dacier and Vuaflart 1922-29	E. Dacier, J. Hérold, and A. Vuaflart, *Jean de Jullienne et les graveurs de Watteau au XVIIIe siècle*, vol. 1-4 (Paris 1921-29).
Engwall 1935	G. Engwall, "Catalogue descriptif des dessins de Watteau du Musée de Stockholm," *Gazette des Beaux-Arts*, 6:13 (1935), 1, pp. 336-44.
Heawood	E. Heawood, *Watermarks, Mainly of the 17th and 18th Centuries* (Hilversum, Holland 1950).
Hoppe 1930	A. Gauffin and R. Hoppe, *François Boucher* (Malmö 1930).
Lugt	F. Lugt, *Les Marques de collections de dessins et d'estampes* (Amsterdam 1921).
Lugt S.	F. Lugt, *Les Marques de collections de dessins et d'estampes . . . Supplément* (The Hague 1956).
Parker and Mathey 1957	K. T. Parker and J. Mathey, *Antoine Watteau, Catalogue complet de son oeuvre dessiné*, 2 vols. (Paris 1957).
Schönbrunner and Meder	J. Schönbrunner and J. Meder, *Handzeichnungen alter Meister aus der Albertina und anderen Sammlungen*, 12 vols. (Vienna 1896-1908).
Sirén 1902	O. Sirén, *Dessins et tableaux de la Renaissance italienne dans les collections de Suède* (Stockholm 1902).
Sirén 1917	O. Sirén, *Italienska handteckningar från 1400- och 1500-talen i Nationalmuseum* (Stockholm 1917).

Catalogues Cited in Appreviated Form

Cat. 1712	*Catalogue des livres, estampes et desseins du Cabinet des beaux arts et des sciences, appartenant au baron Tessin* (Stockholm 1712).
Cat. 1730	Manuscript catalogue drawn up by Carl Gustaf Tessin sometime between 1728 and 1739 (Nationalmuseum).
Cat. 1749	Manuscript catalogue drawn up by Carl Gustaf Tessin sometime between 1749 and 1755 (Nationalmuseum).
Cat. 1785	*Catalogue d'une collection* (Tessin's) . . . *dont la Vente au plus offrant se fera le* (8.) *du mois de* (Mai) *1786. . .* (Stockholm 1785).
Cat. 1790	Manuscript catalogue drawn up by Fredrik Sparre while the collection belonged to the Kongliga Biblioteket (Royal Library). The original manuscript is in the National Archives; a copy in the Nationalmuseum.

Copenhagen 1976	*Johan Tobias Sergel 1740-1814*, Thorvaldsens Museum (Copenhagen 1976).
Copenhagen 1982	*Sergels rejse til Kobenhavn 1796-97. Tegninger af Ehrensvärd, Sergel og Abildgaard.* Statens Museum for Kunst, Kobberstiksamlingen exh. cat. no. 19 (Copenhagen 1982).
Hamburg 1975	*Johan Tobias Sergel 1740-1814.* Hamburger Kunsthalle, (Hamburg 1975).
List 1739-42	Manuscript list of the items that Tessin brought back from his stay in Paris, 1739-42 (Kungliga Biblioteket Ms. S. 12).
London 1959	*The Romantic Movement.* The Tate Gallery and The Arts Council Gallery (London 1959).
Mariette	Pierre-Jean Mariette, *Description sommaire des desseins des grands maistres . . . du cabinet de feu M. Crozat* (Paris 1741).
New Haven 1979	*The Fuseli Circle in Rome. Early Romantic Art of the 1770s.* Yale Center for British Art (New Haven 1979).
New York 1981	*Sculptors' Drawings Over Six Centuries 1400-1950.* The Drawing Center (New York 1981).
New York, Boston, Chicago 1969	*Drawings from Stockholm. A Loan Exhibition from the Nationalmuseum.* The J. Pierpont Morgan Library, New York; Museum of Fine Arts, Boston; The Art Institute of Chicago, 1969.
Paris 1935	*Le Dessin français dans les collections du XVIIIe siècle,* Gazette des Beaux-Arts (Paris 1935).
Paris 1947	*La Suède et Paris,* Musée Carnavalet (Paris 1947).
Paris 1950	*Dessins du Nationalmuseum de Stockholm. Collections Tessin et Cronstedt.* Bibliothèque Nationale (Paris 1950).
Paris 1956	*Théâtre et fêtes à Paris. XVIe et XVIIe siècles. Dessins du Musée National de Stockholm.* Musée Carnavalet (Paris 1956).
Paris, Brussels, Amsterdam 1970-71	*Dessins du Nationalmuseum de Stockholm. Collection du Comte Tessin 1695-1770.* Musée du Louvre, Paris; Bibliothèque Royale Albert Ier, Brussels; Rijksmuseum, Amsterdam.
Rome 1980	*La Svezia e Roma, quattro momenti della cultura svedese a Roma.* Palazzo Braschi (Rome 1980).
Stockholm 1922	*Carl Gustaf Tessins franska handteckningar från 18:e århundradet.* Nationalmuseum 1922, Cat. no. 15.
Stockholm 1926-27	*Utställning omfattande arbeten av Augustin Ehrensvärd och Carl August Ehrensvärd.* Nationalmuseum 1926-27, Cat. no. 23.
Stockholm 1933	*Exposition d'un choix de dessins du quinzième au dix-huitième siècle.* Nationalmuseum 1933, Cat. no. 43.
Stockholm 1942	*Arkitekturritningar, planer och teckningar ur Carl Johan Cronstedts Fullerösamling.* Nationalmuseum 1942, Cat. no. 79.
Stockholm 1943	*Fem stora gustavianer.* Nationalmuseum 1943, Cat. no. 92.
Stockholm 1950	*Elias Martin och hans krets.* Liljevalchs Konsthall, Nationalmuseum 1950, Cat. no. 168.
Stockholm 1953	*Dutch and Flemish Drawings in the Nationalmuseum and Other Swedish Collections.* Nationalmuseum 1953, Cat. no. 200.
Stockholm 1958	*Fem sekler fransk konst 1400-1900.* Nationalmuseum 1958, Cat. no. 247.
Stockholm 1962	*Konstenes Venedig.* Nationalmuseum 1962, Cat. no. 269.
Stockholm 1976	Per Bjurstöm, *Sergel tecknar.* Nationalmuseum 1976 (new edition 1985).
Stockholm 1982	*Svenska 1700-talstecknare.* Nationalmuseum 1982, Cat. no. 460.
Stockholm 1984-85	*Breugels tid.* Nationalmuseum 1984-85, Cat. no. 480.
Venice 1974	*Disegni Veneti del Museo di Stoccolma.* Fondazione Giorgio Cini (Venice 1974).
Zurich 1926	*Johann Heinrich Füssli.* Kunsthaus (Zurich 1926).

INDEX OF ARTISTS

The numbers refer to catalogue entries

Anonymous Drawings